Environmental Criticism for the Twenty-First Century

Environmental Criticism for the Twenty-First Century

**1. Environmental Criticism for the
Twenty-First Century**
Edited and Introduced by Stephanie
LeMenager, Teresa Shewry,
and Ken Hiltner

Environmental Criticism for the Twenty-First Century

Edited and Introduced by Stephanie LeMenager, Teresa Shewry, and Ken Hiltner

Routledge
Taylor & Francis Group
New York   London

First published 2011
by Routledge
711 Third Avenue, New York, NY 10017

Simultaneously published in the UK
by Routledge
2 Park Square, Milton Park, Abingdon, Oxon OX14 4RN

Routledge is an imprint of the Taylor & Francis Group, an informa business

First issued in paperback 2012

Typeset in Sabon by IBT Global.

Library of Congress Cataloging-in-Publication Data
  Environmental criticism for the twenty-first century / edited and introduced by Stephanie LeMenager, Teresa Shewry, and Ken Hiltner.
     p. cm. — (Routledge interdisciplinary perspectives on literature ; 1)
  Includes bibliographical references and index.
  1. Ecocriticism. 2. Environmental protection in literature. 3. Environmental policy in literature. 4. Nature conservation in literature. 5. Ecology in literature.
  I. LeMenager, Stephanie, 1968– II. Shewry, Teresa. III. Hiltner, Ken.
  PN98.E36E58 2011
  809'.9336—dc22
  2010049328

ISBN13: 978-0-415-88630-7 (hbk)
ISBN13: 978-0-203-81491-8 (ebk)
ISBN13: 978-0-415-81638-0 (pbk)

Environmental Criticism for the Twenty-First Century
is dedicated to the environmental critics of the twentieth century, who deeded us fertile ground.

Contents

PART II
History

PART III
Scale

Acknowledgments

All work rests on other work, sometimes evident in the final product and sometimes invisible. First, we want to thank Shannon Brennan for her meticulous indexing and Catherine Zusky for her painstaking transcription of our interview with Elaine Scarry. We want to thank Elaine Scarry for her generous commitment to the interview, during a busy season of winter holidays. We also wish to acknowledge the dual conferences that gave birth to the interview and to this volume. In May 2009, Elaine Scarry gave a keynote lecture at "Beyond Environmentalism: Culture, Justice, and Global Ecologies," a conference organized by Stephanie LeMenager at the University of California, Santa Barbara, with major funding from the UC Humanities Research Institute. Six other chapters from this volume reflect the intimate and challenging conversations that took place at this conference, which also featured a brilliant keynote by Ursula Heise. In March 2009, Jill Casid offered a keynote lecture at "Before Environmentalism," a conference organized by Ken Hiltner and sponsored by the Early Modern Center at the University of California, Santa Barbara. Several chapters in this volume reflect the central goal of that conference, to explore early modern literary and cultural responses to the environmental issues that preceded and gave shape to modern environmentalism. Without the collegiality and vitality of our conference participants in both venues, this collection would not have gotten off the ground. Lawrence Buell's stunning lecture on environmental memory at UC–Santa Barbara, offered in November 2007, first inspired our ambition to attempt the impossible—e.g., anthologizing a rapidly growing field. Finally, we wish to thank the Association for the Study of Literature and Environment (ASLE), the professional organization that has made possible environmental criticism and our earnest conversation with it. Without the guidance of the good people at Routledge, too, we never would have found voice.

Foreword

Lawrence Buell

The first question facing the author of a foreword: how strongly to recommend this book? For *Environmental Criticism for the Twenty-First Century*, it's an easy call. Anyone who wants to know what literature studies are saying of importance *now* about environmental aesthetics, history, and theory should read this smart, inventive, eye-opening collection. Those who fancy themselves already well-informed are in for some salutary jolts. These essays present new work by a cross section of scholars, many in early or mid-career and on rising trajectories. Their overall strength and internal heterogeneity dramatize the momentum that "ecocriticism," the more customary term for contemporary literature-and-environment studies,[1] has been gathering during the two decades since its inception as a self-conscious initiative in the early 1990s.

The first and most basic point to make about that "momentum" is simply its rapid emergence, especially during the past dozen years. Environmental history and philosophy/ethics started a generation before, but literature-and-environment studies are catching up fast. From an original concentration on British Romantic poetry, Thoreauvian nature writing, and their filiations, environmental criticism now extends itself to every chapter and branch of Anglophone writing and beyond to the point that it now engages—as this volume attests, even though most of its contributors remain focused on Anglophone archives—all major Europhone cultures including their (post)colonial diasporas and many of those of the global non-West or "south," including a number of the first peoples of both hemispheres. The ASLE (Association for the Study of Literature and Environment) has burgeoned from a subgroup within the Western Literature Association into a worldwide network. The hundred or so of us who assembled for ASLE's first (1995) biennial gathering in Fort Collins, Colorado, hoped it would be a takeoff moment; but none could have predicted more than a smidgen of what would follow. That 1995 horizon of perception was limited by more than just the generic fallibility of prophecy as against hindsight. As *Environmental Criticism for the Twenty-First Century* shows, notwithstanding various linking threads, the prevalent assumptions about what ecocriticism/environmental criticism should be have markedly changed.

For one thing, this book's contributors articulate a very different critique of human exceptionalism from early ecocriticism's view of the intervolvement between *Homo sapiens* and the biogeological universe. In particular, early ecocriticism's enthusiasm for restoring contact between modern humans and the natural world—and for preservationist initiatives advocating this in the public sphere—has to a large extent given way to indictment of preservationism as an imposition of the privileged (white, affluent, Eurocentric) and of the conception of the "natural world" itself *qua* space apart as a specious artifact of cultural nostalgia that seems all the more bogus and retrograde as accelerating anthropogenic environmental change and contemporary science force recognition of the always-already fusion of human with nonhuman in *natureculture* (Bruno Latour's term). Indonesia has been described as a perpetual catalyst for French revolutions in anthropological theory, from Clifford Geetz to Anna Lowenhaupt Tsing. Judging by the first two essays in this collection, the same might be said of Romanticism *vis-à-vis* ecocritical theory, from phenomenology to deconstruction to new historicism to first-wave ecocriticism to the revisionisms still ongoing. For the "Anthropocene" dispensation that most of the authors of Part I see us living in now, the "monster" in Mary Shelley's *Frankenstein* seems a likelier Romantic-era touchstone than the wishful neoprimordialism with which Thoreau invests Walden Pond.

A particularly striking barometer of the shifting winds of ecocritical doctrine exemplified by *Environmental Criticism for the Twenty-First Century* is its much keener interest (essays four and five especially) in the phenomenon of "chimeras" both fictive and actual—from classical mythology to the transgenic fabrications of contemporary bioengineering—relative to the state or fate of rare and endangered nonhuman species, a prime concern for first-wave ecocritics. This shift is doubtless in no small part a by-product of environmental criticism's increasingly close engagement, following the lead of N. Katherine Hayles, with science studies, with the work of Latour and Donna Haraway in particular. If we humans are all cyborgs now and if everything on earth subsists within an unstable "mesh" (Chapter 1) of natureculture, then the very idea of an "endangered species" is an epistemological mistake if not also a potentially culpable distraction from environmental macro-concerns that might matter more. From this standpoint, the path to environmental criticism's future would seem to lie not in allying itself with any sort of environmental restorationist ethico-politics but rather through recognition of humanity's posthuman condition, whatever its risks, whatever the as-yet-unforeseen, mutagenic transformations of natureculture, be they happenstance or engineered.

But this volume also suggests that hardly less important than science studies theory to the furtherance of such a revisionary script, at least up to a point, is the cross-pollination of environmental criticism by minority/diasporic and post/colonial studies (chapters 4–5, 7–10, 15). Through these lenses, protection of rare species and creation of "wilderness" sanctuaries stands indicted *prima facie* as dominationist double-think, at best an inadequately belated compensatory first-world-initiated response to the rapacious plundering of the global "south" throughout the past half millennium. Accordingly, Rachel Carson's *Silent Spring*, whose opening "Fable for Tomorrow" invokes the pastoral-nostalgic memory of an idyllic middle-American town as ecoethical norm to counter the health hazards of chemical pesticides, seems a less pertinent text for today's filiations of "toxic discourse" than Indra Sinha's novel *Animal's People* (2007). Based on the worst pesticide disaster in history, a horrific 1984 Union Carbide factory explosion in Bhopal, litigation of which drags on to this day, *Animal's People* is the mordantly sardonic memoir of a feisty but traumatized youth grotesquely deformed by the catastrophe through whose eyes *both* foreign do-gooders *and* native environmental justice advocates seem flawed and impotent, however well-meaning and endearing, and a wary survivalism perhaps the best coping strategy at last.

The increasing interpenetration between literary-environmental and post/colonial studies during the past decade can be told as a cautionary tale of belated entry on either side but deserves mainly to be celebrated for reanimating both. For ecocriticism, its most crucial benefit has been, first and most patently, to quicken the felt urgency to deparochialize its scope beyond its original Eurocentric base, bringing with it significantly revised accounts of what deserves to count as "environmentalism" and "environmental writing" (*v.* chapters 9 and 14 especially). In addition, this new work requires rehistoricization of the timescape of accelerated anthropogenic environmental change that backdates it at least several centuries, from industrial revolution (the baseline for most first-wave ecocriticism) to the fifteenth century (*v.* Chapter 7 especially). Indeed, even before 1492, Chapter 6 shows, home-country pillaging of timber and other resources that later became a prime incentive for global colonization incentivized nostalgic propagation of green-world mythology. In such ways *Environmental Criticism for the Twenty-First Century* exemplifies the finer, staged-out calibration that recent historicist work has given such more sweepingly panoramic earlier ecocritical accounts as Robert Pogue Harrison's *Forests: The Shadows of Civilization* (1993) and Louise Westling's *The Green Breast of the New World* (1996), both of which start by invoking the mythicized rendition of the agro-pastoral revolution's irreversible environmental impact in the ancient Sumerian epic of *Gilgamesh*.

So far I've been sounding as if this book speaks in single voice. Not so, fortunately. The downside of ecocriticism's laudable desire to make its forums inclusive has been a penchant for letting civility preempt disputation. Now that there are at least six specialized journal venues for ecocritical work on three continents, not to mention dozens of "special issues" featuring ecocritical gatherings since *New Literary History*'s in 1999, the time for supposing that environmental criticism ever might or should be constituted as a closely coordinated program is long since past. *Environmental Criticism for the Twentieth-First Century* is all the more attractive because it so often bites. Its essays tend to be edgy and contentious, and what's more to pull against each other in a number of ways.

Here are a few examples. The scripts for the posthumanist dispensation offered in Part I are more discrepant than I have made them seem. Nor are Part II's versions of minoritarian and postcolonial environmentalism and ecodiscourse by any means identical. In Part I, environmental justice concerns are muted and, when engaged, in rather oblique and guarded fashion. In Part II, they become much more salient. Even though the theorizations of posthumanism in Part I are mostly on the same page with the postcolonial and minoritarian revisionisms of Part II in dissenting from first-wave preservationism, "nature" emerges in Part II as a substantive as well as phantasmal category, as a palpable actuality pilfered or despoiled by the dominant at the expense of the disempowered. (One recalls political theorist Partha Chatterjee's charge, in *The Nation and Its Fragments,* that Western gurus seem to have rendered nationalism disreputable just in time to deprive emergent nations of its legitimacy. Might some such be said of the deconstruction of "nature" by revisionist ecotheory?) Finally, the quintet of essays in Part III, focused in one way or another on matters of "scale," in itself and in juxtaposition with certain essays in other sections, offers perhaps the most striking case of this book's radiant energy of internal dissonance. Questions of place-attachment and place-(re)construction have been central to ecocriticism since the movement's inception, but the high valuation it initially set on local or bioregional allegiances has been seriously roiled by its recent engagement with postcolonial and "ecocosmopolitan" models of thinking, most influentially Ursula Heise's *Sense of Place and Sense of Planet* (2008). The reader will find both shrewd critique (Chapter 14) and equally shrewd defense (11–12) of local/bioregional thinking here, as well as sharply contrasting appraisals of ecotopian urbanism (the qualified hopefulness of Chapter 5 *versus* Chapter 13's emphasis on the irony of a grandiose scheme derailed by slipshod follow-through and arrogant insouciance of ecocontextual conditions).

"Radiant energy of internal dissonance" is no euphemistic ploy. That these essays pull against as well as with each other is a great intrinsic virtue. It's proof of the vigor and vitality of the underlying project. Those who read this collection as carefully as it deserves will find themselves both equipped and more energized to carry that project on.

NOTES

1. Like editors LeMenager, Shewry, and Hiltner, I prefer "environmental criticism" as the better omnibus term for an array of practices never driven by a single model of inquiry to "ecocriticism's" implication of resting on "ecology" and its implication of some underlying philosophical holism. But I would not dogmatize: tastes differ, "ecocriticism" admittedly translates better across some linguistic borders (e.g., Chinese) as well as being better established within literature studies as well as within some other branches of arts and humanities (e.g., "ecoart," "ecotheology," etc.), not to mention its biblio-canonization since 2002 as a Library of Congress catalogue subject heading.

Introduction

Stephanie LeMenager, Teresa Shewry, and Ken Hiltner

In her introduction to the now classic *Ecocriticism Reader* of 1996, Cheryll Glotfelty cautioned against defining the field of environmental criticism too narrowly, remarking not only the breadth of ecocritical endeavor as it stood in the mid-1990s but also directions for its further development. In the generous spirit of that first must-read collection, we offer an anthology that represents the diverse concerns of environmental criticism in the twenty-first century and, in so doing, charts the considerable distance that the field has traveled since its founding. *Environmental Criticism for the Twenty-First Century* showcases the explosive recent expansion of environmental criticism, which is actively transforming three areas of broad interest in contemporary literary and cultural studies: science, history, and scale. By "science," we mean environmental criticism's sophisticated engagement with science and technology studies through the discourses of evolutionary biology, biotechnology, cybernetics, medicine, and ecology. By "history," we indicate the expanded temporal dimension of ecocritical practice, as environmental critics rethink history as an ecological as well as human drama and uncover the complex relationships between nonhuman systems, foundational ideas such as nature, and historical literary practice. By "scale," we evoke the complex geographical imaginaries of some of the best new ecocritical writing, which recognizes that ecological systems offer rich ground for transnational and translocal analysis. Taken together, these three areas, which form the three parts of *Environmental Criticism for the Twenty-First Century*, represent major, exciting directions in the future of environmental criticism. They also suggest that environmental criticism has taken a leading role in literary and cultural studies through interdisciplinary practice.

We draw together contributors who deal with texts from the Medieval period through the twenty-first century as a way to bring into sharp focus the long durations through which environmental imaginations are shaped. The works in this collection engage ecocritical issues from a range of regional, national, and transnational perspectives, rethinking environmental literature in response to ecology's own regions and borders. We choose to speak of "scale" rather than charismatic current terms, such as "the global" or "the planetary," because we want to interrogate the sometimes facile global-local dichotomy through case studies of collapse, contamination, translation, and community that call attention to the dynamism of place, as well as to the particular difficulty of imagining global or planetary space and time. Contributors pursue the concerns for language, history, cultural difference, and spatial mapping that are crucial to such work. As critical nodes, "science," "history," and "scale" overlap and interpenetrate one another; so, for example, our authors imagine the transgenic hybrids of eighteenth-century English botany enabling the contemporary vision of European BioArtists, or a young Sigmund Freud's response to the landscapes of postwar Europe naming an explicitly African American ecomelancholia. The tripartite structure of this volume assumes the porosity of boundaries and the relational constitution of bodies, including fields of knowledge. Our scholars are interested in creating a transdisciplinary zone of engagement that draws on both the capacities of the sciences and the humanities, in order to find compelling aesthetics, stories, and languages for engaging ecological processes such as global climate change (GCC) and the linked contemporary threats of peak oil production, nuclear proliferation, and food and water scarcity. *Environmental Criticism for the Twenty-First Century* offers powerful proof that cultural criticism is itself ecologically resilient, evolving to meet the imaginative challenges of twenty-first-century environmental crises.

SCIENCE

Science has been a site of conflict and gestation for ecocritical thought since Joseph Meeker's engagement with Darwinian evolution as a comedic mode in what may be called the first work of environmental criticism (Meeker 1972). Understood in terms of situated knowledges and material practices, science complements the environmentalist imperative that matter *matters,* even though environmentalists have recognized the sciences as also objectifying nonhuman agents, speaking for and therefore muting the incommensurable, wild world in the service of capitalism, industrialization, imperialism, and the new empires of globalization. The critiques of disembodiment, transcendent human subjectivity, and decontextualized scientific labor that emerged in science and technology studies in the work of Bruno Latour, Donna Haraway, and N. Katherine Hayles, among others, undergird a strong ecocritical rapprochement with the histories, cultures, and methods of science. At the turn of the twenty-first century, leading ecocritics called for deeper investment in the sciences, citing the necessity of scientific literacy in assessing contemporary environmental risks, such as global climate change and toxic pollution, in understanding the biological underpinnings of human consciousness, and in respecting the material resistance of the nonhuman to incorporation through discursive and information technologies, from literature to digital media (Heise 1997; Love 1999; Phillips 2003; Fromm 2009). The proliferation of environmental criticism in dialogue with science and technology in the last decade testifies to the robust future of environmental science studies, a field that will be sustained by a sharpening of its key conflicts and concepts.

A crucial shift in ecocriticism's engagement with science involved the critique of metaphoricity as a means of interdisciplinary knowledge (Heise 1997; Phillips 2003). Nominating science as a critical area for expansion in ecocriticism, Ursula Heise suggested that the metaphorical transfer of scientific terminology into literary criticism neutered scientific description and literary textuality, creating a false consilience. The apparent wholeness, orderliness, or progressive sequence of a literary text granted the appearance of similar qualities to ideas from the life sciences, such as *the ecosystem;* likewise, the apparent balance or closure implicit in scientific terms, such as *the organism,* granted the appearance of similar qualities in literary texts. Scientific metaphor, dislocated from the bodies and contexts of scientific practice, allowed for a conservative mode of reading literature as Nature when Nature is understood as presence, in other words reading against the challenges to stable origins and objects offered by deconstruction. We see in early iterations of biological ecocriticism a resistance to "theory," as well as an interest in sociobiological arguments for art that may have provoked exaggerated alarm in poststructuralists. Dana Phillips's early-twenty-first-century challenge to the truth of ecology offered a defense of the contingency of literary language and scientific concept alike, built on the back of a criticism of the science of ecology as itself haunted by metaphor, a weak science of macro- or metanarrative. Beckoning ecocritics into "nature-culture, a region where surprising monsters dwell," Phillips signaled what is in fact the new metaphoricity of ecocritical conversations with science, wherein the critical terms of science studies act as heuristics and mediators. If it is not possible for ecocritics to reject metaphor altogether in their interdisciplinary projects, and E. O. Wilson's notion of consilience among the disciplines depends upon such formal reductionism, then at least we might choose metaphors, e.g., *natureculture,* that are lively agents, tropes which turn away from fantasies of pure referentiality.

Bruno Latour's *We Have Never Been Modern* (1993), an argument against modernity as an epochal break with the messiness of matter, generated *natureculture* as a spur to fresh thinking in both science studies and ecocriticism about interpenetration and emergence, or the means by which apparently separate domains, such as the material and the social, are continually reconstituted in relation to one another. Latour's contribution to Actor Network Theory (ANT), which posited both the practice of science and the natural "fact" as effects of network-building among humans, nonhuman beings, and material or institutional infrastructures, challenged the hierarchy of beings and monolithic concepts of Science and Nature which fail to account for the historical entanglements of bodies (Latour 2005). From ANT, the term *network* joined Gilles Deleuze and Félix Guattari's *rhizome* to reinvigorate epistemological thinking. The dismantling and rematerializing of Nature (e.g., indisputable, scientific fact) was, to an extent, always a feminist project, and it found its most popular figuration in Donna Haraway's *cyborg*, a trope for the machinic, organic, and textual constitution of hybrid subjectivities which have never been modern *or* human—in the sense of transcending matter or interdependence (Haraway 1991). Of course the cyborg remains open to its original Cold War–era formulation, as "human-bot" that can survive in space or nuclear war. Haraway has experimented with other figures that resist delusions of human mastery. Her *companion species*, which applies to dogs and their owners, to genetically engineered lab animals like OncoMouse™, and to all life as defined through coevolution, places the cyborg on a continuum with the household pet and the avian flu, opening the door to further considerations of transgenic influence and play. In sympathy with Latour and Haraway, N. Katherine Hayles (1999) made *the posthuman* a crucial metaphor for rethinking embodiment in the digital age, when human identity might be conceived as informational code (e.g., DNA) that can be downloaded into any material substrate. Before the posthuman solidifies into a version of the disembodied, rational "human" of classical liberalism, Hayles invites readers to consider how human consciousness might both be distributed across organic/machinic systems and embodied—an invitation compelling to ecocritics.

The productive, slippery metaphors that came out of science and technology studies in the late twentieth century enabled breakthroughs in twenty-first-century ecocriticism, freeing ecocritics to tinker with the whole toolbox of literary theory, from mimesis through deconstruction, as they reencountered the sciences as, if not exactly textual, at least historical, contingent fields. Stacy Alaimo's interpretive practice of "trans-corporeality," or thinking across bodies, ties environmental science to queer studies and disability studies to allow for strong theorizations of environmental health as a material-semiotic problem (Alaimo 2009). From urban pockets of childhood asthma to the disputed condition of multiple chemical sensitivity (MCS), environmental disease signifies within bodies, as an intimate form of untranslatable, essentially poetic, ecological knowledge. Memoirs associated with what Lawrence Buell identifies as the tradition of "toxic discourse" that sprang from the environmental justice movement, such as Susanne Antonetta's *Body Toxic* (2001), exhibit both the fatal embodiment of environmental intelligence and the necessity of scientific literacy, for example familiarity with oncology, for inhabitants of a modernity birthed in actuarial logic (Buell 1998). Ecocriticism's conversation with science complements the larger project of making science public and participatory—a project Ulrich Beck suggests will be crucial to enlisting humans in our own survival (Beck 1995). Further, ecocritics can assist the efforts of

BioArtists to reunite techno-scientific practice with sense experience, where the fabrication of new flesh stimulates new ecological affect, and transgenic experimentation is reconceived as a *poiesis* that might sustain the human condition beyond its waning hydrocarbon infrastructures.

While science often has been framed as migrating from the "West" to the rest of the world, many postcolonial scholars have challenged this narrative, considering colonial, non-Euro-American, indigenous, and global South locations in which science is made (e.g., Anker 2001; Kathirithamby-Wells 2005; Lowe 2006). Focusing on the generation of scientific stories about forests in colonized Peninsular Malaysia, Jeyamalar Kathirithamby-Wells examines how scientists drew on indigenous and Malay peoples' knowledge in identifying species and medicinal properties, navigating through the environments of the peninsular, and in the telegraphic and insecticidal revolutions (Kathirithamby-Wells 2005). Considering more recent contexts, Celia Lowe engages work by Indonesian conservation biologists in the Togean archipelago, arguing that European and American scientists no longer commonly hold authoritative positions in scientific projects in the tropical world (2006, 5). Scientific work in the global South has been productive of key terms known to transnational science today, such as biodiversity (2006, 14). The flow of scientific intelligence from the global South to the global North stands as a necessary postscript to the histories of Euro-American imperialism with which some of our contributors engage.

Contributors to "Science" move from Charles Darwin's entangled bank, the leading metaphor of **Timothy Morton's** chapter "The Mesh," through strong ecological figures of risky attachment (the posthuman, the network, the cyborg, companion species, the chimera) to articulate the porosity of the human as matter and philosophical category. "The Mesh" offers perhaps the clearest articulation to date of Morton's larger project of ecocritique, putting deconstruction in the service of ecology—the dark ecology that Morton suggests may open a more genuine relationship among humans and nonhumans by emphasizing the desire and lack which structures human being in relation to other life. Moving far from the antitheoretical bias that defined early biological ecocriticism, Morton offers an ingenious Interdependence Theorem by which natural selection can be seen as an arbitrary system of negative difference, without telos or spatiotemporal edge, a mesh/snare in which humans must come to the humiliating realization that we have no idea where we are and, at best, await the (unexpected) arrival of other life among and within us. This rendering of biological evolution as a type of horror story, essentially, where anxiety overwhelms expectation—as what is expected will be unexpected!—is echoed in **Paul Outka's** "Posthuman/Postnatural: Ecocriticism and the Sublime in Mary Shelley's *Frankenstein*." Outka finds in the transatlantic culture of the Romantics a prehistory of posthumanism, explicitly in a recurrent experience, available in scientific and literary discourse, which he defines as the organic sublime.

The organic sublime occurs when an individual becomes suddenly, painfully aware of her radical material identity, her likeness to Earth; in short, the organic sublime counters the expected Romantic epiphany, which reinforces the transcendence of the human. As materialist polemic, *Frankenstein* forces the question of whether the monstrous has been a misdirection taken up by environmentalists, allowing for false epochal distinctions between "humanity" and "posthumanity," "nature," and "postnature." If, as Outka suggests, the monster is us and/as other life, how might we revise an environmentalist ethic of care?

Reconsideration of the unexpected histories and futures of an environmentalist ethic of care enfolds, too, in **Beth Fowkes Tobin's** "Revisiting the Virtuoso: Natural History Collectors and Their Passionate Engagement with Nature." Complicating familiar characterizations of the Enlightenment project as the desacralization of nonhuman nature, Tobin examines the culture of shell collecting in eighteenth-century Britain to reclaim the "virtuoso" or collector as a passionate scientist. Margaret Cavendish Bentinck, the second Duchess of Portland, defies caricatures of antisocial male "classifiers" or female "accumulators," evincing a love for the muck of local undeveloped wetlands and a nascent ecological sociality. Collecting can be ecological practice, even a profound and destabilizing form of desire, and Enlightenment collectors may have been more scientifically informed "nature lovers" than the Romantics who repudiated them. Shuttling from the colonialist projects of eighteenth-century scientific rationalism into the often ironic installations of twenty-first-century BioArt, **Jill H. Casid** offers a series of theoretical riffs upon the potent figure of the chimera, from ancient myths of bestiality to contemporary transgenic creatures such as "shoat" and "geep." Following Donna Haraway's suggestion that "the transgenic is not the enemy," Casid thinks of the chimera as both a product of colonial-paternalist regimes of species, racial, and heterosexual dominance and as a productive site for reanimating sustainable, queer impurities (Haraway 2004). Moreover, Casid suggests that figuration itself, as performed by the theorist and her array of artists, from Miguel Cabrera to Aziz+Cucher, constitutes ecological practice insofar as it generates embodied forms of life and affects which extend the human.

Taking up this promise of the transgenic as imaginative resource, **Allison Carruth** considers the urban design group *Terreform ONE*, whose projects include sustainable structures decoupled from hydrocarbon technologies such as "In Vitro Meat Habitat," a building fabricated from pig cells grown in vitro. Carruth queries the possibility of the genetic engineering of urban infrastructures in relation to the idea of the mutagenic, already chimerical city as it is theorized by novelist Indra Sinha in *Animal's People* (2007), where the fictional Khaufpur, India, stands in for Bhopal after the Union Carbide gas leak. Sindra's recognition that toxified environments are resilient insofar as they foster biological adaptations that may be considered mutations puts into question, again, environmentalists' (mis)use of monstrosity. Here, we ask whether or not sustainability can be considered beyond normative-speciesist concepts of life.

HISTORY

In 1967, in an essay on "The Historical Roots of Our Ecological Crisis," Lynn White Jr. opened with an anecdote, relating a conversation in which he disabused Aldous Huxley of the notion that Europe's environmental crisis is a relatively recent phenomenon (1996). As White would repeatedly make clear throughout the essay, such a belief is far from accurate. For example, he drew attention to London's smog problem, which was already an issue in 1285. Moreover, as we now know, over 85 percent of England had been deforested by the same time. White was not, of course, the first writer to consider the history of environmental crises. George Marsh's tome on *The Earth as Modified by Human Action*, first published as *Man and Nature* in 1864, is just one of many earlier examples (1874). Nonetheless, given that White's essay became enormously influential and controversial (largely because of its blistering indictment of Christianity on environmental grounds), it would have seemed that the time had come to radically reassess the long history of the West's relationship to the environment.

While it is true that a number of works, such as Carolyn Merchant's 1980 *The Death of Nature* (which is a sweeping intellectual history from the Classical period through the Renaissance), set out to do just that, when scholars—and especially literary critics—began to consider specific moments of our environmental history in detail, they frequently looked to more recent periods, often beginning with the so-called Industrial Revolution (Merchant 1980). If Friedrich Engels was correct in arguing that the history of the mass exploitation of the working class in England began with the introduction of the steam engine and machinery for working textiles, then perhaps the history of environmental devastation might begin there as well (1958). Even in 1864 and 1967, respectively, Marsh and White knew that this was not the case. Certainly, as White repeatedly argued, Europeans had been radically modifying their environment for well over a thousand years. Even a cursory look to English Medieval and Renaissance literature makes this clear. For example, consider the issue of plant diversity. Not only did Andrew Marvell famously question why "the world was searched, through oceans new" for exotic plants to import into England, in the previous century the Belgian theologian Justus Lipsius noted that affluent collectors "vaingloriously hunt after strange hearbs & flowers, which having gotten, they preserve and cherish more carefully than any mother doth her child" (1939, 134). As we now know, in the year 1500 there were fewer than 200 nonindigenous species of plants in England; by 1700 that number grew to a staggering 20,000. Alternately, in the seventeenth century George Herbert considered the loss of indigenous species:

"More servants wait on man / Than he'll take notice of; in ev'ry path / He treads down that which doth befriend him, / When sickness makes him pale and wan" (1941; "Man," lines 43–46). This is a strikingly modern argument in favor of plant diversity, suggesting that the plants we are forcing into extinction may have medicinal value for human beings.

Canonical European literatures provide only a small window onto the long durations of environmental imagination, stories of which are reworked by scholars and activists who engage alternate traditions and histories. The archives of global south, non-Euro-American, and indigenous peoples offer important possibilities for apprehending and engaging environmental crisis. Many histories of literary, theoretical, or critical thought related to the environment have not been undertaken in the name of ecocriticism. Ecocritics might, and do, enter heterogeneous, uneven fields of critical engagement. Deborah Bird Rose argues that such work involves learning different modes of ecological relationship with the past. She writes of stories that she learned from Aboriginal Australian peoples about Dreamings, "creative ancestral beings" who moved across the land and changed themselves into entities like trees in sacred sites (2008, 159). This way of engaging time and of recognizing entangled being and becoming is a mode of historiography that is "relational, ethical, inclusive, open and responsive to the vulnerability of the living Earth" (2008, 159, 167). Similarly diverse genealogies for the "ecological" praxis theorized by figures like Bruno Latour in the Western tradition have emerged from Native American and formerly colonized settler cultures within the United States, including African American and Chicano/a culture. In this section, we emphasize the multiplicity of historical trajectories of environmental thought, across varied regions of the globe and beyond the traditional epochal breaks (e.g., the Industrial Revolution) that once stabilized Euro-American environmental imaginaries.

Contributors take up Medieval (Siewers), Renaissance (Test), eighteenth-century (Beth Fowkes Tobin and Jill H. Casid, in the *Science* section) texts, as well as reflect on African (Caminero-Santangelo), Native American (Test), Mexican American (Ybarra), and African American (James) cultures. Keeping with the theme of this History section, many of these chapters also reexamine what we thought we knew about history from an environmental perspective.

For example, a generation ago Northrop Frye famously coined the phrase "green world," describing magical worlds entwined with the natural world, which has become something of a critical mainstay. In this section, **Alfred K. Siewers** reconsiders Frye's green world from an ecocritical, as well as ecosemiotic, perspective, with the larger goal of helping us better understand the environmental function of narrative. In order to do so, Siewers offers a striking green reading of some very canonical Medieval texts: *The Canterbury Tales, Sir Gawain and the Green Knight*, and Malory's *Le Morte d'Arthur*. Moving forward into the Renaissance, **Edward M. Test** meditates on the fact that ever since Columbus's first voyage, the so-called New World was thought by many to contain somewhere the fabled biblical Paradise, while Amerindians were thought to inhabit an Edenic, prelapsarian world. As Test suggests, such fantasies may in large measure have been in response to environmental changes sweeping across Europe, and even a symptom of the desire for new environmental thought. In the French poet Guillaume de Saluste Sieur du Bartas, Test discovers an ecocosmopolitan whose surprisingly unbiased embrace of Amerindian cosmologies counters Paradisiacal imagining, rewriting European natural philosophy.

Moving from the Medieval and Renaissance history of Europe, **Priscilla Solis Ybarra** queries the environmental legacy of the colonial Mexicans of California, known as *Californios,* in Chicano/a and U.S. environmental histories. Ybarra reads the nineteenth-century novels of María Amparo Ruiz de Burton as an archive of Mexican American environmental knowledge, particularly of agricultural practice in the arid environments of the North American Southwest. While John Muir was refining the wilderness ideal in the service of creating the U.S. national parks, Mexican American *hacendados*, such as Ruiz de Burton's protagonists and her own *Californio* family, lamented the forsaken opportunity of Mexican-U.S. cooperation in sustainable stewardship which presented itself, if briefly, in the wake of the U.S.-Mexico war. Focusing on the early-to-mid-twentieth century, **Byron Caminero-Santangelo** illuminates a history of environmental writing by Africans, challenging assumptions that African literary environmentalism emerged in the wake of environmentalisms in the West. He ties the work of Kenyan writer-activist Wangari Maathai to the African anticolonial pastoral tradition of *Negritude* and specifically to the writing of Ugandan poet Okot p'Bitek and Kenyan writer Ngugi wa Thiong'o. In varying but connected ways, these writers affirm indigenous approaches in ecology and address colonial upheavals to their cultures and lifeways. Weaving together concerns for ecology with decolonization, social justice, livelihood, and power hierarchies, African writing reconfigures the ways in which we might understand environmental literature and ecocriticism.

Finally, **Jennifer C. James** offers a breathtaking overview of African American environmental thought, in which she challenges assumptions that legacies of trauma and injustice interrupt African American pleasure in, or understanding of, nonhuman nature. Shuttling amongst poems of the early and late twentieth century, pop music (notably, Marvin Gaye's classic "The Ecology"), and contemporary media, including David Simon's HBO series *The Wire,* James constructs a green African American imaginary populated with nonhuman beings who share, with black Americans, a history of colonization and violence. James's theory of African American ecomelancholia as an unresolved process of grieving that enables black environmental stewardship makes a powerful contribution to both ecopsychology and U.S. environmental history.

SCALE

Attention to scale leads us to deeply powerful forms of territorial organization that impact the environment in uneven ways. It also takes us towards concern for marginalized, illegitimated ways of interacting with space. Spatial arrangements are made in everyday practices among people and other life and are tapped into broader processes such as time, imperialism, global economy, ecology, evolution, and memory. Spaces of literary environmental imagination are not simply about what is said to be present by dominant discourses. Literatures commonly layer environmental spaces with memories and seek to dream up other worlds. Scale is an expansive term that we use to draw together these investigations and to affirm the continued range and contention in ecocriticism's work on space.

It is difficult to understand the spatial processes at work in the environmental changes that are engulfing the world in which we live. Environmental critics are in search of adequate spatial frameworks to understand how literature and the arts engage processes such as the loss of ice from polar ice sheets; the stagnations and movements of entities like oil around the planet; or the unevenly related genealogies of thought that authors often gather together to frame the environment. In *The Ecocriticism Reader*, Cheryll Glotfelty presciently suggested that ecocritical work would become increasingly international and involve thought about the global scale of environmental problems (1996, xxv). There are now multiple affiliate organizations to the Association for the Study of Literature and the Environment (ASLE) around the world. As Michael Branch and Scott Slovic write, observing the expansion of ecocriticism as of the early twenty-first century, "a mere decade ago, few had any idea how vast this scholarly movement might become" (2003, xiv). So the problem of scale, and its exhilarating possibilities, has been instantiated at the institutional level through the growth of environmental criticism's key professional organization in terms of both its numbers and the distribution of its sites. Among environmental critics' theoretical efforts to understand scale, a number of scholars have directed attention to global entanglements (for example, Buell 2001; Garrard 2004; Heise 2008). Greg Garrard engages with varied imaginaries of the planet, such as images of Earth from space, the globe as capitalist marketplace, and the global discourse of biodiversity (2004). Ursula Heise challenges ecocritics in the U.S. to complicate their disproportionate focus on local struggle by considering global connection and cosmopolitanism, forms of attachment that stretch across national borders (2008). Scholars' understandings of the past and present geographic parameters of ecocritical work, as well as of important environmental scales, vary with their social and historical vantage points.

While moving beyond emphasis on allegorically contained, local worlds, ecocritical work on the meaningful textures of specific places remains crucial. Such work explores place as the performance of varied zones of affective intensity. It critically engages questions such as how rainforests have been framed in conservation as sacred places apart from civilization, or how the movements of migrant peoples along train tracks and over waters have at times been envisioned by environmentalists as deeply threatening to beloved places. Lawrence Buell undertakes this kind of relatively focused spatial work when he explores the watershed as a site of unsettled interpretation in U.S. literatures of bioregionalism (2001). Buell considers how literary materials about watersheds address the local and translocal qualities of water, the impossibility of self-enclosure in the contemporary reality of global capitalism, and the colonial practices that suppress indigenous claims on waterways.

Ecocritics are currently engaging the architectures of unevenness, erasure, and collaboration among environmental imaginations around the world. Drawing on varied critical approaches, including comparative and postcolonial, these scholars explore differences and overlaps in environmental thought in distinct communities globally. As well as emphasizing that environmental literatures are nationally and regionally diverse, they explore alternate social-scalar categories through which to situate environmental literatures, such as environmentalisms of the poor or of indigenous communities (e.g., Nixon 2005; Cilano and DeLoughrey 2007; Watts 2007; Huggan and Tiffin 2007; Bird Rose 2008; Yuki 2008; Mukherjee 2010). Attention to the social scales in which we frame environmental literatures is important because certain conceptions of social and environmental space have been dominant in the nationalisms, imperialisms, and corporate capitalist practices of the twenty-first century. Other spaces, imagined and lived through varying species-related, linguistic, social, and geoeconomic practices, are little apprehended or acknowledged. Writers making claims about "national" environments and imaginations, for example, have at times elided the specific, different experiences and environmentalisms of minority communities (Nixon 2005, 237). To begin to work against some of this unevenness, Rob Nixon suggests, we cannot do twenty-first-century ecocriticism through homogenous terms, such as the understandings of nature developed in mainstream U.S. environmentalism; instead, we must negotiate common ground among distinct approaches to the environment that are not easily put into dialogue with one another (2005, 246).

Following Anna Tsing (2005), we might explore in detail the frictions that both trouble and enable the making of environmental stories over vast spatial expanses. Migrating, universal stories, such as decolonization, freedom, or science, are important to environmentalism (Tsing 2005; Chakrabarty 2009). Tsing suggests that we see how such environmental stories are worked out through specific encounters, where they are made unpredictable by cultural differences and status inequalities. Environmental stories of the universal and the common are never homogenous everywhere. Ecocriticism offers a rich site from which to create dialogues and to share frameworks. For example, Masami Raker Yuki describes the labor through which an "intimate intellectual community of ecocritics who are willing to listen to each other" is being created in East Asia and beyond (2008).

Environments are "timescapes," to use Buell's term, reshaped over and over through various durations (2007, 227). It is important to ask what spatial concepts are lit up or erased by particular temporal frameworks (Buell 2007; DeLoughrey 2007; Chakrabarty 2009; Nixon 2009). Time is a vector of scale. Dipesh Chakrabarty shows that thinking in relation to geological time illuminates parameters on life at the scale of the human (2009). He notes that human writing, agriculture, and urban spaces developed as Earth shifted into the relatively stable, warm conditions of the Holocene. This deep species history reminds us that certain geological and biological conditions are necessary for the survival of cultural practices such as the writing of environmental histories or environmental criticism. Wielding a geologic, species-scale force since the Industrial Revolution, humans are changing the conditions that nurtured human life and ecological imaginaries.

Contributors to this collection work with particularly dominant or compelling spatial scales, but they also move among spatial scales. **Michael G. Ziser** engages spatial imaginations of community in U.S. literatures that seek grips on the future beyond reliance on coal and oil. He argues for ecocritical exploration of the environmental costs of communities that operate at different material scales. Desires for materially global forms of life are historical to the current, unsustainable, oil-saturated moment of life. Ziser considers the bioregional imaginations that emerged in U.S. environmentalism and literature in relation to the oil crises of the 1970s and early 1980s. In their explorations of the spatial possibilities for communities living without fossil fuels, these literary visions are an important site through which ecocritics can think about spaces that are yet to come.

Cheryll Glotfelty explores the geographic unevenness present in struggles over nuclear power, looking at the cultural imagination of spaces of abandonment associated with radioactive waste. Plans for the Yucca Mountain nuclear waste repository, Nevada, show the uneven targeting of certain expanses of the world for environmental destruction. Glotfelty analyzes activist cartoons associated with communities that seek to block the disposal of waste. These cartoons' political claim that "you do not put that in my backyard," sometimes maligned as a NIMBY politics, shows politically pragmatic and flexible ways of framing spaces of concern. **Julie Sze and Yi Zhou** also engage processes of spatial differentiation in environmental transformations, analyzing plans for Dongtan eco-city, near Shanghai. This eco-city was dreamed up in the environmental culture of transnational corporations and articulated through a contradictory discourse that emphasizes the significance of local place while assuming that capitalist, techno-scientific values can be compellingly applied everywhere on the planet. Desires for the eco-city were negotiated in relation to Chinese and regional developmental contexts, transnational corporations, and reworked by local people, in conditions of huge power disparities.

Susie O'Brien emphasizes that understandings of scale are always limited in her investigation of North American local food narratives. Literature about the U.S. and Canadian local food movement reflects settler-invader politics through its selective containment of how we might understand space in relation to colonialism. O'Brien argues for awareness of partiality in understandings of locality, because places are shot through with uncertain temporal and spatial qualities, produced not only by care but also by colonial and capitalist violence in ways impossible to fully account for. **Teresa Shewry** also considers how stories about environmental scale are shaped in conditions of power disparities, focusing on collaborative projects among New Zealand writers and artists. She analyzes work by artists whose concerns for social spaces of the sea are marked by histories of colonialism and by artistic, species, and linguistic differences. These artists concentrate not only on entrenched spatial scales but also on how scale is always a site of multiple interpretations, of partly failed understandings. Much falls away from the dominant spatial arrangements in which environments are often understood, and so scale is an important but never exhausted concern.

AFTERWORD: AN INTERVIEW WITH ELAINE SCARRY

Elaine Scarry, the Walter M. Cabot Professor of Aesthetics and the General Theory of Value at Harvard University, does not identify herself as an environmental critic. She is a long-time antinuclear activist with environmental concerns. However, Scarry's strong interest in the relationship of aesthetics to justice makes her work generative for environmental criticism, and volumes such as *The Body in Pain* (1985) and *On Beauty and Being Just* (1999) testify to the deep significance of matter and its injury. In this collection, the relationship of aesthetics to embodiment, everyday practice, and artistic figuration appears variously, for example, within analyses of the future distribution of fossil fuel, the fate of ocean commonwealths, and the development of sustainable cities. The field of aesthetics has been assumed too easily by environmental critics in the past, as if aesthetics were a route into a universal Nature that stands apart from frames of ecological knowledge such as science, history, and scale. We asked Elaine Scarry for this interview to complicate our understanding of how aesthetics might serve environmental justice, abetting constitutional concerns and the immediate policy goals of activists. In the process of the interview, Professor Scarry expounds upon her conviction that nuclear weaponry represents the single greatest threat to environmental health and futurity.

REFERENCES

Alaimo, Stacy. 2009. "MCS Matters: Material Agency in the Science and Practices of Environmental Illness." *Topia* 21: 7–25.
Alaimo, Stacy, and Susan Hekman. 2008. *Material Feminisms*. Bloomington: Indiana University Press.

Anker, Peder. 2001. *Imperial Ecology: Environmental Order in the British Empire, 1895–1945*. Cambridge, MA: Harvard University Press.

Beck, Ulrich. 1995. *Ecological Enlightenment: Essays on the Politics of the Risk Society*. Trans. Mark A. Ritter. New York: Humanity Books.

Bird Rose, Deborah. 2008. "On History, Trees, and Ethical Proximity." *Postcolonial Studies* 11: 157–167.

Buell, Lawrence. 1998. "Toxic Discourse." *Critical Inquiry* 24: 639–665.

———. 2001. *Writing for an Endangered World: Literature, Culture, and Environment in the U.S. and Beyond*. Cambridge, MA: Harvard University Press.

Chakrabarty, Dipesh. 2009. "The Climate of History: Four Theses." *Critical Inquiry* 35: 197–222.

Cilano, Carla, and Elizabeth DeLoughrey. 2007. "Against Authenticity: Global Knowledges and Postcolonial Ecocriticism." *ISLE: Interdisciplinary Studies in Literature and Environment* 14: 71–87.

DeLoughrey, Elizabeth. 2007. "Quantum Landscapes: A 'Ventriloquism of Spirit.'" *Interventions: International Journal of Postcolonial Studies* 9: 62–82.

Engels, Friedrich. 1958. *The Condition of the English Working Class in England in 1844*. New York: Macmillan.

Fromm, Harold. 2009. *The Nature of Being Human: From Environmentalism to Consciousness*. Baltimore: Johns Hopkins University Press.

Garrard, Greg. 2004. *Ecocriticism: The New Critical Idiom*. London: Routledge.

Glotfelty, Cheryll. 1996. "Introduction: Literary Studies in an Age of Environmental Crisis." In *The Ecocriticism Reader*, edited by Cheryl Glotfelty and Harold Fromm, xv–xxxvii. Athens: University of Georgia Press.

Haraway, Donna J. 1991. *Simians, Cyborgs, and Women: The Reinvention of Nature*. New York: Routledge.

———. 2004. *The Haraway Reader*. New York: Routledge.

Hayles, N. Katherine. 1999. *How We Became Posthuman: Virtual Bodies in Cybernetics, Literature, and Informatics*. Chicago: University of Chicago Press.

Heise, Ursula K. 1997. "Science and Ecocriticism." *The American Book Review* 18.5: 4.

———. 2008. *Sense of Place and Sense of Planet: The Environmental Imagination of the Global*. Oxford and New York: Oxford University Press.

Herbert, George. 1941. *The Works of George Herbert*, edited by F. E. Hutchinson. Oxford: Clarendon Press.

Huggan, Graham, and Helen Tiffin. 2007. "Green Postcolonialism." *Interventions* 9: 1–11.

Kathirithamby-Wells, Jeyamalar. 2005. *Nature and Nation: Forests and Development in Peninsular Malaysia*. Singapore: NIAS Press.

Latour, Bruno. 1993. *We Have Never Been Modern*, translated by Catherine Porter. Cambridge, MA: Harvard University Press.

———. 2005. *Reassembling the Social: An Introduction to Actor-Network-Theory*. Oxford: Oxford University Press.

Lipsius, Justus, John Stradling, Rudolf Kirk, and Clayton Morris Hall. 1939. *Tvvo Bookes of Constancie*. New Brunswick, NJ: Rutgers University Press.

Love, Glen A. 1999. "Ecocriticism and Science: Toward Consilience?" *New Literary History* 30.3: 561–576.

Lowe, Celia. 2006. *Wild Profusion: Biodiversity Conservation in an Indonesian Archipelago*. Princeton, NJ: Princeton University Press.

Marsh, George. 1884. *Man and Nature*. New York: Scribner.

Marvel, Andrew. 2003. *The Poems of Andrew Marvell*, edited by Nigel Smith. London: Pearson Longman.

Meeker, Joseph W. 1972. *The Comedy of Survival: In Search of an Environmental Ethic*. Los Angeles: International College Guild of Tutors Press.

Merchant, Carolyn. 1980. *The Death of Nature; Women, Ecology, and the Scientific Revolution*. San Francisco: Harper One.

Mukherjee, Upamanyu Pablo. 2010. *Postcolonial Environments: Nature, Culture and the Contemporary Indian Novel in English*. New York: Palgrave Macmillan.

Nixon, Rob. 2005. "Environmentalism and Postcolonialism." *Postcolonial Studies and Beyond*, edited by Ania Loomba, Suvir Kaul, Matti Bunzl, Antoinette Burton, and Jed Esty. Durham: Duke University Press. 233–251.

———. 2009. "Neoliberalism, Slow Violence, and the Environmental Picaresque." *MFS Modern Fiction Studies* 55.3: 443–467.

Phillips, Dana. 2003. *The Truth of Ecology: Nature, Culture, and Literature in North America*. Oxford: Oxford University Press.

Slovic, Scott, and Michael P. Branch. 2003. "Introduction: Surveying the Emergence of Ecocriticism." In *The ISLE Reader: Ecocriticism, 1993–2003*, edited by Michael P. Branch and Scott Slovic, xiii–xxiii. Athens: University of Georgia Press.

Tsing, Anna Lowenhaupt. 2005. *Friction: An Ethnography of Global Connection*. Princeton, NJ: Princeton University Press.

Watts, Richard. 2007. "Contested Sources: Water as Commodity/Sign in French Caribbean Literature." *Atlantic Studies* 4.1: 87–101.

White, Lynn Jr. 1996. "The Historical Roots of Our Ecological Crisis." In *The Ecocriticism Reader*, edited by Cheryl Glotfelty and Harold Fromm. Athens: University of Georgia Press, 1996.

Yuki, Masami Raker. 2008. "Towards the East Asian Network of Ecocriticism." *ASLE-Japan: The Association for the Study of Literature and Environment in Japan*, 2010. http://www.asle-japan.org/english/2008/11/joint_plenary_speech_at_intern.html#more (accessed August 27, 2010).

Part I
Science

1   The Mesh

Timothy Morton

ENTANGLED

> It is interesting to contemplate an entangled bank, clothed with many plants of many kinds, with birds singing on the bushes, with various insects flitting about, and with worms crawling through the damp earth, and to reflect that these elaborately constructed forms, so different from each other, and dependent on each other in so complex a manner, have all been produced by laws acting around us. These laws, taken in the largest sense, being Growth with Reproduction; Inheritance . . . ; Variability, from the indirect and direct action of the conditions of life, and from use and disuse; a Ratio of Increase so high as to lead to a Struggle for Life, and as a consequent to Natural Selection, entailing Divergence of Character and the Extinction of less-improved forms (Darwin 1996, 395–396).

Over two hundred years after the birth of Charles Darwin, his ideas still appear strange, even dangerous: hence the title of Daniel Dennett's book *Darwin's Dangerous Idea*. In part, this has something to do with the very form of his writing. Notice how Darwin's prose slides from the specific—the life-forms in the "entangled bank"—to the general: the evolutionary trends and forces that determine how that bank appears to us. By the time we get to the end, we seem to have lost track of the specific "entangled bank." Now look back at the "specific" part—just how specific is it? The description, the final paragraph of *The Origin of Species*, is vivid yet curiously vague: "an entangled bank, clothed with many plants of many kinds, with birds singing on the bushes, with various insects flitting about, and with worms crawling through the damp earth." Which birds? What color? It is as if we are already seeing the life-forms blurred and morphed in time, like watching the flow of turbulent currents in a stream—already, that is, before we get to the generalizations that make even this picture seem like a crisp and vivid snapshot.

Darwin's language itself shows magnificently what the trouble is. The trouble is that when you take an evolutionary view of Earth, an astonishing reversal takes place. Suddenly, things that you think of as real—this cat over here, my cat, whose fur I can stroke—become the abstraction, an approximation of flowing, metamorphic processes, processes that are in some sense far more real than the entity I am stroking. The fact that we at present call this flow a cat is a mere matter of convenience. This is not simply about nominalism—a cat by any other name would meow as prettily. The cat as such, no matter what we call it, is not really a cat. The real thing is the evolutionary process—the cat is just an abstraction! The discovery of evolution is nothing less than a Copernican revolution, in which what we take to be immediate and real turns out to be an abstraction of a deeper reality.

There is indeed something humiliating about this reversal of immediacy into abstraction, in the same way Copernicus and Galileo brought humans down to Earth by insisting that the Universe was not rotating around us. In their era, "common sense" told you that the Sun went around the Earth once a day—this is what your eyes seem to indicate. Eyes see the same phenomenon today. It is just that Galileo and Copernicus taught us that our immediate experience is a workable approximation that makes sense only on a very limited island of meaningfulness—the island on which the word *sunrise* has meaning. It's not so much that we mistrust our eyes (bad, mistrustful moderns!). It is that we are able to contextualize our immediate perception within a wider framework. What disappears is the common-sensical idea that what appears to be immediate is also real. In Galileo's age, common sense also told you that weird old ladies offering herbal remedies who did not drown when you threw them in water should be burnt, because they're witches. Common sense has a lot to answer for.

Evolution strikes another great nail into the coffin of common sense. It is worth pausing briefly to let this stunning conclusion sink in. We cannot see, touch, or smell evolution. It evades our perception—it takes place on spatiotemporal scales far in excess of one, or even a million, human lifetimes, and it involves processes such as DNA replication that are too small to be seen with the naked eye. Of course we might see small changes in the ears of any kittens our cat bore. But would the slightly smaller ears count as a significant variation? "Significant" in this case means that the trait is passed on—so in effect, significance is always in the future, always to come. DNA agrees with Hegel that for something to happen, it must happen at least twice (Dennett 1996, 100). Darwin systematically undermines the idea that there are thin, rigid boundaries between species, between species and variants of a species, and between variation and monstrosity (Darwin 1996, 9, 94, 109, 131, 133; Morton 2010, 60–68). The words *origin* and *species* in his title are almost jokes. If Darwin had possessed access to e-mail he would probably have written it as *The "Origin" of "Species" ;)*. It gets even weirder when you realize that it is the very operation of evolution that makes it illegible. Successful species are what create gaps in the fossil record, pages torn from the book of nature—Darwin himself is fond of revising the old topos of the book of nature (Darwin 1996, 100, 141, 251). In other words, even if you assimilated all the information you could ever gather at some point in time about life-forms, your picture would necessarily be incomplete. Of course, in the time it would take you to assimilate the information, new life-forms would have evolved, but for the sake of argument let's just imagine that we possess the ability to gather knowledge instantaneously. Even if this were the case, evolution would still be illegible in some sense. No one could predict the evolution of cats (or of humans) from a snapshot of all the evidence from a time before cats (or humans) appeared. Stranger still, and this is a major topic in *The Origin of Species*, there occurs no moment at which cats become totally distinct from their ancestors. This is Darwin's version of Zeno's paradox, which he calls the problem of "incipient species" (Darwin 1996, 44). Even stranger, if you rewound the evolutionary tape and played it back, you would not necessarily see cats (or humans) appear. DNA is a set of instructions like a recipe (an algorithm), and we all know that if you make a meal twice it would not necessarily turn out the same.

There is thus no place outside of evolution from which to view it objectively—that is, as a totally determined process whose features we can readily predict. In Lacanian jargon, this means that "there is no metalanguage," and that the "Big Other"—some idealized reference point from which everything makes sense—does not truly exist. You simply cannot see the whole thing at once—it has no outside—yet it consists precisely in an unbroken flow of DNA (and other replicators). It's not as if there is nothing there—there is an astonishing variety of life-forms. "Nature" is surely a good candidate for a Big Other from whose vantage point you can assess life-forms. But if you look for Nature, all you'll find are trees, butterflies, oceans, primates . . . Ironically, it's evolution and ecology that put an end to the concept of Nature (I capitalize it to make it seem strange and artificial).

Reconsider our cat having kittens. The DNA mutation visible in those slightly smaller ears is random with respect to current need. In other words, there is no adaptation to an environment in a strong sense. Of course the smaller ears might come in useful. If the kittens who have them do not die before they reproduce, their descendants can keep them: neo-Darwinist theory calls this "satisficing" (Dawkins 1999, 156). If it means anything, "fittest" (as in "survival of") means happening not to die before you have kids. So there exists a huge variety of vestigial organs, nonfatal traces of past mutations. "Fittest" does not mean having six-pack abs or being a cunning, aggressive Wall Street cat. Ducks have webbed feet, and television natural history shows are tempted to talk about how webbed feet are beautifully adapted to water. But coots do not have webbed feet, and they also swim in water—so evolution does not care about webbed feet. Thinking that evolution does care is an error called "adaptationism" (Dawkins 1999, 30).

Furthermore, the environment to which the kitten adapts consists of other life forms, which are also adapting. The very oxygen we breathe, the concentration of iron in Earth's crust, are the excretions of ancient bacteria. Within life-forms, all the way down to the DNA level, there are other life-forms—the fact of symbiosis (Margulis 1979, 1998). Animal cells contain mitochondria, which are bacterial symbionts, like chloroplasts (which make plants green). There exist plant–animal hybrids such as the green sea slug *Elysia chlorotica,* which can photosynthesize (Margulis 1998, 9–10). Life-forms refuse to stay within thin, rigid boundaries. There is no neutral, static background against which specific life-forms could become meaningful. Evolution means that this furry four-legged being that purrs is not strictly a cat . . . In a Darwinian world we can see around the edges of life-forms, and into their strange ambiguous depths—these shadowy hidden sides undermine the coherence of what we took to be our immediate, commonsense perception.

All of this is profoundly antiteleological. Wherever we look, up close or far away, over very short or very long timespans, we fail to find a point, goal, origin, or terminus in the process of evolution. Consider Copernicus again. Discoveries about Earth's place in the Universe did not replace one teleology with another one, making us feel even more secure because one center was replaced with a stronger, better one. The possibility opened up that teleology as such is always an abstraction from what is the case. It is just the same with Darwin. The lack of teleology is humiliating—literally, it brings us down to Earth, which must be good news for ecology.

Notice how Darwin's "entangled bank" suggests that we visualize interconnected life-forms as a whole—and what is ecology if not the study of the fact of this interconnection? Yet what is this whole if not a flowing, shifting, entangled mess of ambiguous entities—entities that become even more ambiguous the closer we look? Or, as I shall be arguing here, the whole is a *mesh*, a very curious, radically open form without center or edge.

Ecological science holds that all life-forms are interconnected, but what are the philosophical and cultural implications of this interconnectedness? The mesh is even more deeply interwoven than biocentric ideas such as the web of life imply, because it does away with boundaries between living and nonliving forms. At the same time, symbiosis ensures that boundaries between life-forms are never rigid and thin; rather, they are wide and permeable. The concept of the mesh gives rise to an ethics and politics based on (1) the utter singularity and uniqueness of every life-form and (2) the lack of fixed identity anywhere in the system of life-forms. Though they seem radically different, (1) and (2) actually entail each other.

THE INTERDEPENDENCE THEOREM

Now let's think about ecological interconnectedness in a more formal way. Imagine an Interdependence Theorem, containing the following two axioms:

Axiom (1): $\forall a: \exists a: a = {\sim}({\sim}a)$
Axiom (2): $\forall a: \exists a: a \supset {\sim}a$

We shall gradually discover that the Interdependence Theorem tells us a lot about what we want to know about how things are interconnected in ecological systems.

Axiom 1 states that for every *a*, the existence of *a* is such that *a* consists of things that are *not not-a*. In other words, *a* is made of *not-a's*, and thus must be defined negatively and differentially. In other words, *a* is *a* because it *isn't not-a*, while *not-a* is only *not-a* because *it is not a*. In this sense, *a* and *not-a* are mutually determining. Axiom 1 states that things are only what they are in relation to other things.

Axiom 2 states that things derive from other things. While Axiom 1 makes statements about how things are (synchronically), Axiom 2 talks about origins (diachrony). In every case, things like *a* only exist such that a *not-a* exists. Nothing exists by itself and nothing comes from nothing.

Axioms 1 and 2 define interdependence across a range of phenomena. They summarize structural linguistics, for instance, because structuralism's model of language is that signs are completely interdependent. The Interdependence Theorem also describes life-forms. Diachronically, no life-form exists that did not arise from another life-form. And synchronically, life-forms are different from each other in arbitrarily negative ways: there is no human-flavored DNA as opposed to daffodil-flavored DNA, for instance. In fact, since life-forms are expressions of DNA, they differ from each other negatively rather than positively, since DNA is of course a language, and can thus be modeled by structuralism.

Since life-forms depend upon each other the same way signs depend upon each other, the system of life-forms is isometric with the system of language. This means that since language as a system is subject to deconstruction, the system of life-forms must also be subject to deconstruction. What happens when we subject the system of life-forms to deconstruction?

Let's remind ourselves what happens when we subject the system of language to deconstruction. Derrida describes this as thinking "the structurality of structure" (Derrida 1978, 280). What kind of structure? It's open-ended: it has no center and no edge. Because language is an arbitrary system of negative difference, there is no sign that stands somehow outside the system to guarantee the meaning and stability of the other signs. This means language is infinite, in the strong sense that we can never fully account for its meanings or effects. It also means that meaning depends upon meaninglessness. And that language as a system is not a thing, not an object, but a strange infinite network that has neither inside nor outside. This is how thinking structuralism leads to the discovery of textuality. The process that makes signs manifest as appearance and meaning is *différance*: the process of difference (synchronic) and deferment (diachronic). The meaning of a word is another word, and strings of signs only gain significance retroactively. The meaning of a sentence is a moving target. You will never be able to know exactly what the end of this sentence is until after you have read it elephant. This means that coherence, in order to be coherence, must contain some incoherence.

We can apply exactly the same view to the system of life-forms. Life-forms are made up of other life-forms (the theory of symbiosis). And life-forms derive from other life-forms (evolution). It is so simple, and yet so profound. Because of the ecological emergency we have entered, we are now compelled to take account of this mind-changing view.

The implications of a deconstructive view of life-forms are manifold:

(1) Life forms constitute a *mesh* that is infinite and beyond concept—unthinkable as such.
(2) Tracing the origins of life to a moment prior to life will result in paradoxes.
(3) Drawing distinctions between life and nonlife is strictly impossible, yet unavoidable.
(4) Differentiating between one species and another is never absolute.
(5) There is no "outside" of the system of life-forms.
(6) The Interdependence Theorem is part of the system of interdependence and thus subject to deconstruction!
(7) Since we cannot know in advance what the effects of the system will be, all life-forms are theorizable as *strange strangers*.

Let's sift through these implications.

(1) *Life-forms constitute a mesh that is infinite and beyond concept—unthinkable as such.* This is not just because the mesh is too "large" but also because it is also infinitesimally small. Differentiation goes down to the genomic level. There is no human-flavored DNA, no daffodil-flavored DNA.

Most of the words for interconnectedness are compromised by references to the Internet—"network," for example. Either that, or they were compromised by vitalism, the belief in a living substance. *Web* is a little bit too vitalist, and a little bit Internet-ish, so I guess it loses on both counts. "Mesh" can mean both the holes in a network and the threading between them. It suggests both hardness and delicacy. It has uses in biology, mathematics, and engineering, and in weaving and computing—think stockings and graphic design, metals and fabrics. It has antecedents in *mask* and *mass*, suggesting both density and deception (*Oxford English Dictionary*, "mesh," n.1.a–c.). By extension, "mesh" can mean "a complex situation or series of events in which a person is entangled; a concatenation of constraining or restricting forces or circumstances; a snare" (*Oxford English Dictionary*, "mesh," n.2.). In other words, it is perfect.

If everything is interconnected, then there is no definite background and therefore no definite foreground. Darwin sensed this startling loss of coordinates while thinking through the implications of the theory of natural selection. You can feel his palpable amazement:

> It is a truly wonderful fact—the wonder of which we are apt to over-
> look through familiarity—that all animals and all plants throughout
> all time and space should be related to each other in group subordinate
> to group, in the manner which we everywhere behold—namely, variet-
> ies of the same species most closely related together, species of the same
> genus less closely and unequally related together, forming sections and
> sub-genera, species of distinct genera much less closely related, and
> genera related in different degrees, forming sub-families, families, or-
> ders, sub-classes, and classes. The several subordinate groups in any
> class cannot be ranked in a single file, but seem rather to be clustered
> round points, and these round in other points, and so on in almost end-
> less cycles. (Darwin 1996, 105–106)

Every single life-form is literally familiar, in that we are genetically
descended from them. Darwin imagines an endlessly branching tree—*mesh*
does not suggest a clear starting point, and those "clusters" of "subordi-
nate groups" in the quotation above are far from linear (they "cannot be
ranked in a single file"). Each point of the mesh is both the center and edge
of a system of points, so there is no absolute center or edge. Still, the tree
image marvelously closes out Darwin's chapter on natural selection, with
its evocation of "the Great Tree of Life, which fills with its dead and broken
branches the crust of the earth, and covers the surface with its ever branching and beautiful ramifications" (Darwin 1996, 107). A "ramification" is a
branch and an implication, a branching thought.

(2) *Tracing the origins of life to a moment prior to life will result in
paradoxes.* Sol Spiegelman's discoveries concerning RNA show how it is
impossible to draw a rigid narrow boundary between "life" and "nonlife."
In order for life-forms to begin, there had to be a strange, paradoxical "preliving life" made of RNA and another replicator, such as self-replicating
silicate crystals (how strange that silicon may be the element in question).

RNA world abolishes the idea of a palpable, fetishized life substance, the
sort Naturephilosophy imagines as *Urschleim* or protoplasmic gel (Grant
2008). Curiously, the fantasy thing of idealist biology turns out to be this
existential substance, as if idealism depended for its coherence on some
metaphysical materiality. RNA world, by contrast, is structured like a language. At bottom, it is a set of empty formal relationships. This is the basis
of a genuinely materialist biology.

(3) *Drawing distinctions between life and nonlife is strictly impossible,
yet unavoidable.* This brings us to our third paradox. If "preliving life" is
necessary for imagining the origins of life, then it is also the case that in the
present moment, the moment of "life" as such, the life–nonlife distinction
is also untenable. When we start to think about life, we worry away at the
distinction between nature and artifice. Viroids, for instance, are entities
that are ten times smaller than virus, consisting of a circle of RNA code.
Their origins are very ancient, probably dating from RNA world. These

little circles of code do not eat or metabolize as such—what they do is make copies of themselves via other DNA systems they find, such as those inside a plant in the case of the potato tuber spindle viroid. If you believe that viroids are alive, you should probably believe that a computer virus is alive. A computer virus is also just a string of code that tells other code to make copies of itself.

(4) *Differentiating between one species and another is never absolute.* This is the lesson of Darwinism. Darwinism is truly a great "humiliation" of the human, up there (or down there) with Copernicus, Freud, and Marx. "Species" is a label that must be applied retroactively to life-forms. There are no species as such, no species-to-be, no point in evolutionary history to which we can point and say, "Here is the origin of (say) *Homo sapiens*." Darwin declared that his observations of mockingbirds and turtles might "undermine the stability of Species." What an understatement.

(5) *There is no "outside" of the system of life-forms.* Once life gets going—we have already shown how thinking this origin is practically impossible—everything else becomes linked with it. This is what most of us mean when we think ecologically: that everything is connected to everything else. There are strong metaphysical versions of this consequence (such as Gaian holism), and weak reductionist ones. I am on the weak reductionist side.

This point is actually very profound, because it also implies that there is no environment as such—that what we're talking about today is the phenotypical expression of DNA. Your DNA does not stop expressing itself at the ends of your fingers. A beaver's DNA doesn't stop at the ends of its whiskers, but at the ends of it dam (Dawkins 1999). A spider's DNA is expressed in its web. The environment, then, from the perspective of the life sciences, is nothing but the phenotypical expression of DNA code. This includes oxygen (anaerobic bacterial excrement). And it includes iron ore (a by-product of archaic metabolic processes). You drive and fly using crushed liquefied dinosaur bones. You are walking on top of hills and mountains of fossilized animal bits. Most of your house dust is your skin. The *environment* is beginning to look like not a very successful upgrade of the old-fashioned term *nature*.

(6) *The Interdependence Theorem is part of the system of interdependence and thus subject to deconstruction!* This is recursivity in action. Since the Interdependence Theorem is also only possible to state in language, and since the Interdependence Theorem describes language itself, the theorem itself falls prey to its own premises.

The First Axiom states, "Things are made of other things." The Second Axiom states that "Things come from other things."

Implication 4 asserts that we cannot rigorously differentiate between one species and another. Wait a moment. In order for Axiom 2 to be valid, we must be able to distinguish one species from another! Since "Things come from other things," there must be a distinction we can draw between one thing and another thing. Yet if we draw this distinction—that is, if we think the word *distinction* means something—then there is no way one species can arise from another species. A dinosaur, a bird: there is a continuity between them. And yet a dinosaur is not a bird. Studying how life-forms are differentiated involves Zeno's paradoxes of this type.

Axiom 2 is in more trouble than this, because it applies readily to things that are not life-forms. Think of a candle and its flame. If there were no difference between the candle and its flame, then the flame could not arise, distinct from the candle. But if the candle is indeed different from the flame, then there is no way the flame can arise from it! Thus "different from" and "comes from" are now reduced to something meager. The very terms of Axiom 2 have shrunk. They are themselves subject to Axiom 2!

Now consider Axiom 1, "Things are made up of other things." Think of a car: it's made of wheels, chassis, steering wheel, windows, and so on. Where is the car-ness in these components? Nowhere. Yet we can't say that just any old thing will do to put a car together: a car is made of just these components, not other ones. We have reduced Axiom 1 to bareness, by using Axiom 1 itself!

Human beings are made up of arms, legs, heads, brains, and so on. So are birds, duck-billed platypuses, and sharks. These organs are made up of cells. So are plants, fungi, amoebae, and bacteria. These cells contain organelles. These organelles are modified bacteria such as mitochondria and chloroplasts. They themselves contain DNA. This DNA is a hybrid fusion of bacterial DNA and viral insertions. DNA has no species flavor; moreover, it has no intrinsic flavor at all. At the DNA level it becomes impossible to decide which sequence is a "genuine" one and which is a viral insertion. In bacteria there exist plasmids that are like pieces of viral code. Plasmids are a kind of parasite within the bacterial host, but at this level, the host–parasite duality becomes impracticable. It becomes impossible to tell which being is a parasite, and which a host. We have discovered components without a device of which they are the components. We could call them organs without bodies (Žižek 2003). Consider, for instance, the endogenous human retrovirus ERV-3. ERV-3 sits in your genome and may well bestow immunosuppressive properties upon the placental barrier. You are reading this, in other words, because a virus in your DNA told your mom not to abort you (Boyd et al. 1993). At the DNA level, the whole biosphere is highly permeable and boundaryless. How do we know that we haven't learnt how to sneeze because rhinoviral DNA codes directly for sneezing as a means to propagate itself? And yet we have bodies with arms, legs, and so on, and every day we see all kinds of life-forms floating and scuttling around, as if they were independent. It isn't an undifferentiated goo.

(7) *Since we cannot know in advance what the effects of the system will be, all life-forms are theorizable as "strange strangers."* The Interdependence Theorem does not reduce everything to sameness; it raises everything

to the level of wonder. The way things appear is like an illusion or magical display. They exist, but not that much. And how they exist is at the same time utterly unmysterious and unspeakably miraculous.

I use the phrase *strange stranger* because Derrida's notion of the *arrivant* is the closest we have as yet to a theory of how the mesh appears up close and personal. The *arrivant* is a being whose being we can't predict, whose arrival is utterly unexpected and unexpectedly unexpected to boot (Derrida 2000). The strange stranger is not only strange, but strangely so—uncanny, to use Freud's term. They could be us. They are us—the conclusion to be drawn from the life sciences is that we've got others—rather, they've got us, literally under our skin.

SOME IMPLICATIONS

In conclusion, let's think about how we might apply the mesh to the analysis of works of art such as literature and music. Darwin's "entangled bank" is in some sense profoundly organic, having to do with a total intimacy of form and content—not just a hand-in-glove fit (this would be more like decorum) but an "enactive" dance in which the form directly *is* the content (Varela, Thompson, and Rosch, 1992). Life-forms directly are maps of DNA's unfolding over time. On the other hand, Darwin's image, like his view in general, is also deeply nonessentialist. Nothing is self-identical.

In the humanities, normative ecological criticism such as ecocriticism tends to be organicist, but it also tends to be essentialist. Ecocriticism is highly suspicious, for instance, of deconstruction and "theory," precisely because thinking in these ways might put skids under the immediacy that is so much a part of environmentalist rhetoric. I propose that in order to accommodate Darwin, and all that Darwinism entails, given that Darwinism is highly congruent with how life-forms actually appear, ecological criticism in the humanities must embrace nonessentialism. (Likewise, deconstruction can be unnecessarily hostile to organicism, assuming that it is always essentialist and that it fetishizes substantiality as palpable, living presence. But I'm not as concerned about this assumption because, on the whole, deconstruction likes surprises.)

The Romantic poets, oft claimed by ecocriticism as part of their lineage, were organicists who were also nonessentialists. When Wordsworth is writing about a profound experience, he is also always asking, "Who was having this experience? Was it an experience at all? What is an experience, anyway?" So Wordsworth chooses forms, such as blank verse, first-person narrative, minimalist imagery, and Miltonic syntax, which will best unfold the openness he sees at the heart of experience. It is deconstruction that holds the nonessentialist piece of the Romantic puzzle, the piece that ecocriticism likes to shove under the carpet in case anyone comes looking for it (see, e.g., Kroeber 1994, 42; Bate 2000, 175). And so it is to deconstruction that ecological criticism must turn if it is to broaden its scope beyond the kinds of thinking, feeling, and writing that I here term *environmentalism*. Scholars must reimagine ecological literary criticism based on the nonessentialism and intimate entanglement of all life-forms that the life sciences discover on many levels, from evolution to symbiosis. The surprising result is that far more texts become available for ecological criticism, since that criticism is no longer restricted to pregiven canon of acceptably "environmental" content.

One goal of environmental writing is to be congruent with "Nature." But what if the concept *Nature* were one of the main things impeding genuine congruency? Contemporary life science constructs a view of the interdependence of life-forms that is remarkably similar to deconstruction's view of the complex interdependence of signs in a text—a phenomenon often called "textuality." This is not a holistic vision, in which parts combine to form a whole that is greater than their sum. Rather, this is a disturbing view of something that is both "less" than our usual categories and far more profound in another way. Life-forms are so intricately interconnected that it is impossible to determine where one ends and another begins. Yet curiously this implies that all life-forms are unique. It is holism that shares with modern mechanistic outlooks the idea that the parts of the whole are ultimately replaceable: if the whole is greater than their sum, this must be the case. Since the whole is at least to some extent different from its component parts, even holism is a form of fragmentation (Bohm 2008, 21, 227). By contrast, a nonessentialist view provides a platform for recognizing each life-form as a unique being, a temporary manifestation of an indivisible whole.

The University of California, Davis

REFERENCES

Bate, Jonathan. 2000. *The Song of the Earth.* Cambridge, MA: Harvard University Press.

Bohm, David. 2008. *Wholeness and the Implicate Order.* New York: Routledge.

Boyd, Mark T., Christopher M. R. Bax, Bridget E. Bax, David L. Bloxam, and Robin A. Weiss. 1993. "The Human Endogenous Retrovirus ERV-3 Is Upregulated in Differentiating Placental Trophoblast Cells." *Virology* 196: 905–909.

Darwin, Charles. 1996. *The Origin of Species.* Edited by Gillian Beer. Oxford: Oxford University Press.

Dawkins, Richard. 1999. *The Extended Phenotype: The Long Reach of the Gene.* Oxford: Oxford University Press.

Dennett, Daniel C. 1996. *Darwin's Dangerous Idea: Evolution and the Meanings of Life.* Harmondsworth, UK: Penguin.

Derrida, Jacques. 1978. "Structure, Sign and Play in the Discourse of the Human Sciences." In *Writing and Difference*, 278–293. Translated by Alan Bass. London: Routledge & Kegan Paul.

———. 2000. "Hospitality." Translated by Barry Stocker with Forbes Matlock. *Angelaki* 5.3 (December): 3–18.

Grant, Iain Hamilton. 2008. "Being and Slime: The Mathematics of Protoplasm in Lorenz Oken's 'Physio-Phyilosophy.'" *Collapse* 6: 287–321.

Kroeber, Karl. 1994. *Ecological Literary Criticism: Romantic Imagining and the Biology of Mind*. New York: Columbia University Press.

Margulis, Lynn. 1979. *Symbiosis in Cell Evolution*. San Francisco: Freeman.

———. 1998. *Symbiotic Planet: A New Look at Evolution*. New York: Basic Books.

Morton, Timothy. 2010. *The Ecological Thought*. Cambridge, MA: Harvard University Press.

Oxford English Dictionary. Edited by John Simpson et al., http://www.dictionary.oed.com (accessed August 9, 2010).

Varela, Francisco, Evan Thompson, and Eleanor Rosch. 1992. *The Embodied Mind: Cognitive Science and Human Experience*. Cambridge, MA: MIT Press.

Žižek, Slavoj. 2003. *Organs without Bodies: Deleuze and Consequences*. New York and London: Routledge.

2 Posthuman/Postnatural

Ecocriticism and the Sublime in Mary Shelley's *Frankenstein*

Paul Outka

In the nineteenth-century transatlantic culture of Europe and the U.S., a range of scientific discourses—medical, evolutionary, chemical, and environmental—began to suggest that human identity was physical rather than spiritual, a particularly complex expression of the natural. We became what we had always been in fact: a part of the earth that learned to talk, rather than Beings who transcended the earthly. Such discourses were reflected in a wide range of texts throughout the nineteenth century, as varied as Whitman's cycling between corpse and poetic text throughout his poetry, Thoreau's comparison (in *Walden*) of a thawing river bank to the human body, Bryant's "Thanatopsis," to the defensive characterization of evolutionary theory as suggesting that humans evolved *from* animals, rather than humans themselves *being* animals.[1] I call such moments the "organic sublime," episodes when an individual experienced and recorded an often profoundly disconcerting awareness of the radical material identity between his or her embodied self and the natural world.

This constitutive similarity between self and world was, I argue, an early version of what contemporary theorists of biotechnology call the "posthuman." This nineteenth-century sense of being organic, a mechanism among mechanisms, of a radical equivalence between self, body, and environment closely, if unexpectedly, resembles cyberpunk's conceit that the human is "wetware," data encoded biologically, but uploadable into an electronic form, into a digital self made of precisely the same stuff as the digital environment it inhabits. In both cases a definitional difference between the "human" subject and the land/datascape—humans are not nature, are mind rather than body, have souls, are somehow ineffable, etc.—is supplanted by the assertion of a definitional identity. While for some time now computational biology, genomics, neuroscience, and other related fields in biology and computer science have assumed a broad interchangeability between materiality and code, the implications of the collapse of this distinction for human identity showed up much earlier. Rather than being a twentieth- or twenty-first-century development, a nascent posthuman consciousness first emerged more than a century earlier in ways that profoundly affected the construction of both the natural and the human.

Such a reading complicates contemporary characterizations of the post-human as almost always involving a merge between the human and the technological, insisting instead on a view that sees nature, the human, and the technological as all differently realized, but fundamentally and qualitatively similar material constructions. In what follows, I want to define the posthuman as a mechanization and materialization of human identity, to read nineteenth-century developments in evolutionary theory and organic chemistry as both producing a materialist Origin for the human and asserting a radically material identity between humans-as-bodies and the material world.

In doing so I push against what seems to me two largely unacknowledged, even "naturalized," assumptions in contemporary posthuman theory: first, that the posthuman is necessarily a cyborg, that the critical unsettlement of the borders of the human is accomplished via a merge with nonnatural technology—what Marquard Smith and Joanne Morra (2006) call the "prosthetic impulse"—and, accordingly, second, that the posthuman is something utterly new, indeed Modern, indeed Postmodern, that our age is disjunctive, the End of History, or other versions of (to me) ahistorical hubris. In contrast, my emphasis on the organic sublime asserts that the critical question for posthumanism is not the unsettlement of the borders of the human by technology, but the materialist identity that such an unsettlement depends on, the radical connection between self, body, earth, matter that emerged so forcefully at this moment in the nineteenth century.

This assertion compliments N. Katherine Hayles's observation that much of contemporary posthumanism depends on seeing "information and materiality as distinct entities," on "information losing its body" (Hayles 1999, 13). Treating information as an entity separate from the accident of its material instantiation is, for Hayles, at the heart of a particular posthuman fantasy of doing away with the (mortal) body, treating "embodiment . . . as if it were a supplement to be purged from the dominant term of information, an accident of evolution we are now in a position to correct" (1999, 12). Under such a view the human body is merely a "wet computer," an all-too-fragile device on which our software/data-based identities "run," hardware we might upgrade or replace altogether without suffering a meaningful loss. For Hayles, this disembodiment of posthuman identity ironically aligns the supposedly disjunctively new subject with liberal humanism and its similar erasure of the body's importance in constituting the subject in favor of enlightened reason, the soul, the human spirit, or whatever other version of ineffability serves to sever the subject from the historical and political and material mess of the flesh. By looking to the nineteenth century, a century before the emergence of the electronic computer and the ready-made way its hardware/software combination serves as a concrete (and false) metaphor for the mind/body "distinction," we can see more clearly what an embodied posthuman might look like, and how profoundly it challenged the category of the liberal subject.

The nineteenth-century experience of the posthuman was deeply disturbing to the subject immediately involved and to the wider ideological formations prevalent in the nineteenth century—most particularly essentialist forms of identity—that depended on a disjunctive relationship between human and nature. The collapse of that disjunction did more than rewrite the human in natural terms, however; it also worked in the opposite direction, making nature itself part of the human. This reading of posthuman theory helps us see how nature began to pivot in the nineteenth century from its early status as an unchanging realm that functioned as a material Other to our transcendent ineffability, to an evolving and utterly material system no longer metaphysically different from other "artificial" mechanisms, and did so in a way that mirrored a similar redefinition of human identity from soul to body.[2]

Hence, Darwin opens his 1859 *Origin of Species* with an extensive comparison of the process of natural selection to the earliest human biotechnology, the domestication of animals and plants. The first chapter of his book discusses domestication, the second, natural variation as the key variable of which human breeders take advantage, and the third, natural selection in which the breeder's choice is replaced by billions of individual creatures' competition for resources and mates accumulated over many hundred millions of years. Domestication and Natural Selection—one an "artificial" form of genetic engineering, the other what nature is, or rather, how it produces and reproduces itself in an endless flux—are in fact both facets of the same process for Darwin:

> I have called this principle by which each slight variation, if useful, is preserved, by the term Natural Selection, in order to mark its relation to man's power of selection. We have seen that man by selection can certainly produce great results, and can adapt organic beings to his own uses, through the accumulation of slight but useful variations, given to him by the hand of Nature. But Natural Selection, as we shall hereafter see, is a power incessantly ready for action, and is as immeasurably superior to man's feeble efforts, as the works of Nature are to those of Art. (Darwin 2003, 60)

This is not a ranking so much as a procedure for ranking; the difference between Nature and Art(ificial life), for Darwin, is not absolute or even fixed, but resides only in the quality of "works" each produces. Nature and Art are up to the same thing in other words, an unsettling fact that Mary Shelley had made the central conceit of her first novel thirty years before Darwin wrote his theory.[3] Both nature and the human collapsed towards each other in this period; we became posthuman; nature became postnatural. Or rather, since Darwin was right, we started to realize what we and nature always were—material, natural, artificial, made not found, always in flux, varied expressions of the same thing. The human was always built on a repression of materiality, a repression that in turn was in a definitional, reciprocal, and binary relationship to a wholly physical Nature both fixed and Other. Change one, change both.

THE ALPINE SUBLIME AND THE ORGANIC SUBLIME IN *FRANKENSTEIN*

In the reading of Mary Shelley's *Frankenstein* that follows, I want to flesh out—literally—the collapse of an earlier version of human/nature built around an oppositional binary between transcendent ineffability and Othered materiality, and its replacement by the nineteenth-century posthuman organic sublime. The novel is structured around a series of supposedly horrific juxtapositions between natural and unnatural environments and bodies: the sublime landscapes of the arctic and the Alps inhabited by the Romantic figures (Robert Walton, Henry Clerval, Victor Frankenstein) who thrill to them versus the creature with its uncanny immunity to those landscapes' physical challenges; human reproduction via Elizabeth's virginal womb versus Victor Frankenstein's "filthy workshop," the biotech lab of the early nineteenth century; normative human embodiment versus the oversized patchwork of human and animal corpse parts stitched together that comprise the creature. Throughout the novel, the horror the monster is meant to inspire is part of a more generalized shudder at the "unnatural" itself in all its various second-term-of-the-binary manifestations.

The critical temptation, if not the critical reflex, is to resolve this structuring natural/unnatural binary in a way that preserves it, by demonstrating how the monster is "really" the repressed part of the first term or by making "nature" capacious enough to include even the creature's unnaturalness. However, to do so misses the more radical collapse of nature and the human that Shelley is recording. To the extent that the category of the "natural" here itself represents an early nineteenth-century binary that juxtaposed an ineffable human and a nonhuman materialized nature, the creature promises the destruction of more than just Victor's family and friends. It spells the end of the very structure of their subjectivity and the nature that (didn't) give it birth.

This earlier structure finds its quintessential expression in the novel's repeated staging of the Romantic natural sublime, experiences that both construct and reflect the central male characters' normative identity. Reflecting the Kantian template laid out in *The Critique of Judgment* some thirty years earlier, the scenes of the natural sublime in the novel dramatize a repeated movement from a carefully controlled confusion in the borders between human and natural to a hierarchized restabilization of that relationship in which the human is rendered utterly different, essentially immaterial, and transcendent. As Kant describes the process, both the idea of the infinite (what he calls the "mathematical" sublime; think the ocean or the night sky) and the sight of immense power (he calls this the "dynamical" sublime; think mountain or storm) only initially destabilize the human subject; the resolution of that instability comes in a realization of utter difference from the material world:

> Now, in the immensity of nature and in the insufficiency of our faculties to take in a standard proportionate to the aesthetical estimation of the magnitude of its *realm*, we find our own limitation, although at the same time in our rational faculty we find a different, nonsensuous standard, which has that infinity itself under it as a unity, in comparison with which everything in nature is small, and thus in our mind we find a superiority to nature even in its immensity. And so also the irresistibility of its might, while making us recognize our own physical impotence, considered as beings of nature, discloses to us a faculty of judging independently of and a superiority over nature, on which is based a kind of self-preservation entirely different from that which can be attacked and brought into danger by external nature. Thus humanity in our person remains unhumiliated, though the individual might have to submit to this dominion. In this way nature is not judged to be sublime in our aesthetical judgments in so far as it excites fear, but because it calls up that power in us (which is not nature) of regarding as small the things about which we are solicitous (goods, health, and life), and of regarding its might (to which we are no doubt subjected in respect of these things) as nevertheless without any dominion over us and our personality to which we must bow where our highest fundamental propositions, and their assertion or abandonment, are concerned. Therefore nature is here called sublime merely because it elevates the imagination to a presentation of those cases in which the mind can make felt the proper sublimity of its destination, in comparison with nature itself. (Kant 1951, 101)

Both the mathematical and dynamical versions of the sublime result in the same sort of recovery for the subject; the assertion of absolute difference from both nature and embodiment, from the material/phenomenal itself. "Considered as beings of nature," we are "physical[ly] impotent" against the "irresistibility of [nature's] might," and can "be attacked and brought into danger by external nature"; our embodied selves do not "remain[] unhumiliated" but "have to submit to this dominion." In sharp contrast to this material submission, however, is "the proper sublimity of [the mind's] destination, in comparison with nature itself." The meaning of the sublime comes not in the momentary confusion of the borders between self and nature, but in their absolute restoration as the subject realizes the fundamental difference between himself (or, much less often in Kant, herself), and his embodied existence in an utterly material natural world. The meaning of the natural landscape is transformed in this process from an overwhelmingly powerful other that threatens the subject's physical existence, to a symbol of the subject's metaphysical difference and fundamentally greater immaterial essence. The ocean or the mountain shift from signifying nature's physical power to signifying the radically empowered subject.[4] So, for example, in "Mont Blanc," after several hundred lines describing the mountain's awesome physical sublimity, Percy Shelley turns sharply, and predictably, in a Kantian direction, asking of the mountain in the poem's final sentence:

> And what were thou, and earth, and stars, and sea,
> If to the human mind's imaginings
> Silence and solitude were vacancy? (Shelley 1977, 93)

Shelley's question here is rhetorical; this is not a proto-Deep Ecological moment but a radically anthropocentric one. The answer to "what were thou?" is not given directly, but rather subsumed under a second question about what meaning humans give to silence and solitude. The significance of Nature's material presence is transmuted into a question about the human meaning of the absence of other humans. It is difficult to imagine a wider gulf between a material, extrahuman nature and a human conceived as an imagining mind than what Shelley opens here, or a more thoroughgoing dominance of the human/immaterial. Mont Blanc's immense physical presence and power is celebrated in awestruck language earlier in a way that ultimately serves to emphasize, as it does in Kant, the complete transcendence of the human from the physical.

Again and again, *Frankenstein* sets up such moments of sublimity for its central male character, only to consistently interrupt the expected Kantian resolution with the arrival of the creature. Indeed, after building the creature, *every* time Victor tries for the sublime the creature shows up immediately, whether mushing on a dog sled, bounding up an alpine cliff, or demanding a long conversation in a hut with his maker. Within a novel so profoundly concerned with the definition of the human, and the ontological and epistemological status of the natural, such interruptions represent more than the individual failure of Victor Frankenstein; Shelley calls into question both that definition and that status, and does so by substituting the creature for the traditional anthropocentric resolution of the sublime. The creature disrupts the sublime formation of the human/natural binary, and in doing so changes the definition of both.

Take, for example, the pivotal moment in the novel when Victor Frankenstein first interacts with his spurned creation. He is on an alpine hiking trip with his father and Clerval on Montavert, in view of Mont Blanc. Despondent, Victor sets out alone to scale the summit in the midst of a rainstorm, hoping that the sublime scene will restore him, as it has in the past:

> I remembered the effect the view of the tremendous and ever moving glacier had produced upon my mind when I first saw it. It had then

filled me with a sublime ecstacy that gave wings to the soul and allowed
it to soar from the obscure world to light and joy. The sight of the awful
and majestic in nature had indeed always the effect of solemnizing my
mind and causing me to forget the passing cares of life. I determined
to go alone, for I was well acquainted with the path, and the presence
of another would destroy the solitary grandeur of the scene. (Shelley,
2009, 120)

And, initially, the setting succeeds in producing the sublime in Victor,
which is to say in producing its own dematerialized departure and Victor's
immaterial transcendence, giving "wings to [his] soul" and allowing him to
"soar from the obscure world to light and joy." The familiar human/imma-
terial versus natural/material binary is proffered here, only to collapse with
near-comic rapidity as the creature arrives:

It was noon when I arrived at the top of the ascent. . . . From that side
where I now stood, Montavert was exactly opposite at the distance of
a league, and above it rose Mont Blanc in awful majesty. I remained in
a recess of the rock, gazing on this wonderful and stupendous scene.
The sea, or rather vast river of ice, wound among its dependent mountains whose aerial summits hung over its recesses. Their icy and glit-
tering peaks shone in sunlight over the clouds. My heart, which before
was sorrowful, now swelled with something like joy. I exclaimed—
'Wandering spirits, if indeed ye wander and do not rest in your narrow
beds, allow me this faint happiness or take me as your companion away
from the joys of life.' As I said this, I suddenly beheld the figure of a
man at some distance advancing toward me with superhuman speed.
(2009, 122)

Not exactly a wandering *spirit* here, the "figure of a man" proves to be an
animated amalgam of corpse parts, one without any bed, narrow or otherwise, and as reciprocally committed to Victor's profound unhappiness as
Victor is to rejecting him utterly as a "companion." At the precise moment
when the Kantian sublime is poised to convert the landscape's materiality
into a vast mirror of Victor's own transcendent narcissism—as if the Alps
existed to relieve him of his sorrows upon request!—the creature shows up,
interrupts, changes the subjects, and the objects, too.

POSTHUMAN/POSTNATURAL: THE NATURE OF THE CREATURE

In the place of the mutually defining human/ineffable versus natural/
material binary produced by the traditional hierarchic resolution of the
Romantic sublime, Mary Shelley insistently proffers what I have called the
organic sublime, in which subjectivity and materiality are fused. Rather

than resolving as an absolute division, the profound instability between self and world that marks the initial moment of the sublime collapses altogether in the (putatively) horrifying monster. He/it merges each side of the binary of the traditional sublime, at once uncannily material—he's meat, composed of dead human and animal body parts—and uncannily immaterial—he talks, has consciousness, emotions, desire, despite, or while, being meat. The horror he inspires stems, then, from contradictory sources: he's at once *too* natural and *un*natural, both an excessively organic, material, fleshy other, and the artificial posthuman creation of nineteenth-century biotechnology.

This contradiction is, indeed, constitutive of the context that gives birth to the creature, Victor's "workshop of filthy creation" (2009, 78), a place that substitutes manufacture for womb, and conjoins artifice and filth.[5] Victor insists that the process of creating the creature involved not only the pursuit of forbidden, if not blasphemous, knowledge, but also excessive and inappropriate contact with the materiality of nature and the body: "I pursued nature to her most secret hiding places . . . dabbled among the unhallowed damps of the grave or tortured the living animal to animate the lifeless clay. . . . I collected bones from charnel houses and with profane fingers meddled with the secrets of the human frame. . . . [t]he dissecting room and the slaughterhouse furnished many of my materials" (2009, 78–79).[6] The result is a creature for whom identity and embodiment are synonymous, an eight-foot-tall being in whom physicality is excessively, if not monstrously, dominant:

> His limbs were in proportion, and I had selected his features as beautiful. Beautiful!—Great God! His yellow skin scarcely covered the work of muscles and arteries beneath; his hair was of a lustrous black and flowing; and his teeth of a pearly whiteness; but these luxuriances only formed a more horrid contrast with his watery eyes, that seemed almost of the same colour as the dun white sockets in which they were set, his shriveled complexion, and straight black lips. (2009, 81)

Half of what makes the creature frightening, indeed what makes all the stereotypically "normal" individuals in the book immediately attack or flee in horror at the mere sight of him, springs from the way Victor/Shelley's construction so absolutely foregrounds his fleshy materiality. He's not just enormous with nonnormative facial features, not merely different or ugly; he produces, as Lennard Davis puts it, a "disruption in the . . . sensory field" itself (Davis 1995, 128). This disruption stems not simply from his surface appearance, in other words, but from the way his surface fails to signify, fails to make him a readily comprehensible object. A "normal" embodiment in the book signifies anything but materiality; the body's surface leads the viewer immediately away from the body and into its cultural/representative function, signifying, for example, Elizabeth and Clerval's perfect incarnation of Europeanized gender, not the flesh that underlies that gender, Safie's heteronormative desirability "despite" her race, Victor's bourgeois happiness or lonely romantic suffering, and so on, not his masturbatory sexuality or gynophobic nausea.

In every "normal" case, then, the material body "means" the immaterial self. In sharp contrast, the monster's surface signifies his literal, material interiority. His lips, the primary entrance to the inside of the body, are the "wrong" shape and color; his eyes, the "windows of the soul," are gray with gray pupils; his face is "shriveled"; his skin "scarcely cover[s] the work of muscles and arteries beneath." Put another way, he's the natural sublime— but the organic version, not the Kantian/Romantic one. Like the mountain or ocean, his dominant materiality produces a representational crisis for the viewer. However, rather than the definitional bifurcation between an immaterial human self and a wholly material natural Other that resolves the latter sublime, the creature collapses that binary, unifying the self and nature under the sign of materiality in a way that aligns the (post)human with the natural and material.

Furthermore, as Lennard Davis (1995) claims in his insightful Lacanian commentary on the novel, the horror the monster's body inspires in "normal" people is in fact a repression of the fragmentary quality of all our embodied experience, of our "true" patchwork selves. For Lacan, as infants, our physical experience of the body is not unified: our limbs flail, we burp, excrete, vomit, and so forth without voluntary control; we have to "find our toes" again and again. But when, in Lacan's "mirror stage," we witness our reflection, and our well-meaning parents point to the image of our bodily wholeness and repeat "that's you!," we learn that our physical experience of materialized fragmentation is at odds with the specular unity that we are (supposed) to be. As Davis puts it, in an analysis that links the disabled body to the creature's:

> The process extends from a fragmented body-image to a form of its totality . . . and, lastly to the assumption of the armour of an alienating identity. When the child points to an image in the mirror . . . the child recognizes (actually misrecognizes) that unified image as his or her self. That identification is really the donning of an identity, an "armor" against the chaotic or fragmentary body.
>
> In this sense, the disabled body is a direct *imago* of the repressed fragmented body. The disabled body causes a kind of hallucination of the mirror phase gone wrong. The subject looks at the disabled body and has a moment of cognitive dissonance, or should we say a moment of cognitive resonance with the earlier state of fragmentation. Rather than seeing the whole body in the mirror, the subject sees the repressed fragmented body; rather than seeing the object of desire, as controlled by the Other, the subject sees the true self of the fragmented body. (1995, 139)

Hence, for Davis, the horror and violence that the creature's appearance universally precipitates is a repressive operation, the forceful denial of the fact of our own materiality, of the various body parts we unify and repress under the sign of Elizabeth Lavenza or Paul Outka. The monster's body is our own writ (literally) large. The horror the monster produces, the eruption of the organic sublime, the emergence of the posthuman, is a repressed moment of self-recognition, the awareness of an identity between the self and the material body. Meet your meat.

This alignment not only changes the human into the posthuman, but changes the identity of the second term as well; nature becomes postnatural in the organic sublime. Shelley is not *simply* collapsing the human into the physical as later versions of the story do, making the creature a lumbering and inarticulate figure with a bolt through its neck. Her excessively physical creature is also an autodidact who speaks beautifully, reads Milton, Plutarch, and Goethe, insistently and articulately demands his rights from Victor. He's Percy Shelley (if anyone), not a mentally deficient Herman Munster. The creature is horrific both because he is excessively natural/physical/material—meat—*and* because he is *un*natural, artificial, a blasphemous incarnation of human technology. He's *talking* meat, a soulless, speaking materiality, what Timothy Morton memorably calls "a horrific abject that speaks beautiful Enlightenment prose, a piece of butcher's meat with blinking eyes" (Morton 2007, 194).

Donna Haraway claims, in her justly famous "Manifesto for Cyborgs," that this combination is a quintessential characteristic of the posthuman/postnatural:

> Late twentieth-century machines have made thoroughly ambiguous the difference between natural and artificial, mind and body, self-developing and externally designed, and many other distinctions that used to apply to organisms and machines. Our machines are disturbingly lively, and we ourselves frighteningly inert.
>
> In short, the certainty of what counts as nature—a source of insight and promise of innocence—is undermined, probably fatally. (Haraway 1991, 152–153)

Haraway locates this change 175 years later than I do, largely because, along with so much of the subsequent posthuman theory her Manifesto inaugurated, she's committed to seeing the cyborg as created by technological disjunction rather than by a more fundamental and much earlier materialism exemplified in Shelley's creature and that has already rendered the natural/artificial distinction moot.[7] The creature's biotech organic materialism and the horror it provokes suggests that what is most deeply unsettling about the human/technology merge in the common image of the cyborg—the Borg in *Star Trek*, say—is not the machine/human combination per se, but what the possibility of that combination reveals about the materiality of the human before the merge. It's the mechanistic, not the materials used to make the mechanism, that is the central issue at this historical moment.

This difference with Haraway aside, her comment captures precisely the collapse between "natural and artificial, mind and body, self-developing and externally designed," that the creature incarnates, and how that incarnation in turn undermines the uncreated "certainty of what counts as nature." The creature, in other words, doesn't stop being nature when he starts talking, or become less natural because he's artificial. What changes, or should change for the reader, is the definition of nature itself. Less an uncreated given, less an abjected materiality that serves ultimately only to reinforce a transcendent human immateriality, in the form of the creature, nature itself looks and talks back, challenges that transcendent subject, insists on its own self-developing *and* externally designed status. In doing so it issues a metaphysical and physical threat—an evolutionary one, indeed—to "human" hegemony.

Shelley underscores this shift in the definition of nature by making the artificial creature so conspicuously—if not, indeed, "unnaturally"—at home in it. He easily survives the alpine sublime landscape and the polar ice; as he says, "The desert mountains and mournful glaciers are my refuge. . . . The caves of ice, which I only do not fear, are a dwelling to me and the only one which man does not grudge" (2009, 123). Indeed, the creature promises Victor that he will relocate to the American wilderness with his mate if Victor agrees to create her, where he will be more at home than any "man":

> If you consent, neither you nor any human creature shall ever see us again. I will go to the vast wilds of America. My food is not that of man; I do not destroy the lamb or the kid to glut my appetite. Acorns and berries afford me sufficient nourishment. My companion will be of the same nature as myself and will be content with the same fare. We shall make our bed of dried leaves; the sun will shine on us as on man and will ripen our food. You are moved. The picture I present to you is peaceful and human. . . .
>
> I swear by the earth which I inhabit, and by you that made me, that with the companion you bestow I will quit the neighborhood of man and dwell, as it may chance, in the most savage places. . . .
>
> I swear . . . by the sun and by the blue sky of heaven, that while they exist you shall never behold me. (2009, 171–172)

The creature at once promises voluntary exile from the human community in favor of a wilderness where only he and his companion will be at home, while at the same time insisting he's offering a "peaceful and *human*" picture of a Rousseauian harmony with nature, one that, by exemplifying stereotypically Romantic values, "moves" Victor. The creature's repeated oaths sworn to nature in the place of God—to "the earth which I inhabit," "the sun and . . . the blue sky of heaven"—and his gleaned vegetarian diet further underscore his unnatural alliance with both the natural world and with the atheist, nature-worshipping, and vegetarian Percy Shelley.

Unable to incorporate the contradictory creature within the ineffable/material binary established by the traditional Romantic sublime, that traditional sublime collapses—or evolves—in favor of an artificial/natural creature that speaks as and for the earth. The posthuman/postnatural union supplants the human and natural, leaving Victor, on his walk back at the conclusion of the interview, unable to accomplish the traditional sublime and make the natural world signify his subjectivity:

> It had long been night when I came to the half-way resting place and seated myself beside the fountain. The stars shone at intervals as the clouds passed from over them. The dark pines rose before me, and every here and there a broken tree lay on the ground; it was a scene of wonderful solemnity and stirred strange thoughts within me. I wept bitterly, and, clasping my hands in agony, I exclaimed, "Oh! stars, and clouds, and wind, ye are all about to mock me. If ye really pity, crush me; but if not, depart; depart and leave me to darkness." These were wild and miserable thoughts, but I cannot describe to you how the eternal twinkling of stars weighted upon me, and I listened to every blast of wind as if it were a dull ugly siroc on its way to consume me. (2009, 173)

The once grand alpine vista is now darkened, the stars and clouds and wind neither mock him, nor depart, nor crush him, but, like Stevens's indifferent clouds, "go nevertheless in their direction." Rather than nature coming to signify the "human mind's imaginings," Victor "cannot describe . . . how the stars weighted upon" him; the aeolian harp becomes like a "dull ugly siroc on its way to consume" a failed definition of human and natural. The creature, though, is celebrating his triumph, his future, the promise of a companion and, most important, of a mate.

THE CREATURE'S PENIS

Why is it there, or more precisely, what could have possessed Victor to sew one on him? How about his monstrous testicles? What exactly was Victor thinking when he hung those on the front of his creation? Similarly, why doesn't Victor just make a sterile female mate for the creature? Skip the womb, snip the fallopian tubes, whatever; certainly it couldn't be any less complicated than making a creature in the first place. Put another way, why, in a novel so willing radically to question human nature, does gendered sexual reproduction play such an unquestioned "natural" role? More specifically and to my purposes here, what's at stake for ecocriticism in the text's total suppression of such obvious questions?

Certainly Shelley, via Victor, makes clear that the creature's reproductive capacity is central to the species-level existential threat he poses to the hegemony of the human over the rest of nature. After first speculating that the female creature might be (even) more vicious than the male, or might be attracted to "human" men rather than the creature, Victor, in a rare moment, thinks about the larger possible consequences of his actions:

> Even if they [the creature and his new mate] were to leave Europe and inhabit the deserts of the new world, it was their intention to have children, and a race of devils would be propagated upon the earth from whose form and mind man shrunk with horror. Had I any right for my own benefit to inflict this curse to everlasting generations? . . . I shuddered to think that future ages might curse me as their pest, whose selfishness had not hesitated to buy its own peace at the price perhaps of the existence of the whole human race. (2009, 189)

This speculation leads him to "t[ear] to pieces the thing on which I was engaged" (2009, 189) as the creature looks on from the window, thereby precipitating the novel's conclusion and the ultimate death of Clerval, Elizabeth, Victor's father, and Victor himself—aka the rest of the Frankenstein gene pool. The narrative nonnegotiability of the creature's reproductive capacity, even when sterilization is the obvious solution to the problem Victor notes above, is, I would argue, part of Shelley's broader commitment to having the creature mark the shift I have described as the transition to the posthuman/postnatural. Unlike Victor's conspicuous lack of sexual interest in Elizabeth, his designated partner since childhood (an absence both his father and Elizabeth ask him about explicitly), the creature "ardently desire[s]" a mate so that he "shall feel the affections of a living being and become linked to the chain of existence and events from which [he is] now excluded" (2009, 171–172).[8] By making the monster fertile, Shelley moves the creature's threat from individual violence and horror to evolutionary competition with normatively embodied humans on the ecosystemic level. The problem is not ultimately that the creature is a horrifying Other with a nonnormative and intensely physical embodiment, but that he might make many more like him in numbers enough to redefine what counted as "non-normative," if not, indeed, in numbers sufficient to become the planet's dominant species.[9] The threat inherent in the creature's fertility, then—why the monster *must* have reproductive organs—is directly connected to the way the organic sublime supplants the romantic sublime in the novel. The creature represents a materialist understanding of human identity—a posthuman—at home in, and an expression of, a nontranscendent materialist nature—a postnature. Moreover, that postnature stops signifying the transcendent human and instead literally incorporates the "artificial" creature as its own, indistinguishable from a "natural" being. Change one, change both.

POSTHUMAN, POSTNATURAL, AND THE ETHIC OF CARE: ECOCRITICISM AND THE ORGANIC SUBLIME

I have been arguing throughout this chapter that we should understand the "human" as fundamentally involving a repression of materiality and embodiment, and its counterpart, the "natural" as an abjected, static, and utterly material Other to that first term. In my analysis, the Romantic sublime serves as a template for producing this binary as the resolution of a prior moment of instability in the borders between self and world. In contrast, the organic sublime, as exemplified in the creature, resolves that instability by collapsing the human and the natural into each other as expressions, in both the literal and metaphorical sense, of a larger material field. Both sides of the binary produced in the Romantic sublime merge: the human becomes material, and nature incorporates the human, becomes unfixed, artificial.

The posthuman/postnatural, then, is only "post" in the sense that it follows the illusion of an ineffable human identity produced in contradistinction to a materialized nature. But it also precedes the human on a factual, evolutionary level, if not a cultural one; we have always, in fact, been posthuman, always been part of a postnatural world. However disjunctive the posthuman/postnatural might seem, in other words, the organic sublime in fact names a return to the "truth" of our "nature," a nature and a truth that are dynamic, unstable, self-generated, the product of eons of incessant evolution and furious self-modification. The ontological (and not simply practical) horror many ecocritics and environmentalists display at the development of genetically modified organisms and other "artificial natures," often conjoined with a pious nostalgia for a pure and stable wilderness referent that never existed, is not only misplaced but blocks the discipline and the movement from caring for the "actual" world with which we are more than just in "contact," but of which we are a material, constituent part. Rather than a Romantic sublime process that endlessly turns flux into definition, (re)producing subjects and objects, the human and the natural, the transcendent and the material, the organic sublime collapses the whole series of binaries into the creature who is all of these things and, as result, a paradigm shift inexplicable in the terms of the previous regime. The demand the creature makes again and again is fundamentally different than the definitional query the earlier paradigm returns to like a skipping CD: a horrified "What are you?" is replaced by the creature's insistent "Care for me!"[10]

This shift is one ecocriticism should embrace; we've been postnatural for a long time now, if we weren't always. As a range of critics from Bill McKibben (1989) to William Cronon (1996) to Timothy Morton (2007) have noted, our pressing environmental questions are more about care than definition, about what we should do where we are and not about which places and entities have status and which don't. If global warming means the end of an untouched nature, if the trouble really is with wilderness, if we should in fact try for an ecology without nature,[11] then the creature's postnatural demand for an ethic of care in the place of some eco-ontological normative/purity quest should be understood as much more than the sui generis pleadings of a lonely freak. Rather, it's the harbinger (or a harbinger) of a much larger shift in environmental thought, one that eschews categorical questions, isn't organized explicitly or implicitly by a natural/unnatural binary or a human/natural one, is largely uninterested in utopian/dystopian environmental discourse, but is, rather, busy asking local, political, and practical questions about how best to care for the fallen world that we make and that makes us.

The difficulty of making this shift fully, however, is underscored by the continuing legibility of the horror the monster inspires. Whether or not we feel the same way a nineteenth-century reader might, their reaction— "unnatural! talking meat!"—remains readily comprehensible, at least in part because we retain both a concept of Nature as something found rather than made and of the human as essentially immaterial. The limited sympathy we might feel for the creature's predicament is falsely patronizing, a strictly bounded acceptance of its abandoned alterity, one that denies our similitude under the guise of accepting "even" him.[12] We're still, in short, approaching nature and the human through the binary paradigm produced by the Romantic sublime rather than the collapse of the human, the artificial, and the natural in the organic sublime. We still identify ourselves with Victor and nature with his beloved Alps, still hear the creature's pleas and threats as if they were not our own. The creature's nature, the/our real one, remains largely abandoned and uncared for, and the apocalyptic threats the creature makes in response to that abandonment resonate far beyond Victor's immediate family and Mary Shelley's own moment.

NOTES

1. See my own "(De)Composing Whitman" (2005) and "Whitmanian Cybernetics" (2001) for an examination of Whitman's cycling between language and physical embodiment, an analysis that presages some of the work I do here, and plan to do in a larger project on the nineteenth-century posthuman. I want to acknowledge the generous help I have already received in moving that project forward and making this essay better, especially from my wife Uma Outka, my sister Elizabeth Outka, my research assistant Jennifer Leigh Moffitt, and the very brilliant students in my spring 2010 graduate seminar at Florida State on the nineteenth-century posthuman. Particular thanks are also due to Stephanie LeMenager and the other editors of this volume for their terrifically insightful comments on the first draft of this chapter, comments that made several critical points in the argument considerably clearer and more carefully thought through.
2. In claiming that early evolutionary theory and the publication of works like *Frankenstein* mark a critical turn in the understanding of nature, I do not mean to imply that such a turn was universally embraced. Far from it—as I

suggest in the chapter's conclusion, the implications of such a shift are still resisted, not only in the long-standing and fierce opposition to evolutionary theory by a range of religious groups, but in the largely uncritical deployment of the Romantic sublime as a sort of naturalized and unconscious procedural framework for creating both nature and subjectivity that extends from Muir through twentieth-century "mainstream" environmentalism. If anything, the disconnection between scientific and humanist understandings of nature has deepened since Shelley's novel, a novel that, like the monster itself, is created in the intersection between the two.

3. As many commentators have noted, evolutionary theory didn't start with Darwin; he was the first to demonstrate convincingly and (mostly) correctly how it worked. Hunter (2008) provides an excellent summary of the influence of pre-Darwinian theories of evolution on Shelley's work.

4. I discuss the ecocritical and racial resonance of the Kantian sublime at greater length in *Race and Nature from Transcendentalism to the Harlem Renaissance* (2008), especially 14–20 and 201–203. Weiskel's (1976) study of the Romantic sublime and its connection to the Kantian tradition remain invaluable.

5. This substitution of workshop for womb invites a broader gender critique outside of my immediate focus here; as Marcus notes, "In the unconscious mental 'workshop of filthy creation,' sexuality, incest, primal-scene material, and the aborted birth of monstrous babies are all conflated, condensed, and annealed" (2002, 197). Marcus's essay in general provides a helpful recent overview of the extraordinarily wide range of critical response the novel has inspired.

6. See Marshall (1995) for an analysis of the connection between the fictional constructions of dead bodies and scientific anatomical representations during this period.

7. Indeed, in her manifesto Haraway explicitly criticizes Shelley's creature as a failure to realize the fully cybernetic: "Unlike the hopes of Frankenstein's monster, the cyborg does not expect its father to save it through a restoration of the garden; that is, through the fabrication of a heterosexual mate, through its completion in a finished whole, a city and a cosmos. The cyborg does not dream of community on the model of the organic family, this time without the oedipal projects. The cyborg would not recognize the Garden of Eden; it is not made of mud and cannot dream of returning to dust" (1991, 151). While I couldn't admire Haraway's groundbreaking work more, as should be clear from my chapter, I do think this critique relies on a distinction between "mud" and technology that my argument is predicated on questioning, and misses the posthuman and postnatural implications of the creature's fertility.

8. For more on Victor's gynophobic relation to female bodies, both dead and alive, see Liggins (2000).

9. For a well-researched and engaging study of the ways the creature came to resonate as a racial imago, an anxiety that certainly also hovers behind the prospect of the creature's reproductive powers, see Young (2008).

10. See Hustis (2003) for an insightful and carefully reasoned analysis of the interplay between obligation and sympathy in the relationship between Victor and the creature, an analysis that ultimately argues for Shelley's "recasting of the Prometheus myth . . . as a meditation on the responsibility that accompanies the creative act" (2003, 856).

I should note here too that I recognize how "identity" and "care" are inevitably interlinked. That interlinkage does not make them synonymous, however, and I think too much focus on the precise nature of that interlinkage risks putting the focus back on identity and away from praxis. That said, my assertions here undoubtedly reflect my own intellectual affiliations with

American pragmatism and its eagerness to elevate questions about practice over questions about truth.

11. For readers less familiar with the ecocritical canon, the three previous phrases refer, respectively, to McKibben's *The End of Nature* (1989), Cronon's "The Trouble with Wilderness" (1996), and Morton's *Ecology without Nature* (2007), the authors referenced in the previous sentence.

12. As Morton says, "Far from standing in for irreducible particularity—and hence ironically generalizing that very particularity—the creature represents alienated generality. . . . But insofar as this nature is abject and its stitches are showing, this 'essence' includes arbitrariness and supplementarity. The creature is made out of any body, anybody" (2007, 194). Morton's work on the novel is enormously valuable in its own right, and particularly for readers interested in questions of the postnatural. See especially 188–195.

REFERENCES

Cronon, William. 1996. "The Trouble with Wilderness; or, Getting Back to the Wrong Nature." In *Uncommon Ground: Rethinking the Human Place in Nature*, edited by William Cronon, 69–90. New York: W.W. Norton.

Darwin, Charles. 2003. *The Origin of Species by Means of Natural Selection.* 1859. New York: Barnes & Noble Classic Editions.

Davis, Lennard. 1995. *Enforcing Normalcy: Disability, Deafness, and the Body.* London: Verso.

Haraway, Donna. 1991. "A Manifesto for Cyborgs." In *Simians, Cyborgs, and Women: The Reinvention of Nature*, 149–181. New York: Routledge.

Hayles, N. Katherine. 1999. *How We Became Posthuman: Virtual Bodies in Cybernetics, Literature and Informatics.* Chicago: University of Chicago Press.

Hunter, Allan K. 2008. "Evolution, Revolution and Frankenstein's Creature." In *Frankenstein's Science: Experimentation and Discovery in Romantic Culture, 1780–1830*, edited by Christa Knellwolf and Jane Goodall, 133–149. Aldershot, UK: Ashgate.

Hustis, Harriet. 2003. "Responsible Creativity and the 'Modernity' of Mary Shelley's Prometheus." *SEL* 43.4: 845–858.

Kant, Immanuel. 1951. *Critique of Judgment.* Translated by J. H. Bernard. New York: Hafner Press.

Liggins, Emma. 2000. "The Medical Gaze and the Female Corpse: Looking at Bodies in Mary Shelley's *Frankenstein.*" *Studies in the Novel* 32.2: 129–146.

Marcus, Steven. 2002. "*Frankenstein*: Myths of Scientific and Medical Knowledge and Stories of Human Relations." *Southern Review* 38,1: 188–201.

Marshall, Tim. 1995. *Murdering to Dissect: Grave-Robbing*, Frankenstein, *and the Anatomy Literature.* Manchester, UK: Manchester University Press.

McKibben, William. 1989. *The End of Nature.* New York: Random House.

Morton, Timothy. 2007. *Ecology without Nature: Rethinking Environmental Aesthetics.* Cambridge, MA: Harvard University Press.

Outka, Paul. 2001. "Whitmanian Cybernetics." *The Mickle Street Review* 14. Accessed February 15, 2011, http://www.micklestreet.rutgers.edu.

———. 2005. "(De)composing Whitman." *ISLE: Interdisciplinary Studies in Literature and the Environment* 12.1: 41–60.

———. 2008. *Race and Nature from Transcendentalism to the Harlem Renaissance.* New York: Palgrave Macmillan.

Shelley, Mary. 2009. *Frankenstein, or the Modern Prometheus.* 1816–17. Edited by Charles E. Robinson. New York: Vintage Books.

Shelley, Percy. 1977. "Mont Blanc." In *Shelley's Poetry and Prose*, edited by Donald H. Reiman and Sharon B. Powers, 89–93. New York: Norton.

Smith, Marquard, and Jonanne Morra, eds. 2006. *The Prosthetic Impulse: From a Posthuman Present to a Biocultural Future*. Cambridge, MA: MIT Press.

Weiskel, Thomas. 1976. *The Romantic Sublime: Studies in the Structure and Psychology of Transcendence*. Baltimore: Johns Hopkins University Press.

Young, Elizabeth. 2008. *Black Frankenstein: The Making of an American Metaphor*. New York: New York University Press.

3 Revisiting the Virtuoso
Natural History Collectors and Their Passionate Engagement with Nature

Beth Fowkes Tobin

Before Charles Darwin became the epitome of what it meant to be a naturalist and before Wordsworth, Emerson, and Thoreau established that the "proper" way to engage with nature was through spiritual communion, there was the Enlightenment with its armies of collectors and classifiers who were eager to collect and name every species of botanical and zoological life. The Enlightenment's project, which has been characterized as the disciplining of Nature, has received attention of late, and most of it negative. Londa Schiebinger in her *Plants and Empire* has argued that Linnaean systematics, the cornerstone of Enlightenment classification, can be viewed as a form of "linguistic imperialism," with Linnaean nomenclature evincing "a politics of naming that accompanied and promoted European global expansion and colonization" (Schiebinger 2004, 195). Susan Parrish has portrayed the impact of metropolitan Enlightenment rationalism with its goal of "imperial imposition of an abstract system" on American naturalists, whom she depicts as a feisty heterogeneous bunch of individuals who held their own against Britain's monolithic but impotent Royal Society and its desire to subsume the natural world under its scientific gaze (Parrish 2006, 315). Moreover, some cultural historians (Tobin 2005) have suggested that such Enlightenment scientific practices as classification were mechanisms by which plant life was stripped of local cultural legibility, a process that enabled the commodification of plant matter and its circulation in a globalized economy. These anti-Enlightenment positions share the Romantic and Transcendentalist critique of the Enlightenment's mechanistic and systematizing approach to nature, and imply that the Enlightenment, with its strategies of collection and classification, was responsible for, or, at least, set the stage for what Carolyn Merchant has called "the death of nature" (Merchant 1989).

At the risk of seeming perverse and counterproductive, I am questioning the validity of such accusations and the assumptions that underlie them by examining closely the natural history collecting practices of a group of shell collectors, of whom the most prominent was Margaret Cavendish Bentinck, the 2nd Duchess of Portland (1715–1785). If the core of the Enlightenment project was the collection and classification of natural life, then studying collectors is a way to grasp what actually occurred in this process and to access the kind and quality of the relationship a natural history collector had to the natural world. What I am after is an answer to the question of whether a natural history collector's relationship to nature was qualitatively different from that of a Wordsworth or a Thoreau. To put it bluntly, did collectors of natural history specimens love nature any less than the Romantic poets and Transcendentalists claim they did?

As a way to confront our stereotypes about the Enlightenment's scientific practices of collecting and classification, it will prove helpful to begin an examination of natural history collecting with the early modern period's own caricatures of natural history collectors. Eighteenth-century print culture was not any more generous than Emerson when describing these collectors, who were depicted in a range of poems, essays, and plays as secretive, possessive, and perverse accumulators of natural objects.

FICTIONAL NATURAL HISTORY COLLECTORS

When Mr. Knightley in Jane Austen's *Emma* (Austen 1816, 2002) invites his friends to Donwell Abbey for an "al-fresco party," he very thoughtfully provides the elderly Mr. Woodhouse with "the most comfortable room in the Abbey" (2002; 286) and a range of activities to keep him entertained while others wander in his gardens and enjoy strawberry picking. "Books of engravings, drawers of medals, cameos, corals, shells, and every other family collection within his cabinets had been prepared for his old friend, to while away the morning" (2002; 290). Mr. Woodhouse is delighted with these collections as they suit his temperament perfectly: "he was slow, constant, and methodical," and like "a child," "he had a total want of taste for what he saw" (290). With this passage, Austen suggests that appreciating a collection of natural and artificial objects does not require taste, intelligence, or knowledge, that it is an activity suited for children or the child-like adult. Though this passage conveys the sense that a "family collection" can be of value in displaying the trappings of gentility, functioning as a marker of lineage and heritage, Austen's depiction of collecting seems quite dismissive as she relegates it to child's play. This dismissive attitude toward collecting was not unusual for this period, and for many, including Austen apparently, these family collections were perceived as old-fashioned, dull, and at best quaint relics of a bygone era when natural history and antiquarian collecting were deemed polite forms of entertainment and education.

The real-life counterparts of the fictional Mr. Knightley would have inherited collections, like Mr. Knightley's hodgepodge of antiquarian and natural history specimens, from relatives who were amateur collectors. Such a collection would have most likely dated from the mid- to late-eighteenth century when natural history collecting was all the rage with the educated elites who were eager to display their interest in botany and zoology. "Polite science" (Sutton 1995), the term that historians have given to this enthusiasm among wealthy amateurs for scientific activities, manifested itself in a range of activities to include collecting dead birds, bugs, and dried leaves, planting botanical gardens, building greenhouses, and filling menageries with exotic animals.

Austen's mildly sardonic depiction of Mr. Woodhouse's pleasure in a cabinet of curios—its drawers filled with coral, cameos, coins, and shells—partakes of a long literary tradition that mocked natural history collectors and their collections. Beginning in the Restoration with Thomas Shadwell's play *The Virtuoso*, extending through the eighteenth century and into the nineteenth, the collector of natural curiosities has been represented in a negative light, ranging from images of the antisocial miser more in love with things than people to images of petty-minded, fussy, scatterbrained, and ultimately nonproductive types incapable of understanding the significance of the objects they collect. The latter type, the fussy old fool, is captured in Austen's Mr. Woodhouse, with his courtly old ways and gentlemanly refusal to engage in useful activities. The former type, the antisocial person who substitutes things for people, is mocked, for instance, in a late seventeenth-century lampoon on virtuosos, which has as its chief target Dr. John Woodward, whose fossil collection is still to be found at Cambridge University. In this anonymous lampoon, a virtuoso is defined as: "one that has sold an Estate in Land to purchase one in Scallop, Conch, Muscle, cockle Shells, Periwinkles, Sea Shrubs, Weeds, Mosses, Sponges, Coralls, Corallines, Sea Fans, Pebbles, Marchasite and Flint Stones; and has abandon'd the Acquaintance and Society of Men for that of Insects, Worms, Grubbs, Maggots, Flies, Moths, Locusts, Bettles, Spiders, Grashoppers, Snails, Lizards and Tortoises" (1696, 91). A *Tatler* essay, entitled "The Will of the Virtuoso" (1710), takes up Shadwell's character Sir Nicholas Gimcrack, depicting him as someone who is *so* cut off from normal social ties that he bequeaths his most valued possessions—a hummingbird's nest and a rat's testicles—to his family, not realizing that what he values possesses no value for them (Bond 1987, 3, 134).[1]

Collectors of natural history specimens were depicted as antisocial, miserly, prone to hoarding and secrecy, and bizarre in their passionate engagement with dried flowers and leaves, skins and feathers, fossils, bones, and shells—the detritus of the living natural world. Not engaged in production or even in the accumulation of money, collectors of natural history objects were viewed even more negatively than art collectors or antiquarians whose objects possessed either some intrinsic aesthetic value or could be linked to patriotic narratives of national origins. Natural history collectors were portrayed as exclusively male and privileged, and engaged in useless activities that only a leisured lifestyle could support.

Hinted at in these portraits is the idea that collectors were engaged in a perverted and deviant economy of accumulation, perverse because they collected objects, not money or land, and deviant because they took objects out of economic circulation, diverting them from the so-called rational world of commodity exchange, and inserted them into the affective realm of curiosity. These portraits ridicule collectors for having refused the category of the useful and the productive to dwell in an alternative economy, one that placed value on natural objects beyond or outside market value.

Against these satiric portraits of collectors, I examine the natural history-collecting practices of the Duchess of Portland and her network of fellow shell collectors, with the goal of recovering an alternative narrative to counter eighteenth-century print culture's depictions of the natural history collector as a reclusive, perverse, and antisocial male, and to suggest that natural history collecting was not necessarily engaged in practices that reduced nature to a commodity and a resource to be exploited.

POLITE CULTURE AND NATURAL HISTORY

Margaret Cavendish Bentinck, the 2nd Duchess of Portland, began collecting shells as scientific specimens in the mid-eighteenth century when Enlightenment ideals defined inquiry into nature broadly and encouraged free and open exchange of ideas, information, and objects within the republic of letters, which invited the participation of women and men of various ranks, talents, and abilities. This was also a time before hard lines were drawn between art and science, and before the fragmentation of natural knowledge into specialized disciplines. Inquiry into nature was not sequestered in spaces designed explicitly for scientific activity, such as the laboratory or the university, and took place in multiple spaces, from the domestic interiors of drawing rooms, closets, and kitchens to flower gardens, estate parkland, and uncultivated tracts of wasteland, and took on multiple forms from decorative art practices of shell and feather work, needlework, and pencil and ink drawings of plants, shells, and birds to cookery books' recipes for varnish and ink and herbals' plant descriptions, recipes, and remedies for disease. Botany, zoology, chemistry, and medicine were studied and enacted in proximity to domestic crafts and amateur arts.

Men and women of ordinary abilities produced knowledge about nature by making excursions to urban green spaces or to the countryside where they botanized, caught insects such as flies and beetles, and collected mollusks in the form of snails and freshwater bivalves that inhabited streams and marshy areas. They gathered specimens, studied them, described and drew them, and attempted to attach names to these natural objects, some employing Linnaean taxonomy. Seashells gathered at the beach were cleaned, dried, polished, and housed in cabinets; flowers, mosses, ferns, and seaweed were dried and pressed onto paper and bound into volumes; and butterflies and moths were captured with nets, killed carefully, and pinned onto cork-lined wooden boxes and drawers. In addition to producing natural knowledge through a wide range of activities, men and women of the educated upper and middling classes were consumers of scientific knowledge as they eagerly bought books about the Linnaean system of classification, illustrated botanical and zoological books, and the natural histories of local regions and foreign locales. The culture of curiosity about nature was bolstered not only by print culture but also by visiting places where natural history specimens, alive and dead, were on display in museums, private collections, public gardens, auction houses, dealers' shops, and country houses with their botanical and zoological gardens. Nature as a source of commercial activity, artistic inspiration, and scientific inquiry was omnipresent in the lives of the polite classes, appearing in material culture, visual culture, and print culture, three arenas within which the duchess was an active participant as a collector and a patroness.

REAL NATURAL HISTORY COLLECTORS

Although the Duchess of Portland collected fossils, insects, birds, and plants as well as fine art, decorative objects, and antiquities, shells were what she cared about the most. Spending a great deal of time and money on acquiring and organizing her shells, she had plans to publish a catalogue of her shell collection, and if she had lived to see it into print, the catalogue would have made an enormous contribution to the natural history of conchology, as the study of mollusks was called in the Enlightenment. Dying before this project was completed, she had specified in her will that all her natural history specimens, along with many of the fine and decorative art pieces, were to be sold at auction for the benefit of her younger children. The auction, lasting thirty-eight days, took place at her Whitehall residence and drew hundreds of viewers and buyers eager to see the duchess's townhouse filled with her intriguing natural history specimens, 90 percent of which were shells. The duchess's collecting has often been portrayed by scholars as a form of primitive accumulation, as a distracted form of consumption driven by irrational desires, and as an acquisitiveness born of the commercial society she inhabited (Allen 1995; Battacharya 2006; Pascoe 2006). Indeed, if her collecting of natural history specimens had been limited to purchasing them from dealers, bidding on them at natural history auctions, or paying someone to gather them for her, then such a characterization might be correct and her collecting of natural objects could be understood as participating in the commoditization and consumption of nature.

However, the duchess's collecting practices were much more complicated than mere consumption. First of all, she was at the center of a network of amateur and professional naturalists, and Bulstrode, the duchess's Buckinghamshire estate, became an important destination for the study of natural history. Mary Delany, famous for her flower-inspired needlework, lived with the duchess for most of her second widowhood, and it was at

Bulstrode that she did the majority of her exquisitely crafted and botanically correct flower paper mosaics (Laird and Weisberg-Roberts 2009). The great botanical illustrator Georg Dionysis Ehret taught the duchess's daughters how to draw, and during his two-year tenure at Bulstrode he drew hundreds of botanical illustrations for the duchess. Of Ehret's role in the duchess's naturalist activities, Mrs. Delany wrote: "We have Mr. Ehret who goes out in search of curiosities in the fungus way, as this is now their season, and read us a lecture on them an hour before tea, whilst her Grace examines all the celebrated authors to find out their class. This is productive of much learning and of excellent observations from Mr. Ehret, uttered in such a dialect as sometimes puzzles me (though he calls it English) to find out what foreign language it is" (1862, 4: 240). The Rev. John Lightfoot, an accomplished botanist, was her chaplain and would often accompany her on her natural history excursions. Visitors to Bulstrode included such famous naturalists as Sir Joseph Banks, the president of the Royal Society, Daniel Solander, premier taxonomist and British Museum curator, and naturalist Thomas Pennant, the author of *British Zoology*, as well as ordinary people who because of their interest in natural history were just as welcome as the more powerful and prominent guests (Delany 1862). John Timothy Swainson, for instance, a customs officer, was invited to Bulstrode to participate in a shell-collecting expedition; he found a snail "in a canal at Bulstrode," a very rare *Helix polita* (J. T. Swainson n.d.).

Moreover, in addition to playing hostess and patroness to other naturalists, Margaret Cavendish Bentinck was a naturalist who was also a specimen hunter (Tobin 2009). Often in the company of her friends and fellow naturalists, one of whom was Jean-Jacques Rousseau (Cook 2007), she wandered about the countryside, carrying nets, shovels, baskets, and boxes to gather land snails that crept about in the early, dewy mornings and rainy afternoons, hiding within "the hollows of old trees" and "the crevices of rocks, walls, and bones" (W. Swainson 1840, 25), and to gather freshwater snails that clung to reeds in marshy terrain and bivalves that lived in the muddy bottoms of ponds or in shallow streams. In a river near Bulstrode the duchess found a new species of *Tellina*, a small bivalve that had not yet been named. Canals, rivers, marshes, ponds, and the ditches of a wet and soggy countryside were popular places for conchologists to search for new specimens, and Bulstrode proved to be as productive as any place in England to collect freshwater mollusks, her gardener finding an unknown limpet "adhering to the leaves of an iris" (Donovan 1799–1803).

She also traveled to England's southern seacoast, where in her quest for shells she dug in the sand, waded in tide pools, clambered over rocks, and took small boats out a few hundred feet to trawl for live specimens. At Weymouth, she found several new species of mollusks, some of which she most generously gave to her fellow conchologists. Swainson, whom she initially met at Margate, a seaside town, and who later visited her at Bulstrode, kept a record of where his shells came from, including those he collected himself and those that were given to him as gifts. Several of the shells he received as gifts from the duchess were from Weymouth. In his notebook he wrote that his specimen of the *Trochus papillosus* was "found by the D: of Portland at Weymouth & had from her," his *Strombus pespelecani* was found "at Weym: by the D. of P.," his *Bulla patula* was "given me by the D of Pd found by her at Weym," *Venus undata* was "found by Dss. Portland off Weymouth," his *Patella groeca* was "found by the D of P off Weymouth," his *Mya declivis* was "found by the D of P off Weymouth," and of his *Cardium tuberculatum*, he writes: "my large specimen . . . found at Weym by the D. of Portland" (J. T. Swainson n.d.).[2] In one of the few statements issued by the duchess about her own collecting practices, she wrote to the naturalist Thomas Pennant on February 26, 1778, about two shells she had collected herself, one of which was "a new *Solen* or *mytilus* which I found last year at Weymouth which they tell me has not been described" (Pennant Correspondence). She loaned this shell to him so that he could have it drawn and included in his book on British zoology.

The duchess's visits to Weymouth were opportunities for her to indulge in her love of natural history, to collect specimens, and to experience freedom from the demands and restraints of her social rank as she wandered for hours along the shore. While visiting Weymouth in August 1771, she received a letter from Lightfoot, who stated how glad he was to hear that she was in good health and to hear "that Weymouth had wonderfully recovered your Grace's Health & Spirits. . . . Three or four hours daily Exercise or Motion in the open Air, your wholesome sea Breezes, your Sand Grottos, but above all the odoriferous Fragrancy of sea . . . & sea shells, cannot fail to brace up the languid System . . ." (Portland Papers). Not only did the duchess walk along the shoreline; she also went out in fishing boats to oversee dredging the seabed in search of live shellfish. She was considered an expert on dredging, although this practice of dragging a bucket across the sea floor is now considered destructive to the environment and is illegal in some waters today.

The duchess's love of going to the coast to search for shells continued well into her late sixties, though Weymouth's pleasures diminished with the death of her friend Mrs. LeCoq, an expert specimen hunter, who had resided in Weymouth. On July 6, 1782, she wrote to Richard Pulteney: "I propose setting out for Margate next week to try if the sea air has still the same Efficacy, for alas, I can never think of Weymouth again since the loss of my kind affectionate Friend Mrs. LeCoq" (Pulteney Correspondence). At Margate, the duchess continued her practice of walking the shoreline in search of shells. Here she was sometimes not as successful finding shells as she wished, writing to Pulteney on August 21, 1784: "This air is very good & I have found great benefit from it but by way of amusement[.] except very pleasant airings there is none[,] not a shell to be met with tho' I have been very diligent in my searches" (Pulteney Correspondence). Perhaps such disappointments were offset by meeting in Margate Swainson, someone who, though her junior by forty years, shared her passion for collecting shells. She gave him shells, went to his apartments to examine his shell collection, and they probably went out together to comb the shoreline for new specimens.

This sociability of shell collecting that we glimpse in the duchess's correspondence is conveyed in greater detail in Mrs. Delany's letters from the 1750s, when she was an avid shellworker in Ireland: "Do you not wish yourself extended on the beach gathering shells, listening to Phill [Miss Donnellan] while she sings at her work, or joining in the conversation, always attended with cheerfulness?" Mrs. Delany traveled modest distances to gather shells: "The coach is at the door, and we are going to Burdoyl, a strand about six miles off, in search of shells" for making "festoons of shell flowers in their natural colours, that are to go over the bow window." (Delany 1862, 3: 542–543). Shell-hunting expeditions offered much pleasure: "Yesterday at five o'clock in the afternoon we took a boat and went to a shore about a mile off to gather shells, where we found a vast variety of beauties. We were very merry in our work, but much merrier in our return home, for five of us, all mounted a cart, and home we drove as jocund as ever five people were" (Day 1991).[3] Like Mary Delany's shell-hunting expeditions, the duchess's excursions to Weymouth were sociable affairs as they included not only Mrs. Le Coq but also Mr. Lightfoot, who accompanied her when she went out dredging despite his tendency to seasickness, and later when she went to Margate, she hunted for shells in the company of Mr. Swainson. The pleasures of searching for seashells—enjoying the sea air, taking boat rides, and walking on the beach—were heightened and intensified by sharing the experience with others who were also passionate about collecting shells.

In addition to the duchess's activities as a field naturalist, she was also actively engaged in the classification of her shells. Having mastered the principles of Linnaean taxonomy, she was quite adept at identifying her specimens' taxa, a practice that involved comparing the collected specimen against the verbal and visual representation of the same shell found in various reference books, some of which were organized along Linnaean categories. Classification for shell collectors usually meant working indoors with his or her specimens, as shells were often delicate and easy to lose, some so small they required a microscope to see them, and the reference books were often large-format catalogues, too expensive and heavy to carry outdoors as one might a field guide. A witness to these attempts to classify natural history specimens, Mrs. Delany describes how the duchess's passion for natural history transformed space at Bulstrode, turning "her Grace's breakfast room" into a "repository of sieves, pans, platters, and filled with all the productions of *that* nature, [which] are spread on tables, windows, chairs, which with books of all kinds, (opened to their useful places) make an agreeable confusion; sometimes, not withstanding twelve chairs and a couch, it is indeed a little difficult to find a seat" (Delany 1862, 4: 238).

Although classification took place indoors surrounded by shells on sorting trays and other available surfaces and in little boxes and patty pans (cupcake tins), this was also a social activity involving friends conferring about specimens, exchanging information and guesses about the species of new and unnamed specimens.

The duchess performed these activities with the assistance of visiting naturalists and interested members of her household, including Mary Delany, the Rev. Lightfoot, the artist Ehret, and even her gardener Agnew. Although she could recognize and label known species with the assistance of shell catalogues, she left naming new species, new in the sense of never named before within Linnaean systematics, to Daniel Solander because he was the foremost expert on mollusks in Britain. He spent one day every week for over four years working on identifying and naming her shells, using her collection, the largest of its kind, as a means to refine and expand Linnaeus's system as it applied to mollusks.

Further work needs to be done on recovering the practices of classification that the duchess and her network engaged with as they cleaned, sorted, identified, and named their specimens, but it is fairly clear that the duchess was respected by her fellow amateur conchologists, who often consulted her for advice when they were having difficulty labeling their specimens. Henry Seymer, a country gentleman whom she visited occasionally in Dorset on her way to Weymouth, wrote their mutual friend, Dr. Richard Pulteney, in the fall of 1772 in anticipation of one such visit, hoping that the duchess's expertise and mastery of Linnaean nomenclature could rescue him from confusion: "If the Ds does not assist me greatly, I shall jumble them together as formerly" (Pulteney Correspondence). With the amateur naturalist Pulteney, she maintained an active, long-term correspondence about his shell collection, giving him specimens that he could not afford to buy or could not take the time from his duties as a physician to gather shells at the seashore. He would write to her asking advice about shells he was having trouble classifying. Pulteney would often send her boxes of shells for her to examine and compare with those in her cabinet, hoping she would catch whether he had made any mistakes classifying these shells. He wrote on the 24th of March 1779: "I have packed up in a Box, and sent by the Coach today as single Valve (for I have not a pair) of that Shell which I have always taken for the *Venus pensylvania*; and I shall be glad to have it determined from your Grace's Cabinet . . . but as your Grace can . . . recollect such, from having several times honoured my Cabinet with your Inspection, you will easily correct such Errors where they occur" (Portland Papers). Accompanying these little packets of shells were long lists of Pulteney's questions about each shell, and if she did not know the answer and was unable to identify certain shells, she would wait for Solander's weekly visit and ask him to help identify Pulteney's troublesome shells. They carried on this correspondence for nearly two decades, writing several times a year, and sending each other little packets of shells, some breaking on the journey between London, where she kept most of her shell collection, and Bland-ford, his home. Far from the secretive, reclusive stereotype of the virtuoso fondling his bits of natural objects, the duchess and her friends were active, energetic, and sociable as they hunted for specimens and worked together classifying their collections.[4]

CONCLUSIONS

In detailing the material practices of shell collecting, my aim has been to demonstrate that natural history collectors were passionately engaged with nature in embodied ways: walking the shoreline, mucking through coastal mudflats and squishy sandbanks; poking around in ponds for bivalves and scooping up freshwater snails with little nets; rambling through wet fields looking for snails and putting them in wicker baskets; and once home, han-dling specimens, cleaning and polishing them, placing them in little labeled boxes, and storing them in cabinet drawers. In order for us to view this embodied and impassioned engagement with nature in a positive light—complete with its interest in the detritus of the natural world—we must ignore the period's literary caricatures of natural history collectors as well as unlearn our Wordsworthian and Emersonian tendencies to disparage these Enlightenment collectors and classifiers of the natural world. It is common today to see these practices of collecting and classifying as some-how responsible for the death of nature, as Carolyn Merchant has implied; for desacralizing nature, as Horkheimer and Adorno (1947, 2002) have put it, and for reinforcing the Cartesian split between the human subject and nature as inert object.

It should be apparent from the enthusiasm and emotional intensity that the duchess and her circle displayed in their quest for natural history speci-mens that these collectors did not perceive nature as separate, as other, and as an object to harness to economic production and the flows of global capital. In fact, it was the very uselessness of natural history collections that fueled contemporary critiques of virtuosi as indiscriminate collectors of dead bits and pieces of the natural world. Natural history collectors took nature out of the realm of utility and economic production and positioned the natural world as the recipient of their attention, labor, and love. There's no denying that they were passionate about the natural world, even though we may judge their passion to have been misdirected, as in Sir Nicholas Gimcrack's attachment to a rat's testicles. These collectors' thoughts, feel-ings, and sense of self were bound up in the natural world in ways that suggest a permeable boundary between self and nature, between subject and object, a kind of fluid and contingent subjectivity that was dependent on affective bonds with the natural world. That someone could love shells, dried beetles, or dead birds to the degree that they would organize their lives around them suggests a kind of affective relationship with nature that is intense and profound. Though collectors' affective ties to natural history specimens could have earned from Freud the label "polymorphously perverse" (Freud 1991, 15: 209), such passionate engagement competes with Romanticism's cerebral aestheticism and our vigilant environmentalism for the title of who loves nature best.

Collectors, like the duchess and her friends, were deeply engaged with nature—out in rowboats dredging shallow seas, wading in streams looking for tiny mollusks clinging to water weeds, and scooping up muck in ponds with long spoons in search of bivalves. They were perhaps even more engaged with nature than a Wordsworth strolling along country lanes or a Thoreau waiting for the farmer's wife to bring him his evening meal at Walden, for Wordsworth and Thoreau had a tendency to hold the natural world at an arm's length in their aesthetic and philosophical contemplation of nature.

While it is possible to portray eighteenth-century taxonomists and their attempts to name and label the natural world as engaged in a form of cultural imperialism, I do not think that collectors and classifiers, then and now, can be blamed for our current ecological disasters; we must look elsewhere, in particular to ways in which nature has been harnessed to capital and intensive production, specifically to the dominance of monoculture over the local and the diversified, and to the industrialization of agriculture, forestry, and animal husbandry. Natural history collectors were not interested in using or exploiting nature for profit; they wanted to observe, touch, describe, and document what they saw, and it is in these methods of observation and documentation that we can perhaps find solutions to our current environmental crises.

NOTES

I acknowledge the invaluable support of the National Science Foundation Scholars Award.
1. For this literary tradition of ridiculing virtuosi, see Claude Lloyd, "Shadwell and the Virtuosi," *PMLA* 44 (1929): 472–496; Joseph M. Levine, *Dr. Woodward's Shield: History, Science, and Satire in Augustan England* (Berkeley: University of California Press, 1977); and Marjorie Swann, *Curiosities and Texts: The Culture of Collecting in Early Modern England* (Philadelphia: University of Pennsylvania Press, 2001), Chapter 2.
2. The duchess's friend John Timothy Swainson was an enthusiastic field collector, and fortunately for us, a record of his activities can be found in a small handmade notebook, which now resides at the Natural History Museum in London.
3. See David Elliston Allen, "Tastes and Crazes," in *Naturalists and Society: The Culture of Natural History in Britain, 1700–1900* (Aldershot, UK: Ashgate Variorum, 2001) for a discussion of Victorian codes of propriety concerning shell and seaweed collecting on the shore.
4. It is important to note that the duchess was not the only woman who was an active specimen hunter. In addition to her friends Mary Delany and Mrs. LeCoq, there was Mary Anning, the famous shell and fossil hunter of Lyme Regis, and there was a Miss Pocock, who pops up with regularity in Edward

Donovan's volumes on the *Natural History of British Shells* as someone who found many new molluscan species along the coast of Wales.

REFERENCES

Allen, David Elliston. 1995. *The Naturalists in Britain: A Social History.* Princeton, NJ: Princeton University Press.

Austen, Jane. 2002. *Emma.* New York: Bedford/St. Martins.

Battacharya, Nandini. 2006. *Slavery, Colonialism, and Connoisseurship: Gender and Eighteenth-Century Literary Transnationalism.* Burlington, VT, and Aldershot, UK: Ashgate, 2006.

Bond, Donald F., ed. 1987. *The Tatler.* 3 vols. Oxford: Clarendon Press.

Cook, Alexandra. 2007. "Botanical Exchanges: Jean-Jacques Rousseau and the Duchess of Portland." *History of European Ideas* 33: 142–156.

Day, Angélique, ed. 1991. *Letters from Georgian Ireland: The Correspondence of Mary Delany, 1731–1768.* Belfast: Friar's Bush Press.

Delany, Mary. 1862. *The Autobiography and Correspondence of Mary Granville, Mrs. Delany, [first series]: With Interesting Reminiscences of King George the Third and Queen Charlotte.* Edited by Lady Llanover. 6 vols. London: R. Bentley.

Donovan, Edward. 1799–1803. *Natural History of British Shells,* 5 vols. London. Vol. 5., Plate CL.

Horkheimer, Max, and Theodor W. Adorno. 2002. *Dialectic of Enlightenment: Philosophical Fragments* (1947). Edited by G. S. Noerr. Translated by E. Jephcott. Stanford, CA: Stanford University Press.

Laird, Mark, and Alicia Weisberg-Roberts, eds. 2009. *Mrs. Delany and Her Circle.* New Haven, CT: Yale University Press.

Merchant, Carolyn. 1989. *The Death of Nature: Women, Ecology, and the Scientific Revolution.* New York: HarperCollins.

Parrish, Susan Scott. 2006. *American Curiosity: Cultures of Natural History in the Colonial British Atlantic World.* Chapel Hill: University of North Carolina Press.

Pascoe, Judith. 2006. *The Hummingbird Cabinet: A Rare and Curious History of Romantic Collections.* Ithaca, NY: Cornell University Press.

Pennant, Thomas. Correspondence. Warwickshire County Record Office, England.

Portland Papers. Margaret Cavendish Bentinck, 2nd Duchess of Portland. Longleat House. Vol. 14.

Pulteney, Richard. Correspondence. Linnean Library, London.

Schiebinger, Londa. 2004. *Plants and Empire: Colonial Bioprospecting in the Atlantic World.* Cambridge, MA: Harvard University Press.

Sutton, Geoffry V. 1995. *Science for a Polite Society: Gender, Culture, and the Demonstration of Enlightenment.* Boulder, CO: Westview Press.

Swainson, John Timothy. n.d. "MS Catalogue of British Shells in the Possession of J. T. Swainson." Natural History Museum, London, Zoology Library.

Swainson, William. 1840. *Taxidermy: Bibliography and Biography.* London: Longman.

Tobin, Beth Fowkes. 2005. *Colonizing Nature: The Tropics in British Arts and Letters, 1760–1820.* Philadelphia: University of Pennsylvania Press.

———. 2009. "The Duchess's Shells: Natural History Collecting, Gender, and Scientific Practice." In *Material Women, 1750–1950: Consuming Desires and Collecting Practices.* Edited by Maureen Daly Goggin and Beth Fowkes Tobin. Aldershot, UK: Ashgate. 244–263.

4 Chimerical Figurations at the Monstrous Edges of Species

Jill H. Casid

FIGURATION 1: BY WAY OF INTRODUCTION

In a September 3, 2001, *New Yorker* cartoon by Jack Ziegler (Figure 1.1), a toga-wearing man balanced on a walking stick meets a bearded centaur under a tree. The centaur informs his companion, "Being a hybrid, I get to have my way with a variety of species, and at the same time I enjoy a healthy tax credit." This encounter between one "man" who openly declares himself a hybrid and another who depends on an extra appendage made of the same substance as the tree intimates how human-animal-plant interdependence might itself constitute a form of hybridity. And this encounter between different forms of hybrids is crucially staged on the

"Being a hybrid, I get to have my way with a variety of species, and at the same time I enjoy a healthy tax credit."

Figure 4.1 Jack Ziegler, "Being a hybrid," cartoon, *The New Yorker*, September 3, 2001, © Jack Ziefler/The New Yorker Collection/www.cartoonbank.com.

common ground of disputes over same-sex marriage and the special tax credits afforded married couples and couples with children, the characterization of same-sex unions as akin to bestiality, and controversies over human embryonic stem cell transplants.

While the walking, talking, and mating centaur of cartoon humor might seem a chimerical figuration in the sense of a conception without ground in material reality, its setting in the time-space of an ancient Greece where such mythical creatures form an essential part of everyday reality also indicates, as bioethicist and legal scholar Henry T. Greely declared, that "[t]he centaur has left the barn more than people realize" (Dowd 2005). In the public policy context of a 2005 workshop held by the Institute of Medicine to determine what ethical guidelines should constrain stem cell research, Greely turned to the ancient mythological half-human, half-animal centaur to mark the already generated and living transgenic hybrids. But this pointed reminder that the question of "whether or not" is posed in the wake of the materialized realities of the fantastic made flesh does more than resituate ethical questions and public policy deliberations on the heels of the retreating hooves of myth made matter. Greely's phrasing represents such new bioforms as themselves in action, not simply as crosses between species, but also as crossed species that transgress.

The centaur that has left the barn is not a figure of stable hybridity but a roving, even rogue body that moves out of protective or controlling enclosure, traversing, overturning, and even destroying boundaries such as the fence between human and animal to an as yet unimagined and undefined space of future conceptions and consequence. This problem of reckoning with hybridity's own uncontrollable agential destructive and procreative power is at the core of contestation over transplantation, the crossing of species, and the generation of unprecedented forms of life that in current medical, legal, public policy, and environmental discourse goes by the name of another mythological beast, the "chimera," or an organism with the genetic information from two or more different species (Clayton 2007). While the National Academies' *Guidelines for Human Embryonic Stem Cell Research* were modified in 2007, 2008, and 2010, they nonetheless retain the human-animal chimera—still the limit horizon for stem cell transplantation—as the hard edge of the ethical map in the place of the fantastic beasts that inhabited the corners of the world on early modern charts of the earth (Begley 2005; National Academies Human Embryonic Stem Cell Research Advisory Committee 2010).

I do not invoke this cartographic analogy to the place of beast bodies in the history of mapping conventions lightly (Traub 2000). The chimera troubles because what it *is* cannot be separated from what it *does*: the chimera is a figure that performs figure-ground problematics (Winkler 1907). The chimera is more than an unstable taxonomic classification and hybrid form of being (Greely 2003; Robert and Baylis 2003). The promiscuous kinship of the very name "chimera," its mating of different types of hybridity produced by different processes and productive of different outcomes poignantly attests to the power of the chimera as a dynamic, living entity of both destructive and generative potential, a force that severs ties assumed to bind the "normal" and forges alternate bonds of kinship across the divides of difference and the ruptures of death. The chimera traverses the imagined distance between being and doing while altering and even pulling up the ground behind it and casting new terrains ahead. And it does so through its powers of materializing figuration, its potential to give active, viable material form to that which would seem to be without ground because it is taken to be out of order. The chimera troubles as an active conceptual linkage between idea and matter that overturns the relations of body and ground, before and after in its power to potently reconceive groundless abstract, speculative, and fantastic ideas in the form of living matter that makes its own grounds and futures.

While the phrase "chimerical figuration" does the labor of revealing the chimera as active materializing force, the "monstrous edges of species" in my title recalls Anna Tsing's poetic articulation of "human nature" as an "interspecies relationship" with fungi in her powerful "Unruly Edges: Mushrooms as Companion Species" (Tsing forthcoming). But in my invocation, the monstrous edges of species marks the domain of incorporations that exceed companionship and is intended to do some complicated historical and cultural boundary-defying work in pushing us to think human, animal, plant, and environment as a complex and dynamic assemblage without priority, hierarchy, or ground. And it is not just the traversal of bounds but also the very erection and maintenance of such perimeters that may be understood as monstrous, if we consider the history of boundaries that cut, histories of the construction of race in terms of distinct species, slavery's conversion of persons into nonhuman things, the constitution of sexed embodiment as a matter of absolute difference, and environmental transformation and destruction as predicated on the separation of biobodies from the ecologies that support them.

In ancient myth and particularly Ovid's *Metamorphoses*, the body is a biology without destiny and the chimera incarnates changes in substance and aim with the power to fundamentally alter any presumed teleology. Consider the tale of Byblis, whose passion for her likeness in the form of her twin brother Caunus drove her to abandon home, possibilities for marriage, and fatherland for the territory "where the Chimaera prowled with lungs of fire and lion's breast and head and dragon's tail" (Ovid IX, 446–665). From Byblis, whose hot desire melted the bounds of custom and kinship until cooled in the arms of wood nymphs—her human form deliquescing into a spring of shed tears—to the chimera itself and on through the many human-to-plant and human-to-animal transfigurations that characterize the *Metamorphoses*, Ovidian myth continues to provide the rhetorics and visual imaginary not merely for substantial corporeal change but also alterations in form and desire that change the relations of body to place and of figure to ground and violate the regulating bounds governing relations of kind and the presumed trajectories or destinies of biological form.

While the results of transplantation are now figured as monstrous hybrids or chimerical combinations of human, plant, and animal, the action or process of figuration has also been conceived from the early beginnings of modernity in the eighteenth century as the fantastic power to commingle, reshape, and materialize potent, order-defying combinations that transgress the body bounds of species (Bailey 1730). It is the monstrous living reality and destructive as well as conceiving force of the chimera that challenges and haunts not merely futuristically but also historically, insisting that we think past and present, before and after in more dynamic relation. In the work of historian Richard Grove, from *Green Imperialism* to his more recent historicizations of anxieties about climate change, global warming, desiccation, species extinction, and biodiversity decline, we find the argument that contemporary environmentalism and, in particular, conservation as a programmatic response to fears about destructive anthropogenic effects begin with late eighteenth-century "colonial environmentalism" in the practice and form of forest preservation on the plantation islands of the east and west Indies (Grove 1996, 2000). This imperial practice also produced a hybridized or intermixed landscape, combining, at once, the radical transformation of the plantation machine, the transplantation of exotic species (including sugarcane itself), and around it the botanical garden and the forest preserve.

As I have argued elsewhere, this island landscape of both transformation and conservation served to produce imperial power as natural possession through the ostentatious spectacle of preservation and reproduction in the reimagining of the plantation machine as a technics that brings in its wake not destruction of the indigenous environment but rather agricultural improvement figured as the heterosexualized sowing of seed, the preservation of the features of the place (particularly forest), and an effect of "pleasing" variety (Casid 2005). I would still assert that the eighteenth-century discursive and material practices of claiming a right to possession through the materializing metaphor of planting scattered seed as heterosexual reproduction, imperial networks of botanical transplantation, the slave trade, and sugar, coffee, indigo and spice plantations with their transformation and remaking of tropical landscape are not just the devastating "before" of environmentalism: these contradictions of colonial landscaping are embedded in environmentalism's putative origins and its afterlife. Environmentalism's postcoloniality is registered both in the aftereffects of guilt and the very discourse and practice of the preservation of the "natural" order of species in the wake and face of change.

The discourse and imaginary of environmentalism has deeply problematic colonial roots that potentially tie us to discourses of paternal stewardship and constructions of the "natural" order and bounds of species that have historically served to instate heterosexual dominance and imperial power as the order of nature through claims to land and the status of the natural. Yet I want to insist that thinking with this history reveals rich figurations with possibilities for the present and future that are not exhausted by the impurities and even taint of their inception. Thinking critically and, indeed, queerly with and against the eighteenth-century colonial origin story of environmentalism may allow us ethically and politically to reimagine and, indeed, revalue the place of queer species, the hybrid, the monstrous, and the protean in discourse and practice. This chapter accordingly courts and conjures the creative possibilities of monstrosity, activating the work of figuration by practicing the monstrosity of mixture it takes as its subject. It assembles into promiscuous contact a set of protean and unstable figurations from contemporary stem cell transplantation, speculations about transgender neurons and consciousness, and bioart to eighteenth-century experiments in transplantation and materialist philosophy. I enlist these chronologically dispersed instances of materializing figuration to think about the history of the dangers and possibilities of transplantation, asking what this ambivalent colonial history might offer a queered discourse on transplantation and cross-species encounter and transformation (Franklin 2007; Giffney and Hird 2008). In the spirit of the monstrous hybrids I discuss and their challenge to temporality, I will shuttle back and forth between a problematized before and after, then and now. Allen S. Weiss's ten theses on monsters represent the creation of monsters through the "confusion of species" as a dynamic aesthetic and political process that manifests the "plasticity of the imagination" in its wondrous "catastrophes of the flesh" (Weiss 2004). This essay lays out its argument across ten volatile figurations that demonstrate not just the plasticity of the imagination but also the protean propensities of matter itself.

FIGURATION 2: THE SCARECROW ON THE ROAD TO OZ

Experimental and yet also serious—even mortal—boundary play with species is the domain of the ArtScience collaborative Le Laboratoire in Paris. Le Laboratoire has deeply serious aims—for the environment and for world health—but it takes, of all possible and fantastic figurations, *The Wizard of Oz* as the extended metaphor for the laboratory site as both a catalyst and productive environment for the cultivation of change at the level of the stem cell (Edwards et. al. 2008, 16). While Le Laboratoire's move to Oz may surprise many a reader, the path to the yellow brick road in fact makes richly playful sense. *The Wizard of Oz* retells the story of modernity as a shift from gray into a projective color that challenges us to rethink the origins and beginnings of the projected image and scientific method in relation to both Sir Isaac Newton's *Opticks* and Enlightenment alchemy with its investment in the possibilities of substantial alteration (Casid forthcoming). Le Laboratoire's 2007 hybrid catalogue, novel, and manifesto titled *Niche* represent the opening exhibition, a collaboration between artist Fabrice Hyber, who speaks of his work as rhizomes, and chemical engineering

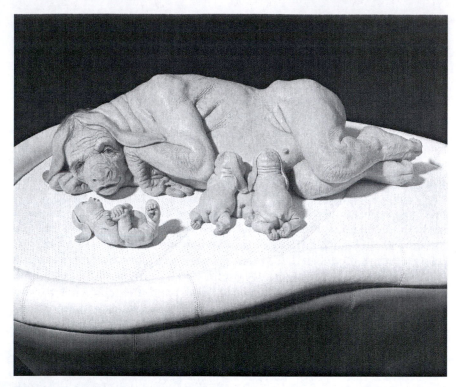

Figure 4.2 Patricia Piccinini, *The Young Family*, 2002-3, installation sculpture from *We Are Family*. Courtesy of the artist.

scientist Robert Langer of MIT, whose work on tissue culture continues to inspire creative bioart projects (Langer and Vacanti 1999). While the subject of the exhibit is the transformation of stem cells and the environment or niche necessary to that process, the image for this process is taken from the scarecrow's song "If I Only Had a Brain" (1939): "I could while away the hours / Conferrin' with the flowers / Consultin' with the rain / And my head, I'd be scratchin' / While my thoughts were busy hatchin' / If I only had a brain." From this image of the semblance of a man made of the very environmental and plant substances with which he is in companionate dialogue comes the manifesto for the creative powers of art-science collaboration on the model of the stem cell that violates these categories in its capacities for transfer and growth between human, plant, animal, and machine. The novel-catalogue-manifesto of art-science collaboration asserts the transformative capacities of science in the discourse of a hybrid form of bioart, proclaiming: "The Artist will be a stem cell-becoming-a-neuron! The Artist shall . . . through the magical art force, become an embryonic stem cell scraped off some available baby embryo blastocyte and figure out his own path to transformation through cell division. Such is the Yellow Brick Road" (Edwards et. al. 2008, 16).

FIGURATION 3: TRANSGENDER CHIMERAS

Figure 4.3 The Tissue Culture and Art Project (Oron Catts, Ionat Zurr, Guy Ben-Ary), "Worry Dolls" from *Tissue Culture & Art(ificial) Wombs: An Installation of Semi-Living Worry Dolls*, 2000, live tissue in incubator. Courtesy of the artists.

Though fanciful and bordering perhaps on the absurd, this winding yellow road of figurations is not the detour from the "real" and consequential materialities of the science and politics of transplantation it might appear. To bring out the consequential materialities of chimerical figuration, let me take a further risk, this time into personal anecdote. In the spring of 2007, my mother was diagnosed with acute myelogenous leukemia, which her oncologist conjectured was induced by the particular chemotherapeutic agent (Adriamycin) used to treat her third round of breast cancer. As they were unable to induce remission with high-dose chemotherapy and she did not have siblings, the only option was determined to be an experimental peripheral blood stem cell transplant from an unrelated donor. Peripheral blood stem cells are considered "hemopoietic," a redolent word which signifies their ability, if the stem cells engraft, to rewrite the blood and recompose their recipient host such that the transplant patient becomes a chimera in another, ostensibly invisible, sense: the recipients are recomposed of both their own DNA and the DNA of their donor. As is typical of unrelated donor transplants, we were told nothing about the donor except, in this case, that he was a man. I raise the issue of this sharing of the donor's attributed sex (and sexuality) because of the framing figuration narrated as comic inversion: my mother's transplant doctor at Baylor University Medical Center joked that we would know that the stems cells engrafted if and when my mother asked for *Penthouse* and started to pump iron (Fay 2007).

However volatilely amusing (or potentially offensive) the use of such sex stereotypes to visually flesh out the invisible transformation of my mother into a genetic chimera, this joking figuration of the chimera's violation of the bounds of binary gender and sexuality also points to some actual transgendering and queering possibilities. The results of a 2004 study conducted at the University of Florida and published in *The Lancet* reported that peripheral blood stem cell transplants performed on three female breast cancer patients who developed leukemia and received transplants from male donors showed the presence of transgender neurons in the brain (Cogle et. al. 2004). The study demonstrated evidence of the plasticity of adult hemopoietic stem cells, that is, their potential to develop into neural cells. But the study also showed the potential recomposition of the patient's brain with transgender neurons. This is, of course, still comfortably distant from the transformation of the consciousness of a sixty-six-year-old woman into that of a twenty-year-old porn-watching, iron-pumping man. But in his own research as well as in conversation with the author, stem cell biologist Clive Svendsen has raised the question of "how neural transplants of stem cells from a wide range of sources may modify the brain of the recipient hybrid in a way that leads to a change in consciousness" (Svendsen 2008).

My interest and concern about the ways in which how we imagine the real and as yet unrealized but potential possibilities of radical transformation frame and constrain how we value and, hence, also practice are animated in no small part by the figuration of my mother as a kind of monster: a queer, transgendered chimera. (This interest is ghosted as well by an acknowledged wish that the experimental stem cell transplant had, indeed, successfully engrafted to sustain life in altered form. The experimental stem cell transplant was performed on July 28, 2008; Susan Casid Miller died on November 11). Figuration is not a second-level concern of representation, but is embedded in how and what we are able to practice. Therefore, the three strands of my project—imaginary, historical, and theoretical—are necessarily as entwined as the strands of DNA.

FIGURATION 4: MONSTROUS MOTHERS

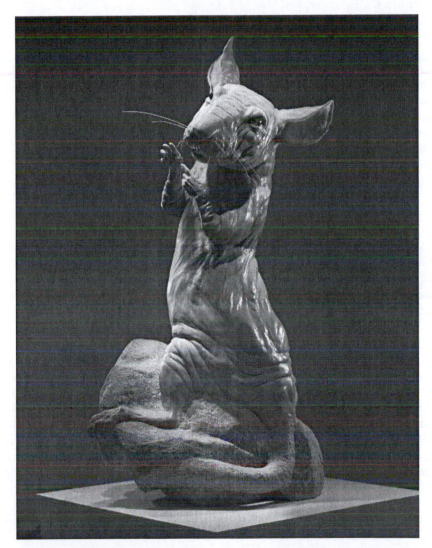

Figure 4.4   Bryan Crockett, *Ecce Homo*, 2000, 6-foot synthetic marble sculpture. Courtesy of the Artist.

It might seem a strictly disciplinary question pertaining to the domain of visual studies to ask how transplantation is visualized in a general sense and, in particular, what social, cultural, and political work the use of the highly visual conceptual image of the chimera does in giving a certain gendered teratological body to the outcome of transplant processes. But the visual power and gendering of the chimera strike in such observations on the figurative rhetoric of the chimera as William Safire's little piece in which he notes with a wry parenthetical, "It's [the genetic hybrid's] always described as a she-monster, you never hear about chimerical he-monsters" (Safire 2005). While not the she-goat of classical mythology, the monstrous hybrid suckling mother she-pig of Patricia Piccinini's sculpture (Figure 4.2) *The Young Family* (2002–3) demonstrates well how the chimera demands a confrontation with the gendering of genre or species. This she-pig incorporates a combination of synthetic and natural materials (silicone, acrylic, human hair, and timber) to stage the porcine parts of organ transplants as potent vehicles that not only remake the maternal body (the figure for reproduction) but also take on the life-giving and transformative powers attributed to sexual reproduction. Piccinini's monstrous mother also allows us to think about the chimera as a powerful discursive figure that, in mobilizing an imaginary of monsters, contributes to the persistent tethering of the products of transplantation to the specter of the monstrosity of reproduction and the vagaries of kinship.

FIGURATION 5: WETWARE WORRY DOLLS

Such familial attachments can also work affectively as practices of a kind of love and not just recoiling horror. This practice of love is strangely palpable in the contestation and play with the possibilities of monsters in such wetware art projects as the "worry dolls" by The Tissue Culture and Art Project (Oron Catts, Ionat Zurr, and Guy Ben-Ary). These seven "semi-living objects" on the model of Guatemalan worry dolls (Figure 4.3) recomposed of human tissue give the monstrous dynamic, volatile, and, as the collaborative team describes it, "gender-less, childlike" form as transporting libidinal carriers with which to play out and with our anxieties about and desires for transformation (Catts and Zurr 2002). The "gender-less, childlike" form and lab setting—which the collaborative team strategically call, in their manifesto on tissue culture, the "artificial womb"—for the dolls' (re)production provide the gestation ground for reinvented sex practices outside the maternal body: "The next sex created in the artificial womb may be a cold, calculated act for the best sex" (Catts et. al. 2000). While it is easy to be suspicious of yet one more project to alienate and colonize the womb, it is harder and yet I think worth the risk to hold onto the possibilities of such chimerical figurations as the she-pig and worry doll not as

Figure 4.5   Miguel Cabrera, *From Spaniard and Indian, Mestiza,* 1763, oil on canvas, private collection.

finalities or endpoints, not as postgender or postsex flesh forms but rather as hybrid sites for the production of queer natures that problematize our ability to distinguish nature and culture, worst and best, and also proffer (semi)living ways of being and becoming beyond the binary oppositions of human and animal, male and female.

FIGURATION 6: THE MONUMENTAL ONCOMOUSE

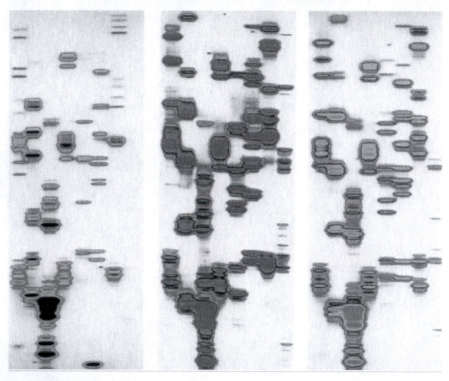

Figure 4.6   Iñigo Manglano-Ovalle, *Glenn, Dario, and Tyrone*, 1998, three c-prints, Collection of the Guggenheim Museum, New York.

Bryan Crockett's human or even greater-than-human-scaled six-foot statue *Ecce Homo* (Figure 4.4) restages in marble and epoxy the witnessing of the body of Christ with the genetically engineered oncomouse in the place of a/the savior. This substitution asks not only what is the difference between science and religion but also what is the difference—not just in body but also in the values attributed to those bodies—between human, animal, and superhuman, even divine. Despite decades of challenges to and efforts to think outside of absolute, binary conceptions of difference from poststructuralist philosophy to postcolonial theory's championing of hybridity, créolité, mélange, and mestizo and feminist and critical race studies scholarship and critiques of science, the question of how difference and sameness are conceptualized remains central to the ethical and political problem of the chimera. When hybridity is figured not as a consequence or product of the crossing or mixture of entirely distinct and opposed entities but rather as combinations that depend for their viability on an affinity or even kinship that make such distinctions difficult, the implications for the practice of transplantation in terms of scientific research, public policy, and ethics begin to change. That is, figurations such as the queer transgender chimera, the she-pig, the wetware worry doll, and the oncomouse might also present opportunities to forge living practices of connection, a kind of monstrous kinship, and alternate forms of embodiment in the present without the assumption that one must or even can know the outcomes in advance. Interdependence, risk, and vulnerability are not choices: they are the chimerical context we inhabit.

FIGURATION 7: CASTAS, CROSSBREEDS, AND QUEER KIN IN THE GARDEN OF DELIGHTS

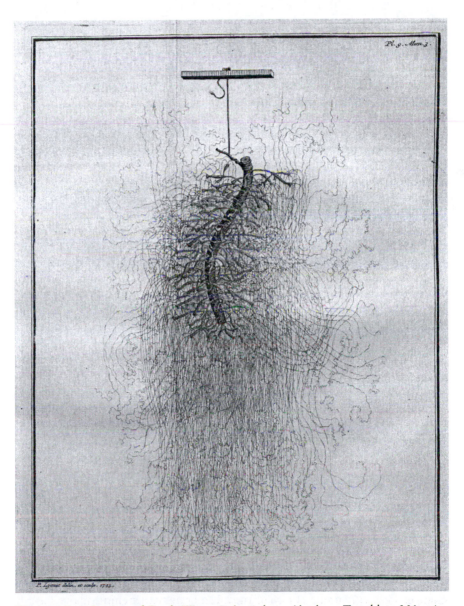

Figure 4.7   "Cutting of Fresh Water Polyp" from Abraham Trembley, *Mémoires pour l'histoire des polypes* (1744). Courtesy of Special Collections, University of Wisconsin-Madison.

The current use of the name "chimera" to designate transplant subjects has a complex history that is inextricably imbricated with colonial taxonomies of race and gender (McLeod 2000; Schiebinger 2004; Schiebinger and Swan 2005; Delbourgo and Dew 2008). Consider the taxonomical elaboration of eighteenth-century Mexican casta paintings such as *From a Spaniard and an Indian Woman, a Mestiza* (Figure 4.5), the first painted panel in a series of sixteen by Miguel Cabrera (Katzew 2005; Carrera 2003). This "genre scene" in multiple senses (quotidian life, species, and gender) represents the bodily crossing and imagined blood mixing of an "Español" with an "India" producing a "Mestiza" as a process of combination that can be seen through the visual analogy of the creation of textiles and their interthreaded tints in the multicolored weavings displayed on and adjacent to the India and Mestiza whose hand she holds. In this material analogy between humans and things, blood and dye, and animate and inanimate exchange commodities, we see how crossbreeding is also intertwined with colonial and neocolonial hierarchies of what is "human" and what counts as "culture." But the reduction of human and plant bodies to alienable parts and the making of bodies into parts of a larger aggregate and ordering scheme also call up the origins of that new form of power in life itself that Michel Foucault called "biopower."

In his lecture "The Meshes of Power," Foucault asserted the eighteenth-century origins of the biopolitics of blood and bodies and the production of power through efforts to control reproduction (Foucault 2001). Foucault may not have posed a colonial origin to this eighteenth-century inception of biopolitics and the forging of ways in which "sex" and procreation would become instruments for the regulation of individual bodies and of bodies as parts and generators of populations. But in "Society Must Be Defended" Foucault argued that one of the principal forms of biopower is developed with colonization, a form he called racism (Foucault 1997). Racism works, he argues, by introducing a rupture into the biological continuum that allows for the conception of society as a whole in terms of a mélange of distinct races while, at the same time, treating particular bodies in terms of fragmenting subdivisions of "species." Foucault dates this cutting practice of biopower to the nineteenth century, but we can see the main techniques at work in the eighteenth-century castas with their simultaneous anatomization of the individual body and its placement within a larger scheme, and their materializing analogy between humans, plants, and things. They situate sex, race, and species, as Foucault phrased it, at the crossroads of disciplines and regulations that turned society into a "machine of production." Further, the castas' human-object analogy of humans as woven cloth seems to anticipate that this (colonial) machine of production would also become a crossroads for forms of generation, kinship, and affinity beyond heterosexual reproduction.

The complex biopolitics of the castas of colonial Mexico have also been given new life as the templates for queer configurations of family and generation in *The Garden of Delights* by Iñigo Manglano-Ovalle, an installation of DNA portrait triptychs. In place of heterosexual pairs of distinct racial identifications and taxonomically positioned mixed-race children, participants in Manglano-Ovalle's project chose their mates and their "offspring." The all-male three-some (Figure 4.6) of *Glenn, Dario, and Tyrone* (1998) are figured as a monumental and abstract blue-on-white arrangement of DNA patterns on three chromogenic prints face-mounted to acrylic that, inspired by the alchemical and transformative couplings of Bosch, reformat the castas as a kind of altarpiece to the possibilities of nonheterosexual reproduction, a reminder that Catholic altarpieces conse-crated to the witnessing of a virgin birth already are such figurative imagin-ings (Zamudio-Taylor and Armstrong 2000).

FIGURATION 8: SENSITIVE MAN-PLANTS, HYDRA POLYPS, AND UNRULY RHIZOMES

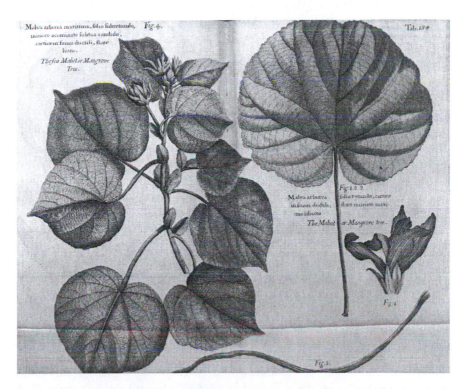

Figure 4.8 "The Mangrove Tree" from Hans Sloane, *A Voyage to the Islands of Madera, Barbados, Nieves, S. Christophers and Jamaica* (London, 1701–25). Cour-tesy of Special Collections, University of Wisconsin-Madison.

Investment in the potential power of bioforms across species (including plants) to act and react, to be both self-moving (even auto-generating) and sensitive, was also at the center of the radical materialism of the metropole and especially the work of Julien Offray de la Mettrie (Vartanian 1960; Wellmann 1992; Thomson 1996). La Mettrie's key text *Man a Machine* has incited controversy since its publication in 1748 for the contention that a noncentralized vital force may govern the actions of the smallest parts of plant, animal, and even human bodies. An essential piece of la Mettrie's argument about the vital commonalities between man, animal, and machine develops in the second part of his treatise *Man a Plant,* which la Mettrie opens with an evocative image of a "natural" metamorphosis based on commonality rather than absolute difference between species:

> Here is man metamorphosed into a plant. But do not think that this is a story such as Ovid might have told. On the contrary, the singular analogy between the plant and animal kingdoms has led me to the discovery that the principal parts of men and plants are the same. And if, herein, my imagination plays sometimes, be assured that it is on the table of truth. My field of battle is that of nature, whose legions I reduce to one (de la Mettrie 1994, 77).

La Mettrie's book did not include literal figurations, but this vivid play on and against Ovid calls to mind such personifications of plants as Robert John Thornton's *Temple of Flora* (1812), which explained Linnaeus's sexual classification system through an extended conceit of Cupid inspiring the plants with love and a full range of forms of love including the myth of the beautiful ephebe Hyacinth, favorite of Apollo, who, killed by jealous lover Zephyr, is turned into a flower by the sun god. A story of alchemical transformation, it is Hyacinth's spilled blood that forms the flowers whose buds are said to be stained by Apollo's tears (Thornton 1812). Such transmutations of life-forms forms the substance of Charles Darwin's father Erasmus Darwin's *The Botanic Garden* (1791), the first book of which is dedicated to an extended discourse on vitalism and the second to a poetic narrative retelling Linnaeus's sexual classification of system as the loves of the plants. The art of transmutation, Erasmus Darwin insists, is consistent with nature itself. Using the rhetoric of restoration, Darwin argues that uncovering the protean, agential powers of trees and flowers is to bring back their "original animality" (Darwin 1799).

While la Mettrie may protest too much against an influence from Ovid (a metamorphic chain that runs through la Mettrie, Thornton, and Darwin), the animating figure for these various efforts to conceive a vital unity between humans, animals, and plants is ultimately more contemporary: Abraham Trembley's self-generating freshwater polyp (Figure 4.7) of his *Mémoires pour l'histoire des polypes* (Trembley 1744). Trembley's experiments with cutting up the hydra and watching it regrow from parts "like branches of a tree" have been hailed as the beginnings of an experimental biology challenging the boundaries of animal, human, and plant (Lenhoff and Lenhoff 1986).

Trembley's work displaying an animal that behaves like a plant and hence the viability of "man a plant" was immediately translated into English and was included, for example, in George Adams's *Micrographia Illustrata*. At issue in Adams's text is not only the continuity of animals and plants in terms of behavior but, even more, in terms of sexuality, an upending challenge to the rule that "there is no fecundity without Copulation" (Adams 1747). In this, the freshwater polyp Hydra behaves like (and prefigures) the rhizomorphic plants theorized by Gilles Deleuze and Félix Guattari as an antihierarchical alternative order to the imperial hierarchies of arborific structures, a concept with real colonial roots, for rhizomorphic plants were the stated enemies of the plantation system (Deleuze and Guattari 1983). Mangrove plants (Figure 4.8), such as those illustrated in Hans Sloane's *Natural History of Jamaica*, represented monstrous asexual (or nonheterosexual) reproduction, a form of generation from any point that betrays hierarchies and produces a root system so difficult to eradicate it came to stand for the potential to undermine or, at least, stall the workings of the plantation-machine (Sloane 1701–25).

FIGURATION 9: LIVE TOOTH TRANSPLANTATION

Fascination and concern with the possibilities for promiscuous asexual or non-heterosexual growth are also at the center of the early modern discourse and practice of human transplantation. The first live human surgical transplantation was done in the eighteenth century by surgeon John Hunter with live human teeth, the results of which were published in Hunter's *The Natural History of the Human Teeth*. In the last chapter, we find the articulation of the principle of a uniting ground of similarity that Hunter argues is consistent with the work of la Mettrie and Trembley. The discovered fact that it is not necessary to find a tooth that fits the cavity because the mouth will grow to accept the tooth, Hunter concludes, is a visible sign that "the living principle exists in the several parts of the body, independent of the influence of the brain, or circulation, and that it subsists by these, or is indebted to them for its continuance ... and in many animals there is no brain nor circulation, so that this power is capable of being continued equally by all the parts themselves, such animals being nearly similar in this respect to vegetables" (Hunter 1771, 127). The mouth that grows around a transplanted tooth provided Hunter the living figuration for the conception of an active force dispersed among and across a continuum of parts from human and animal to vegetable.

While live tooth transplantation from one human to another might not seem to defy bounds between sexes and species, it is important to underscore the hierarchy and order-defying implications drawn in the eighteenth century from such figurations of parts surviving and participating in the transformation of their new host environments. Hunter's surgical experiments were as interested in defying assumed boundaries and hierarchies between top and bottom and male and female as those between human, animal, and plant. The Royal Academy of Surgeons has preserved the

Printed for & Sold by Carington Bowles.   N.º 69 in S.ᵗ Pauls Church Yard London

The LONDON DENTIST.

Published as the Act directs.

Figure 4.9   Robert Dighton, *The London Dentist*, 1784, color aquatint, collection of the British Museum. © Trustees of the British Museum.

artifacts of some of those reordering, even monstrous, transplants Hunter proudly recounted as evidence of the viability of crossing the bounds of species and gender: "Taking off the young spur of a cock, and fixing it to his comb, is an old and well known experiment. I have also frequently taken out the Testis of a cock and replaced it in his belly, where it has adhered, and has been nourished; nay, I have put the Testis of a cock into the belly of a hen with the same effect" (Hunter 1771, 127).

Anxieties surrounding the active potential for transplantation, the vehicle for the creation of chimeras, to interrupt hierarchy-preserving continuities in genus or species and disrupt assumed and hierarchalizing discontinuities between "the races" or "the sexes" play across two satirical British prints of the period: Robert Dighton's 1784 *The London Dentist* (Figure 4.9) and Thomas Rowlandson's 1787 *Transplanting of Teeth* (Figure 4.10). They represent live tooth extraction and transplantation in action and in the form of intimate contact across not just commonality (human to human) but also fetishized differences of color, sex, and class (Blackwell 2004). Blackening plays a triple role as sign of class (the dirt of labor covering the central figure in Rowlandson's print), race (the skin of the young attendant in the Dighton print), and death (the blackened oral cavities where teeth had once been). The precarious potential for disorder is also enacted by the promiscuous assemblage of these scenes of transplantation in the interdependent co-presence in domestic space of bodies marked by difference with fingers and hands gesturing at and almost into the oral boundary between inside and out. The central blackened figures (the laborer in the Rowlandson print and liveried attendant who recalls the slave system in the Dighton print) may also serve as carriers for anxiety that the very need for such transplantation was caused by blackened tooth decay from another costly transplant: slave plantation-grown sugarcane and its domestic consumption in the metropole.

(TRANS)FIGURATION 10: CHIMERAS TO COME

These lines I have traced across time, genre, and geography have taken on new life. "Trembley's polyps have gone transgenic" as the Hydra has proved an important system for the study of stem cells (Steele 2006). Meanwhile, contemporary artists such as Aziz+Cucher invoke Ovid's songs of metamorphosis to articulate their new media practice with transformations in form, as in the digital photography series (Figure 4.11), *Chimera* (1998–99), that confronts the viewer, in the visual idiom of the indexical document, with unknown, illegible, and as yet unrealized variations on the most hypervalued bodily marks of sexual difference. Presenting questions of political and ethical value as indivisible from aesthetic ones, these photographs "of" ultimately unrecognizable organs without bodies or of organs as bodies ask us to reckon with our affective and visceral responses to the violations of sameness and difference, manifesting forms that ambiguate with an almost but not quite. These fleshly proximates look like flesh and even sex organs, but, at the same time, are radically unlike those marks that gender and engender known form. And, yet, in their vague resemblance to organs of procreation, these chimeras also present us with a strange condensation of both the potential outcome and vehicle for the production of further monstrous transformations in the flesh.

Figure 4.10   Thomas Rowlandson, *Transplanting of Teeth*, 1787, color aquatint, collection of the British Museum. © Trustees of the British Museum.

Chimerical figurations are not mere representations and they do not just matter historically: they materialize the dynamic interplay of histories and futures. To argue that the chimera *has* colonial histories of race, sex, breeding, and landscaping behind, around, or even in it (as in, for example, cellular inheritances) might be taken to posit that histories are like baggage just carried along for the ride. But the chimera, as I have attempted to show, is not just a hybrid mixture produced in time. The operations of history may themselves be understood as chimerical to the extent that the chimera challenges priority, order, and biology as destiny. While the embrace of becoming stem cell with which I began this essay may seem absurdly, even dangerously, utopian in the face of climate shift, the capitalization of transgenic hybrids, and prospects of uncontrolled and uncontrollable volatility, I would also insist that strict lines between human, animal, and plant, the dangerous purities of conservation and preservation, or hard and fast distinctions between natural and unnatural cannot and have never served an antiracist, anticolonial, or queer-feminist vision for environmentalism. To put this more positively, we have something to hope from and even inhabit in the protean ontological possibilities of chimeras: from monstrous mothers and she-pigs to transgender transplant subjects, sensitive man-plants, and the almost but not quite flesh forms and organs of generation of what may yet be conceived.

Transplantation and the plasticity of matter that the chimera's viability demonstrates do not just expose the chimerical "nature" of body and

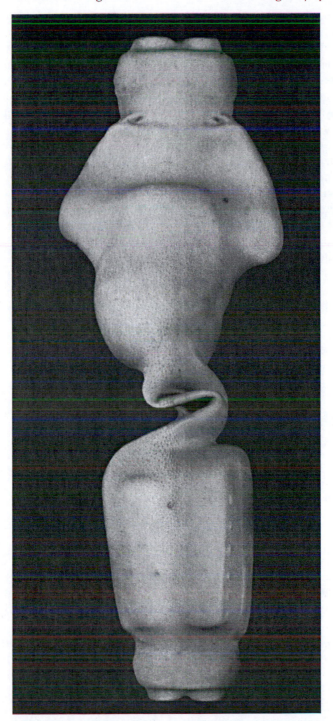

Figure 4.11 Aziz+Cucher, *Chimera #8*, 1998, C-print, 60 X 30 inches. Courtesy of the Arists.

environment but also the chimerical directionalities of history—from political and environmental histories of bodies and land to the histories embedded already in the genomes of human, animal, and plant bodies as the expressed, the not yet, and the may yet become. What might the indeterminate and as yet unnamed, as yet unfigured subjects to come "after" protectionism and "after" conservation bring forth? This afterlife—this living after—of colonialism is not a leaving behind of conflict. It is, or rather it might be, a creative agonistic contact with the colonial history of those many precedents already grown, already developed, and persisting in one form or another at the monstrous edges of species. The futures we can imagine are already in the process of being conceived in the monstrous overlaps of the anachronistic, the unfounded, and the ostensibly past, including that of the colonial. If time will tell, it is through the volatile, materializing power of figuration, which crosses and makes a chimera of time itself.

To Ann Pellegrini.

REFERENCES

Adams, George. 1747. *Micrographia illustrata*. London: Printed for and sold by the author and by Samuel Birt.

Bailey, Nathan. 1730. *Dictionarium Brittanicum*. London: Printed for T. Cox at the Lamb under the Royal-Exchange.

Begley, Sharon. 2005. "Now That Chimeras Exist." *The Wall Street Journal*. (May 6).

Blackwell, Mark. 2004. "'Extraneous Bodies': The Contagion of Live-Tooth Transplantation in Late Eighteenth-Century England." *Eighteenth-Century Life* 28.1, 21–68.

Carrera, Magali Marie. 2003. *Imagining Identity*. Austin: University of Texas Press.

Casid, Jill H. 2005. *Sowing Empire: Landscape and Colonization*. Minneapolis: University of Minnesota Press.

Casid, Jill. Forthcoming. *Shadows of Enlightenment*. Minneapolis: University of Minnesota Press.

Catts, Oron, and Ionat Zurr. 2002. "Growing Semi-Living Sculptures: The Tissue Culture and Art Project." *Leonardo* 35.4, 365–370.

Catts, Oron, Ionat Zurr, and Guy Ben-Ary. 2000. "Tissue Culture and Art(ificial) Wombs." *Ars Electronica*. February 23, 2011. http://www.tca.uwa.edu.au/atGlance/pubMainFrames.html

Clayton, Jay. 2007. "Victorian Chimeras, or, What Literature Can Contribute to Genetics Policy Today." *New Literary History* 38,3, 569–591.

Cogle, Christopher R., Anthony T. Yachnis, Eric D. Laywell, Dani S. Zander, John R. Wingard, Dennis A. Steindler, and Edward W. Scott. 2004. "Bone Marrow Transdifferentiation in Brain after Transplantation: A Retrospective Study." *The Lancet* 363.9419: 1432–1437.

Darwin, Erasmus. 1799. *The Botanic Garden*. London. Printed for J. Johnson, St. Paul's Churchyard.

Delbourgo, James, and Nicholas Dew, eds. 2008. *Science and Empire in the Atlantic World*. New York: Routledge.

Deleuze, Gilles, and Félix Guattari. 1983. "Rhizome." In *On the Line*. Translated by John Johnston. New York: Semiotexte.

Dowd, Maureen. 2005. "What Rough Beasts?" *New York Times* (April 7).

Edwards, David, Jay Cantor, and Daniel Faust. 2008. *Niche*. Paris: École nationale supérieure des beaux-arts de Paris et Le Laboratoire.

Fay, Joseph W. 2007. Conversation with the Author. July 28.

Foucault, Michel. 1997. *"Il faut défendre la société" Cours au Collège de France. 1976*. Paris : Éditions Gallimard.

———. 2001. "Les mailles du pouvoir." *Dits et écrits,1976–1988*. Paris: Éditions Gallimard. 2 : 1012–1013.

Franklin, Sarah. 2007. *Dolly Mixtures: The Remaking of Genealogy*. Durham: Duke University Press.

Giffney, Noreen, and Myra J. Hird, eds. 2008. *Queering the Non/Human*. London: Ashgate.

Greely, Henry T. 2003. "Defining Chimeras." *The American Journal of Bioethics* 3.3, 17–20.

Grove, Richard H. 1996. *Green Imperialism: Colonial Expansion, Tropical Island Edens and the Origins of Environmentalism, 1660–1860*. Cambridge: Cambridge University Press.

Grove, Richard H. 2000. "The Culture of Islands and the History of Environmental Concern." Harvard Seminar on Environmental Values. February 23, 2011. http://ecoethics.net/hsev/200004txt.htm.

Human Embryonic Stem Cell Research Advisory Committee; National Research Council and Institute of Medicine. 2010. Final Report of the National Acadamies' Human Embryonic Stem Cell Research Advisory Committee and 2010 Amendments to the National Acadamies' *Guidelines for Human Embryonic Stem Cell Research*. Washington, DC: National Academies Press.

Hunter, John. 1771. *The Natural History of the Human Teeth*. London: Printed for J. Johnson.

Katzew, Ilona. 2005. *Casta Painting: Images of Race in Eighteenth-Century Mexico*. New Haven, CT: Yale University Press.

Langer, Robert S., and Joseph P. Vacanti. 1999. "Tissue Engineering: The Challenges Ahead." *Scientific American* (April), 62–65.

Lenhoff, Sylvia G., and Howard M. Lenhoff. 1986. *Hydra and the Birth of Experimental Biology, 1744: Abraham Trembley's Mémoires Concerning the Polyps*. Pacific Grove, CA: Boxwood Press.

McLeod, Roy, ed. 2000. *Nature and Empire: Science and the Colonial Enterprise*. Special issue of *Osiris* 15.

Mettrie, Julien Offray de la. 1994. *Man a Machine and Man a Plant*. Translated by Richard A. Watson and Maya Rybalka. Indianapolis: Hackett.

Ovid. *Metamorphoses* IX. 446–665.

Robert, Jason Scott, and Françoise Baylis. 2003. "Crossing Species Boundaries." *The American Journal of Bioethics* 3.3, 1–13.

Safire, William. 2005. "Language: Centaurs, Chimeras, Humanzees." *The New York Times* (May 22).

Schiebinger, Londa. 2004. *Plants and Empire: Colonial Bioprospecting in the Atlantic World*. Cambridge: Harvard University Press.

Schiebinger, Londa, and Claudia Swan. 2005. *Colonial Botany: Science, Commerce, and Politics in the Early Modern World*. Philadelphia: University of Pennsylvania Press.

Sloane, Hans. 1701–25. *A Voyage to the Islands*. London: Printed by B. M. for the Author.

Steele, Robert E. 2006. "Trembley's Polyps Go Transgenic." *Proceedings of the National Academy of Science* 103.17, 6415–6416.

Svendsen, Clive. 2008. Correspondence with the author. February 28.

Thomson, Ann. 1996. "Introduction." In *Julien Offray de la Mettrie: Machine Man and Other Writings*. Cambridge: Cambridge University Press.

Thornton, Robert John. 1812. *Temple of Flora*. London: Dr. Thornton.

Traub, Valerie. 2000. "Mapping the Global Body." *Early Modern Visual Culture: Representation, Race and Empire in Early Modern England*, edited by Peter Erickson and Clark Hulse, 44–97. Philadelphia: University of Pennsylvania Press.

Trembley, Abraham. 1744. *Mémoires pour servir à l'histoire d'un genre de polypes*. Paris: Durand.

Tsing, Anna. Forthcoming. "Unruly Edges: Mushrooms as Companion Species." In *NatureCultures: Thinking with Donna Haraway*, edited by Sharon Ghamari-Tabrizi. Cambridge, MA: MIT Press.

Vartanian, Aram. 1960. *L'Homme Machine: A Study in the Origins of an Idea*. Princeton, NJ: Princeton University Press.

Weiss, Allen S. 2004. "Ten Theses on Monsters and Monstrosity." *The Drama Review* 48.1, 124–125.

Wellmann, Kathleen Anne. 1992. *La Mettrie: Medicine, Philosophy, and Enlightenment*. Durham, NC: Duke University Press.

Winkler, Hans. 1907. "Über Propfbastarde und pflanzliche Chimären." *Ber. Deutsch. Bot. Ges.* 25: 568–576. As cited in Aryn Martin, "'Incongruous juxtapositions.'" *Endeavour* 31.3 (2007), 103.

Zamudio-Taylor, Victor, and Elizabeth Armstrong, eds. 2000. *Ultrabaroque: Aspects of Post-Latin American Art*. San Diego: San Diego Museum of Contemporary Art.

5   The City Refigured
Environmental Vision in a Transgenic Age

Allison Carruth

The cofounder of Terreform ONE, Mitchell Joachim, takes green architecture to task for a "bland" aesthetic that, while founded on sound principles, effects only incremental alterations of the urban environment. By comparison with the popular LEED standards for green building,[1] Joachim envisions a radical "ecological code": design principles that would catalyze a paradigm shift in urban planning by facilitating collaboration among architects, artists, engineers, ecologists, planners, farmers, and geneticists.[2] With respect to this final group, Terreform positions biotechnology as an asset to building sustainable cities. The rise of transgenic organisms—crops, pharmaceuticals, and tissues that cross species at the molecular level—has been of particular interest to Joachim and his collaborators, who are critical of the corporations that control most genetic research and yet curious about whether such technologies can work for the environmental and social "good." Nor is the group alone. An emerging generation of artists, architects, and writers is conceptualizing biotechnology as a resource for reconfiguring twenty-first-century cities to address ecological and social justice challenges. This unorthodox brand of urban environmentalism signals a movement from postmodernism to a new cultural formation, one centered not on the structures of mass media and consumerism but on scientific practices of research and development.[3]

This chapter explores the nascent alliance among environmental ethics, urban aesthetics, and genetic science that shapes the urbanism of Terreform ONE. I begin not with Terreform's conceptual architecture, however, but with Indra Sinha's 2007 novel *Animal's People*, a narrative of an Indian city that takes its inspiration from the 1984 Bhopal gas disaster (Sinha 2007). My pairing of *Animal's People* and Terreform ONE is deliberate, but it is not in the service of tracing thematic or formal commonalities. Rather, I intend the comparison to reveal the conceptual threads between two aesthetic projects that treat the ethical question of how to make cities sustainable—in human and ecological terms and despite irreversible environmental constraints. The rationale for pairing materials more disparate than similar is to tease out my larger hypothesis that a phase change is underway in how literature, art, and architecture imagine the relationship between environmentalism and technology.

Narrating a catastrophe whose long-range effects are ecological and molecular, *Animal's People* depicts the postcolonial city as a contradictory place of social exploitation and community action, toxic soils and resilient bodies. As a story about the possibilities for environmental justice in urban India, the novel calls into question two literary modes—the sentimental and the apocalyptic—that inflect kindred narratives published in the decades since the Green Revolution fueled the development of both chemical and biological technologies. By comparison with environmental texts such as *Refuge, Ceremony*, and *The Hungry Tide*, *Animal's People* offers an unconventional perspective on environmental justice by writing the story of Khaufpur (a city modeled after Bhopal) through the perspective of an irreverent trickster named Animal (Silko 1977; Williams 1992; Ghosh 2005).[4] Through Animal's eyes, the contemporary city seems a verdant environment in which new organisms grow out of industrial disaster. With its particular interest in hybrid bodies, the novel maps a transition in Khaufpur from the chemical age to the age of genetics. In contrast to characters in the novel who apprehend genetic mutation as an emblem of environmental injustice, Animal offers a provocative vision of biochemistry as a means to sustain the human, animal, and even plant communities of Khaufpur. That the site of this regeneration is the abandoned pesticide factory—a sequestered and oddly protected space— suggests that Animal's vision of a mutagenic yet green city may not be possible outside of a controlled environment.

Animal's People shares with Terreform ONE this sense that the future green city may necessitate a closed environment, a view of urban sustainability on display in three recent projects: "Peristaltic City," "NY 2106," and "In Vitro Meat Habitat." These projects employ computer-aided design to create sustainable and, in Joachim's terms, self-sustaining futures for cities like New York and Tokyo. They do so by experimenting with tissue culturing and other areas of biochemistry and molecular genetics that have generated controversy due to the environmental risks and ethical quandaries such technologies pose. Over the last decade, environmental groups have decried transgenic seeds because of their potential to cross-pollinate with other plants and because of the neurotoxins GMOs often contain; legal ethicists and human rights groups have questioned whether tissue culturing and animal cloning may lead to eugenic practices; and both environmental and social justice organizations have mobilized against the enormous political and economic power that major biotechnology corporations wield. In contrast, the architecture of Terreform ONE intimates that the laboratory may provide an ethical alternative to the forest and mine for urban planning; and their designs aspire to create cities as biotechnological environments that grow habitats and greenbelts and that recycle toxins as well as water, food, and fuel. As we will see, Terreform maintains that green architecture can retrofit urban ecosystems for the age of climate change via the very technologies that environmentalists would blame for catastrophes like Bhopal.

ANIMAL'S PEOPLE: ECOLOGICAL RESILIENCE IN THE MUTAGENIC CITY

A novel that has earned the admiration of book reviewers and the attention of postcolonial scholars, *Animal's People* fictionalizes the 1984 disaster at a Bhopal pesticide factory, then owned by Union Carbide, which occurred when a factory leak spread methyl isocyanate gas across the Indian city. The media coverage of the event was global, focusing on the thousands of people who died during or shortly after the event. With the exception of the twentieth anniversary, the gas disaster has since received relatively scant attention in the international press, despite the estimated 135,000–500,000 people who have experienced physical disability, developed congenital disease, or died as a result of the 1984 explosion (Bhopal Medical Appeal 2010; International Environmental Law Research Centre 2010). Bhopal's legacy has given rise to numerous environmental justice coalitions in the region, one of which Sinha has championed: the Bhopal Medical Appeal (BMA). As a London-based copywriter, Sinha developed a publicity campaign for BMA that now runs across the organization's homepage. He has also been a vocal critic of Dow Chemical—the U.S. corporation that purchased Union Carbide in 2001 and then claimed indemnity from legal responsibility for Bhopal (Sinha 2008). *Animal's People* can be read, then, as a political novel that embodies Sinha's commitment to Bhopal as a city that has experienced sustained environmental illness and injustice.

The novel situates the narrative of fictional Khaufpur in the genre of environmental illness memoir. As the dust jacket blurb puts it: "Ever since he can remember, Animal has gone on all fours, his back twisted beyond repair by the catastrophic events of 'that night,' when a burning fog of poison smoke from the local factory (shades of Bhopal) blazed out over the town of Khaufpur, and the Apocalypse visited his slums." These lines hint, however, that Animal's first-person story disrupts the conventions of environmental illness memoir, which include an earnest and intimate narrator, a melding of personal testimony with scientific data, and a call to action. Although Animal speaks directly to the reader, whom he calls "Eyes," his relationship to this imagined Western audience ranges from jocular to antagonistic; and despite Sinha's involvement in the Bhopal environmental justice movement, Animal questions the efficacy of political action against the "Kampani" responsible for Khaufpur's disaster. Insisting that the somatic legacy of the pesticide factory explosion is generative rather than destructive, Animal challenges the basic premise of environmental illness memoirs, which typically depict the "body toxic" as a tragic injustice.

"Ever since he can remember, Animal has gone on all fours." This description of Sinha's protagonist finds expression on the novel's cover, which revolves around a skeletal figure who occupies the margins between biped and quadruped—human being and animal other. The cover design proves an apt backdrop for the primitive yet cyborg figure of Animal, whose hybrid body hovers on the borders between and mixes the attributes of human and animal (Haraway 1991). From this position, Animal rejects both the sentimental and the tragic as tonal registers for his life story. His narrative undercuts the conceptual frameworks of sentimentalism, tragedy, and what Lawrence Buell terms the apocalyptic strains of much "toxic discourse"—all of which the Khaufpur disaster and its somatic aftereffects certainly evoke (Buell 1998; Heise 2002):

TAPE ONE

I used to be human once. So I'm told. I don't remember it myself, but people who knew me when I was small say I walked on two feet just like a human being.

"So sweet you were, a naughty little angel. You'd stand up on tip toe, Animal my son, and hunt in the cupboard for food." This is the sort of thing they say. Only mostly there wasn't any food, plus really it isn't people just Ma Franci who says this. (Sinha 2007, 1)

This passage introduces us to Animal's aging guardian, Ma Franci, and, by extension, to the multiple perspectives on Khaufpur that jockey for our attention and call into question Animal's reliability. It also locates the narrative within a layered technological frame: an ostensibly tape-recorded memoir of Animal, whose body has been transformed at the genetic level by the chemical disaster known locally as "that night" (1). Born a few days before the gas leak, Animal, we learn in Tape One, suffers from an extreme curvature of the spine. As the above description attests, Animal embraces his physical stature by electing to walk on all fours and, in his terms, thus rejects the category of human. In response, other characters insist on Animal's humanity as evidenced in his fraught friendships with two figures: a white American doctor named Ellie, who opens a free clinic in Khaufpur and promises to find a medical treatment for Animal's spine, and a local activist named Zafar, who employs Animal in assisting the legal battle against the U.S. Kampani that owns the defunct factory responsible for the pesticide spill. This cast of characters embodies the competing views of Khaufpur's environmental history that Sinha puts into play. For her part, Ellie tends variously to pragmatism and sentimentalism in her conviction that medical care will correct the somatic consequences of the spill and heal Khaufpur's impoverished communities; for their part, Zafar and Ma Franci draw on apocalyptic discourse to lament—and, in Zafar's case, mobilize people to redress—the original event. Resisting these perspectives, Animal makes the Kampani factory his home and sees in the abandoned chemical plant the seeds of an adaptable, resilient community.

In Tape One, a U.S. journalist (or "Jarnalis" in the novel's vernacular slang) convinces Animal to record his memoirs. Upon beginning this project, Animal conjures a Western audience whom he refers to as the disembodied

"Eyes" that will read the story after the journalist rewrites the tapes as nonfiction. Animal mocks the journalist's lofty claims for their collaboration: "I said, I am a small person not even human, what difference will my story make? . . . I said, many books have been written about this place, not one has changed anything for the better, how will yours be different? You will bleat like all the rest" (3). With the verb "bleat," Animal makes of the journalist an animal figure, confounding any stable relationship between the categories of human and animal. He also insists on the singularity of his body (which is neither human nor animal), even as he reminds us that his story of industrial disaster, carcinogenic soil, and genetic mutation is ordinary rather than extraordinary for poor urban communities like those of Khaufpur.

While dominant, Animal's narrative is only one among many in the novel. Sinha offers us a multivalent imagination of Khaufpur's cityscape as contaminated, exploited, resilient, exceptional, and banal. It is this inconsistency that reviews of the novel tend to cite among its faults (Davies, 2007; Shamsie, 2007; Mahajan, 2008). As one reviewer claims, the novel falters precisely where Sinha strays from Animal's perspective by employing the sentimental language that attends most "socially important" works of fiction (Mahajan, 2008). In thus faulting the novel, however, reviewers demand of it an impossible singularity in telling a story that has, to Animal's point, happened in other cities and to other impoverished communities, if not on the same scale. Put differently, reviewers overlook the novel's productive vacillation between irreverent and sentimental modes of representing both Khaufpur's environmental precariousness and Animal's somatic mutation.

In a 2009 essay, postcolonial scholar Rob Nixon attends to the novel's formal intricacy. Developing the thesis that industrial disasters produce "slow violence," Nixon argues that communities in the global South live within a complex temporality that derives from the lag between an initial disaster and its long-term impact: "Sinha's approach to the aftermath of the catastrophic gas leak at Union Carbide's Bhopal factory . . . throws into relief a political violence both intimate and distant, unfolding over time and space on a variety of scales, from the cellular to the transnational, the corporeal to the global corporate" (Nixon 2009, 444). The twenty-year environmental justice movement in Khaufpur attests that the local community endures the vagaries of regional elections and corporate mergers as forms of slow violence that obstruct legal remediation; similarly, many of the catastrophe's effects take decades to manifest. Nixon, invoking Ramachandra Guha's term "environmentalism of the poor," nonetheless contends that "time is on [the] side" of postcolonial communities, whose movements for justice wait out the legal machinations of multinational corporations: "The Kampani has everything to fear from those with nothing to lose," he writes (Guha and Martinez-Alier 1997; Nixon 2009, 454). Nixon goes on to claim that the slow violence of a disaster like Bhopal inspires narratives that are "slow-paced but open-ended" (445). The form of *Animal's People* turns not on the spectacle of "that night," in other words, but rather on the disaster's slow-moving effects. This "mutagenic theater" avoids the conventions of environmental illness memoirs, which often foreground either the speculative temporality of a toxic future or the nostalgic temporality of a pristine past. The effort to narrate slowly unfolding cellular and genetic mutations qualifies Nixon's claim that "time is on th[e] side" of Khaufpur. As with catastrophic oil spills, the pesticide explosion unfolds over decades rather than days.

Nixon focuses on the formal strategies that Sinha employs to represent Khaufpur's "drama of mutation," a drama about both somatic mutation and the mutagenic character of the institutions that stymie the local environmental justice campaign. He characterizes the novel's form as an amalgam of magical realism, pastoral literature, and picaresque. Nixon views Animal as a *picaro*, who "positions himself at an angle to Khaufpur's environmental justice movement[,] . . . more troubled by his tenacious virginity than by the toxic tenacity of his environment" (Nixon 2009, 453). As a picaro, Animal troubles the long-term outlook of environmental justice activists like Zafar. I would argue that Animal also challenges the idea of slow violence in reminding the reader that Khaufpur's poor live day to day, or at what Animal calls "now o'clock" (185). Animal's disposition toward Zafar's political agenda dovetails with Elizabeth DeLoughrey and Cara Cilano's claim that postcolonial writers tend to "emphasize *the limitations* of representation" when narrating environmental injustices and, hence, tend to adopt multivalent and even satirical perspectives (Cilano and DeLoughrey 2007, 77, my emphasis). We can define *Animal's People* as a postcolonial environmental novel due not just to its tone, however, but also to its peculiar urban geography, by which I mean the map Sinha creates of the toxic and mutagenic landscape of Khaufpur. I would shift the critical lens on the novel, then, from the temporality of *Animal's People* that Nixon elegantly traces to the spatiality of Sinha's fictional city and, especially, of its abandoned pesticide factory. Dwelling on the cultural and physical geography of Khaufpur, we can read the novel as not only a *retrospective* story of industrial disaster but also a *speculative* fiction of what I will term, following Nixon's cue, the mutagenic city.

In a recent lecture, sociologist Ulrich Beck claims that risk "does not mean catastrophe. Risk means the anticipation of catastrophe" (Beck 2006, 332). Beck's definition highlights a limitation of the North American conservation movement, which has focused on preserving natural resources and wildlife while preventing projected risks: the risks of endangered species becoming extinct or of urban land encroaching into wilderness spaces, for example. This framework has tended to neglect urban environmental crises, in part because conservationists rarely apprehend the city as an ecosystem. We might distinguish conservationism from environmental justice along these lines, in that the latter mobilizes communities to redress extant conditions of urban pollution and ecological toxicity as well as the health risks those conditions pose. In the rubric of environmental justice, Khaufpur is a toxic environment whose most impoverished and at-risk communities must struggle for legal reparations and public health services. Yet Beck's paradigm of risk is certainly relevant to this postcolonial story. Evoking the city's uncertain future, Zafar suggests that the gas disaster has not yet revealed its most devastating effects, while Ma Franci (a Catholic nun originally from France) interprets Khaufpur through the religious lens of Revelations.

The apocalyptic rhetoric that characters draw from to make sense of "that night" resonates with much twentieth-century environmentalist discourse about industrial disasters. When Animal describes the abandoned factory where he makes his "lair," for example, Sinha alludes to the apocalyptic fable that opens Rachel Carson's 1962 manifesto against synthetic pesticides: "Eyes, I wish you could come with me into the factory. Step through one of these holes, you're into another world. Gone are city noises, horns of trucks and autos, voices of women in the Nutcracker, kids shouting, all erased by the high wall. Listen, how quiet it's. No bird song" (Sinha 2007, 29). Animal's depiction of the factory's silence recalls *Silent Spring*'s opening chapter, in which Carson invents a bucolic rural town turned eerily quiet when a "blight" of DDT toxins kills off flora and fauna and spreads cancer through the human community.[5] As a postindustrial wasteland, the abandoned pesticide factory in *Animal's People* gives voice to this apocalyptic dread that structures *Silent Spring*.

However, Animal's depiction of silence as a figure for environmental contamination ultimately inverts Carson's; for the silence of the factory stems from an absence not only of "bird song" but also of "city noises, horns of trucks and autos, voices of women in the Nutcracker." In this same scene, the "high wall" separating the factory from the adjacent Nutcracker slum (a wall that proved insufficient to protect the community) separates the contaminated city from a botanical ecosystem growing out of the factory ruins. Animal here disturbs the trope of urban blight, which populates socioeconomic and environmental discourses of cities, to imagine the factory as a site of increasing biodiversity. Against Ma Franci's religious conviction that the factory will usher in the Apocalypse, Animal sees the physical ground for a new urban ecosystem. Through Animal's eyes, the factory is a decaying environment that is technological and biological: "All that's left now is its skeleton. Platforms, ladders and railings are corroding. Its belly is a tangle of pipes like rotting guts. Huge tanks have split, stuff's fallen out that looks like brown rocks" (30). As the factory rots and decomposes, it provides a kind of biochemical humus that supports the growth of flora and fauna. We could interpret this odd appearance of botanical volunteers (the sandalwood trees and vines that are repurposing the urban factory) as either nostalgic or farcical. However, I would argue that the transformation of the factory has a scientific facticity. A number of highly contaminated regions that mark former industrial mines, chemical factories, and nuclear waste treatment facilities—from Hanford, California to Chernobyl—have, through a combination of ecological processes and human interventions, morphed into preserves. These so-called "mutant ecosystems" boast an unexpected biodiversity as flora, fauna, and soils evidently adapt to toxic conditions (Masco 2004).[6] In this context, we can read *Animal's People* as imagining a kindred form of regeneration in the postcolonial city.

Nonetheless, this ecological process is violent; as Animal observes, "a silent war is being waged" in the factory:

> Mother Nature's trying to take back the land. Wild sandalwood trees have arrived, who knows how, must be their seeds were shat by overflying birds. . . . Under the poison-house trees are growing up through the pipework. Creepers, brown and thick as my wrist, have climbed all the way to the top, tightly wrapped woodened knuckles round pipes and ladders, like they want to rip down everything the Kampani made. (31)

The novel puts limits here on the idea of the factory—the chemical technologies and biological mutations it produces—as an urban garden. If Animal redefines sustainability by suggesting that the heart of the city's toxic landscape will sustain its future, the factory environment is one that demands extreme forms of adaptation. Animal's own molecular mutations prove crucial to his adaptability and, as we will see, to his capacity for resilience in a toxic environment. However, Animal and Ma Franci are the only members of the Khaufpuri community who dwell inside the factory. That the factory is partly sealed off from the wider urban environment suggests, akin to the conservationist discourse that the novel seems to eschew, that the city may require enclosure to be ecologically viable in the future.

Animal's vision of the factory—and its metamorphosis into an ecosystem at once biological and technological—foils the aspirations of the environmental justice movement in Khaufpur, for which Animal works while always doubting its goals. Among the novel's magical realist plots, Animal converses regularly with "Khã-in-the-jar," a two-headed fetus that exists in a medical clinic devoted to scientific research of the genetic mutations that the disaster has caused. In one such dialogue, Khã relays that he has formed a coalition to "undo everything the Kampani does. Instead of breaking ground for new factories to grow grass and trees over the old ones, instead of inventing new poisons, to make medicines to heal the hurts done by those poisons, to remove them from the earth and water and air" (237). Khã's reverie envisions a sustainable future defined by ecological regeneration and human health. In that future, industries create not toxins but herbal remedies and construct not factories but greenbelts. In the book's penultimate section, Animal seems to have entered just such a future; there, he narrates his purported afterlife in the forest just outside the city, a highland ecosystem characteristic of central India (specifically, of Madhya Pradesh state) (Manas n.d.). We initially believe that Animal has died in this scene, which follows on the heels of a second explosion at the pesticide factory triggered by fires set during a protest of the Kampani. Animal exploits our assumption, describing the forest as a paradise: "There are animals of every kind, leopards and deer and horses and elephants, there's a tiger and a rhino . . . this is the deep time when there was no difference between anything whole before humans set themselves apart and became clever and made cities and kampanis and factories" (352). The forest—teeming with a magical abundance of wildlife and connecting human to animal—moves Animal into "deep time" and evidently realizes Khã's vision of a future without toxic industries.

The scene proves to be not a magical afterlife but a hallucinogenic vision brought on by Animal's exposure to a spike in atmospheric toxins during the factory fire. After days of searching, Zafar and others locate Animal in the forest and return him to his botanical, if toxic, home within the factory. The novel ends with Zafar's optimism that they will achieve victory against the Kampani and with Ellie's commitment to take Animal to "Amrika" for reconstructive surgery; but it also ends with Animal's rejection of both legal remediation and physical restoration as frameworks for a sustainable, sustaining future. As the local leaders in the suit against the Kampani continue to battle the corporation's lawyers, who countersue the environmental justice organization after a "stink bomb" goes off at a negotiation meeting, Animal observes that "life goes on" in Khaufpur (361, 365). In contrast to the outrage of Zafar and Ellie, Animal closes his environmental illness memoir on an upbeat note, embracing the mutagenic form of the factory and his body. About the factory, he observes how even after the fire the space continues to sustain new flora: "blackened by fire it's, but the grass is growing again, and the charred jungle is pushing out green shoots" (365 [sic]). About his own body, Animal similarly insists on the viability of his mutated, hybrid form: "Eyes, I reckon that if I have this operation, I will be upright, true, but to walk I will need the help of sticks. I might have a wheelchair, but how far will that get me in the gullis of Khaufpur? Right now I can run and hop and carry kids on my back, I can climb hard trees, I've gone up mountains, roamed in jungles. Is life so bad?" (366). The city's mutagenic form requires, then, physiological adaptations that Animal, the most future-oriented of the novel's characters, is unwilling to resist. With these final words, *Animal's People* concludes by locating the seeds of a sustainable future in Animal's somatic mutation and in Khaufpur's mutagenic urban forest, a future not yet imaginable outside the four walls of the factory. Animal's vision coexists, however, with a sustained focus on the present—on the geopolitical structures of power that attend industries like pesticides as well as on the wider economic system that inhibits environmental and social justice in urban India. However resilient the community and ecosystem of Khaufpur and however provocative Animal's view of chemical toxicity and biological mutation as resources, industrial disasters remain very real sources of economic and ecological vulnerability for urban communities like Khaufpur.

TERREFORM ONE: THE GREEN
FUTURISM OF A PERISTALTIC CITY

From *Animal's People*, I turn to another unorthodox vision of the sustainable city, although one that, in taking us from literature to architecture, looks to the city's distant future. Through a series of conceptual projects, Brooklyn architectural nonprofit Terreform ONE (which stands for Open Network Ecology) has been breaking from established conventions of green urban design. The group accomplishes this break by positing a built environment linked not just morphologically to biological organisms, as is the case in much green architecture. Akin to the Khaufpur factory, Terreform designs habitats and cities to be living-breathing-growing systems in which biological, biotechnological, and cybernetic elements work in concert to generate sustainable urban environments, meaning environments that can sustain communities as well as flora and fauna while addressing two environmental problems: a growing human population and the depletion of natural resources stemming from climate change (Joachim n.d.; Joachim n.d.; Joachim n.d.; Joachim and Oxman 2008). With these problems in view, Joachim looks not to nature but to the laboratory for raw materials. Accordingly, the execution of many Terreform projects must wait for developments in genetics and material science.

This alliance the group is forging between green design and molecular genetics reflects a profound shift in the architectural imagination of urban environments and habitats. Here, the architecture of Terreform ONE dovetails with the art movement known as BioArt, whose practitioners often have advanced training in molecular biology or collaborate with scientists to integrate the practices of conceptual art and interactive media with those of biological science. The formal aims of bioartists—such as the relatively well-known Critical Art Ensemble—are far from consistent; yet practitioners do share a transdisciplinary approach to artistic production. Consider an early example of BioArt: a 1997 diorama by New York–based artist Alexis Rockman entitled "Romantic Flower" (Figure 5.1).

A three-dimensional shadow box, "Romantic Flower" exemplifies the conceptual origins of BioArt. Rockman's diorama incorporates everyday, commercial biotechnologies into an artistic pastiche. The materials that Rockman assembles include digitized photographs, oil paint, and salvaged wood along with a household garden hose, latex rubber, spray paint, and, finally, the durable reactive polymer Envirotex, a plastic made possible by both the petroleum industry and a biotech laboratory. Rockman's amalgamation of these objects within his depiction of floral sexuality ruptures ideas

Figure 5.1 "Romantic Flower," Alexis Rockman (1997).

of the natural world as "out there," beyond the boundaries of an urban-centered, technology-driven culture. Of course, I have not accounted for perhaps the most striking element in Rockman's materials list for the diorama: pleistocene. Listed in lower case in the diorama's caption, the term can slip past viewers, blending in with the plastic polymers that comprise "Romantic Flower." The diorama's significance deepens, however, if we pause on the implicit allusion to the Pleistocene geological period, a period marked by climate fluctuations as well as the emergence of many modern species, including early *Homo sapiens*. A palimpsest of late-twentieth-century biotechnologies, "Romantic Flower" juxtaposes the Pleistocene period with our own epoch of anthropogenic climate change. While suggesting that the contemporary era may lead to more *loss than gain* of biological diversity, Rockman invites us to contemplate that future ecosystems may inhere less in biological species than in chemical and synthetic organisms.

Artists like Rockman thus blur habituated distinctions among bodies, ecosystems, and codes in ways that echo Joachim's concept of an "ecological code" for urban design. Bioartist Jennifer Willet, for example, calls for the movement to eschew representational forms in favor of participatory ones (Willet 2009). A recent special issue of *New Literary History* also claims for BioArt an inherently transformational politics. The issue's editors suggest that bioartists help to produce scientifically literate citizens who are better prepared to vote on "stem-cell research, nanotechnology, genomic and genetic screening, and even energy consumption" (Davis and Morris 2007). Practitioner George Gessert goes still further by identifying BioArt as the only ethical aesthetic for confronting contemporary environmental challenges. In a 2009 essay, Gessert argues that anthropogenic climate change demands that contemporary art "contribute to the integrity, sustainability, and diversity of life, especially nonhuman life"; he concludes, "art that does not [do this] is bad for us" (Gessert 2008, 403). Such manifestoes for the ethical stakes of BioArt do not sufficiently account, however, for the material practices of most bioartists. We might query whether the ends justify the means in the case of BioArt, and whether the environmental risks and labor politics that trouble environmentalists about transgenic crops (or cloned animals) should be ethical problems for bioartists too. We might also question the critical framing of BioArt as unassailably environmentalist, a framing that does not account for the movement's use of molecular biology labs, which ties bioartists to corporate structures of science funding, to energy resources that fuel such research, and to the uncertain environmental risks that biotechnology poses.

Returning to Terreform ONE, let me suggest that Joachim's architectural work shares these ethical tensions with BioArt. Terreform's futuristic projects aim variously to transform, enclose, or jettison entirely the contemporary city; the group premises its projects on a future of irreversible climate change and, in response, offers aesthetic and technical strategies that prepare for a future in which fossil fuels, forest resources, and even entire urban grids are unavailable for use. Terreform sees in biotechnology not only scientific but also imaginative resources for addressing these environmental concerns, a vision that informs Joachim's speculative designs for New York, Shanghai, and an enclosed city of the future that he models on the human digestive system (Figure 5.2):

> [The Peristaltic City] is a tall building made of a cluster of shifting pod spaces. The pod skins alter the volume locations within. This soft, pliable, sealed, and non-mechanical innovation encapsulates volumetric structures. . . . By employing a dynamic spatial application against the traditional organization of core and space, we dissolved the dichotomy between circulation and habitable environments. (Joachim and Oxman 2008)

This Peristaltic City (or Peristalcity) can be understood as conceptual architecture for a "sealed," "pliable," "breathable" city that relies for its execution on advancements in genetics as well as nanotechnology. If vernacular architecture makes use of accessible and inexpensive materials, the Peristalcity draws instead on the still experimental science of carbon nanotubes. Just as Animal defines the enclosed pesticide factory as an urban ecosystem, Joachim defines the Peristalcity as a chimera that combines the technology of an elevator with the biology of a digestive system, or rather, the engineering of vertical transportation with the genetics of cultured tissue. These principles—avant-garde in the context of contemporary green design—also shape the project "NY 2106" (Figure 5.3). This plan for Manhattan's future imagines that biotechnology, combined with advanced engineering of water and waste recycling and urban farming projects, will serve to incubate massive urban greenbelts. In Joachim's words, such projects offer "a new model: the socioecological

Figure 5.2 "Peristaltic City," Terreform ONE (2009).

condition. It's part cultural, part science, half and half . . . a great way to think about solving the problems that man has created" (Joachim n.d.). Recalling *Animal's People*, we can see in these architectural forms a kindred idea of hybridity—of mixing chemical and genetic technologies with biological organisms—as a framework for redesigning cities to adapt to current and anticipated environmental problems.

Architecture critic Mimi Zieger follows up on Joachim's stated aims for "Peristalcity" and "NY 2106." She contends that these designs present a new model of sustainability in which biotechnology along with cybernetic

Figure 5.3 "NY 2106," Terreform ONE (2009).

structures coexist and help to sustain biological systems: "the scope of a Terreform ONE project is often as big as the man-made problem at hand. For instance, the proposal *New York 2106: Self Sufficient City* asks that the city go far beyond efficiency, actually producing all of its own necessities, from food and energy to housing and waste processing" (Zeiger 2009). Building on this analysis, we can interpret Joachim's maxim that "everything is used in designing an ecological city" as requiring not only renewable energy, urban gardens, and next-generation recycling programs but also computer-regulated systems, genetically modified tissues, and even waste (Joachim n.d.). As Joachim puts it, "we can no longer throw things (resources), away; there is no 'away'" (Joachim n.d.).

The melding of nature and technology expand in Terreform's projects to include biotechnology in general and tissue culturing in particular, as seen in the "breathable skin" that encloses the "Peristalcity" while allowing this urban ecosystem to circulate air, water, energy, and people. Although radically different in style from Terreform's other projects, the "In Vitro Meat Habitat" similarly combines organic forms with cybernetic and genetic technologies (Figure 5.4). A collaboration of Joachim, biochemist Oliver Medvedik, and a LEED-certified urban planner, "In Vitro Meat Habitat" proposes to construct urban dwellings out of biological tissues cultured in a lab environment. Extracting its materials neither from bamboo forests nor from industrial salvage yards, the building would be fabricated from what the group describes as "three-dimensional printed extruded pig cells."[7] As with much genetically based art and architecture, the technical process for culturing pig cells in a laboratory and then transforming them into the walls of a future urban habitat is admittedly fuzzy. In terms of the ethical claims of the project, the design team presents the meat habitat as a "victimless shelter," because its raw materials would derive from a molecular

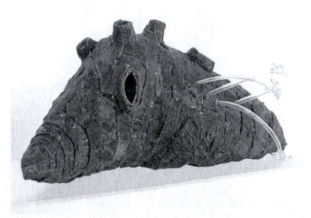

Figure 5.4   "In Vitro Meat Habitat," Terreform ONE (2009).

genetics lab rather than from pigs living either in a natural ecosystem or a confined feedlot. The cells are grown in vitro, that is, rather than extracted from extant organisms and ecosystems.

The negotiation between environmental ethics and genetic science that Terreform's projects embody is noteworthy. An architectural solution to deforestation, the "In Vitro Meat Habitat" connects with a range of Bio-Art projects that offer analogous ideas of sustainable habitats and food systems. Critical Art Ensemble's "Free Range Grain," for example, puts genetic science to work for a radical environmental politics. The ongoing art project tests food samples for genetically modified elements, a project that integrates the methods of a biotech lab into a conceptual art space in order to generate what the group terms a genetic public sphere. Closer in spirit to "Disembodied Cuisine" than much built green architecture, Terreform's lab-generated habitat—ostensibly biological in form—imagines a near future in which ecological sustainability all but requires the geneticist's lab. The sustainability of the "In Vitro Meat Habitat"—the claim that it models a sustainable, if ultimately enclosed, urban environment—resides in the mutation (the "extrusion") of biological tissue into computer-generated and genetically cultured building matter. Put simply, the pig cells are "printed out" rather than "grown." Joachim's recent manifesto for the future green city drives this concept home, suggesting that "tomorrow's" urban environment is one where genetic codes will be the crux of not just technology-driven industries (like the one responsible for Bhopal) but also human creativity. Despite the risks that we will not responsibly develop this area of scientific research and technological development, Joachim holds out the potential that the "codes" of biochemistry and molecular biology may offer a foundation for "fully sustainable cities":

> City architecture, even as a model of information, will reveal astounding insights when somebody tweaks it at the genetic level, i.e. Code. . . . How can we open Pandora's box responsibly? Should we institute a Bill of Rights that would ensure a humanist directive over this Code? Imagine a genetic green algorithm that enables us to test and design fully sustainable cities. (Joachim n.d.)

CONCLUSIONS AND SPECULATIONS

If biotechnology and green politics have been largely at odds in contemporary environmental politics, Terreform ONE and *Animal's People* reveal that this ideological divide is unlikely to last. The sustainability of the "In Vitro Meat Habitat" and the Kampani factory inheres precisely in the capacity of toxic spaces and synthetic technologies to support urban ecosystems. Terreform ONE is on the forefront of green architecture, a position based on the group's commitment to familiar environmental-ist goals like natural resource conservation, alternative energy, and spe-cies preservation. At the same time, Joachim's status as an environmental visionary suggests that the project of greening cities—in the context of either environmental catastrophes like Bhopal or environmental risks associated with climate change—will increasingly make use of (and make good on) biotechnologies. More to the point, the urban body and urban habitat of these twenty-first-century projects are founded both literally and figuratively on the transgenic.

This phase change, as I have termed it, in how contemporary "green cul-ture" interacts with technological production invites environmental critics to expand our methodological horizons. If, to date, interdisciplinary meth-ods within ecocriticism have turned to the philosophy of nature, on the one hand, and the science of evolution and ecology, on the other, the projects I have examined here suggest a new line of inquiry for the field. Engaging with the fields of molecular biology and material science will shed new light on how humanist forms—from the novel to architecture—are today devel-oping new frameworks for environmental ethics, broadly, and for socially as well as ecologically sustainable cities, especially.

NOTES

1. LEED, which stands for Leadership in Energy and Environmental Design, is the accreditation certificate that the U.S. Green Building Council offers to builders, developers, and architects.
2. Joachim elaborates on this concept for avant-garde green cities: "The core idea is the elaboration of a series of patterns, like codes, inherent in the way we build any habitation. . . . These patterns are not blueprints for construc-tion. They are more about behavior than about decoration, more about rela-tionships than about dimensions" (Joachim n.d.).
3. I refer here to Jameson's argument that postmodernism accompanies the development of late capitalism and takes its formal tendency toward pastiche from the practices of consumer culture and broadcast media (Jameson 1991, 2002).
4. The sentimental and apocalyptic modes are prominent in North Ameri-can environmental narratives, exemplified by Tempest Williams's memoir and Silko's novel. However, contemporary Anglophone texts also draw on these two traditions. As one example, Amitav Ghosh's *The Hungry Tide* employs the sentimental in his narrative of the fragile Sundarbans ecosystem and the conflicts between the local community and outsider environmentalists.
5. "There was a strange stillness. The birds, for example—where had they gone? . . . On the mornings that had once throbbed with the dawn chorus of robins, catbirds, doves, jays, wrens, and scores of other bird voices there was no sound; only silence lay over the fields and woods and marsh." (Carson 1962, v, 2)
6. I am indebted to Erica Elliott for bringing to my attention ecological restora-tion at former nuclear and atomic testing sites (Mercer 2002; Masco 2004; Kirsch 2007).

7. Notably, however, the initial model that the group designed appears to have been constructed from beef jerky, as a recent interview with Joachim and Mevedik in *Harpers* reports (Smith 2010).

REFERENCES

Beck, U. 2006. "Living in the World Risk Society." *Economy and Society*, 35.3, 329–345.

Bhopal Medical Appeal. 2010. Bhopal 1984 until Today, http://www.bhopal.org/index.php?id=155 (accessed November 7, 2009).

Buell, L. 1998. "Toxic Discourse." *Critical Inquiry*, 24.3, 639–665.

Carson, R. 1962. *Silent Spring*. Boston: Houghton Mifflin.

Cilano, C., and E. DeLoughrey. 2007. "Against Authenticity: Global Knowledges and Postcolonial Ecocriticism." *Interdisciplinary Studies in Literature and Environment*, 14.1, 71–87.

Davies, S. 2007. Man Booker 2007 Prize: *Animal's People. Telegraph UK*, http://www.telegraph.co.uk/culture/books/fictionreviews/3667306/Man-Booker-2007-Prize-Animals-People.html (accessed November 10, 2009).

Davis, L., and D. Morris. 2007. "Biocultures Manifesto." *New Literary History* 38.3, 411–418, http://muse.jhu.edu/journals/new_literary_history/toc/nlh38.3.html (accessed August 29, 2009).

Gessert, G. 2008. "Unnatural Wonders: Essays from the Gap between Art and Life." *Leonardo Reviews*, 41.4, 402–403, http://muse.jhu.edu/journals/leonardo/summary/v041/41.4.gessert.html (accessed August 29, 2009).

Ghosh, Amitav. 2005. *The Hungry Tide*. Boston: Houghton Mifflin.

Guha, R. 1989. "Radical American Environmentalism and Wilderness Preservation: A Third World Critique." *Environmental Ethics*, 11.1, 71–83.

Haraway, Donna. 1991. "A Cyborg Manifesto: Science, Technology, and Socialist-Feminism in the Late Twentieth Century," in *Symians, Cyborgs and Women: The Reinvention of Nature*. New York: Routledge, 149–181.

Heise, U.K. 2002. "Toxins, Drugs, and Global Systems: Risk and Narrative in the Contemporary Novel." *American Literature*, 74.4, 747–778.

International Environmental Law Research Centre. 2010. Bhopal Gas Disaster, http://www.ielrc.org/india/bhopal.php (accessed April 16, 2010).

Jameson, F. 1991. *Postmodernism or, The Cultural Logic of Late Capitalism*. Durham, NC: Duke University Press.

———. 2002. *A Singular Modernity: Essay on the Ontology of the Present*. London and New York: Verso.

Joachim, M. "Ecological Code: A Collage of Quantum Informatics in Living Automata Cities." *Archinode*, http://www.archinode.com/text2.html (accessed September 5, 2009).

———. "The Rhetoric of Good City Bromides: Ecology, Eschatology, and American Values." *Archinode*, http://www.archinode.com/text3.html (accessed July 17, 2010).

———. "Tilling Education: An Eco-Tech Aesthetic Approach." *Archinode*, http://www.archinode.com/text.html (accessed July 17, 2010).

Kirsch, S. 2007. "Ecologists and the Experimental Landscape: The Nature of Science at the US Department of Energy's Savannah River Site." *Cultural Geographies* 14.4, 485–510. Available at: http://cgj.sagepub.com/cgi/content/abstract/14/4/485.

Mahajan, K. 2008. Review: *Animal's People* Toxically Twisted. *San Francisco Chronicle*, http://www.sfgate.com/cgi-bin/article.cgi?f=/c/a/2008/03/11/DD7LUFMQ0.DTL&type=books (accessed November 20, 2009).

Manas Database. n.d. "Indian States: Madyha Pradesh." http://www.sscnet.ucia.
edu/southasia/Landscapes/MadhyaPradesh.html (accessed March 11, 2011).

Masco, J. 2004. "Mutant Ecologies: Radioactive Life in Post-Cold War New
Mexico." *Cultural Anthropology* 19.4, 517–550, http://dx.doi.org/10.1525/
can.2004.19.4.517 (accessed July 14, 2010).

Mercer, D. 2002. "Future-histories of Hanford: The Material and Semiotic Production of a Landscape." *Cultural Geographies* 9.1, 35–67, http://cgj.sagepub.
com/cgi/content/abstract/9/1/35 (accessed January 26, 2010).

Nixon, R. 2009." Neoliberalism, Slow Violence, and the Environmental Picaresque." *Modern Fiction Studies* 55.3, 443–467, http://muse.jhu.edu/login?uri=/
journals/modern_fiction_studies/v055/55.3.nixon.html (accessed November 1,
2009).

Shamsie, K. 2007. Review: *Animal's People* by Indra Sinha. *The Guardian UK*,
http://www.guardian.co.uk/books/2007/sep/15/featuresreviews.guardianre-
view22 (accessed November 20, 2009).

Silko, L. M. 1977. *Ceremony*. New York: Penguin Group.

Sinha. 2007. *Animal's People*. London and New York: Simon & Schuster.

———. 2008. "Abandoned to Their Fate." *Guardian UK*, http://www.guardian.
co.uk/commentisfree/2008/apr/09/abandonedtotheirfate (accessed November 7,
2009).

Smith, Heather. 2010. "Squeal Estate." *Harper's Magazine*, http://www.harpers.
org/archive/2010/05/0082919 (accessed August 12, 2010).

Willet, J. 2009. "Bodies in Biotechnology: Embodied Models for Understanding
Biotechnology in Contemporary Art." *Leonardo*, http://leoalmanac.org/jour-
nal/Vol_14/lea_v14_n07–08/jwillet.asp (accessed November 5, 2009).

Williams, T. T. 1992. *Refuge: An Unnatural History of Family and Place*, 1st ed.
New York: Vintage.

Zeiger, M. 2009. "Urban Renewal–Urban Development." *Architect Magazine*,
http://www.architectmagazine.com/urban-development/what-is-the-future-of-
american-urbanism.aspx (accessed August 5, 2010).

Part II

History

6 Ecopoetics and the Origins of English Literature

Alfred K. Siewers

When the Green Knight in vegetative attire and hue bursts into King Arthur's court in *Sir Gawain and the Green Knight*, he sparks a serious disruption of the feudal order. Arthur's best knight, Gawain, ends up traveling into imaginary wilds of the Celtic borderland of western Britain, a journey that will subvert his previously well-defined and highly armored subjectivity.

> Hade he no fere bot his fole bi frythez and dounez,
> Ne no gome bot God bi gate wyth to karp,
> Til þat he need ful neghe into þe Norþe Walez.
> Alle þe iles of Anglesay on lyft half he haldez,
> And farez ouer þe fordez by þe forlondez,
> Ouer at þe Holy Hede, til he hade eft bonk
> In þe wyldrenesse of Wyrale. Wonde þer bot lyte
> Þat auþer God oþer gome wyth goud hert louied.
> And ay he frayned, as he ferde, at frekez þat he met,
> If þay hade herde any karp of a knyt grene,
> In any grounde þeraboute, of þe Grene Chapel;
> And al nykked hym wyth 'Nay!'—þat neuer in her lyue
> Þay see neuer no segge þat watz of suche hwez
> Of grene. (Andrew and Waldron 1996, 34, ll. 695–708)

> He had no friend but his horse by forests and hills,
> Nor anyone but God on the way with whom to speak,
> Until he went deep into North Wales.
> Along his left side he kept the islands of Anglesey,
> And he traveled across the fords by the lowlands,
> Over by Holy Head, until he came on the bank again
> In the wilderness of Wirral. Few lived there who
> Either God or a man with good heart loved.
> And always he asked, as he traveled, any man that he met,
> If they had heard tell of a green knight,

> In any land thereabout, of the green chapel;
> And all answered him nay, that never in their life
> Ever had they seen any knight such a hue of green.

Ironically, the geography of the route into the mysterious visitor's "green world" that Gawain seeks proves to be much more specific than that of the vanishing tracks of the "real" feudal world of Arthur's court. As the Green Knight's realm comes into focus, it even leaves a physical mark on an unarmored part of Gawain's body, in the ritual nick to his neck. Gawain travels off the grid from the actual imaginary into the virtual real, to borrow terms from the geophilosophers Gilles Deleuze and Félix Guattari (Goodchild 1996, 198–199). If the road to Camelot is obscure, we can trace on a map Gawain's trip to the Green Knight's fantasy domain, just as we can trace the foundational fantasy history of the twelfth-century *Mabinogi* on a map of Wales today, or that of the otherworldly tales of the early medieval Ulster Cycle on Ireland's geography, even to bicycle and hike story paths on the modern-day "Táin Trail." If the poem ends in mystery at the mound that is the Green Chapel, there are specific sites "on the ground" for that Chapel in England's northwest that scholars connect through folklore and place-name study with legends that likely shaped the fantasy overlay geography (Elliott 2002, 115). And as the beginning of the poem puts it:

> As it is stad and stoken
> In stori stif and stronge,
> With lel letteres loken,
> In londe so hatz ben longe. (Andrew and Waldron 1996, 208, ll. 33–36)

In other words, the poem stands enclosed in story firm and strong, with its true letters linked or enshrined in the land where it has been so long.

Reimagining pre-Scholastic sources of Christian mysticism and native pre-Christian traditions in relation to natural landscape, *Sir Gawain and the Green Knight*—like its fellow fourteenth-century poetic masterpiece *The Canterbury Tales* and the longest fantasy prose text in Middle English, Thomas Malory's later *Le Morte Darthur*—evokes an experientially dynamic sense of place as mystery that includes what environmental philosophers call nature's hidden "other side" (Davis 2008). The resulting overlay of landscapes—wilds associated with the Green Knight amid actual geography of the island of Britain, with French Arthurian realms that seem to be disappearing from view in the aftermath of the Black Death and emergence of a textual landscape of vernacular English—provides a reciprocating and dynamic view of human interaction with the environment that is a noteworthy but ignored tradition for environmental cultural studies today.

Indeed, while the literary critic Northrop Frye defined a similar pattern of overlay landscape in later Elizabethan texts under the label the "green world" (Frye 1967), those texts often show genealogical links or at least analogues to earlier Middle English literary materials, which he instead attributed to folklore. In Frye's model, green-world texts brought two worlds into contact through art, leaving any assumed totality of human life in doubt by its interface with an alternate realm melding nature and imagination. Middle English prototypes unexamined by Frye in turn had adapted an even earlier Insular model of overlay landscape, the so-called Celtic Otherworld, which emerged from a mix of native tradition and Christian asceticism adapted from Eastern deserts to a northwestern European Atlantic archipelago with intensely intermingled realms of sky, sea, land, water and wind—reflected in the entwined worlds of those stories (Siewers 2009). In early patristic imagery, the biblical Paradise formed a mountain encompassing the earth, an analogue to the Otherworld. Middle English literature adapted the latter with a more central focus on forest and countryside, echoing accelerated deforestation that left vanishing Insular woods a symbol of magical engagement with nature in prefeudal times (Cantor 1993, 554), while the sea perhaps had become negatively associated with the colonial and transmaritime *ancien régime*.

In any case, the late-medieval "green world" trope in many ways models what environmental philosopher Bruce Foltz called "nature's other side," ignored by the modern "idea of a universe that is self-subsistent—standing entirely on its own, fully operational and intelligible, independent of anything outside itself . . . inimical to any salutary relation between humanity and the natural environment (Foltz 2004, 330). Foltz, adapting Martin Heidegger's critique of Being as univocal presence, asks:

> What if it is scientific objectivity (as metaphysics, and hence as irretrievably bound up with technology and control, reflected strikingly in the cybernetic notion of "ecosystem") that is itself at the root of the problem? It cannot be emphasized too often that it is not a matter of giving up technological devices or of not paying heed to scientific findings, but simply of refusing their claims of metaphysical ultimacy . . . seeing that for those who would learn how to re-inhabit the earth, it is only poetic discourse and modes of sensibility—not as something rarefied but as they infuse the everyday—that are capable of bringing about and maintaining the new relations that the earth itself and all the modes of nature call for. (Foltz 1995, 176)

Foltz's vision evokes an ecopoetic practice or worldview. But how do we define such ecopoetics from the early green-world tradition? The following sections seek to unpack briefly the meaning of ecopoetics and illustrate it by readings from this early English literature.

ECOPOETICS DEFINED

The literary scholar Jonathan Bate defined *ecopoesis*, from which comes the term *ecopoetic*, as poetic expression "which may effect an imaginative reunification of mind and nature," a psychosomatic and experiential inhabiting of nature linked to language that goes beyond a pastoral or technological literary setting (Bate 2000, 245). The term comes from the Greek *oikos*, meaning house or dwelling place, or habitation, and *poesis*, forming or shaping, evoking premodern views of words as in a sense magically entwined with the world. The meaning comes into further focus when considering how the related term *ecology* includes an ending derived from *logos*, one interpretation of which can be story, enabling a reinterpretation of ecology itself as "the story of home." In early medieval Christian cultures that influenced development of the Celtic Otherworld in Irish and Welsh literatures, the *logoi* of the Creator Logos simultaneously constituted both cosmos *and* divine energies of grace shaping and redeeming the world and human beings, a sparkle of creation in a network of cosmic language that can be thought of as iconographic, incarnational harmony (Thunberg 1985, 140; Farrell 1989, 181, 191; Maximus 2003, 45–74; Stăniloae 2003, 209; Siewers 2009, 69–81): The Logos and the logoi are one.

This is what ecosemiotics (or the study of the relation between nature and culture in relation to signs or meaning-making) refers to as a pansemiotic worldview (Nöth 1998, 334–335), but one significantly more interactive than Scholastic binaries of archetype and analogue (Aquinas 1997, 112–134), which would help form the basis for the modern scientific metaphysics decried by Foltz. In early Christian ascetic practices of nature, echoed in the archipelago around the Irish Sea, the environmental framework of cosmic logoi evoked a range of meanings: "words," "discourses," "stories," "purposes," and "reasons" in the relational context of "harmonies." These logoi of the Logos thus engaged creation as "the harmonies of the Harmony," and so forth. The overlay landscape of the words of God in Genesis 1, interacting with "actual" biblical geography of earth including the four Middle Eastern rivers of Eden, combined with liturgical and Hesychastic-style chanting in "desert" asceticism as it spread to the British islands, and melded with native pre-Christian traditions.

A variant spelling *ecopoiesis* means actual physical shaping of an ecosystem (see, for example, Todd 2004), highlighting the relation between ecological restoration and narrative (Siewers 1998; Kull, Kukk, and Lotman, 2003). And A. Kent Hieatt detailed a "mythopoeic" tradition in early English fantasy landscapes expressing an underlying set of values opposed to objectification of self and others (Hieatt 1975, 1–2), which could be summed up by the concept of empathy in neurophenomenological terms valorized by mind philosophy with an environmental bent (Thompson 2007, 118–122 and 382–411).

In any case, ecosemiotics, ecocriticism, ecophilosophy, and environmental ethics combine to articulate four key aspects of literary ecopoetics:

1. *Triadic overlay.* Ecosemiotics draws heavily on the work of Charles
   S. Peirce, the nineteenth-century American semiotician, whose triadic

model of the process of meaning-making or semiosis arises from interaction of sign, object, and interpretant-meaning (Nöth 1998; Peirce 1998; Kull 1998; Maran 2007). In this process the "object" often consists of physical environment. In Celtic Otherworld stories, the sign of the story engages the "object" of physical geography in relation to the interpretant of traditions of a spiritual realm or overlay landscape. Such literary expressions could be part of an "ecosemiosphere" if reflecting regional culture closely associated with an ecosystem. Peirce's triadic approach contrasts with the dyadic or analogous model for semiosis found in Scholastic notions of *analogia* (Aquinas 1997, 112–134), but it correlates with early Trinitarian "energy doctrine" whose cosmology influenced the Otherworld trope (Kristeva 1989, 209–211; Siewers 2009, 17–19).

2. *Metonymic imagery.* Ecocriticism examines "how artistic representation envisages human and nonhuman webs of interrelation" as Lawrence Buell notes (Buell 2005, 138). This can highlight a metonymic effect involving metaphor entwined with physicality, as in the image of "desert" standing for monasticism or "sweat" for labor. Thus in *Sir Gawain and the Green Knight* the green knight's raiment, hue, and horse all suggest vegetation, *and* the knight himself personally embodies the Otherworld associated with nature and a transformative magic immanent in native landscape beyond the court's feudal culture. In *The Canterbury Tales* the pricking in the hearts by "nature" in the opening to the General Prologue involves energy with physical effects, not just metaphor or an abstract allegorical figure of Nature.

3. *Time-plexity.* Articulation of the plexity or interwoven and multi-stranded nature of time explicates nature's "other side," breaking down human conventions to indicate ecophenomenologically the coexistence of nonhuman times and even nontime (Wood 2003, 213–217). Non-Augustinian patristics influential on the early Irish involved four modes of time and nontime: Human, nonhuman natural, created eternal (angels and demons), and the everlasting nontime of uncreated divine energies in nature (Mantzaridis 1996; Romanides 2007, 274–275). Overlapping modes of time and nontime emerge from the General Prologue in *The Canterbury Tales* and the overlay calendars of *Sir Gawain and the Green Knight*—seasons, church year, dual new years (one at Gawain's departure on All Hallows, considered the pre-Christian Irish "new year"), spiritual overlay. Neither replicates the transcendentally subjective Augustinian eternal present found in Dante's pilgrim-comedy.

4. *Environmental ethos.* Aldo Leopold's land ethic extends the liminality of time to the intersection of ethos as "place" and ethical behavior (Leopold 1986, 237–263), calling for an understanding of the land itself as having rights. This sense of ethos also involves a personal dialogue of responsibility that extends the ethical dialogics of Mikhail

Bakhtin and Emmanuel Lévinas to the nonhuman (Pevear 1995, xviii–xix; Lévinas 2002). We see this in the empathy implicit in Hie-att's textual genealogy. Thus, for example, the laughter of the Green Knight in his rural realm puts a face on nature.

THE "GREEN WORLD" AND ELVISH WRITING
IN THE CANTERBURY TALES

Chaucer's overlay landscape leads us on a "green world" journey along an identifiable route outdoors in the English countryside, reaching no linear destination. It shapes an edge of text and ecology, a textual ecotone engaging both the inner human and outer natural worlds on their shared border. This is apparent from its beginning. Modern editors of *The Canterbury Tales* inserted parentheses in the famous opening of the General Prologue, obscuring the presence of this overlay landscape evoked by a key line (11): "so prick-eth him nature in her corages" (in other words, "so nature energizes them in their hearts" or "sparkles in them so"). The line was taken by many modern commentators to refer exclusively to birds mentioned immediately before, prompting the addition of the parentheses (Stanbury 2004). But the lack of parentheses in the original enables the meaning to flow across all the famous opening lines, punctuated below with a semicolon to suggest how the line in question easily reads as pivot point for the whole:

Whan that Aprill with his shoures soote
The droghte of March hath perced to the roote,
And bathed every veine in swich licour
Of which vertu engendred is the flour;
Whan Zephirus eek with his sweete breeth
Inspired hath in every holt and heeth
The tendre croppes, and the yonge sonne
Hath in the Ram his halve cours yronne,
And smale foweles maken melodye,
That slepen al the nyght with open eye;
So priketh hem nature in hir corages—
Thanne longen folk to goon on pilgrimages,
And palmeres for to seken straunge strondes,
To ferne halwes, kowthe in sondry londes;
And specially from every shires ende
Of Engelond to Caunterbury they wende,
The holy blisful martir for to seke,
That hem hath holpen whan that they were seeke. (Chaucer 1988,
    23, ll. 1–18)

The poem here at its start evokes a palimpsest of cultural interactions with the land in rich layers of time and nontime. This move forms the heart of Chaucer's poetic answer in *The Canterbury Tales* to the Scholastic feudalism of the tottering Norman *ancien régime*. The pilgrims move along what apparently is the old Roman road between London and Kent in springtime. Their route from the London suburb of Southwark and their ending in the seat of the medieval church in England at Canterbury (a destination itself named for an old Romano-Celtic tribe) can figure a transition from materialistic to spiritual concerns. But both termini are "real" earthly places, and the pilgrims never actually arrive at the Cathedral in Canterbury as a spiritual space. (The assumption that *The Canterbury Tales* is unfinished as opposed to unpolished, as argued also for the masterwork of Chaucer's acolyte Edmund Spenser, *The Faerie Queene.* is belied thematically by the order of tales found in the Ellesmere manuscript, with its culmination in *The Parson's Tale.*) Rather than an entry into the interiorized virtual reality of the Gothic cathedral, the work remains "on the road," always in process in the natural world, and indirectly but ultimately reflecting on older Insular ascetic projects of grounding the mind in the heart and realizing the human in larger cosmic connections beyond any objectified ego.

Nature pricks the hearts of humans and nonhumans in spring, including birds and zodiac and rain and plants and cycles of season and life, all elementally interwoven. The atmospheric climate and creatures of the air, the emergence of plants in the spring, the astronomical realms—these are all part of nature's energizing or sparkling, which links to the second part of the opening in terms of the parallel springtide migrations of people on pilgrimages, and the incorporation of the spiritual realm into this movement of nature, including Canterbury with the presence of Thomas Becket. Becket's martyrdom occurred at the hands of the Norman feudal regime, which implicitly is called into question by Chaucer's entire project—from the poet's use of the vernacular to his existentially ironic subversion of a social hierarchy and worldview on its last legs in the wake of the Black Death, the Peasants' Revolt, and other social and religious upheavals.

Chaucer's landscape similarly grounds human personas in larger cosmic networks, subverting any sense of discrete subjectivity at odds with or controlling the natural world. This is evident in the holocaust of the grove and its nature spirits in the first actual story of the poetic cycle, The Knight's Tale (and in that entire tale's arguable send-up of chivalry for its objectification of both people and nature [Jones 1994]). Yet this is already apparent too in the Prologue's implicit comic contrast of the pilgrims' self-projected identities with contextualization of them in larger networks of the poem's environments. The characters that seem most honest are those most grounded in the countryside, namely the Parson and Plowman, and perhaps the Franklin, together with the Clerk, who would contextualize his interiority in teaching others. This extrasubjectivity is highlighted by Chaucer's use of the Otherworld-related term of *elvishness* as a key concept in two central stories, and in reference to his poetic project itself. The wife of Bath in beginning her tale recalls a time when the landscape of England was inhabited by an elf queen and "fairies" (geocentric beings known from romances often derived from Celtic sources that Chaucer references also in The Franklin's Tale). The sovereignty goddess in early Irish traditions was the necessary partner of a successful king, and the wife's tale draws heavily on the motif of the Sovereignty goddess (or elf queen) as bestowing authority (and, in the case of Chaucer's tale, freedom) upon the man who can ignore her initial appearance—in effect avoid objectification of her, as a force of nature—and partner with her in allegiance. Chaucer's own persona later in the lead-in to the Tale of Sir Thopas is identified as elvish, embodying a magic of poetry in the landscape.

Likewise, immediately preceding The Wife of Bath's Tale and sharing with it a central position in Chaucer's collection based on the Ellesmere Manuscript, The Man of Law's Tale includes a reference to the saintly heroine of that tale, Constance, as elvish. Constance's Christian otherworldliness thus is identified with a native pre-Norman elvishness, and also with a type of Christianity linked to a mythical native Celtic Christianity through a "British" Bible. Her otherworldly power rejects and surmounts the imperialistic ambitions of various monarchs, aristocrats, and regimes in favor of a radically therapeutic Christianity (Robertson 2001). Constance embodies a different type of sovereignty figure, still within a tradition likely adapted typologically by its monastic literary compilers, related both to traditions of the Mother of God (in Ireland linked to St. Brigit) and the feminine figuring of biblical Wisdom. The Wife of Bath's Tale, together with The Man of Law's Tale, can be read as offering a response of sorts to the objectified courtly love satirized in The Knight's Tale, and to the ribald materialism of the so-called bawdy tales involving both Scholastic clerks and rising capitalist notions of love, also emphasized in the Wife of Bath's prologue. Both with their "elvish" references provide an alternative to objectified relationships amid the whole work's vernacular assertion of an English countryside. Partnership in marriage in The Wife of Bath's Tale and sacralized marriage in The Man of Law's Tale through associations to the natural world via "elvishness" lend an ecofeminist edge to the poetry (Plumwood 1993). In Wendell Berry's terms, such a premodern sense of marriage in the land figures how "one can become whole only by the responsible acceptance of one's partiality . . . the double sense of particularity and generality: one lives in marriage and in sexuality, at home and in the world . . . it is impossible to care for each other more or differently than we care for the earth" (Berry 1977, 123).

OVERLAY LANDSCAPE AND LAUGHTER IN
SIR GAWAIN AND THE GREEN KNIGHT

The color of the Green Knight is clearly associated through his clothing and bough of holly with the natural world, but also in poetic tradition with the "green pastures" of biblical Paradise as it had become entwined with a native Otherworld in Insular traditions. While the color green in the late Middle Ages had overtones of the otherworldly veering toward the demonic, sometimes associated with lust and envy, the "green street of Paradise" as a motif associating natural verdure with Paradise (although perhaps also a difficult path) had a venerable genealogy stretching back into Old English poetry (Randall 1960; Keenan 1970, 1973; Doane 1973; Sajavaara 1975), a meaning echoed elsewhere in the corpus associated with the *Gawain* poet (*Cleannness* l. 767; *Pearl* l. 37), and it also carried meanings of charity. The color term in effect, analogous in this partly to the early Irish term *glas*, spanned the sensual and the spiritual (Siewers 2005a).

Similarly, the juxtaposition of the animal-hunting scenes with the scenes in the bedroom in the Green Knight's castle vividly evokes the entanglement of human life with the earth. As Gawain and his host's wife go through their flirtatious chivalrous quasi-courting rituals, the role of his ideal persona as the prey of physicality on many levels becomes more apparent. To save his physical life he seemingly abandons his trust in Christ and the image of the Virgin Mary on his shield for the sake of the green girdle of Bertilak, given by his wife to Gawain as part of a scheme by the "goddess" Morgan le Fay, a figure of the elvish sovereignty goddess again. Meanwhile, the status of the beasts keeps getting more common (from royal deer to boar to rodent-fox) and the boudoir situation more desperate.

On the one hand there is the hunting, with grisly butchering (in this case of the deer):

> Syþen þay slyt þe slot, sesed þe erber,
> Schaued wyth a scharp knyf, and þe schyre knitten;
> Syþen rytte þay þe foure lymmes, and rent of þe hyde,
> Þen brek þay þe balé, þe bowelez out token . . .
>   (Andrew and Waldron 1996, 256–257, ll. 1330–1343)

> After they slit the throat-hollow, seized the gullet,
> Shaved it out with a sharp knife and knit the white flesh;
> Then they cut the four legs and rent the hide;
> They then broke open the belly, took out the bowels.

Meanwhile, in the supposedly cultured "other world" of the castle, in an illusory mirroring of the "real world" contrast between Arthurian court and green world in the poem's larger frame, Gawain finds his identity subverted:

> "Bot þat e be Gawan, hit gotz in mynde."
> "Querfore?" quoþ þe freke, and freschly he askez,
> Ferde lest he hade fayled in fourme of his castes;
>   (Andrew and Waldron 1966, 255, ll. 1293–1295)

> "But that you are Gawain is questionable."
> "Why?" said the knight, eagerly asking,
> Afraid lest he had failed in the manner of his speech.

The capstone of the poem in Passus 4 provides a complex back-and-forth, integrating the binarized hunt and bedroom with the contrast between the peripheral rural geography of the Green Knight's realm and Arthur's Frenchified and quasi-colonial court. The laughter of the Green Knight and his green girdle catalyze the integration. The Green Knight in effect tells his alter ego Gawain to "lighten up" and realize his grounding in physicality. Gawain becomes in effect the new disruptive visitor to Arthur's court, although now bearing symbols that will remain there through the laughter and sashes of green and the story itself. Gawain's confession and penance in the countryside at the Green Chapel become also a kind of fantasy echo of extra-Catholic Lollardism. As the Green Knight says:

> "Bot for ye lufed your lyf; þe lasse I yow blame"
> (Andrew and Waldron 1996, 294, ll. 2368).

> But because you loved your life; the less I you blame.

The laugher of the Green Knight melding into that of the court, going beyond words in a kind of redemptive environmental semiosis from the green world, recalls both the same poet's description of Sarah's laughing and God's response in *Cleanness* and Julian of Norwich's contemporary words on laughing in her mystical *Shewings*: "But in God may be no wreth, as to my syte. . . . I thowte that I wold that al myn evyn Christen had seen as I saw and than should thei al lauhyn with me" (Crampton 1994, 510–520). Unlike Augustinian theology, which saw nonbeing fundamentally as evil, nonbeing or nature's "other side" becomes a source for joy when seen as divine, an insular cosmological thread traceable back to John Scotus Eriugena's early Hiberno-Latin philosophy of nature. (Siewers 2009, 67–95).

ENVIRONMENTAL ETHOS AND LE MORTE D'ARTHUR

The Wasteland that emerges in Book 2 of Caxton's edition of Malory's opus figures the mix of the sinister and the redemptive in the forests of adventure of this fantasy history, and the spiritual realm that entwines them. Malory rehistoricizes and regrounds Arthurian legends that had been heavily allegorized and idealized in French romances at a remove from their mythic Welsh and fantasy-history Cambro-Latin origins. The grail cycle becomes placed more integratively within English geography and a quasi-chronicle framework, mirroring dimly the Wars of the Roses and struggles of the Welsh-rooted Tudors to claim legitimacy. The broken systems of the

Middle Ages and chivalry in ruins around him, Malory the prisoner-author looks to a mythic native time and ultimately the complexly layered story landscape of Glastonbury in southwestern England for reweaving a magical geography of Britain. Written immediately after the fall of Constantinople, like its heir *The Faerie Queene*, Malory's work harkens back implicitly to a lost Christian *ecumene* integrating native landscape, traditions, and historical and spiritual realms in a cosmic geography of relational desire, with the story of the Sangreal itself likely a reimagined Byzantine cosmic mystery mingled with early Irish Otherworld traditions (Scavone 1996). In the process, its central landscape takes shape in the green-world tradition.

Balin's Dolorous Stroke to the Maimed King in Book 2 of Caxton's edition emerges from offenses to feminine figures identified with an Otherworld associated in turn with nature, magic, danger, and redemptive mysteries. The underlying story pattern follows that identified by the Celticist John Carey (2007) in early Irish prototypes that influenced Welsh and Breton Arthurian legends, in which otherworldly treasure is seized from disrespected feminine guardians in magical natural landscapes, resulting in environmental catastrophe (only if the treasure is granted as a result of due respect and what could be called a mutual empathy does it grant fertility to the land rather than shape a wasteland). Balin seizes a magic sword against the will and warning of a lady sent from Avalon (a place associated in Malory's time both with a native Otherworld and with Glastonbury), and then in revenge beheads the Lady of the Lake, who had given Excalibur to Arthur. Fleeing, Balin slays an Irish knight pursuing him, whose lady then commits suicide, where suicide becomes the magical pretext for the Dolorous Stroke. "O Balyn, two bodyes thou hast slayne in one herte, and two hertes in one body, and two soules thow hast lost" (67). Merlin explains that because of the death of the lady due to his killing of her love, Balin will commit the Dolorous Stroke (68).

When King Pellam fights Balin, the Dolorous Stroke connects the Otherworld realm of the grail with both the forests of adventure and the deadly feuds of late-medieval English chivalry. Balin runs through Pellam's mysterious chambers and takes the spear of Longinus and delivers the Dolorous Stroke to Pellam, causing the castle to fall atop them. As Balin rides forth again, "alle that were on lyve cryed, O Balyn, thow hast casued grete dommage in these countrayes; for the dolorous stroke thow gauest vnto Kynge Pellam thre countreyes are destroyed, and doubte not but the vengeaunce wil falle on the at the last" (75).

In the ambiguities of Malory's adaptation, Pellam and Pelles seem confounded in the figure of the Maimed King, whose Castle Carbonek connects with an Otherworld identified in turn with Avalon and geographic place in the Glastonbury area of the Somerset Levels, while on a larger scale juxtaposed with Camelot. This back-and-forth landscape focus disrupts any sense of the land of Britain as ontological object, and places limits on those who would possess it. (The line of Pellam-Pelles is also identified with that of St. Joseph of Arimathea, who traditionally brought the Sangreal to the

Glastonbury area in dim mists of mythic time. The earliest extant identifications of a pre-Christian Otherworld of Avalon with Glastonbury and its legends of ancient Christianity date to the thirteenth century [Siewers 1994, 2002]. Chaucer also may have touched on Glastonbury-related tales of Joseph for his ancient British-related figure of Arvirargus in the "Celtic" Franklin's Tale, who shares a name, mythic time frame, and geographic orientation with a ruler in the legends.)

Geraldine Heng (2004) argues persuasively for a "feminine subtext" in Malory's work, pointing to land-goddess-like figures such as the Ladies of the Lake and of Avalon, and Morgan le Fay, related through their magic to the natural landscape as Otherworld. Indeed, Irish traditions referring to the Otherworld as "the land of women" had morphed into aspects of the Arthurian cycle. In some respects the structure of the overlay landscape trope itself matches the literary theorist Luce Irigaray's sense of a double-enfolded or relational feminine landscape, and Deleuze and Guattari's quest for an ecosophical redefinition of desire as relational rather than lack (Deleuze and Guattari 1987, 157; Casey 1998, 321–320; Siewers 2009, 3). Associations of a goddess of the land with the earth (Herbert 1992) parallel both apparently pre-Christian Celtic tradition and Christian identification of the Mother of God and earth (Miller 1992). The quest for the Sangreal emerges as a subversion of what, in ecofeminist terms, could be called the male-centered domination ethos of the Round Table.

Yet the Sangreal also brings resolution of sorts in the healing of the Maimed King. Galahad (bearing the sword of King David in a girdle woven from the spindles of Eve) anoints the Maimed King at Castle Carbonek with the blood of the spear and heals him. A voice addresses the gathering there as "my sones and not my chyef sones, my frendes and not my werryours, goo ye hens where ye hope best to doo and as I bad yow" (502), seemingly releasing them from feudalism. When the Sangreal is taken up to heaven, Joseph of Arimathea appears, reopening the connection to the landscape of Glastonbury.

At the end, Arthur on the brink of death comforts Bedivere by saying "Comfort thyself . . . and doo as wel as thou mayst, for in me is no truste for to truste in, for I wyl into the Vale of Auylyon to hele me of my greuous wounde," and thence is taken in a boat with magical queens including Morgan le Fay as his sword is taken back by the waters (591). Bedivere takes to the forest and encounters the exiled Bishop of Canterbury at his hermitage near Glastonbury, where lies Arthur's tomb (593). But Malory-as-narrator notes that "somme men say in many partyes of Englond that Kyng Arthur is not dead, but had by the wylle of our Lord Ihesu into another place" (592). Skeptical, he still indicates a lack of supporting evidence "of the veray certente of his deth" (592).

In any case, Lancelot at the end of Malory's cycle takes final leave of Guenever, into the forest again, and ends up at the Glastonbury hermitage and chapel "betwyxte two clyffes" (595). Later he and his posse bring

Guenever's body back to Glastonbury to be buried next to Arthur. After Lancelot's own burial elsewhere, his knightly friends return to the Glastonbury hermitage for a month before separating to live as "holy men" (599). The new King Constantine sends for the bishop-hermit from Glastonbury for his coronation, in perhaps another echo of Britain as a kind of Insular mystical heir to Byzantium in this story-landscape, St. Constantine the Great having had legendary British roots.

The overlay landscape of Malory's work never totally unifies Glastonbury and Avalon as objective space. The two, like the Otherworld and this-world, entwine through the historicized grail tradition as a kind of antidote to the crumbling medieval worldview, shadowing each other even from the inception of Arthur's realm. Malory's comments about the ambiguity of Arthur's death suggest Avalon could be "irretrievably outside the temporal boundaries of the narrative's world" (Parry 1997, 147). Yet the dynamic of Glastonbury landscape in relation to the forest hermitage as final setting of the fantasy history suggests an immanent "other side" both to nature and human history in the early English green world. Subsequent writers from Spenser to the Romantics would take up the pattern, influencing in turn yet others such as the foundational American landscape writer James Fenimore Cooper, whose translation of the green world to the vanishing Eastern Woodlands of America would help inspire early conservationists such as Theodore Roosevelt (Brinkley 2009, 40–41). Later adapters of the green-world tradition, most popularly J. R. R. Tolkien's fantasy history with its Ents and Elves in an ancient European overlay landscape (Siewers 2005b), would steer the trope into environmental contexts more immediately recognizable as such to modern audiences. But its roots provide an important early model of ecopoetics, still relevant amid the pressing need for more ecologically centered cultural narratives today.

REFERENCES

Andrew, Malcolm, and Ronald Waldron, eds. 1996. *The Poems of the Pearl Manuscript*. Rev. ed. Exeter, UK: University of Exeter Press.

Aquinas, Thomas. 1997. *Basic Writings of Thomas Aquinas*. Vol. 1. *God and the Order of Creation*. Edited and translated by Anton C. Pegis. Indianapolis: Hackett.

Bate, Jonathan. 2000. *The Song of the Earth*. Cambridge, MA: Harvard University Press.

Berry, Wendell. 1977. *The Unsettling of America, Culture and Agriculture*. San Francisco: Sierra Club Books, 123.

Brinkley, Douglas. 2009. *The Wilderness Warrior: Theodore Roosevelt and the Crusade for America*. New York: HarperCollins.

Buell, Lawrence. 1995. *The Environmental Imagination: Thoreau, Nature Writing and the Formation of American Culture*. Cambridge, MA: Harvard University Press.

Cantor, Norman F. 1993. *The Civilization of the Middle Ages: The Life and Death of a Civilization*. New York: HarperCollins.

Casey, Edward S. 1998. *The Fate of Place: A Philosophical History*. Berkeley: University of California Press.

Chaucer, Geoffrey. 1988. *The Riverside Chaucer*. 3rd ed. Edited by Larry D. Benson. Oxford: Oxford University Press.

Crampton, Georgia Ronan, ed. 1994. *The Shewings of Julian Norwich*. Kalamazoo, MI:

Medieval Institute Publications, http://www.lib.rochester.edu/Camelot/teams/julianfr.htm

Davis, Carmel Brendon. 2008. *Mysticism and Space: Space and Spatiality in the Works of Richard Rolle, the Cloud of Unknowing Author, and Julian of Norwich*. Washington, DC: Catholic University of America.

Deleuze, Gilles, and Félix Guattari. 1987. *A Thousand Plateaus. Capitalism and Schizophrenia 2*. Translated by Brian Massumi. Minneapolis: University of Minnesota Press.

Doane, A. N. 1973. "'The Green Street of Paradise': A Note on Lexis and Meaning in Old English Poetry." *Neuphilologische Mitteilungen* 74. 456–465.

Edwards, Paul N. "Cyberpunks in Cyberspace." *The Cultures of Computing*. The Sociological Review monograph series. Edited by Susan Leigh Star. Oxford: Wiley-Blackwell, 69–84.

Elliott, Ralph. 2002. "Landscape and Geography." *A Companion to the Gawain-Poet*. Edited by Derek Brewer and Jonathan Gibson. Woodbridge, UK: D. S. Brewer/Boydell & Brewer, 105–117.

Farrell, Joseph P. 1989. *Free Choice in St. Maximus the Confessor*. South Canaan, PA: St. Tikhon's Seminary Press.

Foltz, Bruce V. 1995. *Inhabiting the Earth: Heidegger, Environmental Ethics, and the Metaphysics of Nature*. Amherst, NY: Humanities Books.

———. 2004. "Nature's Other Side: The Demise of Nature and the Phenomenology of Givenness." *Rethinking Nature: Essays in Environmental Philosophy*. Edited by Bruce V. Foltz and Robert Frodeman. Bloomington: Indiana University Press, 330–341.

Frye, Northrop. 1967. "The Argument of Comedy." *Shakespeare: Modern Essays in Criticism*, rev. ed. Edited by Leonard F. Dean. London: Oxford University Press, 79–89.

Goodchild, Philip. 1996. *Deleuze and Guattari: An Introduction to the Politics of Desire, Theory, Culture & Society*. London: Sage Publications.

Heng, Geraldine. 2004. "Enchanted Ground: The Feminine Subtext in Malory." *Sir Thomas Malory, Le Morte Darthur*. Norton Critical Edition. Edited by Stephen H. A. Shepherd. New York: W.W. Norton, 835–849.

Herbert, Máire. 1992. "Goddess and King: The Sacred Marriage in Early Ireland." *Women and Sovereignty*. Cosmos Yearbook 7. Edited by Louise Olga Fradenburg. Edinburgh: University of Edinburgh Press, 265–275.

Hieatt, A. Kent. 1975. *Chaucer Spenser Milton: Mythopoeic Continuities and Transformations*. Montreal: McGill-Queen's University Press.

Jones, Terry. 1994. *Chaucer's Knight: Portrait of a Medieval Mercenary*. Rev. ed. London: Methuen.

Keenan, Hugh T. 1970. "*Exodus* 312: The Green Street of Paradise." *Neuphilologische Mitteilungen* 71, 455–460.

———. 1973. "*Exodus* 312a: Further Notes on the Eschatological Green Ground." *Neuphilologische Mitteilungen* 74, 217–219.

Kristeva, Julia. 1989. "Dostoevsky, the Writing of Suffering, and Forgiveness." *Black Sun: Depression and Melancholia*. Translated by Leon S. Roudiez. New York: Columbia University Press, 175–217.

Kull, Kalevi. 1998. "Semiotic Ecology: Different Natures in the Semiosphere." *Sign Systems Studies* 26, 344–371.

Kull, Kalevi, Toomas Kukk, and Aleksei Lotman. 2003. "When Culture Supports Biodiversity: The Case of the Wooded Meadow." *Imagining Nature: Practices of Cosmology and Identity.* Edited by Andreas Roepstorff, Nils Bubandt, and Kalevi Kull. Aarhus, Denmark: Aarhus University Press.

Leopold, Aldo. 1986. *The Sand County Almanac with Essays on Conservation from Round River.* New York: Ballantine.

Lévinas, Emmanuel. 2002. "Ethics and the Face." Translated by Alfonso Lingis. *A Phenomenology Reader.* Edited by Dermot Moran and Timothy Mooney. London: Routledge, and New York, 515–528.

Malory, Thomas. 1983. *Caxton's Malory: A New Edition of Sir Thomas Malory's* Le Morte Darthur *Based on the Pierpont Morgan Copy of William Caxton's Edition of 1485.* Edited by James W. Spisak and William Matthews. Berkeley: University of California Press.

Mantzaridis, Georgios I. 1996. *Time and Man.* Translated by Julian Vulliamy. South Canaan, PA: St. Tikhon's Seminary.

Maran, Timo. 2007. "Towards an Integrated Methodology of Ecosemiotics: The Concept of Nature-Text." *Sign Systems Studies* 35.1/2, 269–294.

McTurk, Rory. 2005. *Chaucer and the Norse and Celtic Worlds.* Aldershot, UK: Ashgate.

Miller, Dean A. 1992. "Byzantine Sovereignties and Feminine Potencies." *Women and Sovereignty.* Cosmos Yearbook 7. Edited by Louise Olga Fradenburg. Edinburgh: Edinburgh University Press, 250–263.

Nöth, Winfried. 1998. "Ecosemiotics." *Sign Systems Studies* 26, 332–343.

Peirce, Charles S. 1998. *The Essential Peirce, Volume 2: Selected Philosophical Writings, 1893–1913.* Edited by Peirce Edition Project. Bloomington IN: Indiana University Press.

Parry, Joseph D. 1997. "Following Malory out of Arthur's World." *Modern Philology.* 95.2. 147–169.

Pevear, Richard. 1995. "Foreword." *Demons.* Fyodor Dostoevsky. Translated by Richard Pevear and Larissa Volokhonsky. New York: Vintage Books, xviii–xix.

Plumwood, Val. 1993. *Feminism and the Mastery of Nature.* London and New York: Routledge.

Randall, B. J. 1960. "Was the Green Knight a Fiend?" *Studies in Philology* 57, 479–491.

Robertson, Elizabeth. 2001. "The 'Elvyssh' Power of Constance: Christian Feminism in Geoffrey Chaucer's The Man of Law's Tale." *Studies in the Age of Chaucer* 23, 143–180.

Romanides, John. 2007. *Patristic Theology: The University Lectures of Fr. John Romanides.* Translated by Alexios Trader. Thessaloniki, Greece: Uncut Mountain Press.

Sajavaara, K. 1975. "The Withered Footprints on the Green Street of Paradise." *Neuphilologische Mitteilungen* 76, 34–38.

Scavone, Daniel. 1999. "Joseph of Arimathea, the Holy Grail and the Edessa Icon." *Arthuriana* 9.4, 3–31.

Siewers, Alfred K. 1994. *"A Cloud of Witnesse": The Origins of Glastonbury Abbey in the Context of Early Christianity in Western Britain.* Unpublished M.A. dissertation. Aberystwyth: University of Wales.

———. 1998. "Making the Quantum Culture Leap: Reflections on the Chicago Controversy." *Restoration & Management Notes* 16, 8–15.

———. 2002. "Gildas and Glastonbury: Revisiting the Origins of Glastonbury Abbey." *Via Crucis: Essays on Early Medieval Sources and Ideas in Memory of J.E. Cross.* Morgantown, WV: West Virginia University Press, 423–432.

———. 2005a. "The Bluest-*Greyest*-Greenest Eye: Colours of Martyrdom and Colours of the Winds as Iconographic Landscape." *Cambrian Medieval Celtic Studies* 50, 31–66.

————. 2005b. "Tolkien's Cosmic-Christian Ecology: The Medieval Underpinnings." *Tolkien's Modern Middle Ages: The New Middle Ages*. Edited by Jane Chance and Alfred Siewers. New York: Palgrave Macmillan, 138–153.

————. 2009. *Strange Beauty: Ecocritical Approaches to Early Medieval Landscape*. . New York: Palgrave Macmillan.

Stanbury, Sarah. 2004. "Ecochaucer: Green Ethics and Medieval Nature." *The Chaucer Review* 39.1, 1–16.

Stăniloae, Dumitru. 2003. *Orthodox Spirituality: A Practical Guide for the Faithful and a Definitive Manual for the Scholar*. Translated by Jerome Newville and Otilia Kloos. South Canaan, PA: St. Tikhon Seminary Press.

St. Maximus the Confessor. 2003. *On the Cosmic Mystery of Christ*. Translated by Paul M. Blowers and Robert Louis Wilken. Crestwood, NY: St. Vladimir's Seminary Press.

Thompson, Evan. 2007. *Mind in Life: Biology, Phenomenology, and the Sciences of Mind*. Cambridge, MA: Belknap-Harvard University Press.

Thunberg, Lars. 1985. *Man and the Cosmos: The Vision of St. Maximus the Confessor*. Crestwood, NY: St. Vladimir's Seminary Press.

Todd, Paul. 2004. *Final Progress Report on Robotic Lunar Ecopoiesis Test Bed for the NASA Institute for Advanced Concepts*. Greenville, IN: Space Hardware Optimization Technology.

Wood, David. 2003. "What Is Eco-Phenomenology?" *Eco-Phenomenology: Back to the Earth Itself*. Albany, NY: State University of New York Press, 211–233.

7 Amerindian Eden
The *Divine Weekes* of Du Bartas

Edward M. Test

When Izaak Walton writes in *The Compleat Angler* (1655) about the "truths by Du Bartas and Lobel . . . and laborious Gerard in his Herbal" (261) he places the knowledge of the natural world of French poet Guillaume de Saluste Sieur du Bartas (1544–1590) on par with the great English herbalists John Gerard and Mathias de L'Obel. Indeed, England's renowned natural philosopher, Sir Francis Bacon, corresponded with Du Bartas, and Ann Bradstreet's poem "In Honour of Du Bartas, 1641" praises his "Art in natural Philosophy." Readers of Du Bartas's Christian epic, *La Sepmaine; ou, Creation du monde* (1578–1584)—or *Divine Weeks*, as Joshua Sylvester's 1605 complete translation of the first and second weeks is known in English—would agree with Ms. Bradstreet: the poem contains an encyclopedic knowledge of worldwide flora that has rightly earned him the moniker of a "Natural-Philosophical" poet.[1] Du Bartas, however, has a second, more prominent moniker as a "divine poet." He celebrates a natural philosophy through Scripture, creating what Sir Francis Bacon disparages as "this unwholesome mixture of things human and divine [from which] arises not only a fantastic philosophy but also a heretical religion."[2] In this sense, the wide-ranging and perhaps mildly heretical (if we are to believe Bacon) French Huguenot Du Bartas belongs to a particular segment of Natural Philosophy called Mosaic or Christian Philosophy, which uses the Bible, particularly Genesis, as the source and "book of nature" for all natural philosophical inquiry.[3] The first week of the *Divine Weekes*, in which Du Bartas rewrites Genesis, epitomizes the poetic expression of this sacred Mosaic philosophy, but unlike other Christian philosophers, Du Bartas extends his allegorical reading of Genesis beyond the Bible to incorporate the Amerindian cosmologies and environment of the New World.

Du Bartas, then, considers an indigenous understanding of nature and the physical universe, adding to Mosaic and natural philosophies a third component that we might label somewhat anachronistically an "ethnographic philosophy." Like the great sixteenth-century herbalists, he reveals a surprising amount of practical knowledge about the natural New World garnered from the Amerindian environment and culture, which does not emphasize differences between the Old and New World but a continuity, or sameness. From an ethnological viewpoint, Du Bartas's *Divine Weeks* is a sheer marvel in its originality, astounding the reader with a straight-forward embrace of extra-European cultures. Du Bartas rewrites Scripture to include the Amerindian environment, especially Mesoamerica, in such a manner that his recontextualization extends far beyond the popular speculations that the Amerindians are the lost tribe of Jews, the source of King Solomon's golden Ophir, or descendants of Noah dropped off the ark to form a colony. For Du Bartas, Mesoamericans were not exception to, but rather *part of*, the biblical story, not different from, but *part of*, Christianity.[4] The Garden of Eden in Du Bartas, for instance, contains Mesoamerican maize, metl (the Nahuatl spelling for maguey, or agave plant), cochineal (Renaissance Europe's preferred crimson red dye, also solely found in Mexico), and after the fall, Eve weaves together a Mexica feather mantle and places it upon Adam's shoulders. While the 1935 edition of Du Bartas's work (the standard for many years) notes that "his interest in the Americas was exceptionally keen" (Holmes 1935, 148), no scholarly work attempts to reconcile natural and Mosaic philosophies in Du Bartas with the overwhelming presence of the natural New World in the *Divine Weeks*. By considering the presence of three New World materials in Du Bartas—the ceiba tree, gold, and feathers—this essay reveals Du Bartas's understanding of Mesoamerican cosmology and their environment, emphasizing how these natural resources retain a vestige of their original Amerindian meaning, albeit reconstituted in Europe in a syncretic coupling of Amerindian and Christian myth. In this manner, the natural and Mosaic philosophies of Du Bartas are complemented by an early modern ethnographic and environmentalist understanding of the New World's "book of nature."

Before beginning my analysis, something needs to be said about the current place of Du Bartas in literary studies. He is—sadly—rarely read and, until recently, rarely studied in the Anglophone world.[5] Despite Du Bartas's importance to Sir Francis Bacon, King James I (who knew him personally and translated his work), and Sir Philip Sidney (who also translated the first week of *La Sepmaine*, though it is now lost); despite Sylvester's 1605 edition of the *Divine Weeks* containing prefatory material from renowned writers, such as Ben Jonson and Samuel Daniel; despite the effusive declaration by Gabriel Harvey that Du Bartas was as great as Homer, Virgil, and Dante; despite the *Divine Weeks*' undeniable influence on Milton's *Paradise Lost*, his work has dropped into the darker recesses of the literary canon in England.[6] Why the continued disregard by Anglophone readers and scholars?

Interest in Du Bartas first began to wane in the Restoration (the last edition of Sylvester's *Divine Weeks* appeared in 1641), when "John Dryden," Anne Lake Prescott notes, "renounced his earlier admiration and called the *Sepmaines* 'abominable fustian'" (Prescott 1968, 144). His disappearance from the literary canon is further due to the use of hexameter verse, a metrics that never caught on in early modern Europe (Sylvester uses pentameter verse in his translation), and also because the *Divine Weeks* exemplified an older, pre-empirical mode of thought. "Whatever one thinks of Du Bartas's poetry," writes Anne Lake Prescott, "in Renaissance Britain he was read, translated, imitated, and quoted" (Prescott 2004, 1). If writers in Renaissance England praised Du Bartas, then our understanding of literary and cultural history can only be enriched by likewise embracing one of the most valued—and strangely forgotten—of Renaissance writers. Moreover, if Du Bartas's reputation fell into decline precisely because of the seemingly disjunctive blend of a harmonious universe with empirical knowledge of the natural world, then perhaps this is exactly the juncture—where Mosaic, natural, and ethnographic philosophies meet—that can help restore Du Bartas to his rightful place among Renaissance writers and Anglophone scholars.

Du Bartas's Mosaic and natural philosophical approach to describing the human and the divine on earth has roots in both European and indigenous cosmologies. Unlike Copernicus, for Du Bartas Mother Earth is the only possible center. Even today, given our knowledge of a relative and ever-expanding universe, where no place (or every place, for that matter) is the center, calling earth a sacred center is completely reasonable—it is, after all, the only place we inhabit. Almost fifty years after the publication of Du Bartas's *Divine Weeks* in England, John Milton, who is considered "perhaps the most Baconian poet of the seventeenth-century" (Martin 2001, 231), similarly stresses a Ptolemaic universe, and like Du Bartas, Milton configures a geocentric universe because it places humankind in a central relation to the divine. To make an analogy, Milton and Du Bartas view the world like the medieval T-O maps, which place the sacred city of Jerusalem at the divine center of the known world and the universe: Milton and Du Bartas may be astronomically backward, but they are spiritually centered (and in the case of Du Bartas, environmentally centered as well). Du Bartas describes the cosmological center as follows:

> In all the world, God could not place so fit
> Our Mother Earth, as in the midst of it.
> On Fire and Aire, and Water divers wayes,
> Dispiersing so, their powerfull influence
> On, in, and through these various Elements:
> But on Earth, they all in one concurr,
> And all unite their severed force in her:
> As in a Wheele, which with a long deepe rut,
> His turning passage in the durt doth cut,
> The distant spoakes neerer and nearer gather,
> And in the Nave unite their points together. (1.2.355–366)

For Du Bartas, the feminine Mother Earth (in French "ayuele feconde," or literally "fecund grandmother") is the center where the spokes of the spiritual universe gather, ultimately uniting in the "Nave" of the church. Similarly, Amerindian traditions viewed earth and their religious centers as the spiritual hub of the universe. To continue the cartographic analogy, across the Atlantic in the Peruvian Andes, Guaman Poma created a map in 1610 (*Mapamundi del Reino de las Indias*) which places the Peruvian cosmological, sociological, and spiritual center, Cuzco, in the middle of the map.[7] Thus, while Du Bartas ignores the astronomic advancements of Western science, his spiritual centering places him firmly in line with contemporary Amerindian cosmologies.

As suggested earlier, Du Bartas develops his unique ethnographic cosmology at a time when "the common union between knowledge of nature and of its creator," writes Walter Mignolo, "began to be replaced with a more rigorous experimental method whose final destination was knowing the laws of nature rather than using nature to know its creator" (Mignolo 2008, 475). In the Americas, of course, the creator was still known through the natural environment. Some scholars consider Christianity (particularly Protestantism) as a partner in the rise of secular science because of the abstraction of a God above and outside of the earth, which not only separates humans from God, but also removes God from the natural world; and few would contest the direct relationship between the rise of empirical sciences (Mignolo's "laws of nature") and capitalistic resource exploitation.[8] As Marx bemoans in *Das Kapital*: "Christianity with its religious cult of man in the abstract, i.e. in Protestantism" leads to a society of commodity producers, which in turn limits "relations between man and nature" (Marx 1977, 173). Du Bartas and other Mosaic philosophers, however, oppose this trend and celebrate the natural world as a way of knowing the creator—the *All*, as Du Bartas labels God (like pagan Roman Lucretius before him). Similar to Amerindian traditions, Du Bartas fuses together God, nature, and humans into a complete whole, or "universall city," as he calls it, and does not divide the human soul from God, whose breath/spirit/soul is in all creation (like the Hebrew *ruah*, Hindu *atma*, Hawaiian *aloha*, or Amerindian animism). As Kathryn Banks notes, "Du Bartas asserts that God does not divide his divinity, yet also that man is given 'some small' stream of it" (Banks 2008, 42), thus separating Du Bartas from many Christian theologians, such as St. Augustine and Calvin (who argued that the breath or spirit of God cannot exist in humans because it implies that every time humans sin God sins also).[9]

In addition to maintaining that God's spirit resides in humans, Du Bartas echoes the Stoics and the Greek concept of Gaia (goddess of earth and its cities) by maintaining that we are all part of the same organism (connected to God and nature), which he expresses through an analogy to a tree:[10]

And as with us under the Oaken barke
The knurrie knot with branching vaines, we marke
To be of substance all one with the Tree,
Although farre thicker and more tough it bee:
So those guilt studs in the upper stories driven,
Are nothing but the thickest part of Heaven. (1.4.91–96)

The use of a tree as a symbolic representation of a divine cosmology that unifies the earthly with the sacred also exists throughout Mesoamerica. For instance, in Maya culture the physical embodiment of this sacred tree is the ceiba: a tall, large canopied and impressively rooted tree known by Europeans as the God-tree. The *OED* notes that the ceiba is found in the West Indies, and provides this pertinent usage: "one who . . . kneels before an oak as the wild Indian [from Guiana] does before his ceiba."[11] The *OED* recognizes Sylvester's 1598 translation of the *Divine Weeks* as the tree's first occurrence in the English language; defined as "a supposed tree of vast circumference, formerly rumoured to grow in the West Indies." Significantly, after the Tree of Knowledge and Tree of Life, Du Bartas elects the ceiba, or *Cerba*, as the first tree to amaze Adam as he walks like an Amerindian through a Garden of Eden laden with Mesoamerican flora:

Then up and downe a forest thicke he paceth,
Which selfelie opening in his presence baseth
Her trembling tresses never vading spring,
For humble homage to her mightie king:
Where thousand trees, waving with gentle puffes
Their plumie tops, sweepe the celestiall roofes.
Yet envying all the massie *Cerbas* fame,
Sith fiftie paces can but clasp the same. (Eden, 575–582)

By viewing humanity "to be of substance all one with the Tree" of God, and placing the West Indian "Cerba" as the largest and most envied tree in the Garden of Eden, Du Bartas combines his Mosaic view of Christianity with an Amerindian veneration of nature.

Importantly, Du Bartas's religious reverence for the natural world of the Americas occurred at a time when the economics of colonialism enabled rampant resource exploitation. By featuring Mother Earth as the sacred center of a divine cosmology, Du Bartas not only opposes Copernican and Baconian science, but also challenges the capitalist approach toward natural resources—it is rather hard to exploit a natural world overtly embodied by God. Before Bacon, "the earth was alive and considered to be a beneficent, receptive, nurturing female," Carolyn Merchant writes, "in general, the pervasive animism of nature created a relationship of immediacy with the human being . . . in much the same way, the cultural belief-systems of many American-Indian tribes had for centuries subtly guided group behavior toward nature" (Merchant 1983, 28). Du Bartas celebrates a worldview not different from, but similar to, the Amerindians when most Europeans pushed indigenous belief systems to the margins as they ravaged the New World for profitable commodities—especially gold.

No other New World resource piqued the interest of Europeans more than American gold. While this earthly "specie" was obviously found, forged, and venerated throughout the history of Western civilization, its abundance in the New World (especially in Peru and Mexico) developed into a virtual metonym for the Americas: Raleigh's El Dorado, Solomon's Ophir, America's "golden fleece," people of the Golden Age.[12] Even the golden apples that Hercules obtains from nymphs in the garden of the Hesperides (depicted on the title page to the herbalist Rembert Doedens *Crudyboeck*, 1554) were transformed from Greco-Roman myth to Mesoamerican reality: in Italy the name *pomodoro* (or *pommi d'oro*), "golden apple," is still used as the name for the Mesoamerican tomato. The predominant Edenic correlation between Ovid's mythic Golden Age and the Native Americans, reflected in Arthur Barlowe's narrative of the 1584 Virginian voyage—"we found the people most gentle, loving, and faithful, void of all guile and treason, and such as live after the manner of the golden age"—carries the metonymic weight of gold, albeit with the inverse relation to European avarice: the Amerindians appreciated gold for adornments and religious uses only, but did not understand the value of gold as a pure commodity. Indeed, one of the first major chroniclers of the New World, Peter Martyr, notes in his *Decades de Orbe Novo* how the Amerindians "had the golden age, *mine* and *thine*, the seeds of discord, were far removed from them."[13] The European perception that Amerindians misvalued gold occurs in the earliest of encounters: Columbus notes in his first letter that the natives "bartered, like idiots, cotton and gold for fragments of bows, glasses, bottles, jars" (Columbus 1893, 8), and Martyr further celebrates the Mexican use of cacao beans instead of gold as money: "O felicem monetam," he writes, "which exempts its possessor from avarice, since it cannot be long hoarded nor hidden under ground"—so much for the principle of capital accumulation![14]

While Europeans primarily viewed New World gold as valuable for financial gain (granted its abundant use in churches), in Mesoamerica the yellow metal was linguistically linked to the gods, like many other natural substances. A 1571 dictionary of Spanish and Mexica languages, written and published in Mexico by the friar Alonso de Molino, translates "oro," or gold, as "cuzticteocuitlatl."[15] The key root in this word is "teo," which means "God" or "divine." Even the word for "money," which in its European sense did not technically exist in Mexico (and likely came into existence in the Mexica language after the conquest), contains a connection to the divine in Molino's translation: "teocuitlacocoualoni."[16] In Mesoamerica, then, gold was related to the divine, while in Europe it was related to the profane accumulation (despite its use in churches) of worldly wealth that ultimately led to the tragic demise of Amerindian culture. As David Hawkes writes rather acutely, we can "acknowledge what was obvious to most people in the sixteenth and seventeenth centuries: that the conquest of the world by capital was an unmitigated disaster, an irremediable injustice, and an unadulterated tragedy" (Hawkes 2001, 261). Bartolomé de Las Casas notes in his 1552 *Devastation of the Indies* (a text that is severely critical of his fellow Spanish Christians and helped foment the infamous 'Black Legend') that the "reason for killing and destroying such an infinite number of souls is that the Christians have an ultimate aim, which is to acquire gold" (Las Casas 1992, 31), and in an ironic scene Las Casas describes an Indian with a basket "full of gold and jewels" commenting sadly: "You see their God here, the God of the Christians" (Las Casas 1992, 44), essentially revealing gold as the focus of Christian idol worship. According to Gómara, Cortés wryly explained to Moctezuma, when asked why he wanted so much gold, that the Spanish "suffer from a disease of the hart which can be cured only with gold"—a disease better known as avarice, for which there is no cure (Gómara 58).

In Renaissance Europe, gold was synonymous with the Americas, and as such the New World kindled an inordinate desire for it (both metal and land), leading to the death of countless Amerindians in massive mining operations that early modern writers, such as Las Casas, frequently deride. A disdain for mining, especially its damaging effect on Earth, has a history in Western civilization: Agricola, Ovid, Seneca, and Lucretius all write about the horrors of mining mother earth.[17] Contemporaneous to Du Bartas, the English herbalist John Gerard echoes Lucretius in the preface to his *New Herball* (1597):

> Although my paines have not been spent (courteous Reader) in the gracious discoverie of golden mynes, nor in the tracing after silver vaines. . . . I confesse blinde Pluto is now adaies more sought after, than quicke sighted Phoebus, and yet this dustie mettall, or excrement of the earth (which was first deeply buried, least it should be an eyesore to greeve the corrupt hart of man) by forcible entrie made unto the bowels of the earth, is rather snatched at of man to his owne destruction, than directly sent of God, to the comfort of his life.

Gerard's condemnation of mining in a book about plants may seem odd; however, in the Renaissance gold was considered a plant that grew underground. In ancient Greece, philosophers believed that all metals grew as underground plants and that veins of gold were like branches of trees, as Peter Martyr echoes when he writes "the seams of gold are like a living tree."[18] Not surprisingly, Du Bartas associates gold in the *Divine Weeks* with the Indies through his fantastic creation of an Indian Griffin, a refiguring of a Greco-Roman creature (part eagle, part lion) used to characterize European avarice and the raping of Mother Earth. The griffin, like dragons, were quite real to Europeans, but existed in the past or faraway places. Edward Topsell's *The History of Four-Footed Beasts and Serpents* (1607) contains drawings of dragons based on Conrad Gesner's *Historiae Animalium* (1563), and on his travels through Mexico in 1599, Samuel Champlain produced a watercolor of a Mexican dragon that resembles a griffin (see Figure 7.1).

Champlain notes that this dragon, "ayants la teste approchante de celle d'un aigle" (it has the beak of an eagle), is just like a Griffin. Champlain was also probably influenced by images of the Mexican god, the plumed serpent, or Quetzalcoatl, which was integral to Mexican religion throughout Mesoamerica, its image appearing on pyramids and in codices

In Du Bartas, the Indian Griffin first appears with "fierce talons" and "with these, our Grandames fruitfull panch he pulls, / Whence many an Ingot of pure Gold he culls, / To floor his proud nest" (1.5.719–722), suggesting that the Griffin is guilty of pillaging the earth and hoarding the gold. Although Du Bartas ultimately figures the Indian Griffin as a protector of Mother Earth, here the Griffin stands in for greed (John Milton's comparison of Satan to a Griffin in *Paradise Lost* likely stems from Du Bartas). Importantly, the use of the word *ingot* implies a European transformation of gold, such as the Spanish mining ventures in the New World, thus suggesting that the Indian Griffin's "proud nest" is not Amerindian but rather Spanish. The hoarding of gold in a treasure trove, like Spenser's Mammon, who hoards his wealth and does not know the "right usance" of gold, is symptomatic of the Spanish protecting their American mining operations from intruders, as Du Bartas further notes: "He guards against an Army

PLANCHE XLVII.

Figure 7.1   From *Brief discours des choses plus remarquables que Samuel Champlain de Brouage á reconneues aux Indes occidentals.* JCBL.

bold / The hollow Mines where first he findeth Gold" (1.5.723–724).[19] The following stanza, to which Sylvester adds the marginalia, "Detestation of Avarice, for her execrable & dangerous effects" (Du Bartas 1979, 177), associates the valiant Indian Griffin with the Western tradition of abhorring mining practices:

> O! ever may'st thou fight so (valiant Foul)
> For this dire bane of our seduced soule . . .
> . . . O odious poyson! for the which we dive
> To *Pluto's* dark Den: for the which we rive
> Our Mother Earth; and, not contented with
> Th' abundant gifts she outward offereth,
> With sacrilegious Tools we rudely rend-her,
> And ransak deeply in her bosom tender. (1.5.727–738)

It is worth noting that in the original French Du Bartas uses the word "ame idolatre," or "idolatrous soul," in lieu of Sylvester's "seduced soul," which carries a notable anti-Catholic (and anti-Spanish) sentiment for Du Bartas's Protestant readers. When Du Bartas notes how this "valiant foule" (now associated with Amerindians) fights to keep the greedy humans from "riving" mother earth, "not contented with / Th' abundant gifts she outward offereth," he emphasizes how the Amerindians view mother earth similar to the antimining tradition espoused by European writers such as Gerard.

For Du Bartas, then, gold does not carry the mythical overtones of the Golden Age but rather the cold fact of European resource exploitation in the Americas and the distortion of the Amerindian relationship with the natural world. For the majority of Europeans, gold was extracted solely for its use as a commodity, but Du Bartas also imported the cultural knowledge of the Amerindian environment into his poetry. In addition to the ceiba and gold, the featherwork of the Mexica, or *arte plumaria*, attracts Du Bartas in a way that his onetime friend, King James I, derides in his *Counterblaste to Tobacco*, when he questions, "why doe we not as well imitate [Amerindians] . . . in preferring glasses, feathers, and such toyes, to golde?" (King James 1604, 02). True, for Amerindians feathers were preferred to gold, especially in Mesoamerica where plumage was connected to the divine, a connection that Du Bartas depicts through Eve's weaving of a Mesoamerican feather mantle for her mate, Adam.

> But, while that Adam (waxen diligent)
> Wearies his limbs for mutuall nourishment:
> While craggy Mountains, Rocks, and thorny Plains,
> And bristly Woods be witness of his pains:
> Eue, walking forth about the Forrests, gathers
> Speights, Parrots, Peacocks, Estrich scattered feathers,
> And then with wax the smaller plumes she sears,

And sowes the greater with a white horse hairs,
(For they as yet did serue her in the steed
Of Hemp, and Towe, and Flax, and Silk, and Threed)
And thereof makes a medly coat so rare
That it resembles Nature's Mantle fair,
When in the Sunne, in pomp all glistering,
She seems with smiles to woo the gawdie Spring.[20]
    (First Week, the Seventh Day, Handicrafts, 141–154)

The artisanal process is identical to the feather mantles made by the Mexica. In this manner, Du Bartas transforms Biblical Eve into a Mesoamerican feather-maker in the manner of the noblewomen of Montezuma, as described in the Spanish Chronicles. The conquistador Bernal Diaz de Castillo, for instance, writes that "at the house of great Montezuma, all the nobleman's daughters whom he kept to be his mistresses wove wondrous garments, and many other commoner's daughters, all of so decorous a bearing that one might take them to be nuns, also wove, all from feathers."[21] To understand further why Du Bartas might describe Eve as a Mexica feather artist, we must return to the country of origin, Mesoamerica, where feathers were among the most valued and religiously significant of natural resources: feathers were symbols of fertility, riches, nobility, martial strength, and divine power. According to Diego Durán, the "main idolatry [of the Mexica] was founded on the adorations of . . . feathers, which they called 'the shade of the gods."[22] The Mexican god of war, Huitzilopochtli ("left-winged hummingbird") was conceived immaculately when a ball of feathers landed upon the belly of his mother, Coatlicue (similar to the dove with Mary). The feather, then, was an integral part of Mexica religion and society, and an appropriate symbol for Eve to adopt, given Du Bartas's appreciation for Amerindian cosmology. The European chroniclers and Du Bartas, however, don't inform us what the Mexica believed in their own words. Returning to Molino's 1571 Spanish and Nauhatl dictionary reveals an astounding array of words which use the etymological root for bird: "tototl." "Totochiquiuitl" is a bird's nest and "Totoltetl" is a bird egg, and more significantly "Totomiquiliztli" means male impotence, and "Totonal" is the sign of something born with soul or spirit. It is worth noting that this last word is quite unlike the abstract notion of the Christian "soul" and its separation from the physical body. While the Christian religion can be considered an incarnational religion that looks to the resurrection of the *body*, the Mexica refer to the "soul" as something material, emphasizing the organic union of body and spirit, much like the Mosaic philosophers of Europe across the Atlantic.

    This conjunction of body and spirit is a form of organicism that is prevalent in Amerindian religions, where the natural world is imbued with the spirit of the cosmos. Du Bartas echoes Amerindian organicism, Mosaic philosophy, and the European Hermeticism of Giordano Bruno, who similarly linked body and spirit, unifying man with the cosmos and nature. According to Bruno, every human being was "a citizen and servant of the world, a child of Father Sun and Mother Earth,"[23] reflecting a unity between the cosmos and every living being on earth much like Du Bartas's vast tree. This holistic cosmology, "contrary to Christian and secular ones," writes López Austin, "brings to the foreground the interactions and "common union" of the body and the cosmos rather than the separation of body and spirit" (López Austin 1980, 470). And Walter Mignolo likewise states: "Amerindian epistemology . . . presupposed an interaction among living organisms rather than a separation between human beings and nature that [humanity] . . . could know, exploit, and use" (Mignolo 2008, 476). In short, the Amerindian animism, Mosaic and ethnographic philosophy of Du Bartas's poetry offered an alternative to the burgeoning capitalistic economy of Europe, which, along with monotheism, the emancipation of thought from myth, and the abstract separation of God from earth, stripped the sacred from nature and helped transform the natural world into a marketable resource. And perhaps more remarkably, Du Bartas's engagement with the natural world and inhabitants of America realigns the Christian narrative with a new global age of the mestizaje, or mixing of cultures. In this manner, while Du Bartas may seem scientifically backward in his understanding of the cosmos, he was perhaps more modern in his affirmation and recognition of a rapidly hybridizing world.

Although Du Bartas celebrated the faith of Mesoamerican featherwork, the emergence of this Atlantic Network of cultural and material exchange had, and still has, profound consequences on the environment of the Americas: the "Golden Age must have an iron ending," as Fletcher presciently writes in his *Sea Voyage*. Rather than stress the exploitation of the New World, the cultural coupling described in this essay reveals a relationship between Europe and the New World that precludes the traditional system of binaries—colonizer/colonized, civilized/barbarian, pagan/Christian, devilish/angelic, metropole/periphery—and rather explores a continuity or sameness that existed in the transatlantic world. While seemingly anathema to a European worldview, du Bartas's particular brand of cosmology espoused in the *Divine Weeks* views the entire earth and its inhabitants as part of the *All* (his preferred word for God), thus acknowledging the New World as *similar to* rather than different from Europe.

NOTES

1. Kathryn Banks, *Cosmos and Image in the Renaissance*, 13.
2. Bacon, *New Organum*, aphorism 65. It is worth noting that even though Bacon labels it heresy, he likewise mixes the biblical and scientific in odd ways throughout the *New Atlantis* (1624).
3. See Ann Blair, "Mosaic Physics . . . ," 33.

4. While medieval scholars will point out that the mixing of Christianity with pagan religions occurred in medieval Europe (where religious systems interacted and blended together over several centuries), the discovery of the New World in the Renaissance provided a completely foreign, new, unknown, and nonlocal paganism with which Christianity assimilated with new vigor. The transition and confrontation was immediate. Du Bartas reflects one of the more syncretic approaches toward indigenous peoples by incorporating their beliefs as opposed to supplanting them.

5. Most of the recent work on Du Bartas comes out of France, not surprisingly. For recent scholarship in English not mentioned in this article, see: Banderier, Gilles, "Linguistic and Ideological Stakes in the Translations of Du Bartas," *Neuphilologische Mitteilungen* (2005), 106.3, 337–348; Heather, Noel, "Number, Symmetry and Order in Du Bartas' Semaines: Reform of Church and Sky?" *Renaissance Studies: Journal of the Society for Renaissance Studies*, (1991), 5.3, 288–300; Parker, Ian C., "Marvell's Use of Sylvester's Du Bartas, II.iv.4," *Notes and Queries* (2006), vol. 53.2, 172–178.

6. Gabriel Harvey's assessment of Du Bartas is mentioned in Prescott (1978), 194. The influence on Milton is noted in Snyder, 84, and Prescott (1978), 191.

7. For a detailed analysis of *Mapamundi*, see Mignolo, 471–493.

8. For the Christian split with the natural world, see Watson, Mignolo, and Merchant.

9. For theological disputes on humans containing the breath of God, see Kathryn Banks, *Cosmos*, 41–47.

10. Walter Mignolo discusses Amerindian versions of Gaia, 478.

11. The cerba, or ceiba, is described in Fernández de Oviedo's *Historia Natural de las Indias*, 9.2; in Chapter 13 of Jean de Léry's *Voyage to Brazil*; and in José De Acosta's *Historia Natural y Moral de las Indias*, book 4, Chapter 30.

12. El Dorado is the mythic "Golden Man" who Sir Walter Raleigh sought in his Discovery of Guiana; "Of Solomon's Ophir or the Lande of Perue" (ms. 494, Lambeth Palace, UK) uses biblical quotes to prove that Peru is source of Solomon's gold; see also Edmund Campos, "West of Eden," 254, for an analysis of Solomon's Ophir in Richard Eden's writings. William Vaughan wrote *The Golden Fleece* (1626), which discusses the commodities of Newfoundland, especially codfish.

13. As qtd. in Greenblatt, 228.

14. Martyr, *Decades*, Decade 5, Chapter 4.

15. See Fol 91r of Molino's *Vocabulario En Lengua Castellana y Mexicana*. Casa de Antonio de Spinosa. Mexico, 1571. This text is housed at the John Carter Brown Library.

16. Fol 87r.

17. See Merchant, *Death of Nature*, 3, for antimining tracts by Agricola, Ovid, Seneca, and Lucretius.

18. The philosophers are: Anaxagoras (500–428 BC), Theophrastus (370–278 BC), and Dionysius of Perigetes (fl. AD 86–96). See Merchant, 29, 73. Martyr, *Decades de Orbe Novo*, III, 7; III, 8.

19. See Campos and David Read, *Temperate Conquests*. Karen Edwards notes that Sir Walter Raleigh defines the griffin in terms of the colonial activities in the New World (Edwards, 103).

20. Sylvester changes Du Bartas's original by replacing "L'Oriot" (Oriole) feathers with "Estrich" feathers.

21. Yturbide, 80; Durán, *Historia de las Indias* 2, 206.

22. Yturbide, 40; Durán, *Historia de las Indias* 2, 206

23. Merchant, 25.

REFERENCES

Acosta, José de. 1988. *Historia Natural y moral de las Indias*. Ed. José de Alcina Franch. Madrid: Cronicas de America.

Bacon, Sir Francis. 1620. *Novum Organum*. London. John Bill.

Banks, Kathryn. 2008. *Cosmos and Image in the Renaissance: French Love Lyric and Natural-Philosophical Poetry*. London: Legenda.

Blair, Ann. 2000. Mosaic Physics and the Search for a Pious Natural Philosophy in the Late Renaissance. *Isis* 91.1, 32–58.

Columbus, Christopher. 1893. *Letter of Christopher Columbus*. Chicago: W.H. Lowdermilk.

Dodoens, D. Rembert. 1554. *Cruydeboeck*. Antwerp: Jan vander Loë.

Du Bartas, Guillaume de Saluste Sieur. 1935. *The Works of Guillaume de Saluste Sieur Du Bartas: A Criticial Edition with Introduction, Commentary, and Variants*. Edited by Urban Tigner Holmes Jr., John Coriden Lyons, and Robert White Linker. 3 vols. Chapel Hill: University of North Carolina Press.

———. 1979. *The Divine Weeks and Works of Guillaume de Saluste Sieur du Bartas*. Edited by Susan Snyder, translated by Joshua Sylvester. Oxford: Clarendon Press.

Durán, Fray Diego. 1967. *Historia de las Indias de Nueva España e Islas de la Tierra Firme*. 2 vols. Mexico: Porrua.

Gerard, John. 1597. *The Herball or Generall Historie of Plantes*. London: Edm. Bollifant for [Bonham Norton and] Iohn Norton.

Gesner, Conrad. 1563. *Historiae Animalium*. Zurich: Christoffel froschauer.

Gómara, Francisco Lopez de. 1964. *Cortés: The Life of the Conqueror by His Secretary*. Translated by Lesley Byrd Simpson. Berkeley: University of California Press.

Greenblatt, Stephen. 1980. *Renaissance Self-Fashioning: From More to Shakespeare*. Chicago: University of Chicago Press.

Hawkes, David. 2001. *Idols of the Marketplace: Idolatry and Commodity Fetishism in English Literature, 1580–1680*. New York: Palgrave.

James, I, King of England. 1604. *A counterblaste to Tobacco*. Imprinted at London: By R. B[arlter].

Las Casas, Bartholomé de. 1992. *The Devastation of the Indies: A Brief Account*. Edited by Bill Donovan. Baltimore: Johns Hopkins University Press.

López Austin, Alfredo. 1980. *Cuerpo humano e ideologia: Las concepciones de los antiguos náhuas*. Mexico City: Universidad Nacional Autónoma de México.

Martin, Catherine Gimelli. 2001. "'What If the Sun Be Centre to the World?': Milton's Epistemology, Cosmology, and Paradise of Fools Reconsidered." *Modern Philology* 99.2, 231–265.

Martyr, Pedro de Anglería. 1944. *Décadas del Nuevo Mundo*. Argentina: Editorial Bajel.

Marx, Karl. 1977. *Capital*. Vol. 1. New York: Vintage.

Merchant, Carolyn. 1983. *The Death of Nature: Women, Ecology, and the Scientific Revolution*. San Francisco: HarperCollins.

Mignolo, Walter D. 2008. "Commentary" in José de Acosta's *Historia Natural y Moral de las Indias*. Ed. Fermín del Pino-Díaz. Madrid: Consejo Superior de Investigaciones Científicas.

Molino, Fray Alonso de. 1571. *Vocabulario En Lengua Castellana y Mexicana*. Mexico: Casa de Antonio de Spinosa.

Prescott, Anne Lake. 1968. "The Reception of Du Bartas in England." In *Studies in the Renaissance* 15, 144–173.

———. 1978. *French Poets and the English Renaissance: Studies in Fame and Transformation*. New Haven, CT: Yale University Press.

———. 2004. "Du Bartas and Renaissance Britain: An Update." Ed. Yvonne Bellenger. *Oeuvres & Critiques* 29.2, 27–38.

Topsell, Edward. 1658. *The History of four-footed Beasts and Serpants*. London: Printed by F. Coles for G. Sawbridge, T. Williams, and T. Johnson.

Walton, Izaak. 1655. *The Complete Angler*. London: Printed by T. M. for Rich Marriot.

Watson, Robert N. 2006. *Back to Nature: The Green and the Real in the Late Renaissance*. Philadelphia: University of Pennsylvania Press.

Yturbide, Teresa Castello. 1993. *The Art of Featherwork in Mexico*. Houston: Wetmore & Company Press.

8 Erasure by U.S. Legislation

Ruiz de Burton's Nineteenth-Century Novels and the Lost Archive of Mexican American Environmental Knowledge

Priscilla Solis Ybarra

Young, intelligent, and beautiful, albeit powerless, Mexican women play the central roles in María Amparo Ruiz de Burton's two novels, *Who Would Have Thought It?* (1872) and *The Squatter and the Don* (1885). Ruiz de Burton's young Mexican women, the most important protagonists of her two novels, demonstrate the ways that the U.S. took advantage of a vulnerable population in order to erase the Mexican American contribution to shaping the land we now call the U.S. Southwest. As their names suggest, the young women suffer cruel trials associated with land and its resources in the years following the 1848 U.S.–Mexico War. Dolores, of course, means "sorrows," and Mercedes can mean "mercy" and also "land grants." In this context, the secondary meaning of Mercedes's name becomes more significant because the Mexican American population gained their lands through Spanish and Mexican-era land grants that were often invalidated in the U.S. courts after 1848, transforming a ranching aristocracy into a laboring class in a few short years (Montejano 1987, 50–74; Griswold de Castillo 1990, 62–107). Ruiz de Burton herself was a young woman during this time of transition, so it is not surprising that she writes indignantly about the injustices that she witnessed (and suffered) first hand (Aranda 2003, 95). Scholars recognize that hers was a voice of opposition to the U.S. political collusion with Anglo-American businessmen to exploit Mexican Americans and to take over their lands (Aranda 2003, 81–117; Rivera 2006, 82–109; Alemán 2004). Scholars also agree that Ruiz de Burton articulated a feminist argument in her novels, showing how women's powerlessness occasions needless harm (Sanchez and Pita 2005; Casas 2007, 159–167). However, little attention has been given to the way that Ruiz de Burton's writings comprise an early Mexican American environmentalism.

Ruiz de Burton's novels were written and set in the early days of national parks, some of which—like the iconic Yosemite—the U.S. established in newly acquired Mexican territories. Indeed, John Muir's descriptions of Yosemite convinced many U.S. politicians, including President Theodore

Roosevelt, to approve the preservation of natural spaces, making Yosemite a benchmark in the development of wilderness parks (Fox 1981, 103–147). Environmental historian William Cronon notes, in his now well-known critique of the wilderness idea, "Yosemite was deeded by the United States government to the State of California in 1864 as the nation's first wild-land park, and Yellowstone became the first true national park in 1872" (Cronon 1998, 474). Yosemite became a national park in 1890. But before the U.S. could deed Yosemite to the State of California and then later make it an iconic national park, the U.S. had to start and win the U.S.–Mexico War. Neither environmental studies nor Chicana/o studies make note of this war as a key transition relevant to *environmental* history, yet the take-over of Mexican lands helped make possible one of the most important ideas that we have used in the twentieth century to inspire environmental sentiment: wilderness. For the idea of wilderness to work, the U.S. had to erase not only the Native American but also the Mexican American transformation of the natural environment in California, Nevada, Utah, New Mexico, Texas, Arizona, and parts of Wyoming, Colorado, Utah, and Kansas—all former territories of Mexico.

Moreover, environmentalism's active promotion of wilderness has served to alienate people of color (Guha 1989). Cronon notes that "[t]he removal of Indians to create an 'uninhabited wilderness'—uninhabited as never before in the human history of the place—reminds us just how invented, just how constructed, the American wilderness really is" (Cronon 1998, 482). In the case of Mexican Americans, wilderness and the national parks serve as a stark reminder of what Ruiz de Burton puts at the center of both her novels: that nineteenth-century American imperialism disenfranchised and dispossessed the Mexicans who chose to stay on their lands, lands suddenly located in the U.S. after 1848. Important for an environmental analysis of Ruiz de Burton's two novels, the imperial attitude also kept the U.S. from gaining the significant skills, knowledge, and loyalty of the new Mexican Americans, estimated to be approximately 100,000 in number (Griswold del Castillo 1990, 62). This lost repository of knowledge and loyalty becomes ecologically significant when one considers the fact that landholding Mexicans had learned a great deal about how to profitably and sustainably manage their haciendas.

U.S. imperial fervor obscured Mexican American environmental knowledge in favor of two broadly environmental goals that would develop over the later nineteenth century: ultimately, to create national parks in "wild" areas that would help establish a U.S. national identity based on iconic places; and more immediately, to use what Anglo-American farmers considered underdeveloped Mexican American ranchlands to implement tried and true agricultural practices—tried and true in the well-watered North American East and Midwest—that were unfortunately inefficient and unsuitable to the climate and terrain beyond the hundredth meridian. Concerning the goal of creating wilderness, Americans felt they had lived too long in the shadow of ancient European civilizations, and they looked to the newly acquired West and its monumental scenery to compete. Historian Alfred Runte says of this period that "[t]he agelessness of monumental scenery instead of the past accomplishments of Western Civilization was to become the visible symbol of continuity and stability in the new nation" (Runte 1997, 12). Ruiz de Burton's Dolores in *Who Would Have Thought It?* exposes U.S. hypocrisy, especially through violations of the Treaty of Guadalupe Hidalgo, concerning the lands and peoples it abused in order to provide these national symbols.

As to the latter goal concerning competing land-use approaches, Mike Davis has observed that, in contrast to the American Indian cultures as well as the Spanish and Mexican colonizers, the "Anglo-American conquistadors . . . were riven by confusion and ambivalence" concerning the semiarid climate of the newly acquired territories (Davis 1995, 224):

> Immigrants from the humid states, moreover, brought with them deeply engrained prejudices about climate and landscape that had been shaped by the environmental continuum of Northwestern Europe and the Eastern United States. (Davis 1995, 225–226)

Ruiz de Burton's *The Squatter and the Don* shows how Mexican American ranchers attempted to educate the newly arrived eastern Americans about the unique challenges of semiarid agriculture, but California state laws supported an imperial agenda that discouraged Anglo-Americans from working with the Mexican Americans.

In the pages of Ruiz de Burton, it is no coincidence that Dolores travels to New England with a treasure trove of gems from the Western U.S. in *Who Would Have Thought It?* and that *The Squatter and the Don* begins with a debate between a Mexican rancher ("the Don") and a group of Anglo squatters—one of whom will eventually court the Don's daughter Mercedes. With her two female protagonists, Ruiz de Burton shows how the U.S.–Mexico War created the possibility for Mexicans to become new and empowered citizens of the U.S. and for Americans to work together with them for a common good: a sound democracy and development of beautiful, fertile, and productive territories. However, U.S. greed for Mexican American citizens' lands and mineral rights resulted in an alienation of the new citizens from their lands as well as from their new nation. We live with the legacy of this forsaken cooperation to this day. Recent studies indicate that Latinos are the ethnic group most exposed to toxic harms. Former Congresswoman Hilda Solis (now Secretary of Labor) states in a foreword to a Natural Resources Defense Council study on urban toxicity: "Our [Latino] children disproportionately suffer from asthma as a result of air pollution, and pregnant women and the elderly suffer from lead and other contaminants in our drinking water" (Solis 2004, iv). A UC–Irvine research team has shown how there is presently a "disproportionate proximity to toxic waste among Latinos" in Southern California (Hipp and Lakon 2010, 681). Moreover, the semiarid climate of Southern California continues to be misunderstood by its current population (Davis 1995). Ruiz de Burton recounts the pain of the initial steps toward these environmental wastes and injustices in her two artfully crafted novels, written in a unique blend of sentimental Victorian romance and matter-of-fact social criticism.

In the opening scenes of *Who Would Have Thought It?* the patriarch of an Anglo New England family, Dr. Norval, returns from a four-year trip out West. He planned these trips as often as possible in order to pursue his amateur science of collecting various rock specimens, and, perhaps, in the hopes of discovering a profitable location for mining. His wife, three daughters, and spinster sister-in-law await his arrival with mixed emotions. They look forward to the long-awaited reunion but dread the intrusion of the geologic samples that Dr. Norval customarily brings back from these trips. Eldest daughter Ruth, upon sighting the heavy wagonload accompanying her father, observes: "More rocks and pebbles, of course. But I don't know where he is to put them: the garret is full now" (13).

Far from depicting a scene where wife, daughters, and sister-in-law clamor to receive gifts and tidings from an exotic place, Ruiz de Burton shows these women to be toughened against such expectations. Judging from the family's disdain, Dr. Norval's samples apparently never before amounted to anything more than burdensome curiosities. This, however, would prove to be an altogether different collection of samples, beginning with the dark little girl at his side. The "rocks and pebbles" eventually transform the Norval women into wealthy socialites, and the dark little girl becomes the reason for their shift in fortune. Nonetheless, all but one of the Norval women choose to hate the little girl, even after she is no longer dark—her skin tone results from her Indian captors' strategy to keep her hidden amongst them by using a dye to color her skin. When she grows up, Dolores Medina, a.k.a. "Lola," becomes beautiful, light-skinned, wealthy, and well bred; but only after years of loneliness in the Norval household.

Lola's story is about as unbelievable as the idea that one nation would take over half its neighbor's territory and then "discover" a wealth of precious minerals and beautiful landscapes within it. In other words, this historical novel's seemingly far-fetched events suit the times in which they occur. Lola's mother was captured by "Indians"—the novel never specifies which tribe—from her wealthy family's hacienda when Lola was still unborn. Lola is born five months after her mother is captured, therefore proving her "pure Spanish blood." The chief wants Lola's mother, Theresa, for his wife, but Theresa only agrees when she gets assurances from the Indians that no one will touch her daughter. When Lola is ten, the Indian chief turns ill and runs across Dr. Norval's explorer party. Dr. Norval agrees to treat the chief and subsequently meets Theresa. Theresa asks Dr. Norval to promise to take Lola with him, away from the "savages," when he returns to New England. Dr. Norval agrees to take Lola with him and to do all he can to reunite the girl with her long-lost family in Mexico. Anticipating Lola's departure, Theresa's health begins to decline. However, before she loses all strength, she manages to collect and deliver to Dr. Norval a cache of rough gold nuggets and raw precious gems. She collected the cache during the tribe's wanderings and saved it to assist in Lola's escape, if such a time ever arrived.

Lola and the rough stones share a fate: upon their arrival in New England, both are belittled and disdained, yet, upon closer examination, the "little girl very black indeed" becomes white, and the "rocks and pebbles" (13) that threaten to "scratch the oilcloth, which was nearly new" become precious stones and metals. Likewise, the economic situation of the family improves, but their morality becomes corrupted as they try to separate the compañeras—Lola and her stones. When they succeed in separating Lola from her riches, they discard her without a care, but remain vigilant of her precious "rocks and pebbles." This plot mimics the Americans' attempts to cheat Mexican Americans and indigenous peoples out of their lands, especially once they learn that the lands contain precious stones and metals.

The only thing between Lola and utter powerlessness in the hands of the Norval family and others that lust after her wealth is a document her mother dictated in the final hours of her captivity to a scribe and translator provided by Dr. Norval. Dr. Norval, in all honesty and honorable intention, planned to rely upon this document to help him locate Lola's father in Mexico. But because he does not speak Spanish, he had to depend on his associate to take down Theresa's story, including the very important names of Lola's family. The associate then translated the document and mailed it to Dr. Norval. However, the document never arrives at the Norval home and instead arrives at the "dead letters" room at a post office in Washington, DC. Without the document that tells him whom to contact about Lola's whereabouts, Dr. Norval must take charge of Lola's care and education as well as her gold and precious gems.

Two significant parallels develop here between Lola's story and the story of Mexican Americans and their lands post-1848. First, the peoples' fate and that of their lands relies upon a single document: in Lola's case it was her mother's narrative; in the case of the Mexican Americans it was the Treaty of Guadalupe Hidalgo, which ended the war and included a pledge from the U.S. to protect the rights and lands of Mexican Americans. Second, because of the U.S. government's careless treatment of the respective important documents (loss of the narrative and violation of the Treaty of Guadalupe Hidalgo), Lola and her precious stones, and the Mexican Americans and their valuable lands, become subject to the whims of the U.S. government, state and local officials, corrupt businessmen, and a cruel social hierarchy. Lola's trajectory in *Who Would Have Thought It?* mirrors the vexed fate of Mexican Americans in the nineteenth century. Ruiz de Burton sees herself, as do all her fellow upper-class Mexican Americans, as racially "white," tracing her lineage back to Spain, and as a member of a privileged and distinguished social class. Yet, she also recognizes that the bulk of Americans in the wake of the U.S.–Mexico War view Mexicans as racially dark, putting them in a class little deserving of distinction or possessions. In her novel, she attempts to show how this perception of Mexican American racial "darkness" is only a temporary effect, like the dye that darkens Lola's skin. The discovery of gold on formerly Mexican territories, such as California and Arizona, and the establishment of wilderness areas and national parks in former Mexican territories only serve to exacerbate the instinct Americans already had to disdain the newest Americans: Mexicans. Likewise, Lola's precious metals and stones make most of the Norvals harbor disdain for her. Ruiz de Burton offers Lola's fascinating tale as a parallel to the cruel reality that many Mexican Americans experienced post-1848.

Despite her portrayal of loss and betrayal, Ruiz de Burton nonetheless writes her narrative in a way that challenges Americans to see the ways that Mexican Americans can still make a positive impact on their adopted nation. For example, on the night of Lola's arrival to the Norval home, Dr. Norval and his wife engage in a tense conversation, "'I think that Lola, instead of being a *burden* to us, will be a great acquisition. Don't you think so?' said the doctor, after his wife had toyed with the gold for some time" (Ruiz de Burton 1995, 25). In this intimate scene between husband and wife, Dr. Norval struggles to convince his harsh wife to welcome the little girl to their home and uses the gold to push her toward generosity. Mrs. Norval, for her own part, initially questions her first response to reject Lola:

> The despised black child she now would give worlds to keep. She would go on her knees to serve her, as her servant, her slave, rather than let her go . . . Thus ran the thoughts of the high principled matron. But never once did it occur to her that she had sent the child to sleep with the cook and the chambermaid, and she did not know that the little girl was now crying as if her heart were breaking, calling her mother between sobs. . . . (Ruiz de Burton 1995, 30)

Here we see Mrs. Norval begin to reason that the little girl can bring distinction to her home and family by means of her riches. At this point in the story it is still possible to associate Lola closely with her accompanying goods. If only the Norval family had continued to think in these terms, Lola would not have suffered a childhood and youth of loneliness and disdain. The Norvals could have worked with Lola to make the most of their fortunes together.

However, Mrs. Norval soon reasons that she can contrive to take the gold and gems from Lola for her own use and even rationalizes that she deserves them as reward for allowing Lola to set foot in her home. She asks her husband, "Didn't her mother give you anything for taking charge of her daughter for life?" (Ruiz de Burton 1995, 29). Later in the novel, Mrs.

Norval further attempts to rationalize her family's use of the riches that Lola does not deserve or even supposedly know how to put to good use: "And would that little nigger be so rich, and her girls so poor? Their new carriages and splendid horses and handsome house, after all, did not make Mrs. N. happy" (Ruiz de Burton 1995, 49). At the same time, Ruiz de Burton editorializes that the family's use of Lola's riches does not increase their happiness: it just makes them want more and care for Lola even less. The way that Americans rejected Mexican Americans in the nineteenth century certainly gave them access to more lands, mineral rights, and freedom to establish national parks, but they lost the opportunity to establish alliances with deserving peoples.

History does not show Mexican Americans escaping a measure of discrimination and inequality until well into the twentieth century, but Ruiz de Burton gives Lola a hopeful future after years of suffering in the Norval clan. Dr. Norval continued to be her protector and confidante, but his increasing frustration with his family's greed and the hypocrisy of his government during the Civil War drives him to take a risky expedition to the African continent. He entrusts Lola to the guardianship of his son Julian, who is beginning to fall in love with Lola but who is also very distracted with his service as an officer in the Union army. This leaves Lola relatively vulnerable to the manipulations of Mrs. Norval and her secret lover, the onetime preacher turned military officer John Hackwell. Lola narrowly manages to escape plots to completely deprive her of her property and self-determination only after Mrs. Norval's younger brother Isaac, of all people, discovers the lost letter containing Theresa's narrative concerning Lola. Isaac finds Lola's father and grandfather in Mexico and brings them to New York where Lola lives with the Norvals. Julian, Dr. Norval, and a few other allies work to foil the plots against Lola and she eventually returns home to Mexico and marries Julian.

The recurring refrain in the novel does not concern social discrimination as much as it critiques government failure to honor its commitments. Indeed, the government of Mexico suffers harsh critique from Ruiz de Burton alongside the U.S. Congress. The narrator comments, "If Mexico were well governed, if her frontiers were well protected, the fate of Doña Theresa would have been next to an impossibility . . . If we were to trace our troubles to their veritable source, we would often reach, more or less directly, their origin in *our lawgivers*" (Ruiz de Burton 1995, 201). Of course, part of what weakens the Mexican government's vigilance over its borders is the U.S. impulse to satisfy Manifest Destiny and expand its own boundaries. The U.S. and especially the Northern abolitionists are subject to constant caricature in this novel, from the bumbling fool who becomes a hero of the Civil War because his horse is spooked to charge into battle, to Mrs. Norval, who crusades on behalf of the enslaved but indulges deep hatred toward Lola. For Ruiz de Burton, the U.S. legislators in their greed and collusion with Anglo-American businessmen kept the U.S. from welcoming

Mexican Americans. Such is also the case in *The Squatter and the Don*, where Ruiz de Burton further argues that Mexican Americans had vital environmental skills and a thriving culture to offer the U.S.

The Alamar family in Ruiz de Burton's 1885 novel *The Squatter and the Don* own an expansive cattle hacienda in the San Diego area. In this novel, the Alamares, especially the patriarch Don Mariano Alamar, make clear their knowledge of California ecology. The title of the novel itself reveals a story of California land use in the late nineteenth century: the Anglo-American squatters came to California from the East Coast of the U.S. in search of lands to settle and farm, while "the Dons," or Mexican American hacienda/ ranch owners, already had land-use practices well developed in California. In *The Squatter and the Don,* the proud Ruiz de Burton, who was born in 1832 into a family who owned lands in Baja California, depicts her compatriots' experiences. Ruiz de Burton contrasts the Mexican hacienda owners' land use to that of the new population of Anglo-American squatters. The point is not to romanticize *Californio* ecological knowledge; history clearly reveals Spanish introduction of invasive species and manipulative technologies. However, the *Californios* had acquired an intimate knowledge of the land they had worked and shaped for at least a century, and they could not help but object to the unwise agricultural practices of the newly arrived Americans.

Ruiz de Burton demonstrates *Californio* authority regarding the land, particularly in an early scene. Don Mariano Alamar proposes a compromise to the Anglos squatting on his land and killing his cattle. A couple of factors contributed to the encroachment of farmers on California ranches—in the novel and in actual historical fact. Squatters settled on ranches that they erroneously believed available for new American settlers on the strength of the recent U.S. takeover. They killed cattle because they claimed the cattle ruined their newly planted crops by wandering among the plants and eating the green shoots. However, killing cattle to protect crops—an activity sanctioned by the "no fence law"—was not just an act of crop defense. The "no fence law," passed by the California legislature in 1874, made the fencing-in of cattle the responsibility of the ranchers, and it protected any farmer who shot cattle that wandered into their crops (Raup 1959, 65). Of course, the ranchers never used fences prior to this law and it would be a huge expense to implement them. The practice of farmers shooting cattle reduced ranch capital and made ranch owners less and less financially capable of defending their lands in the courts.

In response to the above cattle-shooting scenario, Don Mariano calls a meeting to propose a compromise to the squatters. Although he could justifiably consider the squatters greedy invaders, the novel clearly shows him attempting to find common ground by invoking the enterprise in which they are all engaged. He says: "The reason why you have taken up land here is because you want homes. You want to make money. Isn't that the reason? Money! money!" (Ruiz de Burton 1992, 86). The squatters reply in the affirmative to this proclamation, some of them even laughing. Then the Don presents a plan to them with which they can stay on the rancho without paying for the lands they have settled, make more money, and (in his interest) protect his cattle.

In summary, the plan involves an agricultural shift for the farmers from the struggle to cultivate wheat and other grains to the growth of fruit trees and vineyards, after an initial period of raising cattle—he says "plant vineyards, olives, figs, oranges; make wines and oil and raisins; export olives and dried and canned fruits" (Ruiz de Burton 1992, 88). This agricultural shift would enable two key changes for the Don that would also benefit the farmers. First, the farmers would use less land—as orchards and vineyards require less space than grain production—and therefore it would be feasible for them to build fences to keep out the cattle. If the cattle were no longer threatening the farmers' harvests, they no longer would have any right or need to kill the cattle. They would have one less chore on their busy farms. Second, the Don would gain allies in business rather than legal foes, and the farmers would benefit from the Don's local environmental knowledge in order to work towards successful enterprise in the greater San Diego region. In short, the farmers would continue the activity for which they moved west: the cultivation of produce. They would simply change from one kind of cultivation to another more sustainable one, and they would shed the task of shooting helpless cows every evening.

However, several details, left unattended, would surely impede the plan. First of all, the cultivation of successful fruit orchards and vineyards takes years. The farmers would have to find another enterprise to keep them in the black until the orchards and vineyards could yield. The Don answers this query with a practical proposal: he would give each farmer a number of cattle, and give them each five years or so to repay him, at no interest. This meant that as long as they bred the cattle adequately, the reproduction of the cattle themselves would generate enough animals to repay the Don. This question of repayment, of course, suggests that the Don may want the farmers to pay for the lands they were currently squatting. However, the Don assures them that they will all retain their homesteads, at no cost. He promises to quit fighting their claims in the courts and present each of them with a quitclaim deed.

Still, in the face of all these advantages, the squatters reject Don Mariano's proposal. They scorn his plan on the basis of cultural difference, saying "perhaps you understand *vaquering* [cowboying]; we don't," at the same time mocking the Spanish language. Unfortunately, in one of the book's greatest ironies, Don Mariano's plan fails because the Americans cannot imagine themselves as vaqueros, or *cowboys*—an image that these days stands as one of the globally most recognizable symbols of the American West. By invoking their common enterprise, agriculture, and environmental knowledge that can help them work toward their economic goals, Don Mariano hopes to strike a working compromise with the squatters. And this compromise, this bridging of cultures, just may have been possible, if it were not for the existence of a "higher law" which the squatters could invoke in their favor. The law they invoke is not of any environmental or moral origin, but the "no fence law" handed down to them from legislators who sought to promote a familiar Eastern American agriculture that was out of place in semiarid California. Rejecting the Don's proposal that they become ranchers, the squatters also reject the one standard that the Don would hold them to if they insisted on planting wheat: to fence their crops. A squatter named Mathews explains: "I am not so big a fool as to spend money in fences. The 'no fence law' is better than all the best fences" (Ruiz de Burton 1992, 90). More than just protecting crops, the "no fence law" protects an imperial agenda, giving familiar American enterprise an upper hand at the cost of *Californio* culture and environmental knowledge. While the squatters may be benefiting from the laws, the true culprits in the novel are legislators and monopoly capitalists.

Further reflection on the Don's proposal reveals ways that the squatters and the Mexican Americans could have found common ground. Indeed, the Don's plan begs the question: why would Don Mariano propose a plan to the squatters that would enable their acquisition of land that was originally granted to his family by Spain and Mexico? One would imagine that he would be doing everything within his power to run the squatters off his lands. However, the impulse to acquire and settle new territories resonates with him. His ancestors, who originally acquired the Alamar rancho from Native Americans, were pioneers in "unsettled" territory, just as the squatters on the rancho were the most recent wave of pioneers in territory they considered "unsettled," or at least underdeveloped, as well. In his meeting with the squatters, Don Mariano addresses them as equals, and he invokes their common ground. Later, he even says to Clarence, a squatter's son and his daughter's suitor, "I don't find it in my heart to blame those people [the squatters] for taking my land as much as I blame the legislators who turned them loose upon me" (Ruiz de Burton 1992, 161). Indeed, Clarence's many failed attempts to court Don Mariano's daughter Mercedes result from the squatters' rejection of Don Mariano's mutually beneficial plan.

However, the span of time that separates the colonial wave of Spanish and Mexican settlement to California from the imperial wave of U.S./ American settlement to California also represents differences in approach to settlement and cultural traditions. The Mexican Americans and the Anglo-American squatters do not readily recognize their commonalities as outsiders in California. The Spanish colonizers and Mexican settlers who arrived in California in the sixteenth, seventeenth, and eighteenth centuries sought to establish outposts, missions, and eventually a nation-state, in territories already inhabited by American Indians. Perhaps the opportunity for cooperation between Spanish settlers and American Indian settlements existed in early encounters. Yet, the pattern of violent engagements, land takeovers, and imposed religious conversions in the Spanish settlement of the Americas is well known. And the Spanish invoked the same reasoning that the Americans intoned in later years about the Mexican Americans: the previous inhabitants did not adequately develop the resources of the land.

The colonization of the Americas by the Spanish initiated an eco-logical revolution from lower-impact American Indian horticulture and extensive burning to facilitate the growth of plants palatable to game animals to European-style ranching, including the introduction of new species. As environmental historian William Preston, writing about environmental change in colonial California, observes about the American Indians in California:

> These peoples for the most part were not farmers so much as domes-ticators, and in a number of important respects all had domesticated portions of their habitat in order to induce greater subsistence. Instead of relying on the axe, rake, or plow, they skillfully learned to prune, till, coppice, transplant, and burn California's vegetation in order to encourage a greater abundance of plant and animal foods and materi-als. The land yielded its bounty to the ingenuity of native intervention and was substantially transformed in the process. (Preston 1998, 289)

That the colonial Spanish and Mexicans were blind to the Indian domes-tication of California is clear. In the same way, U.S./Americans underesti-mated the Spanish and Mexican knowledge and influence over the land. One of the more significant changes was the way that U.S. imperial settle-ment of California initiated an ecological revolution from a land-grant sys-tem to a land-tenure system. This is a significant shift, in scale, from large landholdings managed by an elite class, to smaller parcels of land man-aged by many more individuals and families of varying class status. This made an ecological impact, to be sure, although arguably this transition was bound to occur sooner or later as the population of North America steadily grew.

The real bit of wisdom to gather from Ruiz de Burton's depiction of this historical moment is the fact that Mexican Americans and their environ-mental knowledge were factored out of the land-management equation at a key moment of transition. And they felt a great deal of betrayal about this process at the initial moment of their acquisition of U.S. citizenship and participation in U.S. democracy, that is, immediately following the U.S.–Mexico War. Indeed, Don Mariano's dying words are not for love of family but for the heartbreak that his new nation caused him. Upon being asked by Mercedes if she can help relieve his pain, he whispers, "Too late. The sins of our legislators!" (Ruiz de Burton 1992, 304). That Ruiz de Bur-ton wrote in the same era that the American Transcendentalists (including Ralph Waldo Emerson and John Muir) were writing foundational environ-mental texts and that the U.S. was initiating a new era of environmental protection for the world is not an irony lost on Mexican Americans—in the nineteenth century and today.

Preserving and communicating the Mexican American perspective on the environment is certainly not Ruiz de Burton's primary goal in *Who Would Have Thought It?* or *The Squatter and the Don*, but she weaves this concern into the complex tapestry of other incisive social critiques. Importantly, she also lays bare the groundwork that will continue to support evolving Mexican American views on the environment. In spite of this early alienation of Mexican Americans from their lands and the attempted erasure of their environmental practices and insights, Chicana/o writers follow Ruiz de Burton's legacy of linking nature and social critique through the twentieth century and into the twenty-first.

Early Chicana/o literary history offers a window into traditional agricultural and ranching methods as well as, importantly, cultural practices that endeavored to keep human impact on local environments in check. These early Mexican American writers include María Amparo Ruíz de Burton, Jovita González, Américo Paredes, Eva Wilbur Cruce, Fabiola Cabeza de Baca, and collections of oral histories edited by Patricia Preciado Martin and Tey Diana Rebolledo. Writers of the dynamic Chicano literary renaissance and Civil Rights era of the 1960s as well as the writers publishing up until the present day offer politically incisive perspectives on Chicana/o experience with the environment by covering topics ranging from pesticide contamination, migrant farmworker abuse, alienation from traditional lands, segregation into toxic urban barrios, and even futuristic portraits of environmental dystopia. Examples of writers who expand "environmental writing" in these ways are Alejandro Morales, Helena María Viramontes, Gloria Anzaldúa, Ray González, Arturo Islas, Pat Mora, Reies López Tijerina, Jimmy Santiago Baca, Ana Castillo, Luis Valdez, Sandra Cisneros, Tomás Rivera, and Cherríe Moraga. These literatures depict the universal themes of balancing the individual with the community, a yearning for intimacy, the evolution of mutual respect, and an endurance of hardship with the environment. Yet these literatures also document a specific and oftentimes threatened Chicana/o way of life in an attempt to make it last, even as it adapts to challenges.

Twenty-first century ecocriticism must engage Mexican American and Chicana/o literature, past and present, to show how racism and the challenge of environmental sustainability have been intertwined for more than a century. Chicana/o authors rewrite the fundamental terms of environmental thought, insofar as Chicana/o environmentalism emerges out of experiences of dispossession, poverty, and racism, suffering the consequences of the ideas of unlimited resources and Manifest Destiny. Moreover, Mexican American and Chicana/o literatures reveal centuries' worth of environmental care carried forward through channels of cultural hybridity and *mestizaje*.

REFERENCES

Alemán, Jesse. 2004. "'Thank God, Lolita Is Away from Those Horrid Savages': The Politics of Whiteness in *Who Would Have Thought It?*" In *María Amparo Ruiz de Burton: Critical and Pedagogical Perspectives*, edited by Amelia María de la Luz Montes and Anne Elizabeth Goldman, 95–111. Lincoln: University of Nebraska Press.

Aranda, José F. 2003. *When We Arrive: A New Literary History of Mexican America*. Tucson: University of Arizona Press.

Casas, María R. 2007. *Married to a Daughter of the Land: Spanish-Mexican Women and Interethnic Marriage in California, 1820–1880*. Reno: University of Nevada Press.

Cronon, William. 1998 [1995]. "The Trouble with Wilderness, or, Getting Back to the Wrong Nature." In *The Great New Wilderness Debate*, edited by J. Baird Callicott and Michael Nelson, 471–499. Athens: University of Georgia Press.

Davis, Mike. 1995. "Los Angeles After the Storm: Dialectic of Ordinary Disaster." *Antipode*. 27.3: 221–241.

Fox, Stephen. 1981. *John Muir and His Legacy: The American Conservation Movement*. Boston: Little, Brown & Company.

Griswold del Castillo, Richard. 1990. *The Treaty of Guadalupe Hidalgo: A Legacy of Conflict*. Norman: University of Oklahoma Press.

Guha, Ramachandra. 1989. "Radical American Environmentalism and Wilderness Preservation: A Third World Critique." *Environmental Ethics* 11, 71–83.

Hipp, John R., and Cynthia M. Lakon. 2010. "Social Disparities In Health: Disproportionate Toxicity Proximity in Minority Communities over a Decade." *Health & Place* 16, 674–683.

Montejano, David. 1987. *Anglos and Mexicans in the Making of Texas, 1836–1986*. Austin: University of Texas Press.

Preston, William. 1998. "Serpent in the Garden: Environmental Change in Colonial California." In *Contested Eden: California Before the Gold Rush*. Edited by Ramón A. Gutiérrez and Richard Orsi. Berkeley: University of California Press.

Raup, H. F. 1959. "Transformation of Southern California to a Cultivated Land." *Annals of the Association of American Geographers* 49.3.2, 58–78.

Rivera, John-Michael. 2006. *The Emergence of Mexican America: Recovering Stories of Mexican Peoplehood in U.S. Culture*. New York: NYU Press.

Ruiz de Burton, María Amparo. 1992. [1885]. *The Squatter and the Don*. Houston: Arte Público Press.

———. 1995. [1872]. *Who Would Have Thought It?* Houston: Arte Público Press.

Runte, Alfred. 1997. *National Parks: The American Experience*. Lincoln: University of Nebraska Press.

Sánchez, Rosaura, and Beatrice Pita. 2005. "María Amparo Ruiz de Burton and the Power of Her Pen." In *Latina Legacies: Identity, Biography, and Community*, edited by Vicki L. Ruiz and Virginia Sánchez Korrol, 72–83. Oxford: Oxford University Press.

Solis, Hilda. "Foreword." 2004. In *Hidden Danger: Environmental Health Threats in the Latino Community*. By Adrianna Quintero-Somaini and Mayra Quirindongo with contributing authors Evelyn Arévalo, Daniel Lashof, Erik Olson, and Gina Solomon, M.D., M.P.H, iv. Washington, DC: National Resources Defense Council.

9 Shifting the Center
A Tradition of Environmental Literary Discourse from Africa

Byron Caminero-Santangelo

In 2005, the Nobel committee surprised the world by giving the peace prize to an environmental activist. Wangari Maathai was a cofounder of the Green Belt Movement, a grassroots organization mobilizing Kenyan women to develop tree nurseries and plant trees in order to combat deforestation. However, she and the Green Belt Movement were also key players in the fight against Daniel arap Moi's kleptocratic authoritarian regime, which plundered Kenya's national resources and risked its future for private gain. Increasingly, the work of the Green Belt Movement highlighted the intersection of environmental activism and issues of human and civil rights, democratic rule, and social justice. It also helped challenge the association of environmentalism in Africa with fortress-style wildlife conservation, driven by the priorities of affluent nations and African elites.

In her memoir *Unbowed*, Maathai draws on what Lawrence Buell refers to as an "indigene pastoral" in order to give narrative shape to her vision for social and environmental regeneration in Kenya. She begins her story with a childhood memory of a beautiful, health-giving, and well-managed natural environment which sustains the human community physically and spiritually and which is itself sustained by that community's care, reverence, and sound ecological practice and knowledge. Maathai erases colonialism's presence from this initial description of her childhood home in the central highlands as a means to emphasize its catastrophic environmental impact resulting from unsustainable "methods of exploiting our rich natural resources" and cultural transformation: "Hallowed landscapes lost their sacredness and were exploited as the local people became insensitive to the destruction, accepting it as a sign of progress" (Maathai 2006, 6). Throughout the rest of her narrative, she repeats this theme, while insisting that redemption can be achieved through the rejuvenation of indigenous cultural values and the struggle against the legacies—especially psychological and ideological legacies—of colonialism.

In using pastoral discourse, Maathai is, of course, following in a long tradition of environmental writing and rhetoric. Despite its many problems, this discourse is "part of the unavoidable ground-condition" for those struggling against the environmental implications of modernity's narrative of development and positing alternatives (Buell 1995, 32). Yet, the particular kind of indigene pastoral Maathai uses also connects her narrative with a long tradition in African letters. The story of "natural," harmonious precolonial African cultures and of the corrupting impact of colonialism was a prominent aspect of Negritude, which began in the 1930s, and remains ubiquitous in African poetry, fiction, and drama. Its purpose is usually explained in terms of counternarrative: the effort to create stories challenging imperial representations in which Africa is defined by negation—the absence of history, development, civilization, and so forth—and in which the coming of the European conqueror represents the advent of a proper ordering of (wild) nature.

The connection between Maathai's rhetoric and this tradition of African anticolonial pastoral writing raises an interesting question: Does Maathai's environmental sensibility indicate a *new* direction for the African indigene pastoral, or might the relation extend to environmental concerns? In beginning to formulate an answer to this question, I will be examining older, now canonical anticolonial literary pastorals also from East Africa, Okot p'Bitek's *Song of Lawino* (1966)/*Song of Ocol* (1967) and Ngugi wa Thiong'o's *A Grain of Wheat* (1967), in terms of their relationship with Maathai's writing. It may be that in many cases, the indigene pastoral has "more to do with reinvention of the non-European world as a mirror-opposite of certain European norms" than with "actual environments" (Buell 1995, 68); however, such narratives, even those from the nationalist period, cannot be lumped together. Ngugi and Okot may not be as focused on environmental degradation or on ecological relationships as Maathai, but, like her (and unlike many of the poets of Negritude), they bring attention to actual environmental changes wrought by colonial ideology and policy and to benefits of (relatively) concretely defined indigenous environmental practice and epistemology. In this sense, their texts may point to a legacy of environmental writing from Africa that anticipates and gives a cultural context for the kind of environmental rhetoric and activism visible today in Africa. The project of establishing a literary pedigree stretching back to the middle of the twentieth century for a form of environmentalism conceptualized and led by Africans challenges the often implicit assumption that (nonsettler) African environmental writing is both belated and scarce, coming well after the rise of popular environmentalism in the West and remaining confined to a very few authors.

Such a project also contributes to the larger, ongoing effort to widen the scope of ecocriticism not only through the diversification of ecocritical canons but also through the use of critical frameworks informed by environmentalism developed by activists working within marginalized communities in the West and majorities in the Global South—activists like Wangari Maathai (Adamson, Evans, and Stein 2002; Nixon 2005). From a certain perspective, *Song of Lawino* and *A Grain of Wheat* would hardly be considered "environmental" at all. These texts prioritize the task of decolonizing culture and psyches in newly independent African nations; they remain focused on social justice, on lived environments and livelihoods, as well as on the relationships among constructions of nature, environmental practice, and structures of power and ownership. They pay little attention to nature and its protection apart from such concerns. As a result, they would probably be considered inadequately focused on nature "in and for itself" (Garrard 2004, 43) for an ecocriticism shaped by mainstream environmental discourse, originating and centered in the West, which separates nature and its defense from systemic inequality among humans. Such discourse often implies that the closer one gets to the truths of ecology and to appreciation and care for "nature," the more one escapes the influence of socioeconomic interests and the more one becomes a true environmentalist. This perspective cannot be separated from notions of objective representation and forms of desire (for the "freedom" of the "wild") associated with relatively privileged positions shaped by four hundred years of European imperialism.

In contrast, viewed from the perspective of a discourse stemming from the environmentalism of the poor, the notion that *Song of Lawino/Song of Ocol* and *A Grain of Wheat* might be "environmental" texts becomes substantially less outlandish.[1] Such a discourse is not focused on a "nature" that is separate from the shaping effects of historical social relationships but precisely on the intersection of the "natural" environment and socioeconomic interest. Concern with environmental change is couched in terms of its relationship with economic inequality and political oppression and in terms of how it impacts the lives—the homes, livelihoods, and health—of the impoverished and disenfranchised. In this kind of discourse, questions of environmental policy can never be separated from issues of social justice and political rights, and understandings of "nature" and "conservation" must be understood as always mediated by socioeconomic relationships. Ultimately, a discourse deriving from the environmentalism of the poor ties ecological concerns with issues of oppression and liberation—issues which are closely related to colonial legacies and anticolonial resistance. Through the lens of such a discourse, texts which do not prioritize the observation of nature and which only reference environmental change fleetingly or indirectly but which point to the relationship between the struggle for decolonization and the efforts to turn back the environmental legacies of colonialism—texts like *Song of Lawino/Song of Ocol* and *A Grain of Wheat*—could still be considered "environmental" and might even be more important rhetorically in the struggle against socially and ecologically destructive processes than texts which pay close attention to "nature" or to "natural" ways of dwelling but which suppress the significance of colonial histories.

The effort to articulate an African environmental literary tradition, and in the process to use an ecocritical framework shaped by those working at the intersection of environmentalism and social justice, is necessarily part of the ongoing project to develop a postcolonial ecocriticism (Nixon 2005; Cilano and DeLoughrey 2007; Vital 2008; Huggan and Tiffin 2010; Wright 2010). Lawrence Buell has claimed that the accommodation of perspectives offered by environmental justice and environmentalism of the poor "may indeed be ecocriticism's greatest challenge during the first part of the twenty-first century" if it is not to "fission and wane" (Buell 2005, 113). Postcolonial ecocritics facilitate this accommodation as they bring a much needed attention to imperialism and to parts of the world often elided by a still predominantly Anglo-American ecocriticism. Like postcolonialists more generally, the postcolonial ecocritic seeks to challenge forms of situated knowledge and representation which are assumed to be objective and universal and which have been crucial components of imperialism as it has sought to establish consent (O'Brien 2007; Cilano and DeLoughrey 2007; Vital 2008). Thus, for example, the postcolonial ecocritic might bring attention both to differing environmentalist discourses—and, therefore, different conceptions of what constitutes an environmentalist text—*and* to the historical relationships between these discourses and imperialism (Huggan and Tiffin 2010, 15).

Ecocritical work on Africa has been scarce, even compared to other areas of postcolonial literary studies, and many of the articles that have been published have focused on very recent texts and/or on a few authors—often white and/or South African.[2] Such work is of course important, but it needs to be broadened in terms of the range of texts, authors, issues, and genres. Doing so will change perceptions of environmentalism and its history in Africa, even as it contributes to bringing into dialogue differing understandings of what constitutes a properly ecocritical practice or an environmental text.

* * *

Ugandan poet Okot p'Bitek's *Song of Lawino* is among the most influential poems in twentieth-century African literature. First written in Acoli, and then translated into English by the poet himself, it was revolutionary in its accommodation of the oral tradition. Okot used the language, imagery, forms of address, and rhetoric of evocation of traditional Acoli "songs," and especially songs of abuse, to develop a new kind of long poem (Heron 1976, 1984; Okpewho 1992, 302–305). He also effectively dramatized the tensions between advocates of tradition and of modernity, and, as a result, was widely read throughout East Africa. In this "song poem," the eponymous character by turns ridicules, refutes, and beseeches her husband Ocol. The Western-educated Ocol parrots colonial discourse, and, in particular, continuously offers up the image of Africa as a savage wilderness with nothing of intrinsic value; he wants to utterly transform the continent by destroying African cultures, environments, and selves and replacing them with their "modern" European equivalents. He has rejected Lawino, the "voice" of tradition, as the representative of all he has come to despise. In her song, Lawino strikes back by depicting the value of Acoli culture and local nature, and by representing Ocol's attitudes as embodying a form of corruption and illness. In a shorter (later) poem, Ocol responds to Lawino; however, *Song of Ocol* mostly reinforces Lawino's perspective by suggesting that his attitudes can only result in self-hatred and are, in fact, leading Africa towards social decay and environmental degradation. Read together, the two "songs" offer a pastoral discourse pointing to the artificiality and destruction brought by colonial modernity and calling for the return to traditional ways of life which are closely tied with environmental conditions and which enable self-sufficiency, health, and an authentic existence.

Lawino's primary argument can be summed up by her song's central, repeated proverb, "The Pumpkin in the old homestead / Must not be uprooted" (p'Bitek 1984, 41). To uproot a pumpkin plant is to destroy the source of a highly valued, nutritious food and to undermine the ability to sustain oneself. Lawino associates the pumpkin with Acoli culture, which she represents as being effective and beautiful precisely because its "roots reach deep into the soil" (p'Bitek 1984, 41). She ridicules the idea of replacing Acoli practices with Western ones that are divorced from local conditions and rendered useless, meaningless, ugly, and/or dangerous in Africa. Often, her criticism of Western culture subtly becomes more universal; she not only ridicules its manifestations in Africa but also suggests that it is, in general, less attractive, more abstract, and, ultimately, less "natural"—less in touch with the sensual world—than Acoli culture.

However, the "pumpkin" refers not only to an Acoli culture rooted in a local natural environment, but also to that environment itself. Accepting the construction of Africa as one vast monstrous wilderness, Ocol conceives of African "nature" as offering nothing of value, even as he acknowledges no effective accommodation of nature by humans before colonization. As a result, he seeks the utter transformation of African environments, as well as cultures and identities. Lawino refutes Ocol by alluding to a vibrant Acoli agro-ecosystem ("an ecosystem reorganized for agricultural purposes" [Worster 1993, 52]), based on indigenous biodiversity, which enables healthy, fulfilling lives. As Don Worster notes, subsistence agro-ecosystems developed by traditional small-scale farmers, "despite making major changes in nature, nonetheless preserved much of its diversity and integrity," an "achievement," he claims that "was a source of social stability, generation following generation" (Worster 1993, 56).

Lawino references the benefits of such an agro-ecosystem when she discusses Acoli food and food preparation. Ocol claims that "Black people's foods are primitive" and "dirty" (p'Bitek 1984, 62). Lawino responds by arguing that knowledge and utilization of local biodiversity embedded in Acoli culture result in effective, even beautiful, food preparation and tasty, health-giving food. For example, she discusses "in detail" the different kinds of firewood "stacked right to the roof" (p'Bitek 1984, 60). She knows "their names and their leaves and seeds and barks," and explains the uses to which each one can be put. In this way, she emphasizes the knowledge entailed in Acoli cooking, the control that it allows, and the value of the indigenous flora. She also explains the advantages of serving and storage technologies her family uses, which are based on local environmental products and highlight the freshness and sensual attraction of local foods. Unlike "millet bread" in "the white man's plates," "a loaf in a half-gourd / Returns its heat / And does not become wet / . . . And the earthen dish / Keeps the gravy hot / And the meat steaming" (p'Bitek 1984, 61). Through such sharp observations, Lawino builds up an (in many ways classically pastoral) image of the wholesomeness of a way of life rooted in local nature; at the same time, this image points to the value of an ecosystem which underpins that way of life—it too is the pumpkin that should not be uprooted.

The threat of environmental uprooting is most fully represented by Okot in the later poem, *Song of Ocol,* which expands on Lawino's warnings about the dangers of a ruling elite whose outlook and desires have been utterly shaped by colonialism and who want only to take the place of the former colonizers within the new nation. Such a situation results in the desire to destroy anything "African" and, ultimately, in self-hatred, since the transformation to a fully Europeanized self is impossible: "Mother, mother, / Why, Why was I born Black?" (p'Bitek 1984, 126). An extreme manifestation of Ocol's hysteria, driven by the contradictions of the colonial discourse he parrots (which simultaneously promises and withholds transcendence), is his desire to annihilate the very geography of the continent: "We will uproot / Each tree / From the Ituri forest / And blow up / Mount Kilimanjaro" (p'Bitek 1984, 146).

As a means for Okot to express his vision of the contradictions, self-hatred, and hysteria of a Western-educated ruling class's colonized condition, Ocol's call for the geographic transformation of Africa works well. However, the apocalyptic imagery is both too improbable and too melodramatic to serve as a warning regarding the threat of actual human-induced environmental degradation. More subtle and more convincing in this regard is Ocol's desire to eradicate the existing agro-ecosystem, as well as his recounting of the "progress" he has made towards this goal. Early in his song, Ocol proclaims his desire to "see an Old Homestead/ . . . All in ruins": "We will plough up / All the valley, / Make compost of the Pumpkins / And the other native vegetables . . ." (p'Bitek 1984, 124). Later, he makes clear that the ploughing and composting he references will be part of the establishment of mechanized monocropping on large, privately owned farms: "When the tractor first snorted / On these hunting grounds / The natives scuttled into the / earth / Like squirrels, / . . . Behold, / Africa's wildest bush / Is now a garden green / With wheat, barley, coffee . . ." (p'Bitek 1984, 141). Ocol embraces a form of capitalist agriculture which includes the enclosure and privatization of the commons (the "hunting grounds") for the production of cash crops; in the process, the land itself has been turned into a commodity which can be concentrated in the hands of the new elite running the freshly independent nation: "We have property / And wealth, / We are in power" (p'Bitek 1984, 142). The hopes of social justice, of a focus on the well-being of all citizens, are mocked, as the new rulers continue processes that began under colonialism. These processes are sanctioned by the language of development, which represents them as turning useless "bush" into a productive "garden."

In her writing, Wangai Maathai has stressed how the kinds of attitudes towards traditional subsistence farming expressed by Ocol, and the concomitant pursuit of "modern" cash-crop agriculture, have been ecologically and socially disastrous. Lawino's warning not to uproot the pumpkin of traditional agro-ecosystems has gone unheeded, much to the peril of East Africa. As farmers have cleared their land for crops such as tea and coffee, they have contributed significantly to deforestation, leading, in turn, to soil erosion, loss of freshwater sources, scarcity of firewood, and destruction of biodiversity (Maathai 2006, 123). As they have ceased to grow crops for consumption, they have been unable to feed themselves and have needed to buy their food, which is often processed and contributes to malnutrition (Maathai 2009, 234–235). Their livelihoods have become more vulnerable to the vicissitudes of both weather and the global economy. Industrial agriculture, particularly on the kind of plantations described by Ocol, has played no small part in vastly uneven wealth distribution, conflict (over land and resources), as well as the impoverishment and disempowerment of the rural poor (Perfecto, Vandermeer, and Wright 2009).

More generally, Okot's "songs" can be read as precursors to Wangari Maathai's narrative regarding the origins and hope for amelioration of the African nation's and continent's ills. Like Lawino, she represents these ills as stemming from the long reach of colonialism. Maathai represents traditional Gikuyu identity as springing from a close relationship with the soil and Gikuyu culture as rooted in ecological wisdom enabling environmental integrity and prosperity. In *The Challenge for Africa*, Maathai extends this representation of an ecologically wise culture to the continent as a whole: "People . . . lived in harmony with the other species and the natural environment, and they protected the world" (Maathai 2009, 162). Many of Africa's current problems, according to Maathai, stem from the denigration of these cultures by colonialism and their replacement by the narrow instrumentalism of colonial modernity. She points, for example, to the long-term damaging results of the kind of attitudes embraced by Ocol which reject indigenous foods and methods of cultivation "in favor of a small variety of cash crops": "The loss of indigenous plants and the methods to grow them has contributed not only to food insecurity but also to malnutrition, hunger, and a reduction of local biological diversity" (Maathai 2009, 175). Like Okot, Maathai suggests that a cure for the ills bred by colonialism lies in a cultural return which will enable reclamation of self and a reconnection with the land. Throughout her song, Lawino tries to reform Ocol and address the threat he represents by reeducating him in the ways of Acoli culture and emphasizing their benefits. Similarly, for Maathai, reeducation is the "missing link in Africa's development" (Maathai 2006, 175). Cultural disinheritance "explained to [her] why many Africans, both leaders and ordinary citizens, facilitated the exploitation of their countries and peoples. Without culture, they'd lost their knowledge of who they were and what their destiny should be" (Maathai 2009, 166–167).

Finally, Maathai and Okot are linked by a sensibility we might associate with the environmentalism of the poor. Both point to the interdependence among precolonial agro-ecosystems, indigenous biodiversity, and the well-being of human communities, and both give the natural world value well beyond that of a narrow economic (monetary) instrumentalism. They also remain focused on issues of resource control and utilization in terms of the well-being of local communities, the economically and politically disadvantaged, and future generations. In addition, they share a perspective on the intersection of gender and environmental concern associated with the environmentalism of the poor, in which women have played central roles both as leaders and participants. This centrality is often explained in terms of women's positions in rural communities as those working most closely with natural resources and most attuned to the impact of environmental change; they are the community members who most often "gather fuelwood, collect water, and harvest edible plants" (Guha 2000, 108). In Kenya, they are also among those most likely to be small-scale farmers. Regarding the centrality of women in the Green Belt Movement, Rob Nixon notes, "as forests and watersheds became degraded, it was the women who had to walk the extra mile to fetch water and firewood, it was the women who had to plough and plant in once rich but now denuded land" (Nixon 2011). Their work has also, of course, given women effective environmental knowledge and practice, as Maathai suggests through the figure of her mother. In this context, Okot's use of Lawino as the voice articulating the benefits of traditional environmental knowledge and agro-ecosystems links his poems with Maathai's writing, as does the suggestion that Lawino will be the one most negatively impacted by the changes wrought by Ocol's form of development.

However, representations of gender also separate Maathai's writing from p'Bitek's "songs." Constructing Lawino as keeper of tradition and embodiment of the land, the poems are part of a gendered essentializing nationalist discourse prominent in male African anticolonial pastoral writing—most obviously in the poetry of Negritude (Stratton 1994). This discourse has been all too frequently used to keep women in their "places," through accusations of inauthenticity, when they try to break from restrictive gender roles and become a threat to patriarchal power. In *Unbowed,* Maathai narrates her own familiarity with this situation; she was accused of being too educated, too Westernized, and too "wayward" to be "a proper woman in 'the African tradition'" (Maathai 2006, 196). As she tells her story, she brings attention to how the kind of gendered discourse of authenticity served up by Okot can be used to squelch women's agency and, more generally, to suppress dissent against men in power who represent themselves as the defenders of tradition.

To argue for this distance between the two writers is not to claim that Maathai's own discourse escapes the political pitfalls of pastoral nativism. She repeatedly offers images of an idealized ecological indigenous identity and makes calls for a return to homogenous cultures unsullied by social contradiction. In fact, her writing is fraught with the tension between discourses challenging and upholding notions of cultural authenticity and purity. This tension separates her from Okot, who mostly offers a monologic (gendered) nativism, but it does not do away with the limitations caused by a discourse which can all too easily elide the impossibility of accessing a culture untransformed by the hybridizing effects of history or the implausibility of such a culture in the past.

Maathai's writing and p'Bitek's "songs" also, of course, differ in terms of the priority given to environmental issues and of concomitant attention to ecological relationships. Maathai's emphasis on the importance of understanding the details of those relationships and on the necessity for Africans to make environmental degradation a central concern is clearly absent from *Song of Lawino* and *Song of Ocol*. To claim that Okot's songs, or Ngugi wa Thiong'o's *A Grain of Wheat*, anticipate Maathai's writing and that they could be considered as part of a legacy of environmental writing in Africa is not to say that they have the same degree of engagement with ecology and actual environmental change. Yet, as I will ultimately claim in my discussion of Ngugi's novel, this difference in focus does not necessarily mean that her writing represents an unambiguous or uncomplicated "progression"—even in terms of environmental discourse.

* * *

Ngugi wa Thiong'o's *A Grain of Wheat* highlights the themes of betrayal and disillusionment in the newly independent African nation, as well as the search for a transformed anticolonial struggle. While writing the novel, Ngugi had become strongly influenced by Franz Fanon, who famously declares in *The Wretched of the Earth* that the goal of national independence was not necessarily identical with the goal of dismantling an unequal, exploitative colonial system and culture because these could live on, albeit in new forms (Fanon 1963, 148). The novel takes place at the moment of Kenya's independence in 1963, but the majority of the narrative focuses on the period between the end of World War II and the defeat of the Mau Mau liberation movement in the early fifties.

The novel begins with a depiction of the present as degraded and corrupt, with the hopes of a new future through independence already blighted. Environmental conditions connote this degeneration; in the first chapter, the land is described as "sick," "dull," "dry," and "hollow" (Ngugi 1967, 6). In the course of the novel, these conditions are associated with the corrosive alienation and isolation caused by colonialism, both among people and between people and land. The degraded present is contrasted with images which allude to a time when, as a result of indigenous Gikuyu cultural identity, communal bonds among people were strong and the land was healthy and beautiful. In this sense, an idealized past and the harm caused by colonialism are represented in fairly mannered pastoral terms. However, the narrative also offers a strong historical vision which focuses on the complicated transformations wrought by colonialism throughout Kenya and suggests the need for adaptation rather than simple "return." Particularly pertinent for an ecocritical reading of the novel are Ngugi's depictions of the environmental impact of specific colonial attitudes, policies, and practices.

In *A Grain of Wheat,* the ideology of geographic difference and the desire for mastery underpinning colonialism are summed up in the title of a book the colonial official John Thompson seeks to write: *Prospero in Africa* (Ngugi 1967, 54). For Thompson, Shakespeare's imperial sorcerer-king invokes the image of the heroic colonial mission to tame and make useful savage wilderness. Instead of magic, however, the British use science; Thompson's final administrative post in Kenya is as codirector of the "Githima Forestry and Agricultural Research Station," created to be part of "a new colonial development plan" (Ngugi 1967, 33). Such stations were part of the project of scientific conservation found throughout the British empire. The proclaimed goal of this work was the development of techniques and policies for sustained yield, the rational use of natural resources resulting in the prevention of unsustainable environmental degradation, particularly from deforestation and soil erosion. However, as environmental historians have shown, conservation and environmental science were a means for colonial governments to exercise control over land, people, and resources (Gadgil and Guha 1993; Leach and Mearns 1996). In the colonies, scientific forestry facilitated the seizure of vast areas of forest already in use by indigenous peoples who, it was claimed, did not know how to take care of and utilize nature's bounty. It also worked closely with capitalist development, often with disastrous environmental results. In the case of agricultural science, the claim that traditional farming practices caused soil erosion became an excuse in Kenya to justify land alienation and resist redistribution (Mackenzie 1998, 2000). In addition, in Kenya "discourses of 'betterment' and 'environmentalism'" were used to deepen administrative control over African farmers (Mackenzie 2000, 699). They were pushed to embrace the practices of scientific agriculture in order to preserve soil and increase yield and, ultimately, to transform the Gikuyu Reserves into spaces which would resemble British rural landscapes (Mackenzie 2000, 701). This transformation had an economic goal: an increase in yield and in marketable crops leading to an increase in tax revenue (Mackenzie 2000, 703). In this sense, colonial environmental science and policy in Kenya encouraged the spread of capitalized agriculture, as well as the class divisions that came with it.

A Grain of Wheat represents the spread of a capitalist ethos among Gikuyu farmers as socially and environmentally destructive. Mugo, who betrays a leader of the resistance to the British, focuses on capital accumulation through his agricultural work, with the ultimate objective of social recognition: "He would labour, sweat, and through success and wealth, force society to recognize him" (Ngugi 1967, 8). In the novel, Mugo's connection with the environment, based on the land's utility for achieving dreams of wealth and power, is associated with the kind of degraded landscape he struggles to cultivate in the opening of the book: "[Mugo] raised the jembe, let it fall into the soil . . . The ground felt soft as if there were mole-tunnels immediately below the surface. He could hear the soil, dry and hollow, tumble down" (Ngugi 1967, 6).

In the course of A Grain of Wheat, such descriptions of environmental desiccation seem primarily to serve as a means to figure the corrupt condition of the nation resulting from the inability to break with colonial capitalism (a reading in line with the growing influence of Marxism on Ngugi). The focus seems to be not so much on actual environmental degradation and its causes as on degenerate social relations characterized by isolation and betrayal which environmental conditions represent. Yet, the ecological significance of the connection A Grain of Wheat makes between the impact of colonialism and an infertile land should not be dismissed, especially in light of what we know about the changes wrought by the colonial environmental attitudes and policies represented in the novel. The images of a dry, unproductive land suggest soil erosion and infertility, inadequate water supply, and poor crops—all of which remain long-term results of the impact of scientific agriculture and conservation in Kenya. In the reserves, new crops and new crop varieties "together with new agricultural practices . . . contributed to the acceleration in loss of soil fertility" (Mackenzie 2000, 702). The deforestation accompanying cash-crop farming also contributed to soil erosion, as did colonial forestry (Maathai 2006, 38–39, 121–122). Thus, the link between the legacies of colonialism and environmental degradation alluded to by Ngugi might be considered historically and ecologically astute rather than simply a recycling of pastoral tropes which downplay issues of real environmental threat.

In A Grain of Wheat, the struggle against the legacies of colonialism necessitates a rejuvenated anticolonial movement. Ngugi suggests it will need to be different from previous manifestations of the movement, since what must change is not foreign, white rule but the structures and psychology it set in place. In this situation the primary task of an anti-colonial movement is to foster self-sacrificial honest dialogue and confession revealing the extent to which the nation and its citizens have become internally colonized. Only through such dialogue and confession will the new nation overcome the atomization, focus on self-interest, exploitation of other people and the land, and betrayal of the hopes for a better future for all Kenyans. Yet, if the movement must be transformed, it will also need to remain closely tied in spirit and principle to the anticolonial struggle of the past. In particular, it must draw from that struggle a mode of understanding the world very different from the one offered by colonialism and capitalism, one based on communal interdependence and responsibility, as well as on a corresponding willingness for self-sacrifice.

Finally, the movement needs to pursue the "bond with the soil" from which anticolonialism's "main strength" always "sprang" (Ngugi 1967, 12). This bond is based on familial love and identification rather than on private ownership. As the resistance leader Kihika proclaims, "This soil belongs to Kenyan people. Nobody has the right to sell or buy it. It is our mother and we her children" (Ngugi 1967, 98). Ngugi links this ethic with Gikuyu culture; in the novel, indigenous dwelling is defined by the interconnection between human habitation and a local nature that has not been repressed through the effort to master it. In the days before the rebellion, "a bush—a dense mass of creepers, brambles, thorn trees, nettles and other stinging plants—formed a natural hedge around" each of "the homes in the village of Thabai" (Ngugi 1967, 75). The connection between the liberation struggle and Gikuyu environmental attitudes and practice is perhaps best exemplified through the use of the forest during the uprising. If, for the colonists, the forest represented all that had to be transformed if Africa was to be rendered useful and livable, for the resistance fighters it was a place of refuge and protection in which they lived and organized; it was a kind of home (Nicholls 2005, 184–186).

The kind of relationship with the land that Ngugi associates with anticolonial struggle and with Gikuyu culture offers the possibility of a different conception of "development" from the one pushed by colonial modernity. The traitor Karanja betrays the resistance because of his desire for "whiteman's power . . . a power that had built the bomb and transformed a country from wild bush and forests into modern cities, with tarmac highways, motor vehicles . . . railways, trains, aeroplanes and buildings whose towers scraped the sky" (Ngugi 1967, 156). In *A Grain of Wheat*, those like Karanja, as they become leaders, betray the land and the majority of the people. A revitalized and healthy new nation requires a model of development based less on technological and economic growth and on mastery and more on an ethics of care and responsibility rooted in reestablished bonds within communities and between people and the land.

Maathai's exploration of independent Kenya's colonial inheritance and of the need for a liberatory movement based on principles from traditional

Gikuyu culture has substantial overlap with Ngugi's. She too suggests that Kenya's ills have stemmed from notions of development based on individual acquisition of wealth and power, on strictly technical and industrial advances, and on GNP. Like Ngugi, she urges a shift from narrow individual or group interests to a larger sense of communal interest, from a conception of development which benefits only a few to one focused on the well-being of all Kenyans and on social equity. Also like him, she encourages an "ethic of selflessness" (Nixon 2011). "Africans," she claims, "must begin the revolution in ethics that puts community before individualism, public good before private greed, and commitment to service before cynicism and despair" (Maathai 2009, 23). Finally, Maathai claims the nation will not be on the path to regeneration unless Kenyans recuperate a set of values based on appreciation for the interrelationship between ecosystemic integrity and communal well-being.

As was the case with Okot, Ngugi does not place nearly the same emphasis on the centrality of ecological awareness for a better future as does Maathai. *A Grain of Wheat* suggests that those who wage an anticolonial struggle automatically speak and fight for nature's interests. In this sense, there is no need to give ecological understanding any primacy; that understanding will come with the rejection of colonial epistemology. In contrast, Maathai emphasizes the need to acquire ecological knowledge if the future is to be secured against what Nixon refers to as "the slow violence" of environmental degradation (Nixon 2011). For her, the fight against colonial values is crucial in the struggle for environmental health, but it is not adequate. Compared with Maathai, Ngugi's romantic pastoral downplays actual environmental degradation, its causes, and effects.

Nevertheless, it might be too easy to represent Maathai's writing as offering a clearly more "advanced" environmentalist sensibility than *A Grain of Wheat* and, concomitantly, to gesture towards a linear, progressive narrative for environmental writing in Africa. For example, she reinforces an ethos of the autonomous individual more than does Ngugi, even in his early writing in *A Grain of Wheat*. As Rob Nixon notes, *Unbowed* is a memoir in which "a group endeavor [is] recast as personal journey with a singular autobiographical self as its gravitational center" (Nixon 2011). This form may be, as Nixon suggests, in large part due to the pressures of Western publishers and audiences, as well as the genre of the struggle memoir, but it still contrasts sharply with the narrative form of *A Grain of Wheat*. The narrator of Ngugi's novel is an unnamed member of a Gikuyu village who speaks as an equal to other members of that village and references shared memories, history, geography, and communal identity. In this sense, there is less focus on individual achievement and importance than in Maathai's memoir (or, for that matter, in *The Challenge for Africa*). She, more than Ngugi, reinforces the notion of the (heroic) autonomous self, a notion that can be problematic for those encouraging notions of ecosystemic interdependence and a transformed conception of individual identity in the fight against environmental change.

The point I make, however, is not so much about the lack of "purity" in Maathai's writing as it is about the value of beginning to explore a tradition of environmental writing by Africans by putting texts and authors in dialogue. Such dialogue can help us not only question potentially colonialist representations of African environmentalism (as belated) and not only continue to push towards a more cross-culturally sensitive ecocriticism, but also resist closure to environmental praxis in Africa.

NOTES

1. In this context, the term *environmentalism of the poor* is more applicable than *environmental justice*, which tends to be associated with issues of race and minority communities in the U.S. In my discussion of environmentalism of the poor, I draw heavily on the work of Ramachandra Guha and Joan Martinez-Alier (Guha and Martinez-Alier 1997; Guha 2000; Martinez-Alier 2002).
2. For work that theorizes the intersection of African literature and ecocriticism, see Caminero-Santangelo (2007); Caminero-Santangelo and Myers (2011); Martin (1994); Slaymaker (2001); Vital (2005, 2008). Much of the literary criticism itself has focused on J. M. Coetzee, Nadine Gordimer, Zakes Mda, and Ken Saro-Wiwa. In a recent issue of *Safundi* focused on ecocriticism and South African literature, all of the critical analysis is on white writers and much of it deals with issues of animals and animal rights (Wenzel 2010, 129–130).

REFERENCES

Adamson, Joni, Mei Mei Evans, and Rachael Stein, eds. 2002. *The Environmental Justice Reader: Politics, Poetics, and Pedagogy.* Tucson: University of Arizona Press.

Buell, Lawrence. 1995. *The Environmental Imagination: Thoreau, Nature Writing, and the Formation of American Culture.* Cambridge, MA: Harvard University Press.

———. 2005. *The Future of Environmental Criticism: Environmental Crisis and Literary Imagination.* Malden, MA: Blackwell.

Caminero-Santangelo, Byron. 2005. "Different Shades of Green: Ecocriticism and African Literature." In *African Literature: An Anthology of Criticism and Theory,* edited by Tejumola Olaniyan and Ato Quayson, 698–707. Oxford: Blackwell.

Caminero-Santangelo, Byron, and Garth Myers, eds. 2011. *Environment at the Margins: Literary and Environmental Studies in Africa.* Athens: Ohio University Press (forthcoming).

Cilano, Cara, and Elizabeth DeLoughrey. 2007. "Against Authenticity: Global Knowledges and Postcolonial Ecocriticism." *ISLE: Interdisciplinary Studies in Literature and Environment* 14.1, 71–87.

Fanon, Frantz. 1963. *The Wretched of the Earth.* New York: Grove.

Gadgil, Madhav, and Ramachandra Guha. 1993. *This Fissured Land: An Ecologica lHistory of India.* Berkeley: University of California Press.

Garrard, Greg. 2004. *Ecocriticism.* London: Routledge.

Guha, Ramachandra. 2000. *Environmentalism: A Global History.* New York: Longman.

Guha, Ramachandra, and Joan Martinez-Alier. 1997. *Varieties of Environmentalism: Essays North and South.* London: Earthscan.

Heron, G. A. 1976. *The Poetry of Okot p'Bitek*. London: Heinemann.
———. 1984. Introduction to p'Bitek, Okot. *Song of Lawino and Song of Ocol*, by Okot p'Bitek, 1–33. London: Heinemann.
Huggan, Graham, and Helen Tiffin. 2010. *Postcolonial Ecocriticism: Literature, Animals, Environment*. London: Routledge.
Leach, Melissa, and Robin Mearns, eds. 1996. *The Lie of the Land: Challenging Received Wisdom on the African Environment*. Portsmouth, NH: Heinemann.
Maathai, Wangari. 2006. *Unbowed*. New York: Anchor.
———. 2009. *The Challenge for Africa*. New York: Pantheon.
Mackenzie, A. Fiona D. 1998. *Land, Ecology and Resistance in Kenya, 1880–1952*. Portsmouth, NH: Heinemann.
———. 2000. "Contested Ground: Colonial Narratives and the Kenyan Environment, 1920–1945." *Journal of Southern African Studies* 26.4, 697–718.
Martin, Julia. 1994. "New, with Added Ecology? Hippos, Forests, and Environmental Literacy." *Interdisciplinary Studies in Literature and Environment* 2.1, 1–11.
Martinez-Alier, Joan. 2002. *The Environmentalism of the Poor: A Study of Ecological Conflicts and Valuation*. Cheltenham, UK: Elgar.
Ngugi wa Thiong'o. 1967. *A Grain of Wheat*. London, Heinemann.
Nicholls, Brendon. 2005. "The Landscape of Insurgency: Mau Mau, Ngugi wa Thiong'o and Gender." In *Landscape and Empire, 1770–2000*, edited by Glenn Hooper, 177–194. Aldershot, UK: Ashgate.
Nixon, Rob. 2005. "Environmentalism and Postcolonialism." In *Postcolonial Studies and Beyond*, edited by Ania Loomba et al., 233–251. Durham, NC: Duke University Press.
———. 2011. "Slow Violence, Gender and the Environmentalism of the Poor." In *Environment at the Margins: Literary and Environmental Studies in Africa*, edited by Byron Caminero-Santangelo and Garth Myers. Athens: Ohio University Press (forthcoming).
O'Brien, Susie. 2007. "'Back to the World': Reading Ecocriticism in a Postcolonial Context." In *Five Emus to the King of Siam: Environment and Empire*, edited by Helen Tiffin, 177–199. Amsterdam: Rodopi.
Okpewho, Isidore. 1992. *African Oral Literature: Backgrounds, Character, and Continuity*. Bloomington: Indiana University Press.
p'Bitek, Okot. 1984. *Song of Lawino and Song of Ocol*. Edited by G. A. Heron. London: Heinemann.
Perfecto, Ivette, John Vandermeer, and Angus Wright. 2009. *Nature's Matrix: Linking Agriculture, Conservation, and Food Sovereignty*. London: Earthscan.
Slaymaker, William. 2001. "Echoing the Other(s): The Call of Global Green and Black African Responses." *PMLA* 116, 129–144.
Stratton, Florence. 1994. *Contemporary African Literature and the Politics of Gender*. London: Routledge.
Vital, Anthony. 2005. "Situating Ecology in Recent South African Fiction: J. M. Coetzee's *The Lives of Animals* and Zakes Mda's *The Heart of Redness*." *Journal of Southern African Studies* 31, 297–313.
———. 2008. "Toward an African Ecocriticism: Postcolonialism, Ecology and *Life & Times of Michael K*." *Research in African Literatures* 39.1, 87–106.
Wenzel, Jennifer. 2010. "Meat Country (Please Do Not Feed Baboons and Wild Animals)." *Safundi: The Journal of South African and American Studies* 11.1–2, 123–132.
Worster, Donald. 1993. *The Wealth of Nature: Environmental History and The Ecological Imagination*. Oxford: Oxford University Press.
Wright, Laura. 2010. *Wilderness into Civilized Shapes: Reading the Postcolonial Environment*. Athens: Georgia University Press.

10 Ecomelancholia
Slavery, War, and Black Ecological Imaginings

Jennifer C. James

"TREE TALK/WATER WORDS"[1]

Paul Laurence Dunbar's 1903 poem "The Haunted Oak" begins with a passerby posing a question to a tree:

> Pray why are you so bare, so bare,
>> Oh, bough of the old oak tree;
> And why, when I go through the shade you throw,
>> Runs a shudder over me? (Dunbar 2003, 89)

As if long awaiting a sympathetic listener, the oak pours forth a story of a lynching that took place on its limbs. With great sorrow, the tree explains that absorbing the mob's violence and the victim's agony has transformed it from its previously "green" state: "I am burned with dread, I am dried and dead." The poem turns on a recurrent trope in the African American artistic imagination: The earth as a site of black memory. Within works from writers as diverse as Charles Chesnutt, Zora Neale Hurston, Sterling Brown, and Toni Morrison, memory permeates black landscape. It walks out of rivers, rises up in oceans, grows in flowers and in fields, rolls back as stone. Memory *becomes* a part of the natural world.

This trope is neither wholly metaphorical nor entirely anthropocentric, however. Much of African American religious thought reflects African beliefs in an animated universe; that is, every entity made from the natural world, be it human, plant, animal, or mineral, is "alive in varying levels of existence" (Teish 1983). In some traditions, animation extends to objects created by human hands. A WPA worker collecting narratives from living slaves in the 1930s noted that an elderly man in Mississippi insisted that even bucket had a spirit. The return of memory through nature, then, is not reducible to instrumentality, as if nature were an archive storing history in the way, say, a pro-drilling politician has claimed the earth is "warehousing" oil for our use. "Natural memory" represents a belief in organic proximity and reciprocity; the lines separating humans from nature, the living from the dead, are scarcely determinable. And just as the passerby's repeated inability to find comfort in the oak's shade prompts his inquiry into the tree's condition, natural memory makes it impossible for humans to indulge in nature while oblivious to the distress they have caused it. The return is thus inherently paradoxical: a reminder of human and nature's essential connectedness and a reminder of the violent forces which threaten that connection. Histories of violence are always shared.

In much the same way, black writers, scholars, and activists in the twentieth and twenty-first centuries have suggested that African Americans' collective memory of slavery and racial violence can engender an empathetic response to environmental destruction. Lucille Clifton expresses this idea in lines from a 1972 poem:

> being property once myself
> i think I have a feeling for it
> that's why i can talk about environment
> what wants to be a tree
> ought to be he can be it . . . (Clifton 1987, 58)

Clifton is not implying that African Americans are "like" nature, as the proslavery advocates argued to claim that blacks were meant for the fields and that this "primitivism" should exclude them from white civilization. The "property" metaphor implies that, similar to nature, African Americans were commodified in what Hortense Spillers has famously characterized as the primal scene of New World slavery: *a theft of the body—a . . . violent severing of the captive body from its motive will, its active desire*" (Spillers 1998, 658). The re-ascription of autonomous existential desire Clifton offers the slaves she extends to the "tree" and any "other things" made object, whether women, men, or nature. Other African Americans have placed environmental activism on a continuum of struggle originating in slavery. Robert Bullard, often called the "father" of the modern black environmental justice movement, views its imperatives as "an extension of the first protest against being uprooted from our homeland and brought to a strange land" (quoted in Smith 2007, 1987). "Uprooted" is intentionally polyvalent here, speaking to black deracination from a "homeland," the difficulties of prospering on new soil, and the forced disconnection from *the* land in its metonymic capacity for the earth. Neither the continued injustices nor the continued mobilization can, he claims, be understood apart from slavery.

But the argument that slavery and racial terror have fostered environmentalism must contend with its ecophobic double: that the legacies of trauma and injustice have attenuated African Americans' connection to nature. Shelton Johnson, an African American ranger at Yosemite National Park, one of only a few nationally, speculates that the "the horrible things that were done . . . in rural America" have caused African Americans to "disassociate from the natural world," preventing them from embracing the "wilderness" particularly (Fimrite 2009). While this speculation might seem wild itself, Johnson is not alone in theorizing that racial terror, symbolized most readily in the lynching in the woods, has deterred blacks from activities removed from urban or exurban spaces. A black parks-and-recreation diversity coordinator in Washington State has admitted that even for him, "going to these rural parks takes you a bit out of your comfort zone . . . I tend to look around and see if there are other blacks around" (Turnbull 2005). An accompanying claim is that the psychological need to repudiate land-based labor has alienated blacks from nature. For instance, the authors of a fascinating study of blacks in the vanishing turpentine industry argue that the blacks' "collective memory" of land-based exploitation has damaged their perception of the natural world and diminished their "knowledge of the forest for sustenance, health and livelihood." The essay ends with a ritual call to overcome: "If African Americans are to return to the land en masse as nature enthusiasts, they must first reconcile with the past and then move forward" (Johnson and McDaniel 2006, 61, 62). The larger implications are plain. Black ecophobics must "get over" the memory of trauma to become realized environmental actors.

Both perspectives underscore the difficulty of *not* referring to the cultural memory of trauma in discussions of African Americans and the environment. While it is tempting to analyze this recourse as the "return of the repressed," I will resist that framing. Repression would require that these memories had been at times unavailable to black collective consciousness, an unsustainable argument. I will instead suggest that this return should be labeled "ecomelancholia" after another Freudian concept of memory, melancholia, a form of mourning marked by its resistance to termination. In so doing, I join other minority critics who wish to rethink Freud's definition of melancholia as an inherently debilitating, pathological condition, who choose to read persistent mourning as missives from politically aggrieved and emotionally bereaved communities. Before fleshing out my claim, I will briefly explain pertinent aspects of the two states as Freud outlines them.

Tammy Clewell notes that Freud began theorizing his economy of mourning as early as the essay "On Transience" (2004, 45), first published in 1915. There he asserts that mourning is a necessary but *temporary* process of grieving which, in his words, "spontaneously" ends after an unspecified period of time. In the duration, the mourner must labor to eradicate the libidinal energy still being directed at the lost love object and memories associated with it. Once the ego has successfully "renounced everything that has been lost," the mourner can "once more [be] free (in so far as we are still young and active) to replace the lost objects by fresh ones equally or still more precious" (Freud 1915). In the more widely read essay which followed, "Mourning and Melancholia" (1917), he adopts a nearly identical position (Clewell 2004). In proper mourning, grieving occurs, then dissipates after the object is relinquished. The termination of mourning is, he says, the healthy restitution of the "normal," individuated ego; the healthy ego can and will distinguish between itself and the lost love object.

For the melancholic subject, however, mourning is seemingly unending. Undone by the experience of loss, incomplete, the ego's libidinal energy scouts for new love objects for the ego before it has fully restored itself. Freud cautions that this is not a genuine quest for new attachments but a destructive need to imagine a precariously diminished ego as whole. The ego does not truly desire a substitute. It wants the former love object, and wants to devour it completely in an effort to make the ego and object one. But with the original love object gone, and the substitutes unsatisfying, the libido turns its appetites inward. It consumes the ego, furthering its disintegration until the subject falls into a melancholic depression. This melancholy is felt more acutely when the love object resembles the ego: "the disposition to fall ill of melancholia lies in the predominance of the narcissistic type of object-choice" (Freud 1986, 587). Once again, we find Freud cautioning against improper attachment to "the same as," a problem queer and feminist theorists have blasted as heterosexist and misogynist. Somewhat contradictorily, he admits in "Mourning and Melancholia" that such "identification is the expression of there being something in common, which may signify love" (587).

If we take the "love object" as the natural world, ecomelancholia can be thought of as the inability or *unwillingness* to "stop mourning" ecological loss and losses associated with "the land" in a present where loss continues.

Tellingly, Freud's ideas about mourning in "On Transience" begin with nature. The essay opens with his recollection of "a summer walk through the smiling countryside" with two friends who were unable to find "joy" in the scenery because they were "disturbed by thought that all this beauty was fated to extinction" with winter's coming. Even after he reminds them that loss in this case will be temporary, they remain inconsolable, leading him to conclude that their disposition toward nature betrayed a general "revolt . . . against mourning" emerging from an unwillingness to accept death. Invoking the principle of "scarcity value," he asserts that an acceptance of transience and finitude would *increase* pleasure rather than diminish it: "Limitation . . . raises the value of the enjoyment" (Freud 1915).

Ecomelancholia disavows mourning's "renewable" economy and the attendant theory that scarcity mitigates loss. The recovery of lost love objects—disappearing lands, species, finite natural resources, ways of life—would prove impossible in many instances. There will be no "fresh" objects to replace the natural world, and certainly none "more precious." It is apparent how those antienvironmental theories of consumption which argue that the earth is replenishing recall Freud's faith in bounty. "On Transience" itself offers evidence that Freud borrowed capitalist theories of human consumption to structure his concept of mourning.

Ecomelancholia's historical and memorial disposition defends against mourning's call to prematurely forget. It responds to the cumulative losses of nature, land, resources, and to traumas tied to those losses, such as death, deracination, and dispossession; it is activated by ongoing and interrelated social and political violence, including the catastrophes of war, genocide, and poverty. Clewell notes that during the twenties, Freud became less adamant about the pathology of the interminable mourning, conceding that mourning can persist if the ego continues to suffer loss and that the ego might never find or accept "substitutions" for the love objects. More significantly, Clewell attributes some of this raised ambivalence to Freud's uncertainty about Europe's ability to psychically recover from the catastrophe of WWI. He worried that the fate of civilization depended on endemically destructive human beings: "Freud concluded that the violence sweeping through Europe was not an anomaly of the war, but an undeniable fact of human existence, a fact that civilization tries but largely fails to restrain. Consequently, the Great War, despite the deprivation and alarming death tolls it produced, fostered an especially productive period for Freud as he worked to revise psychoanalytic theory, including his mourning theory" (Clewell 2004, 57). In "On Transience," Freud had already unwittingly exposed his hope that the end of the war might end his *own* state of mourning: "My conversation . . . took place in the summer before the war. A year later the war broke out and robbed the world of its beauties. It destroyed not only the beauty of the countrysides through which it passed and the works of art which it met with on its path but it also shattered our pride in the achievements of our civilization . . . once the mourning is over, it will be found that our high opinion of the riches of civilization has lost nothing from our discovery of their fragility. We shall build up again all that war has destroyed, and perhaps on firmer ground" (Freud 1915). Freud's early theory of mourning—the ability to forget loss—was bound to a futurist utopia permitting Freud to defer the full psychic impact of the destructiveness of his present era. Civilization will be restored; the earth fully regenerated. Ecomelancholia refuses to take consolation in fantasies of rectification while destruction occurs unabated.

Finally, ecomelancholia complicates mourning's illusion of "discrete" subjectivity. The year "Transience" appeared, in another essay, "Thoughts for the Times on War and Death" (1915), Freud hypothesized that Europeans were surprised that groups who had displayed civilization in "technical advances in the direction of dominating nature" and become "lords of the earth," had nevertheless failed to find peaceful means to "settle misunderstandings and conflicts" (Freud 1981, 592–593). Looked at environmentally, dominating nature would logically presage aggression toward other beings; "lording" validates the kind of hierarchy which disregards ecological inseparability. The ecomelancholic quest to be like the love object, to de-individuate, is the desire which undoes the self/other splitting created in violence.

WALKER, CLIFTON, GAYE:
ECOMELANCHOLIA IN THE TIME OF WAR

Alice Walker's 1976 novel *Meridian* has been praised for its treatment of the Civil Rights Movement and black feminism. Critics less often note its concern with blacks' ethical commitment to nature. Yet, the first significant episode in the work is an instructive one, involving an oral history about a magnolia tree planted by Louvine, a female slave on a Mississippi plantation. Louvine, a passionate creator of stories, defiantly buried her own tongue beneath the magnolia after her master punitively sliced it from her mouth. The magnolia grew wildly thereafter, as did other slaves' faith in its powers. They believed it "could talk, make music, was sacred to birds . . . in its branches, a hiding slave could not be seen" (Walker 2003, 34). After the war, the Saxon plantation was transformed into a black women's college. By the 1960s, when Meridian arrives, the tree has been embraced as the site of lovemaking, storytelling, music. But in the wake of a riot against the administration, the first in Saxon's "placid, impeccable history," the women destroy it: "Though Meridian begged them to dismantle the president's house instead, in a fury of confusion and frustration, they worked all night, and chopped and sawed down, level to the ground, that mighty, ancient sheltering music tree" (39).

The question Walker raises in this episode is clear: how do a people who have received a culture in which trees are sacred destroy the symbol of their history and turn against the land itself? It is a question she will spend the novel answering. In a second early episode in *Meridian*, the protagonist's father, a careful, loving farmer, learns that the land his grandfather obtained after the Civil War contains a Native American burial mound. He is made aware of this after Walter Longknife, a Native American WWII veteran, travels from Oklahoma to reclaim it. Walker calls the father "a mourner" who "wandered," not physically, but "across maps with his fingers" (48). Cut loose from his "homeland," the father instinctively relates to Longknife as another deracinated subject, another wanderer and mourner. While deciding whether to relinquish the land, he shuts himself away in a backyard shed for long periods of time. A child at this time, Meridian sneaks in to discover his activities:

> Her father sat at a tiny brown table poring over a map. It was an old map, yellowed and cracked with frayed edge, what showed the ancient settlements of Indians in North America . . . All over the walls were photographs of Indians: Sitting Bull, Crazy Horse, Geronimo . . . There were also books on Indians, on their land rights, reservations, and their wars . . . As she tiptoed closer to the bookshelves and reached to touch a photograph of a frozen Indian child (whose mother lay beside her in a bloody heap) her father looked up from his map, his face wet with tears, which she mistook, for a moment, for sweat. Shocked and frightened, she ran away (47).

The father tries to understand Longknife's claim almost entirely from a place of remove: the palimpsest of the map, the trace of history, the absence of photograph. It might appear that the father—and Walker—are indulging what Werner Sollors labels "Indian Melancholy," a phenomenon which took hold of the cultural imagination in the mid-nineteenth-century U.S. Socially "dead" to whites, Native Americans became the site of all manner of cultural projection. "Vanishing Indians" appeared in "songs, poems, plays, paintings and sculptures," often representing "the melancholy passage of time" (Sollors 1986, 117–118). Sollors claims that in the 1960s and 1970s, another version emerged, this time from the imaginations of post-Vietnam "ethnohistorians" driven to refute U.S. exceptionalist history in the aftermath of the war. Idealized as peaceful, kind, and connected to nature, Native Americans were made to symbolize all that Americans were not. They remained "a white man's Indian" (103).

Walker is remarking on the "black man's Indian": the fierce foe of white men, the unwavering ally of slaves. The father's immersion in history disorders this romanticized narrative of black and Native American compatriotism when he discovers that some tribes sided with Confederates in the Civil War. With a cross-ethnic identification based in an *imaginary* nullified, what remains for the father is an actual shared experience of loss: home, land, culture, human lives disposed of in "bloody heaps." Moved by empathy for a fellow melancholic man, the father gives the land up. After one summer spent on the land attempting to cleanse himself of war, Longknife returns the deed to Meridian's father. Walker denies the reader a tidy ending, however. The local government seizes the land then quickly transforms it into a Native American "tourist attraction and park." A segregated one. The moral for Meridian lies not in the injustice; she has always thought of whites as "elephants" who crush everything beneath them. The real moral lies in what occurs when "Colored" are allowed in the park. They come, laugh, slide down the side of the mound. The future, Walker intimates, should belong to those melancholics who refused to join in: "Others stood glumly by, attempting to study the meaning of what had already and forever been lost" (54).

Her decision to explore the father's loss through a melancholic pastoral frame reflects Walker's indebtedness to Zora Neale Hurston's critique of modernity in the elegiac pastoral novel *Their Eyes Were Watching God*. Yet neither novel is typically theorized in relation to the pastoral. Black American treatments of nature are more often understood as expressions of "antipastoral" counternarratives, a tendency revealing the extent to which the term *pastoral* has become synonymous with racially oppressive visions of the land. This tendency supports Leo Marx's protest in *The Machine in the Garden* that the definition has been unjustly narrowed to "simple" pastoral sentimentalism exalting "pleasing rural scenery" (Marx 1964, 25) for viewers whose pleasure is spoiled if "laborers" enter the picture, as Emerson once notoriously fretted. Emerson himself aside, Marx contends that the white American canon is replete with "complex" pastorals which "qualify, or call into question, or bring irony to bear against the illusion of peace and harmony" (25). He traces this variation to Virgil's influential but understudied pastoral "Eclogues" (37 BCE), a text to which I argue Walker intentionally alludes. Set against the backdrop of war and imperial Rome, "Eclogue I" begins with the shepherd Titryus lazily, happily playing a flute—enjoying his land—when another shepherd, Melibeous, disrupts his reveries to lament that he has been unfairly dispossessed of his land. While Marx sidesteps the issue of Roman slavery, Titryus is, in fact, a Roman slave who has purchased his freedom from his owner. His pleasure in the land and his "liberty" are thus predicated upon a forgetting and a distance from his former condition, which Melibeous's disruptive presence disallows. The shepherds, Melibeous warns, are doomed to wander: "But we must go hence—some to the thirsty Africans, some to reach Scythia and the chalk-rolling Oaxes, and the Britons, wholly sundered from the world" (line 64). What Titryrus ultimately offers Melibeous at the end of this first bucolic is what the father offers Longknife: comfort. Read in this way, Virgil's Arcadia is best interpreted less as a serious wish for utopia than as a melancholy recognition of its impossibility. The metaphor of Arcadia is the act of dreaming rather than the dream itself; as Walker writes, it represents "the already and forever lost" of the already and forever dispossessed, something Hurston also recognized. As such, Walker places the magnolia and the farm in the foreground of larger landscapes of loss. By the end of the novel, Martin Luther King Jr. has been assassinated and the Vietnam War has begun.

In *Meridian*, she describes that decade as "marked by death" (22). The murders seemed endless: King and the Kennedys, Medgar Evers and Malcolm X; three civil rights workers shot to death and buried in a Mississippi dam; four little girls killed in an Alabama church bombing. King's slaying had moved many urban black Americans to attack their own neighborhoods in violent expressions of self-destructive grief, prompting brutal police backlash. Many there were already suffering the slow deaths of the poor. The numbers dying in the Vietnam War were surging. But the loss was beyond human. In public denunciations of the war in the final year of his life, King decried the damaging of Vietnamese ecosystems as terror: "We poison their water . . . we kill a million acres of their crops. They must weep as the bulldozers roar through their areas preparing to destroy the precious trees" (King 1968). As King was bringing attention to the environmental catastrophe overseas, the grassroots left in the U.S. was warning the American public about the fate of the earth. The first Earth Day would be staged in 1970. During the remainder of the 1970s, Congress enacted broad environmental legislation, including the ban on DDT and the Endangered Species and Clean Water acts. Even as tentative steps were being taken to remediate major ecological problems, the very need for action itself heightened the sense that the world was imperiled.

Clifton published her first book of poetry, *good times*, in 1969, registering this mood. *times* contained poems about the war and the problematic ways sociologists were constructing the "inner-city." The collection also offered "generations," the first of dozens of environmental poems she would publish before dying of cancer in 2010. It begins with Clifton admonishing human beings for abandoning their duty to nonhumans: "People who are going to be / in a few years / the bottom of trees / bear a responsibility to something / besides people":

> but
> this business of war
> these war kinds of things
> are erasing those natural
> obedient generations . . .
>
> and the generations of rice
> of coal
> of grasshoppers
>
> by their invisibility
> denounce us (Clifton 1987, 36)

In these early works, Clifton began to articulate an environmental politics other black artists of this era shared: that corporations, the state, and its institutions were no less than coconspirators in widespread slaughter. She returns to this theme in her second book, *good news about the earth* (1972), where "being property once myself" first appeared. "after kent state" expresses anguish over the unarmed students the police killed during an antiwar protest:

> he kills his cities
> and his trees
> even his children   oh (57)

The "oh"—a vocalization of lament—is the clarion sounding of black mourning. If "white ways," Clifton writes, could include the killing of their own white children and the earth, then African Americans are especially unsafe: "come into the black / and live" (57). Black mourning here acts, too, as a resounding of Clifton's Christianity: a plea for God to hear and have mercy, to spare humans a fate that seems inevitable, and an expression of hope that Christ will at last bring the "good news" believers are awaiting. Clifton's environmental writing will increasingly assume the shape of prophecy, manifesting itself as a full-blown ecojeremiad in *Mercy* (2004).

It is significant that Clifton positions the prophecies of *Mercy* directly after another cycle, "september song: a poem in 7 days." Beginning with "tuesday 9/11/01," each of its seven poems represents her effort to make sense of the attacks on the World Trade Center during the week that followed while she struggles with the contradictory feelings they arouse in her as an African American. "[C]ursed with long memory," her inability to suppress black collective trauma differentiates her from whites, whose faith in an American immuno-exceptionalism has been shaken: "some of us know / we have never felt safe" (2004, 48, 46). Reminiscent of Meridian's father's realization that melancholic loss bound him to Walter Longknife, "tuesday" expresses hope that that U.S. mourning will foster empathy with others who "know" loss here and elsewhere:

>   all fear
> is one   all life   all death
> all one (43)

The closing couplet of the final poem, "monday sundown 9/17/01," subtitled "Rosh Hashanah," asks her readers to recognize the beauty in what *remains*:

> what is not lost
> is paradise (49)

She then shifts to her ecojeremiad to portray the fall which will occur if humans fail to recognize a need for regenesis:

> when you come again
> and you will come again
>
> the air
> you have polluted
> you will breathe
>
> the waters
> you have poisoned
> you will drink (72)

This unified choral of otherwordly voices warns of the folly of a *human* immuno-exceptionalism which mimics the *nationalist* incarnation troubling Clifton in "september": "you / are not chosen / any stone / can sing . . . your tongue / is useful / not unique" (55). The hell she presents is an eternal condemnation to the very world our arrogance will bring to ruination.

Clifton calls this cycle "a message from The Ones (received in the late 70's)," possibly referring to the iconic Marvin Gaye song from the 1970s, "Mercy, Mercy, Me (The Ecology)":

> Oh, mercy mercy me
> Ah things ain't what they used to be no no

Poison is the wind that blows
From the North and south and east

Oil wasted on the ocean and upon our sea
Fish full of mercury (Gaye 1971)

Delivered in the sonic idiom of the spiritual, Gaye captures the fragile state of the earth in pairs of simple, discrete images. It was one of three singles from Gaye's phenomenally successful concept album, "What's Going On," titled after his powerful indictment of the Vietnam War. The third, "Inner-City Blues (Makes Me Wanna Holler)," protested the economic injustices contributing to black urban despair. Not only does he, like Clifton, see the annihilation of lives in the ghetto, in war, and the natural world as coextensive instances of violence; he also views the violence as prophetic.

I offer these instances of black ecological imagination from the sixties and seventies not because they represent the "origins" of the African American environmental thought, which emerged at least as far back as the nineteenth century. I chose them because they are prominent works from celebrated artists from a black cultural milieu which has received sustained scholarly attention. "The Ecology" alone might stand as the most disseminated artistic statement about the environment to date. Even so, reports of the "lack" of African American environmental art still surface, as does a "truism" about its content: that black environmental philosophy, borne out of survival, will always be concerned with the well-being of black people before, say, "grasshoppers." These examples demonstrate otherwise while suggesting that to prioritize ecologically connected life is a fruitless exercise. To read African American literature ecocritically is to encounter black loss. Too, Clifton's and Gaye's concern with fish and trees pushes us to rethink the psychic and geographical terrain of black *urban* environmentalism; both lived most of their lives in cities. If structures of exploitation and domination cut across the imagined boundaries dividing civilization from nature, so does the urban imagination.

It is thus critical to ask why ideas of ecophobic black behavior in the natural world persist and why that perception matters.

Ecophobia I: Fear and Loathing on *The Wire*

The first season of the acclaimed series *The Wire* features a storyline in which a young black male informant who wants to "start over" is temporarily relocated from Baltimore to the rural eastern shore of Maryland where his grandmother lives. The arrival proves farcical: The sounds of crickets make him jump; the "sticky air" overwhelms him. After a brief stay he calls his friends, pleading for rescue in a high-pitched voice barely scratching puberty: "I ain't no country-ass nigger" (David Simon, Ed Burns, and Joy Lusco 2002). When he returns, one of his former allies shoots him in the face. In an episode from the third season, a duo of officers punishes a group of black offenders by dropping them off in the woods and with-holding directions back to the city. The black officer warns that he will take them to West Virginia the next time. In an oblique reference to the skilled relationship with the land that led many slaves to freedom, the white officer quips that he is certain they are unable to locate north from the stars. He points out the Big Dipper for them. As the officers speed away, the boys look around nervously (David Simon and Rafael Alvarez 2004).

The humor of such scenes depends on *The Wire*'s audiences sharing a "common sense" recognition that African Americans' relationship to the natural world is dangerously broken. In the first, it is apparent that the boy rarely sees this grandmother—who is not shown—and perhaps barely knows her. This attenuated kinship is partly the reason the Eastern Shore, a potentially "safe space," feels foreign to him; this unease causes him to return to the streets of Baltimore where he meets his deadly fate. In the second, the officers rely on the absence of natural ways of knowing to taunt the boys while they activate the cultural memory of the woods as a site of the very kind of racial terror which seemingly facilitated black estrange-ment from the land. The fourth season again has boys worried about KKK members lurking in the Maryland countryside.

To be sure, writer/producer David Simon and his team are drawing from African Americans' own mythologies about the effects of post–Civil War migration: most saliently, that the movement to the North and West marked a radical temporal break from the Southern past and a psychic repudia-tion of slavery. The first wave of black migrations occurred at the turn of the century, coinciding with the "machine age"; for some migrants, the urban North symbolized a mechanized future free of black bodies shack-led to land-based labor. Members of the black intellectual class similarly envisioned connections to technological advancement as "supplementing" a race the dominant culture had deemed evolutionary deficients. Racial leader Alexander Crummell argued that embracing science and industrial-ism would create a people embodying "the impulses of irrepressible prog-ress," proclaiming that this new racial character could loosen white beliefs that blackness equaled retrogression (1898, 4, 6–7). Even Booker T. Wash-ington, who infamously propagandized a black future in the South and farming (a position which secured his reputation as a black neo-planta-tionist), encouraged African Americans to explore agricultural science and technology; and while he disdained poor blacks' penchant, in his mind, to fritter money away on unnecessary mechanical goods, such as organs and clocks, he fulsomely praised the efficiency of the washing machine.

What separates Simon and early black techo-enthusiasts is his empha-sis on blacks' alignment with technology as *substitution* rather than sup-plement. While praised for its sometimes complex portraits of African Americans, early seasons of *The Wire* depict the gangbangers of its world as embodying the massive contradictions expressed in the "urban-jungle" metaphor. Simultaneously atavistic and futuristic, their commandeering of high-tech equipment—including pagers, cell phones, semiautomatic weapons, even studying economic science formally—fails to lift them above an environment governed by deterministic "ecological" principles. In this setting, "the latest in yo tech," as a black officer calls it, only speeds their devolution (David Simon and Joy Lusco 2004). At the same time, Simon's sweeping political lens in the series opens to a larger panorama of the American city which allows the viewer to see the deleterious impact of technology on multiple communities and institutions. The implementation of robots threatens dockworkers' livelihoods. The reliance on computers and wiretaps in the misguided "war on drugs" has eroded the human part of police work, including the building of genuine relationships with people in dispossessed communities. But it is only with black Americans that nature is ushered in to make sense of the problems of urban America. This pairing is reflexive and problematic, giving credence to the dichotomy between worlds natural and unnatural. Environmentalism is not the series' concern, yet the force of these representations of blacks, nature, and technology has environmental implications. Afghanistan and Iraq murmur in the background; those "in the [drug] game" call themselves "soldiers," peddle packages named "WMD" while rarely speaking of wars which, given the disproportionate numbers of young black military recruits, must have cut very close. It follows that the *group* of people these characters represent, black urban residents, would be equally insensible to the peril the destruction of nature poses—the machine encroaching upon the garden—because they are so closely identified with the machines, and because the garden, as Simon sees it, holds little meaning for them.

ECOPHOBIA II: OBAMA GOES CAMPING, OR PARKS AND RECREATION

On August 7, 2009, Jeff Zelney published a *New York Times* blog regarding President Obama's plans to take his family to Yellowstone Park and the Grand Canyon. Appended to an official visit to the state of Montana, the Obama administration intended the trip to boost attendance in the national parks system. Zelney's post was accompanied by a single idyllic photograph of the Grand Canyon, with a curious caption printed beneath: "The first family will not be camping when they visit the Grand Canyon later this month." The blog again refers to this speculation within a parenthetical aside: "(No, aides said, they will not be camping.)" (2009). In a separate briefing held during the trip, a reporter posed this question to Press Secretary Robert Gibbs: "On a lighter note, how do you think Obama is doing in terms of being kind of an outdoorsy guy this weekend?" He continued: "It's been interesting to me to watch him, not being from the great American West . . . do you think the family in general has developed more of an appreciation for—I don't know—the outdoors way of life, hiking?" (Gibbs 2009). Gibbs's response is noteworthy: "Well, look, I think he's always tremendously enjoyed being outside . . . Look, he was dying to come here and go fishing. Literally, we—every time we'd been to Montana—the primary, the general election—every time we went he said, I'm going to come back here and learn how to fly fish. He was dying to do that, and finally got a chance to do that, though was a bit frustrated he didn't get to hold one of the fish."

The absurd premise sparking the initial rumor suggests that some press members pursued this angle merely for amusement's sake. It is easy to imagine how the idea of a man caricatured as a Harvard effete partaking of the "great outdoors" could drive others to demand evidence of his "nature creds." But by the end of August, a racist joke involving Obama setting up tent with "Tonto" circulated the Internet, with Tonto getting the better of the hapless president. The image of Obama as a stumbling neophyte so in over his head in the wilderness—a white man's space—that he can't even foil a Native American is an unvarnished expression of the racial irony animating the rumor in the first instance. Placed in this context, Gibbs's "fish defense" appears to be an argument for a black urban president's legitimacy in the role of national steward.

Indeed, the standardized test of blacks' and other minorities' authentic appreciation for the natural world is the "free association" with the outdoors implied in recreation and leisure activities rather than in their environmental behavior or attitudes. As a writer for *The Christian Science Monitor* concluded of the Yosemite trip, "[W]hat's important with the Obama visit, though, is the symbolism. The demography of national park visitors remains overwhelmingly white" (Wilkinson 2009). As I have mentioned, many African Americans themselves subscribe the outdoor recreation test. Framed in the overcoming narrative, it carries the additional burden of proving that blacks have shed a slave past. The *Chronicle* in fact featured the interview with ranger Johnson citing black memory as inhibiting participation only two days after the White House publicized the trip. Shortly thereafter, a man calling himself "The Field Negro" posted a blog entry on a black Web site, *The Daily Voice*, quoting Johnson and repeating the erroneous rumor: "As Obama goes camping," he asks, "why don't more blacks do the same?" He proposes racial terror as one possible reason, then informs the fearful they are missing out on "fun" (*Daily Voice* 2009).

These conversations reveal camping as a racially loaded signifier which points to the reification of spatial imaginaries in discussions of blacks and nature. African Americans' own tendency to cordon off "rural America," "the country," the "wilderness," or "the South" as racial "danger zones" might be understandable, but it is also misleading. It is undeniable that many historical atrocities occurred in these spaces, but they also occurred in towns or their bare outskirts. While they did not always involve hangings, in those that did, bodies were hung from telephone poles, bridges, and other symbols of modernity—not only from trees. Whatever its source, racial zoning exerts a dangerous influence on our collective sensibility about environmental stewardship. It lends power to readings of natural spaces as the domain and therefore responsibility of "whites," and urban spaces as the domain, and therefore the problem, of "blacks." Certainly, the examination of Obama's *feelings* about nature in the 2009 press exchange took precedence over a rigorous examination of his uneven environmental policies. In the wake of the recent oil disaster in the Gulf of Mexico, a major media outlet ridiculed his dress attire as he assessed the southern shoreline and his reliance on scientists, once again construed as signs of his discomfort with the land. Of course, the irony is that former oilman George W. Bush's whiteness may have allowed him to successfully stage photos "working" his ranches to signal his "love of the land" at the same time he was gutting environmental protection. Walker and Clifton are correct: it will fall to the ecomelancholics, those "cursed with long memory," to remind us of the disastrous consequences of forgetting.

REFERENCES

Clifton, Lucille. 1987. *good woman: poems and a memoir, 1969–1980*. Rochester, NY: Boa Editions Ltd.

———. 2004. *Mercy*. Rochester, New York: Boa Editions, Ltd.

Clewell, Tammy. 2004. "Mourning Beyond Melancholia: Freud's Psychoanalysis of Loss." *Journal of the American Psychoanalytic Association* 52, 1.

Crummell, Alexander. 1898. "Civilization: The Primal Need of the Race." *The American Academy Occasional Papers* 3. Washington, DC: The Academy.

Dunbar, Paul Laurence. 1903; reprint, 2003. "The Haunted Oak." In *Witnessing Lynching: American Writers Respond,* edited by Anne P. Rice. New Brunswick, NJ: Rutgers University Press.

Fimrite, Peter. 2009. "Park Ranger Asks: Where Are the Black Visitors?" *The San Francisco Chronicle*, August 9, http://www.sfgate.com (accessed July 28, 2010).

Freud, Sigmund. "On Transience." 1915. Translated by James Strachey, http://www.freuds-requiem.com/transience.html (accessed July 29, 2010).

———. "Mourning and Melancholia." 1986. In Peter Gay, *The Freud Reader*. New York: W. W. Norton and Company.

———. 1981. "Thoughts for the Times on War and Death." Vol. I of *The Major Works of Sigmund Freud*. Franklin Center, Pennsylvania: Franklin Library.

Gaye, Marvin. 1971. "The Ecology" (vocal performance). By Marvin Gaye. *What's Going On*, Tamla Records, May 21.

Johnson, Cassandra Y., and Josh McDaniel. 2006. "Turpentine Negro." In "'*To Love the Wind and the Rain': African Americans and Environmental History*." Edited by Dianne D. Glave and Mark Stoll. Pittsburgh: University of Pittsburgh Press.

King, Martin Luther Jr. 1967. "Why I Am Opposed to the War in Vietnam" (speech). Ebenezer Baptist Church, Atlanta, Georgia, April 30, http://www.lib.berkeley.edu/MRC/pacificaviet/riversidetranscript.html (accessed July 28, 2010).

Marx, Leo. 1964. *The Machine in the Garden: Technology and the Pastoral Ideal in America*. New York: Oxford University Press.

"Press Gaggle by Press Secretary Robert Gibbs." 2009. Air Force One, http://www.presidency.ucsb.edu/ws/index.php?pid=86539 (accessed July 28, 2010).

Smith, Kimberly K. 2007. *African American Environmental Thought: Foundations.* Lawrence: University Press of Kansas.

Sollors, Werner. 1986. *Beyond Ethnicity: Consent and Descent in American Culture.* New York: Oxford University Press.

Spillers, Hortense. 1998. "Mama's Baby, Papa's Maybe: An American Grammar Book." In *Literary Theory: An Anthology*, edited by Julie Rivkin and Michael Ryan. Oxford, UK: Blackwell Publishers.

Teish, Luisah. 1983. "Women's Spirituality: A Household Act." In *Homegirls: A Black Feminist Anthology*, edited by Barbara Smith. New York: Kitchen Table Press.

Turnbull, Lornett. 2005. "Wanted: African-American Campers." *The Seattle Times*, July 5, http://seattletimes.nwsource.com (accessed July 28, 2010).

Walker, Alice. 2003. *Meridian*. New York: Harcourt, Inc.

The Daily Voice. 2009. "As Obama Goes Camping, Why Don't Blacks Do the Same?" http://thedailyvoice.com/voice/2009/08/ (accessed July 28, 2010).

The Wire. Episode no. 11, first broadcast August 18, 2002, by HBO. Directed by Steve Shill and written by David Simon, Ed Burns, and Joy Lusco.

———. Episode no. 31, first broadcast October 31, 2004, by HBO. Directed by Leslie Libman and written by David Simon and Rafael Alvarez.

———. Episode no. 32, first broadcast November 7, 2004, by HBO. Directed by Timothy Van Patten and written by David Simon and Joy Lusco.

Zelney, Robert. 2009. "Obamas to Visit Yellowstone and the Grand Canyon." *The New York Times*, August 7, http://www.nytimes.com (accessed July 28, 2010).

Wilkinson, Todd. 2009. "Like Past Presidents, Obama Celebrates the Grandeur of Yellowstone." *The Christian Science Monitor*, August 15, http://www.csmonitor.com (accessed July 28, 2010).

NOTES

1. Lucille Clifton. 1987. *good woman: poems and a memoir, 1969–1980.* Rochester, NY: Boa Editions Limited, 54.

Part III
Scale

11 Home Again
Peak Oil, Climate Change, and the Aesthetics of Transition

Michael G. Ziser

This order is now bound to the technical and economic conditions of machine production which today determine the lives of all the individuals who are born into this mechanism, not only those directly concerned with economic acquisition, with irresistible force. Perhaps it will so determine them until the last ton of fossilized coal is burnt (Weber 1905/1958, 181).

Ballround, earth-town.
Each street meets
itself at length.
Old are the roads,
long are the ways,
wide are the waters.
Whale swims west returning east,
tern flies north returning south,
rain falls to rise, sparks rise to fall.
Mind may hold the whole
but on foot walking we do not come
to the beginning end of the street.
The hills are steep,
the years are steep,
deep are the waters.
In the round town
it is a long way home
(Le Guin 1985, 395).

One of the peculiarities of reaching a maxima or "peak" in any system is that recently experienced events begin to repeat themselves in reversed order. On a trampoline, the world that was rushing away one minute now resolves itself again; on a train that has stopped and begun to make its return trip, the landscape through the window reappears in a strange dynamic of repetition and erasure. This chapter will argue that in the wake of an imminent, present, or already-past peak in its ability to draw upon fossil-fuel resources—the massive seams of coal and uncontrollable gushers of oil that underlay the astonishing growth in the twentieth century slowly diminishing, generations hence, into insignificance—American modernity will begin to reexperience moments in its cultural past as the materially conditioned facts of its present and future. Certain moments from a generation ago are in fact already returning to the public imagination, filling pages, canvases, airwaves, and bandwidth with untimely images and ideas that provide an index of what under our customarily progressive view of history is an unthinkable change to the material basis of civilization. In particular, current representations of an end to the hydrocarbon age in the U.S. replay key aspects of the oil-shock culture of the 1970s and early 1980s, rehearsing that era's classic bioregionalist themes of utopia, apocalypse, geographic constriction, tribalization, and—perhaps most significantly— informational networking in their struggle to conceive the traumatic loss of a fossil-fuel subsidy that has underwritten an economic culture of near-constant growth.[1] This "repetition," however, is no sign of aesthetic failure or conceptual backwardness, but rather an indication of a "new" spatial and temporal paradigm whose paradoxical novelty consists in a repudiation of spatial and temporal innovation as it was conceived under energy-surplus conditions. Understanding the aesthetics of the new environmental Age of Transition to a lower-intensity energy regime requires us to reflect on the parameters set by what William S. Burroughs (2000, 240) called the "gasoline crack of history" in order to reimagine them for the future.

PEAK OIL AND GLOBAL CLIMATE CHANGE

According to Vaclav Smil, the foremost historian of human energy use, early hunter-gatherer communities relied almost entirely on their own muscle power and a small array of biomass fuels—wood, straw, and dung—to subsist on plants, insects, fish, and animals. Of greatest evolutionary significance during this period were phenotypic changes like bipedality and profuse sweating (which allowed hunters to run their prey down to exhaustion) as well as technological achievements like basic weaponry and cooking fires. The beginnings of agriculture, which slowly introduced deep changes to the size and structure of societies, exploited the benefits of aggregated human and animal labor and basic power multipliers like levers and pulleys, but other than the introduction of limited amounts of wind and water power there was no fundamental change in what Smil calls the "prime mover" or basic power source of human civilization, which remained the sun (1994, 28–156 passim). The limits to growth imposed by the amount of yearly solar radiation striking the earth were decisively overcome only with the advent of a fossil-fuel economy in the late sixteenth century, first based on coal and then on oil and natural gas, through which "fossil sunlight" in the form of chemically transformed organic matter could be mined or pumped and in essence *brought forward in time* to allow human societies to apply forces to their environments that were far in excess of the historical norm and of the ultimately sustainable supply. By the close of the nineteenth century, fossil fuels had surpassed traditional biomass fuels in the global energy supply, and over the course of the twentieth century they surged a further tenfold (187, Figure 5.15). In 2008, the combustion of fossil fuels accounted for between 80 and 90 percent of worldwide power consumption (474 exajoules) (British Petroleum 2009). In the West, this percentage is often even higher, and we depend *almost entirely* on fossil fuels not only for heat, light, electricity, and transportation but also for basic industrial raw materials (plastics and metals), defense, and even the fertilization and protection of food crops. Our Western bodies, homes, communities, governments, arts, and ideologies are— in a sense that is still mysterious and infrequently spoken of—expressions of the mystical surplus of energy that is fossil fuel.

Extensive recent scientific research has made it increasingly clear that this massive fossil-fuel amplification of the human species, amounting to an extra quarter-sun every year, cannot continue indefinitely in the current form. Although the precise amount of recoverable oil worldwide has proved very difficult to determine, the most thorough review of existing studies concludes that "a peak of conventional oil production before 2030 appears likely and there is a significant risk of a peak before 2020" (UK Energy Research Centre 2009, x). As production slowly falls from the peak (approximately 85 million barrels per day) amidst rising consumption, the price and availability of oil are likely to become very unstable, undermining the economic rationale of many of Western modernity's most fundamental material and cultural practices, from industrial food production to air travel, especially those for which no viable replacements currently exist. The projected date for peak coal appears to be significantly further out (between 2025 and 2150, with the most recent forecasts trending toward the earlier date), but the prospect of a coal-based extension of the hydrocarbon regime raises the other horn of the fossil-fuel dilemma: the prospect of massively destructive anthropogenic global climate change (Luppens et al. 2008 and Committee on Coal Research 2007). Over thirty years of focused scientific research have led to the conclusion that historical and continued emission of gases (primarily carbon dioxide, methane, nitrous oxide, and ozone) associated with the production and consumption of fossil fuels is causing significant warming of the global climate system (U.S. EPA 2010). The widespread consequences of this warming may include significant rises in sea levels, increased quantity and duration of heat waves and freezes, shifts in territorial boundaries for many species of animals and plants, changes in rainfall quantities and patterns, crop failure, social upheaval, and permanent and irreversible alteration of the ecological systems upon which contemporary human societies to varying degrees depend (IPCC 2007).

Strictly speaking, peak oil and global climate change are two different phenomena, and in fact they can easily be read as mutually exclusive. If we are indeed about to run out of inexpensive fossil-fuel resources adequate to our current population and energy intensity, as the most pessimistic "peakers" have argued, then global climate change is of little concern, a disease of affluence confronting a civilization about to be reduced to starvation (Kunstler 2005). By the same token, one of the ironies of calls for conservation and alternative energy solutions to reduce atmospheric carbon is that such measures may ultimately extend and deepen world economic dependence on nonrenewable resources by delaying the peak that would otherwise force the issue, particularly if the time lag encourages developing nations to industrialize under a fossil fuel energy regime, however relatively efficient it may be. At the level of our fundamental notions of humankind's relationship to the natural world, the differences are even more profound. The peak oil scenario envisions our species as fundamentally at the mercy of immutable natural laws and geologic facts. In the case of climate change, the problem is precisely the reverse: we have too much power over even the least tamable aspect of the planet, its atmosphere.

In cultural representations of a constrained future, these material distinctions are frequently glossed over. The prospect of peak oil is understood as an additional incentive to act on climate change, which for its part stands as Nature's inflexible corroboration of what most credible observers believe to be the ethically appropriate (albeit economically inconvenient) action. To a surprising degree, postapocalyptic scenarios in popular literature and film involving climate change differ little from those dealing with resource depletion, and both differ in key ways from the many other forms of doom that haunt our public imaginary (nuclear, biological, extraterrestrial). *Mad Max 2: The Road Warrior* (Hayes et al. 1981), which is set in a diminished world characterized by gasoline shortages obviously inspired by the 1973 and 1979 oil shocks, features many of the same essential elements—conflict between anarchic and nomadic bands of survivors distinguished primarily by their attitudes toward resource conservation—as the first major-studio film depicting the aftermath of global climate change, *Waterworld* (Rader and Twohy 1995).[2] The permaculture movement, born of the same historical moment as *The Road Warrior*, has since become the basis of the Transition movement, one of the major proposed solutions to the hydrocarbon crisis (Mollison and Holmgren 1978, 1979; Holmgren 2009). And these elements have left their imprint on the quintessential contemporary vision of apocalypse, Cormac McCarthy's *The Road* (2006), the very title of which points to the crisis of combustion and mobility.[3] As we continue to move into a postcarbon future, the cultural contradictions embodied in this apocalyptic amalgam of Promethean hubris and abject powerlessness will need to be resolved. Neither cornucopian nor catastrophic, the real future is likely to involve changes that require both creative human solutions and acquiescence to physical constraints.

DIE-OFF AND/OR VIRTUALIZATION

The prospect of permanent global fuel shortages and climate change as the primary context for environmental discussions has distributed ecocritics, and the environmental community in general, along a spectrum with two distinct poles. At one end are the localists, whose model of political action primarily concerns the regional impacts of human development on wild or mostly wild conservation areas. The corresponding localist aesthetic, well exemplified by *Orion* magazine's glossy and proudly noncommercial homages to the beauty of nature, tends to favor traditional realist depictions of the natural world or, when a less empirically attentive perspective is called for, first-person reflections on the phenomenology of the (mostly) natural world.[4] When more broadly political topics are broached, they tend to take the form of traditional denunciations of human negligence, insensitivity, and greed. This is the classic environmentalism of Thoreau, Muir, and Carson, and it is the source of much that is both intellectually profound and politically admirable. However, it retains a problematic emphasis on the separability of the human and the natural realms, is often expressed through a melancholic attitude linking natural plenitude with human absence. The contradictions inherent in such a fantasy have recently been made concrete by Alan Weisman's *The World without Us* (2007), a futurist speculation that details the ways that geological, meteorological, and biological forces would carry out the destruction of the man-made world in the event that all human life were to be instantaneously removed from earth. The transcendental pleasures involved in witnessing the unwitnessable— the world without you—derive from the same source as those attending the "wilderness reflection" characteristic of traditional nature writing, where the relinquishment of the human clears a space for the mind to expand to its fullest potential.[5] Even more obviously, *The World without Us* is related closely to a strain of apocalyptic rhetoric that has accompanied the emergence of both peak oil and global climate change as major environmental issues. The notion that the human population will overshoot the carrying capacity of the global environment and crash precipitously, whatever its truth value as a prediction of future events, draws strongly on a deep-seated environmentalist desire to reclaim the natural world as a place in which one may be left alone by society and history.[6]

Opposed to this pessimistic and often nostalgic perspective is an environmental taste that craves texts with a less pious view of nature, takes its cues from ecology's insistence on complex and systemic global interconnection, and problematizes fundamental conceptions of environmentalism, often by calling attention to the histories, conventions, and mediums of environmental representation. Ursula Heise's recent *Sense of Place and Sense of Planet*, for example, invokes the physical senses and the places of classic localist environmental writing as the obsolete backdrop for a new ecocosmopolitan story about virtualization and globalization (Heise 2008). The first chapter of Timothy Morton's recent *The Ecological Thought* is entitled "Thinking Big," an intellectual project he explicitly contrasts with older environmentalist slogans, such as E. F. Schumacher's *Small is Beautiful* and Frances Moore Lappé's *Diet for a Small Planet*, which advocate virtues of inhibition like humility and restraint (2010, 20). While contesting key aspects of traditional ecologism, both Heise and Morton lay claim to the "eco-" prefix on the strength of their fierce adherence to the major ecological precept that "when we try to pick out anything by itself, we find it hitched to everything else in the universe." Their preferred model for this ineluctable interconnectedness is our contemporary infrastructure of information technology: the web, the cell phone, the transoceanic cable, the wireless network. Morton, again on the first page of the "Thinking Big" chapter, describes the human mind as "operating system software" that "boots up our minds to be ready for what we need in thinking democracy . . . [and] ecology." Heise's *Sense of Place, Sense of Planet*, the most direct consideration we have of environmental scale in the arts, likewise turns to the Web for both examples and metaphors suited to the dawning cultural sense of interconnection that accompanied the science of chemical toxicity, radioactive fallout, and global climate change. If traditionalist environmentalism seeks vainly to inhabit a posthumous perspective on nature, this later version maintains a tempered optimism borne of a faith in the power of the digital age to preserve a global ecology reduced to its virtual, disembodied elements.

These apparent alternatives have generated some intra-ecocritical partisan rancor, but what interests me here is the degree to which they draw upon a shared conception of space. The quest for sublimity, which Burke defined as a privation whose affective power is equivalent to the obliterating force it cancels, is frequently recorded in the localist literature as the individual transcendence of the body and local confines towards a generalized sense of becoming ecstatically one with the universe. Nothing could be further from a realist commitment to physical embodiment in a defined natural setting, and this alocality is something Morton's increasingly religious version of ecologism recognizes and celebrates. What is more, Morton's key presumption that everything in the universe is hitched to everything else and Heise's commitment to thinking globally are borrowings from a more explicitly localist moment in environmental history. The "hitched" slogan first came from the lips of John Muir, the man who practically defines the traditional place-based American environmental movement in the nineteenth century. "Think globally, act locally" was a formula coined by an environmentalist—either David Brower or René Dubos—more than forty years ago.

Such barely hidden affiliations between environmentalism and Environmentalism 2.0 (as journalists have tellingly dubbed it) should alert us to the fact that *some* global and local visions of environmentalism, and their attendant ideologies, are in important ways united by a shared understanding of scale, in this case a "glocal" paradigm in which the ultimate interconnectedness of the all components of the terrestrial ecosystem ultimately overpowers the spatial differences and material distances that resist such connection.[7] What the end of the fossil-fuel age discloses, however, is precisely the degree to which such modern models of scale are rooted in the contingent space-annihilating substances and regimes that subtend them. The unacknowledged paradox of archenvironmentalist Bill McKibben's argument, in *The Death of Nature*, that global anthropogenic atmospheric changes have tragically killed any possibility of experiencing the natural world as wholly other, is that this "death" is in fact the logical precondition of any comprehensive global ecological politics of the sort McKibben (1989) has since advocated in defense of localized experience.[8] We cannot consciously and concertedly act upon the atmosphere without implicitly acknowledging that the atmosphere—the wildest venue around—is in fact in some sense already under our control and hence "dead" in the traditional environmentalist sense. Understanding global climate change and peak oil requires us to acknowledge the ways in which our best critical paradigms, avant- and derrière-garde alike, reflect rather than contest our overconsumption of petroleum and the overemission of carbon dioxide and other greenhouse gases.

ANCHORING THE WEB

As I hinted above, some of the trouble for environmental theorists in thinking about the historical energetics of environmental representation stems from the overidentification of ecological connectivity with the network structure of information technology. The phrase "media ecology" as currently used in popular and academic discourse has little to do with the scientific discipline of ecology or even with the larger field of environmental concern that is ecology's constant companion. The coining definition, first given by Neil Postman in 1970—"Media ecology is the study of media as environments"—is still broadly current, at least so long as one understands by "environment" a way of designating the relationship between the tangible technical objects that mediate communication and the subjective interpreters that receive and are affected by that communication (Postman 1970).[9] As Lance Strate, a contemporary media ecologist, has elaborated:

> It is the study of media environments, the idea that technology and techniques, modes of information and codes of communication play a leading role in human affairs.
>
> Media ecology is the Toronto School, and the New York School. It is technological determinism, hard and soft, and technological evolution. It is media logic, medium theory, mediology. It is McLuhan Studies, orality–literacy studies, American cultural studies. It is grammar and rhetoric, semiotics and systems theory, the history and the philosophy of technology.

It is the postindustrial and the postmodern, and the preliterate and prehistoric (Strate 1999).

What it is not, despite its name and its official birth in the year of the first Earth Day, is anything like the materialist disciplines and practices devoted to thinking through, articulating, and acting upon the connection of humankind and the nonhuman world. Nevertheless, Postman underscored his intention to analogize media studies to the natural science of ecology (and not human ecology, as Strate and others have suggested) in a 2000 speech at the first convention of the Media Ecology Association:

> In the early days of our department, we were subjected to a good deal of derision, some gentle and some nasty, about our use of the phrase "media ecology." I think the objection was that the term was too trendy, but more than that, the term was more comfortable in biology than in social studies and ought to remain there. But from our point of view, we had chosen the right phrase, since we wanted to make people more conscious of the fact that human beings live in two different kinds of environments. One is the natural environment and consists of things like air, trees, rivers, and caterpillars. The other is the media environment, which consists of language, numbers, images, holograms, and all of the other symbols, techniques, and machinery that make us what we are (Postman 2000).

Such a defense compounds the original error by insisting on a strict incommensurability between the physical natural world and the symbolic media environment that is noteworthy for: (1) its lack of logical sense, as the very concept of *medium* depends on a constant traffic between or mutual construction of the symbolic and material; and (2) for its consignment of the "natural" to the shrubbery at the margins of what really "make[s] us what we are." To argue thus is to misconstrue Norbert Wiener's famous statement that information is not the same thing as matter and energy to mean that information can exist independently of matter and energy, a fallacy carefully tracked by N. Katherine Hayles in her critique of disembodiment, *How We Became Posthuman* (1999). There is no absolute separation between the world of the electronically manipulated bit and that of "trees, rivers, and caterpillars": computer networks run, by and large, on coal. Despite the ever-growing ratio of information per gram or joule now delivered by computer technology, the "virtual" world of the Internet accounts for between 5 and 10 percent of U.S. energy use. Postman's instructive mistake, deliberate or not, is to remove the media environment from its physical instantiations and the infrastructure that supports it by focusing on the ecosystem/media *analogy* rather than on the ecological *embedding* of information technology within a larger ecological context. The last line of Strate's definition clarifies the historical dimensions of this oversight. The "postindustrial and the postmodern and the preliterate and prehistoric" specifies a context for media ecology that contains all time *except* for the fossil-fuel intensive industrial age. It should be clear why such a worldview will be inadequate to the task of confronting the consequences of an end to that age. Because scientific ecology is in large part the study of the circulation of carbon through a system and ecological politics are increasingly concerned with the global carbon budget, omitting the carbon supplement from a consideration of the new media environment would seem to destroy the utility of the "media ecology" analogy. However, if we dispense with the *analogy* of contemporary media with ecology and proceed ecologically with a material consideration of Web media as a part of the ecological carbon cycle that has particular significance for the way we think about mobility, we can begin to think seriously about the role of information technology in the carbon-constrained future.

TRANSITION AESTHETICS AND THE ECOTECHNIC FUTURE

Key to the project of integrating our cyber advancement with our hydrocarbon decline is moving away from the traditional ontological and hylomorphic distinctions between the "virtual" and the "real" and towards a hard-nosed accounting of the meaning and cost of moving between different scales of experience in a material world that is never *a priori* unified but can be temporarily *made a one* by a physical exertion of perception or representation. As bioregional theorist and practitioner Robert L. Thayer Jr. has noted, the carbon-constrained future forces us to disarticulate the carbon-intensive trade in goods from the carbon-parsimonious trade in global ideas and images.

> The post-"oil peak" future will necessitate a contraction, or relocalization in the source-to-end-use distances of physical goods and resources as transportation fuels become scarce and extremely expensive: for the first time in history, the world perceptually expands, as travel and freight shipping become more difficult and time-consuming. On the other hand, the continued increase in global electronic communication and consolidation of corporate ownership will continue to virtually "shrink" the world and globalize many aspects of culture. Thus, we enter a new perceptual relationship between time, scale, and sense of place unlike that ever previously experienced (Thayer 2008).

Because the revolution in telecommunications happened during the heyday of cheap oil, it is easy to assume that trade in images and ideas is coextensive with trade in more substantial physical goods. Under scarcity conditions, however, this association breaks down, as the relatively low energy cost of information exchange (currently 5–10% of the U.S. energy budget and susceptible to significant future efficiency increases) gives it an economic advantage over commodity shipments. Thayer's vision, shared by prominent oil forecaster Matthew Simmons, entails the principled return of spatial distance (a rough proxy for carbon intensity) as a factor in economic calculations, focuses equally on both the production and consumption sides of the coming change and rigorously refers ethical questions back to a clear determinant in the form of energy. For Thayer and environmental futurists like John Michael Greer (2009), the reality with which any new environmental culture must grapple is one defined by a process of relocalization in which the physical distances traversed by our sustaining networks will contract as their energy costs rise. Heaviness will matter again in the world by which we get our living, but it will matter even less than currently in the symbolic world in which our explicit culture is articulated.

Addressing the full range of psychological, cultural, and environmental effects this new manner of conceiving scale will have is a topic for another venue. What I would like to stress here is the fact that civilizational trends foreseen by Thayer and Greer resemble neither the cornucopianism of some technofuturists nor the apocalyptic collapse of the more extreme peakers but rather the dreams of the first American bioregionalist subculture. Growing out of the countercultural back-to-the-land movement of the 1960s, bioregionalism emerged in the writings of Peter Berg, Gary Snyder, and Kirkpatrick Sale as an infusion of vehemently (if sometimes fuzzily) ecological definitions of human communities as they are constrained and stimulated by their environmental conditions. Snyder called it "the entry of place into the dialectic of history—but not place defined in exclusively human terms." This movement has given us several key statements of ecological ethics and environmental sustainability that take head-on some of the conundrums now posed by academic scholars concerning sustainable living, relocalization, and environmental awareness, Snyder's *Practice of the Wild* (1990) and *A Place in Space* (1995) in particular. Where the earlier bioregional movement would seem to come up short in its applicability to current questions is in its underappreciation of the schism created by the rise of low-energy information exchange and the equally prominent rise of the relocalization of heavier forms of material production (Curtis 2009). After all, isn't bioregionalism a naïve retreat from the global community and the obligations imposed by global environmental problems? Such is the standard critique, but once we begin to recontextualize environmental writing from the late 1960s to the present as a response to climate change and peak oil, bioregional work gains in contemporary relevance. Material localism was and will be imposed by economic and environmental necessity *and* by conscious countercultural choice, but this relocalization was not and will not be accompanied by the return of geographically specific local patterns of knowledge and practice. It was and will be a world in which our stone once again reliably comes from the local mine rather than the freighter but our masonry techniques may be taken from cultures far distant in space and time. Writers in the 1970s and 1980s, particularly those who were focused on questions of the limits of the fossil-fuel economy or the emergence of large-scale environmental degradation, epitomize this sophisticated reconceptualization of scale. So ingrained is our current distinction between urbane twenty-first-century technophiles and "Luddite" 1970s environmentalists that their historical intertwinement is commonly overlooked. Stewart Brand is perhaps the most well-known example of this phenomenon: as the publisher of the *Whole Earth Catalog* he is associated very closely with the back-to-the-land movement of the era, which was itself very closely tied to the efflorescence of bioregionalism. As the founder of the WELL, among the first publicly accessible Internet user groups, he is also heralded as one of the visionaries who foresaw and helped build the Internet age. Even the *Whole Earth Catalog* itself, the ultimate in sustainability and self-sufficiency texts, has been retrospectively described as anticipating the function of search engines like Google. Brand, whose career includes many other influential projects, is not an outlier, and many other thinkers and writers shared his sense that the free flow of information would increase rather than limit people's ability to meaningfully interact with their immediate physical environments in rewarding and sustainable ways.

In the latter half of the Age of Transition, the relative value of global to local knowledge is nevertheless likely to decline. Why focus on the streamed image of a distant landscape when the experience of a local teacher is so much more relevant to survival? Why struggle with the paradoxes of eco-mimesis when practical instruction is more valuable? We can best imagine this scenario, too, by reinhabiting a prior moment in the history of environmentalism, not to reclaim its value system in a fit of nostalgia but to rummage through it for usable principles and establish it as a site for an "archaeology of the future." This phrase—pointing to the enjoyment of the possible futures dormant in the sedimented layers of the history as well as the power of the future to clarify the limits of the present—comes from one of the most imaginatively elaborated fictional visions of bioregionalism, Ursula Le Guin's *Always Coming Home* (1985). The conceit of this fantasy novel is that Le Guin, sometimes going by the name Pandora, has "discovered" evidence of a *future* civilization, Kesh, on the grounds of her current property in what is transparently the Napa Valley of California (Na in the Kesh language). The book is thus an editorial project that consists of a long narrative (told by Kesh citizen Stone Telling) interrupted by a variety of geographical, ecological, ethnographic, linguistic, mythic, and literary notes and capped with multiple explanatory appendices further explaining the Kesh and the other groups they have contact with in the region. Full of references to native Californian lore and saturated with countercultural-ist rhetoric, *Always Coming Home* could serve as a prime exhibit in any contemporary critique of obsolete localist and essentialist modes of environmentality.[10] But if we suspend this critique, we can sift out something of crucial relevance to our hydrocarbon-starved and information-rich future, something that is still largely missing from our environmental literature and our ecocriticism. In telling the story of the Kesh, who "might be going to have lived a long, long time from now in northern California," Le Guin fully immerses us in a world where the two phenomena usually collapsed in discussions of global environmentalism are disarticulated. The one major legacy that the Kesh preserve from our present civilization (called the City of Man in their idiom and considered "outside the world") is a computer network that archives and serves all recorded human knowledge to researchers who access it through "exchanges" like the Library of Wakwaha using a lingua franca called TOK. Running this future-primitive Internet on solar power, the Kesh have almost entirely foregone the parallel material trade that runs on fossil fuels, which are no longer a part of Kesh society. Profoundly bioregional in their material lives, the Kesh and other residents of their world can nonetheless connect at will to the aggregated cultural experience of all past and present cultures.

The mismatch between the Kesh's seeming unworldliness and their astonishing information-technology infrastructure is addressed by Pandora/Le Guin in an unusual narratorial intrusion.

> Have I burned all the libraries of Babel?
> Was it I that burned them?
> If they burn, it will be all of us that burned them. But now while I write this they aren't burnt; the books are on the shelves and all the electronic brains are full of memories. Nothing is lost, nothing is forgotten, and everything is in little bits.
> But, you know, even if we don't burn it, we can't take it with us. Many as we are, there's still too much to carry. It is a dead weight (147).

Here Le Guin is wrestling with the inevitable disproportion between the information available in cyberspace and the material occasions for its application, a gap that will grow as the scope of fossil-fueled human action diminishes. The Archivist at Wakwaha describes the electronic City of Man as a place that "keeps the dead." "When we need what's dead, we go to the Memory. The dead is bodiless, occupying no space or time. In the Libraries [i.e., the living Kesh culture] we keep heavy, time-consuming, roomy things" (152). A generation ago, imaginative writers like Le Guin were already sorting through the consequences of a profound cultural and material shift, conditioned on a shrinking supply of oil, that had not yet even been properly articulated by the professional futurists of the era.

A futurist text like *Always Coming Home*, avant-garde without mortgaging itself to progress defined as geographic or temporal mobility, might be one place to seek an ecopolitics and aesthetics addressed to our highly networked but carbon-constrained future, in which information travels freely but the mobility of materials and goods is diminished. This complex bioregionalism, which never was the kind of naïve essentialism it sometimes stands in for in oil-glutted postenvironmental arguments, comes from our way up to the peak, and it provides our best guide for the trip back down, as we slowly imagine ourselves becoming something other than "migrants of ape in gasoline crack of history" (Burroughs 2000, 240).

NOTES

1. By some estimates, something over half of the current world population owes its existence to the fossil-fuel subsidy of transport costs, agriculture, and industry (Daily, Ehrlich, and Ehrlich 1994).
2. *Waterworld*'s co-screenwriter, David Twohy, has explicitly cited *The Road Warrior* as his major influence, and the two films share the same director of photography (Dean Semler). The evildoers in *Mad Max 2* are those who ostentatiously waste precious gasoline, burning "donuts" in the desert with their monstrous automobiles. In *Waterworld*, the wicked "Smokers" cruise around a planet inundated by the greenhouse-induced melting of polar ice-caps in a tanker called the *Deez* (the resurrected Exxon *Valdez*). Both films (and *The Road*, see next note) feature a relationship between an alienated adult and a vulnerable child.
3. The origin of the holocaust in *The Road* is deliberately obscured by McCarthy, and the novel seems to rule out a simple biological, chemical, nuclear, or ecological catastrophe. The emphasis on the road, the struggle of travel and transport, frequent allusions to fossil fuels (the man and the boy travel with the aid of an "oilcompany map" and make several side trips to scavenge oil), and the pervasive imagery of atmospheric cataclysm, however, help make this very spare and "timeless" tale recognizable as a twenty-first-century production.
4. *ISLE*, the main organ for academic ecocriticism, is unusual among professional journals in dedicating significant space to original lyric poetry and prose and in welcoming narrative criticism.
5. The *locus classicus* of this trope can be found in the closing paragraph of Ralph Waldo Emerson's *Nature* (1836). For the key historical demystification of wilderness, see Cronon (1996).
6. The classic version of this is Ehrlich (1968).
7. The etymology and practical use of the portmanteau term *glocalism* makes its affinities with globalization clear (and in fact one of the first definitions of "globalization," that of sociologist Barry Wellman, was based directly on the term "glocalization"; i.e., the portmanteau preceded one of its components.) Based on a Japanese marketing idea that recognized the need to customize the business practices of large multinational companies to their various branches, "glocalism" today is invoked more broadly to describe a culturally flexible approach to the roll-out of capitalist consumer culture. If globalization denotes the process of establishing worldwide networks of trade and communication, glocalization names the mechanism by which the enormous enterprises thereby created reinsert themselves in human communities (Wellman 2002, 11–25).
8. McKibben 1989. McKibben has awakened to this paradox in his most recent book, *Eaarth: Making a Life on a Tough New Planet* (2010).
9. Heise (2002) is an excellent overview of the history and implicit assumptions of the media-ecology analogy.

10. The novel's claim to native knowledge is strong. The Napa Valley is considered by archaeologists to be one of the oldest and most densely populated native regions in North America prior to the epidemics, massacres, and forced relocations of the colonial period. Le Guin is the daughter of the preeminent California anthropologist Alfred Kroeber.

REFERENCES

British Petroleum. 2009. *Statistical Review of World Energy 2009*, http://www.bp.com/liveassets/bp_internet/globalbp/globalbp_uk_english/reports_and_publications/statistical_energy_review_2008/STAGING/local_assets/2009_downloads/statistical_review_of_world_energy_full_report_2009.pdf.

Committee on Coal Research, Technology, and Resource Assessments to Inform Energy Policy, National Research Council. 2007. *Coal: Research and Development to Support National Energy Policy*. Washington, DC: National Academies Press.

Cronon, William. 1996. "The Trouble with Wilderness, or, Getting Back to the Wrong Nature." *Environmental History* 1.1, 755.

Curtis, Fred. 2009. "Peak Globalization: Climate Change, Oil Depletion, and Global Trade." *Ecological Economics* 69.2, 427–434.

Daily, Gretchen C., Anne H. Ehrlich, and Paul R. Ehrlich. 1994. "Optimum Human Population Size." *Population and Environment: A Journal of Interdisciplinary Studies* 15.6.

Ehrlich, Paul. 1968. *The Population Bomb*. New York: Ballantine.

Emerson, Ralph Waldo. 1836. *Nature*. Boston: James Munroe & Company.

Greer, John Michael. 2009. *The Ecotechnic Future: Envisioning a Post-Peak World*. Gabriola Island, BC: New Society Publishers.

Hayes, Terry, et al. 1981. *Mad Max 2: The Road Warrior*. DVD. Directed by George Miller. Broken Hills, NSW. Byron Kennedy.

Hayles, N. Katherine. 1999. *How We Became Posthuman*. Chicago: University of Chicago Press.

Heise, Ursula. 2002. "Unnatural Ecologies: The Metaphor of the Environment in Media Theory." *Configurations* 10, 149–168.

———. 2008. *Sense of Place and Sense of Planet: The Environmental Imagination of the Global*. New York: Oxford University Press.

Holmgren, David. 2009. *Future Scenarios: How Communities Can Adapt to Peak Oil and Climate Change*. White River Junction, VT: Chelsea Green.

Intergovernmental Panel on Climate Change. 2007. *Climate Change 2007: Synthesis Report: Summary for Policymakers*.

Kunstler, James Howard. 2005. *The Long Emergency: Surviving the End of Oil, Climate Change, and Other Converging Catastrophes of the Twenty-First Century*. New York: Atlantic Monthly Press.

Le Guin, Ursula. 1985. *Always Coming Home*. Berkeley: University of California Press.

Luppens, J. A., D. C. Scott, J. E. Haacke, L. M. Osmonson, T. J. Rohrbacher, and M. S. Ellis. 2008. *Assessment of Coal Geology, Resources, and Reserves in the Gillette Coalfield, Powder River Basin, Wyoming: U.S. Geological Survey Open-File Report 2008–1202*.

McCarthy, Cormac. 2006. *The Road*. New York: Alfred A. Knopf.

McKibben, Bill. 1989. *The End of Nature*. New York: Random House.

———. 2010. *Eaarth: Making a Life on a Tough New Planet*. New York: Times Books.

Mollison, Bill, and David Holmgren. 1978. *Permaculture One*. Tyalgum, NSW, Australia: Tagari Press.

———. *Permaculture Two*. 1979. Tyalgum, NSW, Australia: Tagari Press.

Morton, Timothy. 2010. *The Ecological Thought*. Cambridge, MA: Harvard University Press.

Postman, Neil. 1970. "The Reformed English Curriculum." *High School 1980: The Shape of the Future in American Secondary Education*, edited by Alvin C. Eurich. New York: Pitman.

———. The Humanism of Media Ecology: A Keynote Address Delivered at the Inaugural Media Ecology Association Convention, Fordham University, New York, June 16–17, 2000. 2000. *Proceedings of the Media Ecology Association* 1, 10–16.

Rader, Peter, and David Twohy. 1995. *Waterworld*. DVD. Directed by Kevin Reynolds. Huntington Beach, CA. Kevin Costner et al.

Smil, Vaclav. 1994. *Energy in World History*. Boulder, CO: Westview Press.

Snyder, Gary. 1990. *The Practice of the Wild*. San Francisco: North Point Press.

———. *A Place in Space*. 1995. Berkeley: Counterpoint Press.

Strate, Lance. 1999. "Understanding MEA." *In Medias Res 1*.

Thayer, Robert Jr. 2008. "The Word Shrinks, the World Expands: Information, Energy, and Relocalization." *Landscape Journal* 27.1, 9–22.

UK Energy Research Centre. 2009. *Global Oil Depletion: An Assessment of the Evidence for a Near-Term Peak in Global Oil Production*.

United States Environmental Protection Agency. 2010. *Inventory of U.S. Greenhouse Gas Emissions and Sinks, 1990–2008*.

Weber, Max. 1905/1958. *The Protestant Ethic and the Spirit of Capitalism*, translated by Talcott Parsons. New York: Charles Scribner's Sons.

Weisman, Allen. 2007. *The World Without Us*. New York: Thomas Dunne Books.

Wellman, Barry. 2002. "Little Boxes, Glocalization, and Networked Individualism." *Digital Cities II*, edited by Makoto Tanabe, Peter van den Besselaar, and Toru Ishida. Berlin: Springer-Verlag, 11–25.

12 Reclaiming Nimby
Nuclear Waste, Jim Day, and the Rhetoric of Local Resistance

Cheryll Glotfelty

Nimby, an acronym for "not in my backyard," refers to local resistance to unwanted facilities and land uses. The *Oxford English Dictionary* dates the term to 1980 and defines it as follows:

Nimby, *n.*

orig. *U.S.* Freq. *depreciative*. DRAFT REVISION Sept. 2003

1. An attitude ascribed to persons who object to the siting of something they regard as detrimental or hazardous in their neighborhood, while by implication raising no such objections to similar developments elsewhere. Freq. *attrib.*

"Nimby," in other words, is a pejorative label to pin on someone else, implying that he or she is selfish. Commercial developers whose projects are stalled, stymied, and even scrapped due to local resistance are likely to think of their opponents bitterly as nimbys.[1] Indeed, exasperated builders and developers have bandied new acronyms such as BANANA (build absolutely nothing anywhere near anything) and CAVE (citizens against virtually everything) to express infuriation over what they regard as nimby-*ad absurdum* opposition to developments or changes of any kind. Public planners are similarly frustrated by nimby resistance to public works projects. A 1992 article in the *Journal of the American Planning Association*, entitled "Understanding and Overcoming the NIMBY Syndrome," observes that

> Neighborhoods and political leaders are fighting with increased fervor to prevent unpopular projects from being sited in or near their communities. It's always hard to find places for jails, drug treatment centers, boarder babies, halfway houses, highways and sanitation truck

garages, incinerators, and homeless shelters. But the NIMBY (not-in-my-backyard) syndrome now makes it almost impossible to build or locate vital facilities that the city needs to function (Dear 1992, 1).

Author Michael Dear worries that "we will regress into a new feudalism": "At the very moment when barriers are coming down around the world, we will find ourselves marching backward toward the imaginary safety of feudal fiefdoms defended by NIMBY walls" (Dear 1992, 1).

Nimbyism has been attacked from within the environmental movement as well as from without. Environmental justice leaders, for example, pair nimbyism with racism. Robert D. Bullard's seminal study *Dumping in Dixie: Race, Class, and Environmental Quality* documents racial bias in the siting of toxic waste dumps, a clear example of injustice caused by nimbyism. As he explains, "Given the political climate of the times, the hazardous wastes, garbage dumps, and polluting industries were likely to end up in somebody's backyard. But whose backyard? More often than not, these LULUs (locally unwanted land uses) ended up in poor, powerless, black communities rather than in affluent suburbs" (Bullard 2000, 4). Thus, Bullard and others in the environmental justice movement contend that the nimby phenomenon results in a de facto PIBBY policy: "place-in-blacks'-backyard" (Bullard 2000, 4). Still others argue that identifying with one's local place may be misguided in an era of globalization and environmental problems on a planetary scale, such as global climate change. Ursula K. Heise, for example, in *Sense of Place and Sense of Planet* criticizes American nature writing and ecocriticism alike for being preoccupied with a sense of place—"an excessive investment in the local"—urging that critics should instead engage literature and art that cultivates *The Environmental Imagination of the Global*, as the book is subtitled (Heise 2008, 10).

Collating the points of view expressed above, we might conclude that nimbys are knee-jerk naysayers, hostile to the common good, feudal turf protectionists, racists, and nearsightedly blind to global-scale environmental problems. Given its negative connotations (signaled by the words *depreciative* and *attrib.* in the OED definition), *nimby* is a term that few would choose to describe their own orientation or behavior. Nevertheless, I must now confess that I have on numerous occasions—albeit with mixed results—fought to block LULUs from my region. These have included a dog kennel, a motocross track, a road, a housing development, a gravel quarry, a kitty-litter mine, a 1200-megawatt coal-fired power plant, and a casino. Each of these locally unwanted land uses raises tangled environmental and ethical issues that open me and fellow activists to charges of nimbyism. Rather than defend these actions, however, I want to start a conversation about nimbyism within literary and cultural studies.

The case study that I consider concerns the siting of nuclear waste. Nuclear proliferation and waste disposal is, of course, a global-scale problem, but it carries intensely local implications, namely, *where* on earth will we put radioactive waste? Nuclear energy often surfaces in debates about global climate change (GCC), since it is a "clean" form of energy capable of producing prodigious amounts of power without emitting greenhouse gases. In February 2010, citing concerns about climate change, President Obama announced a federal loan guarantee to build two new nuclear reactors in Burke, Georgia, the first reactors to be built in the U.S. in more than thirty years. The president's climate advisor expressed hopes that the Georgia project would be "the first of many new nuclear projects" (Behr 2010). Energy Secretary Steven Chu agreed, saying, "This is a significant step by the Obama Administration to restart our domestic nuclear industry, helping to create valuable long-term jobs and reduce our greenhouse gas emissions" ("Obama" 2010).

Many green movement leaders, if not thrilled with nuclear energy, are coming to regard it as the lesser of two evils. "It's better than coal" is quickly becoming a nuclear catchphrase. Stewart Brand (2009), for example, in his recent *Whole Earth Discipline: An Ecopragmatist Manifesto*, recants his earlier stance against nuclear power and makes a strong argument for its advantages, citing more than ten other prominent environmentalists as likewise pronuclear. As compelling as the case is for increased reliance on nuclear energy, GCC discourse tends to silence, brush off, or defer questions of nuclear-waste disposal. Brand, for example, feels confident that future generations with new technologies will be able to figure out what to do with spent fuel. However, others are skeptical, fearing that because of its insidiously lethal waste, nuclear energy will prove to be a Faustian bargain.

This essay first reviews the history of the federal plan to build a permanent, high-level nuclear waste repository in southern Nevada. I then propose a critical methodology for analyzing the rhetoric of "nimby lit"— literature of local resistance—illustrating the method by analyzing editorial cartoons by Las Vegas author Jim Day. I conclude by revisiting the vexing question of the ethics and environmentality of nimbyism itself.

HISTORY OF THE PROPOSED NUCLEAR WASTE REPOSITORY AT YUCCA MOUNTAIN

The Atomic Energy Act of 1954 ended government monopoly of atomic energy and enabled commercial development of nuclear power by establishing a licensing and regulatory program.[2] As the United States invested in nuclear power, little thought was given to what to do with the radioactive waste produced as a by-product of nuclear fission, the assumption being that new technology would arise to deal with the waste. For the next several decades, high-level radioactive waste accumulated near atomic power plants throughout the country, creating a dangerous situation as the storage containers aged. Security risks compounded as the number of atomic power plants multiplied, exceeding fifty by 1980. Finally, in the early eighties the federal government committed itself to solving the problem of the nation's nuclear waste—77,000 metric tons of it, radioactive for more than 10,000 years. In 1982, Congress passed the Nuclear Waste Policy Act (NWPA), which tasked the U.S. Department of Energy (DOE) with finding a suitable site for an underground geologic repository. To ensure regional equity, two repositories were to be developed, one on each side of the country. Multiple sites were to be studied before a recommendation was made.

By 1986, due to political pressure rather than scientific evidence, the DOE had narrowed the field from nine candidate sites down to three, all in the American West. A controversial 1987 amendment to the Nuclear Waste Policy Act—a.k.a. the "Screw Nevada" bill—singled out Yucca Mountain in Nevada as the sole site for continued study. For the next twenty years, the U.S. government spent upwards of nine billion dollars studying Yucca Mountain, a six-mile-long, 1,200-foot-high volcanic ridge eighty miles northwest of Las Vegas. The research turned up serious safety concerns, including earthquake activity, volcanic instability, porous rock, and hydro-thermal dynamics. Nevertheless, the proposed project lumbered forward. On Valentine's Day 2002, Energy Secretary Spencer Abraham officially recommended Yucca Mountain as the place to locate the nation's nuclear waste repository. President George W. Bush approved the recommendation the next day. Nevada Governor Kenny Guinn vetoed the decision, but the U.S. Congress overrode Guinn's veto. In 2008 the DOE submitted an 8,600-page license application to the Nuclear Regulatory Commission. By this time Harry Reid, a democratic senator from Nevada, had become Senate majority leader. He used his political clout to slash the project's funding and to broker the support of presidential candidate Barack Obama, who after his election cut funding in 2009 for the Yucca Mountain approval process, if not killing the project at least putting it on indefinite hold. In January 2010, Secretary of Energy Steven Chu announced the formation of a blue ribbon commission on America's Nuclear Future "to provide recommendations for developing a safe, long-term solution to managing the Nation's used nuclear fuel and nuclear waste," going back to square one, with the Yucca Mountain option temporarily tabled ("Secretary Chu" 2010). And in March 2010, in an unprecedented move, DOE attorneys filed a motion with the Nuclear Regulatory Commission to withdraw "with prejudice" its license application to build a nuclear waste repository at Yucca Mountain. Decisions, reversals, lawsuits, and countersuits appear to have no end in sight. Meanwhile, the most studied mountain in the world is where it is, a silent presence under the desert sun, aloof to the rhetorical battles waged in its name, towering above the mountain of paper that has piled up below.

If you consult a map marking the location of nuclear reactors in the U.S., you cannot help but notice that 90 percent of America's commercial nuclear power plants are located east of the Mississippi River—a veritable shotgun spray of sites—while the few plants in the West are dotted along the Pacific Coast and U.S.–Mexican border. There are no nuclear reactors in Nevada.

The Yucca Mountain case qualifies as an environmental justice issue in at least three ways. First, among the seventeen Principles of Environmental Justice, adopted at the First National People of Color Environmental Leadership Summit in 1991, is a principle that states, "Environmental justice demands the cessation of the production of all . . . radioactive materials; and that all past and current producers be held strictly accountable to the people for detoxification and the containment *at the point of production*" (qtd. in Di Chiro 1995, 308; emphasis mine). Second, the people who live near the proposed nuke dump at Yucca Mountain do not themselves benefit from nuclear power, violating the environmental justice argument that environmental costs and benefits be equally shared. And, third, Yucca Mountain is located in the homeland of people of color, a nation the Western Shoshone refer to as *Newe Segobia*, protected by the 1863 Ruby Valley Treaty of Peace and Friendship. However, despite these clear environmental justice appeals, resistance to the proposed Yucca Mountain nuclear waste repository has been predominantly framed as a nimby issue.[3]

Jim Day and the Rhetoric of Nimby

Scholarly discourse on the "NIMBY phenomenon" or so-called "NIMBY syndrome" is well established in the fields of sociology, political science, history, public planning, and psychology, but it appears to be nonexistent in literary studies. At the time of this writing, a keyword search in the MLA bibliography for *nimby* yields no records.

To begin a conversation of nimbyism within literary studies, I want to propose one possible methodology for analyzing how nimby literature works. I posit that the phrase "not in my backyard" is an abbreviated form of the sentence "You do not put that in my backyard." This sentence has three pronouns and one metaphor whose referents are ambiguous:

You do not put **that** in **my backyard**.
  1   2   3   4

1. *You*: Who is the agent? Who has power?
2. *That*: What is the unwanted project, and why is it undesirable?
3. *My*: Who is the person (or group) who will be affected?
4. *Backyard*: Put it where? How is space defined?

The precise character of nimby texts depends on which pronominal element or set of elements authors choose to emphasize and how they construct the referents. Hence, a critical reading of nimby literature examines evasive referents. I illustrate the methodology economically by reading editorial cartoons. I choose editorial cartoons because they are so short that I can cover a lot of ground (you, that, my, backyard) in one essay.[4] But the methodology could be applied to nimby literature of any genre on any issue. A second reason that I choose editorial cartoons is because doing so allows me to draw attention to the work of cartoonist Jim Day, which deserves commendation. Day has worked for the *Las Vegas Review-Journal* for thirty years and has satirized the Yucca Mountain project since 1987. "Day's cartoons have been a favorite for Southern Nevada refrigerators and dart boards for two decades," writes Thomas Mitchell, editor of the *Las Vegas Review-Journal*, Sin City's longest running and highest circulation newspaper (Mitchell 2002, 5). In 2002, Day republished more than one hundred of his cartoons in a book sold throughout Nevada entitled *Screw Nevada! A Cartoon Chronicle of the Yucca Mountain Nuke Dump Controversy.* A nuke green-colored sticker affixed to the book's cover informs readers that "$1 from every book sold goes to FIGHT THE DUMP! NEVADA PROTECTION FUND."

Using humor as his weapon, Day depicts nuclear waste as a deadly threat; he strategically maps *backyard* onto the entire state of Nevada; and he exhibits cunning dexterity in pointing the finger at a host of culprits, including Nevadans themselves. Day's cartoons have helped to keep the nuclear waste dump controversy in the public eye for more than twenty years of state-level nimby resistance.

A 1987 cartoon entitled "Bombs away . . ." appeared in the *Review-Journal* upon the heels of the "screw Nevada" bill. This cartoon pictures a chubby, World War II–style bomber plane whose nose cone resembles the dome of the U.S. Capitol building and whose tail fin sports the logo "US Congress" (Day 2002, 6). The cargo doors of the bomber are still

Figure 12.1   Bombs away.

open, having just discharged a bomb labeled "Nuclear Waste," which begins its fall to earth. The cartoon identifies the *you* as the U.S. Congress. Nuclear waste—the *that*—appears as a bomb, conjuring memories of Hiroshima and Nagasaki and alluding to aboveground atomic testing at the Nevada Test Site. The bomb is shaped like a galvanized garbage can, suggesting that the United States plans to transport its worst garbage to Nevada, more than two thousand miles from the seat of power. Although the 1987 amendment to the NWPA singled out Yucca Mountain for *study* only, presumably willing to nix the project if scientific studies deemed the site unsafe, Day's cartoon portrays the arrival of waste in Nevada as inevitable. Perhaps the most interesting detail in this cartoon is subtle, a little address tag tied to the garbage can lid, labeled "c/o Nevada." The cartoon thus defines *my* as all Nevadans and *backyard* as the state. The tag could have read "Yucca Mountain" or "Nye County" or "The American Southwest" or "The Mojave Desert" or "*Newe Segobia*" or even "Las Vegas's Backyard." However, from its inception the nuclear waste repository siting process became predominantly constructed as a state-level issue. This point is important and one I shall return to below. This bombs-away cartoon sets Nevadans at war with the federal government—recall that Nevada is where the Sagebrush Rebellion took place—figuring Nevada as a target and a victim of federal aggression, never mind that to be a Nevada citizen is also to be a U.S. citizen. Cartoons such as this one encourage Nevada residents to politically identify themselves at the state level ("us") rather than at the federal level ("U.S.").

A 1990 cartoon features two semitrailer trucks speeding along in the desert, belching smoke, having just passed a highway sign that reads, "Now Entering Nevada" (Day 2002, 7). The passenger door of the front truck is labeled "Dept. of Energy." The truck's sole cargo is an enormous screw, while the second truck hauls a humongous screwdriver, labeled "Congress." Visually punning on the "Screw Nevada" theme, Day again defines *you* at the federal level, showing the U.S. Congress and the Department of Energy in cahoots to screw Nevada. Again the state of Nevada figures as *backyard*. As in this image, many of Day's cartoons depict semitrucks as the big, bully-like intruders, barreling along with a seemingly unstoppable momentum. The word *screw* carries connotations of injustice, sexual assault, victimhood—and perhaps defeat, as in "we're screwed." The slogan itself seems to evoke social justice concerns, positioning Nevada as the state that gets harassed. Many readers will be aware that historical precedent supports this view. The nation's atomic testing program in Nevada took place from 1951 to 1992, exploding more than one thousand nuclear devices, making Nevada the most bombed state in the country. In the 1970s, Nevada and Utah were sited for the proposed MX missile scheme, which would have shuttled more than one hundred nuclear warheads around the two states in a shell game, removing land from the public domain and turning this area into a military target. Vigorous public protest eventually scuttled the

Figure 12.2 Now entering Nevada.

MX project, but the MX left an aftertaste of mistrust. Given its history of being targeted for dangerous military maneuvers, it is not surprising that many Nevadans view the Yucca Mountain project as yet another in a series of federal assaults on Nevada: "[Yucca Mountain] reminded us of a painful episode of above-ground weapons testing when they told us it was absolutely safe to drop bombs 60 miles from Las Vegas. Just bring the kids inside and hose down the car, afterward," recalls Richard H. Bryan, former Democratic governor and U.S. senator for Nevada (qtd. in Smith 2010, A1).

Whereas the above cartoons construct *you* to be the federal government and its agencies, others hold politicians and individual decision makers accountable. One cartoon published in June 2000 depicts a George W. Bush-for-President billboard whose slogan is "Putting Science *Before* Politics" (Day 2002, 74). The billboard is illuminated by a string of lights whose power cord zigzags into the background, where it connects to the "Main Generation Plant" of the "Nuclear Energy Industry." Day insinuates that Bush's campaign is powered by the Nuclear Energy Industry, implying that the site studies at Yucca Mountain carried out under a Bush administration would be in the pocket of the nuclear energy industry, with "scientific findings" skewed by special interests. Another campaign-era cartoon entitled "Trojan Elephant" pictures a giant wooden elephant on wheels, holding a Bush-Cheney flag in its trunk, approaching a fort, whose gate reads, "Welcome to Nevada" (Day 2002, 75). The elephant's midsection is emblazoned with the trilobed symbol for radioactivity and is labeled "Nuclear Waste." The cartoon suggests that the Republican Party led by the Bush-Cheney duo will employ deception to smuggle nuclear waste into Nevada. These two campaign cartoons adopt a common nimby tactic, casting the political race as a single-issue election, in this case, Yucca Mountain. Despite their cynicism, these cartoons hold out some hope for the democratic process, reminding readers that their vote counts. After Bush's election in 2000, Day continued to point the finger at Bush, featuring the White House in several cartoons, while other cartoons lambasted Bush's secretary of Energy, Spencer Abraham, whose head is depicted in one cartoon as the handle of a rubber stamp held by the fist of the Nuclear Energy Industry, poised to stamp the words "Site Approved" (Day 2002, 88).

This series of cartoons identifies the *you* as the federal government and its decision makers, with strong ties to the nuclear power industry. This choice may help to rally Nevadans—strange bedfellows as they are— around a common outside enemy, building solidarity by encouraging readers to identify with the state. Yet another strategy Day takes is to implicate Nevadans themselves.

A two-paneled cartoon that takes this approach shows a black silhouette of a mountain on the left. An arrow in the sky points down to the mountain, and words above explain, "One of the primary reasons southern Nevada became the *ideal site* for a nuclear waste dump" (Day 2002, 106). In the

Figure 12.3   Apathetic Nevadans.

next panel the scene is illuminated and what before looked like a dark mountain may now be discerned to be an obese, pointy-headed, double-chinned man, wearing sunglasses, a frilly shirt, several gaudy necklaces, big rings on pudgy fingers, and a costume-jewelry watch. The sedentary hulk of a man is puffing on a cigarette and is buried in a book entitled *Beating the Odds in Vegas*. The arrow in the sky above this man reads, "Apathetic Nevadans." This cartoon caricatures the image that many people have of Nevadans, a stereotype that most Nevadans find insulting. Day implies that if you want to fight the image, then wake up and fight the dump. Whereas Day's federally targeted cartoons evoke anger and righteous indignation, this and similar jeremiads seem intended to arouse a sense of personal culpability and responsibility.

While some of Jim Day's nimby cartoons emphasize the *you* of "You do not put that in my backyard," others focus on constructing an undesirable *that*. The worse *that* can be made to seem, the greater reason for resistance. Some cartoons represent nuclear waste as generic garbage, depicting metal trashcans, garbage trucks, and dumpsters. Is it fair for the nation to dump its unwanted garbage in Nevada? the images seem to ask. Other drawings focus on the dangerous nature of the waste. A Christmas cartoon, for example, shows Santa Claus stuffing a nuclear waste cask into a stocking labeled "Nevada" (Day 2002, 79). Santa manipulates a pair of long tongs to handle the cask, and he is clad in a full suit of protective gear, with thick gloves and a goggled gas mask. Frequently Day invokes the fearful word *plutonium* as a stand-in for nuclear waste as in a Halloween cartoon of a pumpkin patch. A human skeleton lies facedown near a sign that reads, "Yucca Mountain: The Great Plutonium Patch, All Tricks, No Treats" (Day 2002, 8). Like this one, many cartoons equate nuclear waste with human death, reminding Nevadans that their lives—and the lives of their children—are at stake. Several cartoons depict contaminated water, conjuring the truly fearsome prospect—some would say likelihood—that radioactive waste will eventually leak into the groundwater, whose harmful effects would migrate through time and space. Perhaps even scarier than death, genetic mutation, physical deformity, and mental disability are favorite specters in Day's work, linking Yucca Mountain with radiation experiments conducted during the Cold War and with deformities witnessed by downwinders throughout the era of atomic testing.

The Yucca Mountain project presented the DOE with a public relations conundrum. On the one hand, it must argue that a national repository is needed to remove nuclear waste from the sites around the country, where it is accumulating and posing a grave danger to public safety. On the other, it must assure Nevadans that concentrating all this nuclear waste in Yucca Mountain will be safe. In 1991 the American Nuclear Energy Council (ANEC) mounted an aggressive TV advertising campaign in Nevada in an effort to convince Nevadans (who opposed the dump by a four-to-one margin) that a high-level nuclear waste repository would be safe. Some TV ads showed nuclear waste casks surviving a spectacular crash between a trailer truck and a train, while others featured DOE scientists explaining that nuclear spent fuel comes in the form of a safe, little, solid pellet, not a spillable liquid or explosive gas. Jim Day and other local commentators had a field day lampooning the ads, portraying the scientists as dishonest, the seemingly innocuous pellets as lethal, and the claims of transportation safety echoing reassurances that the Titanic was unsinkable. Nimby literature such as Day's cynically unmasked the nuclear industry's public relations campaign, rendering it alarming rather than mollifying. The campaign became a fiasco and was abruptly discontinued. Day's cartoons condition the public to view nuclear waste—the *that* of "you do not put that in my backyard"—not just as everyday, generic garbage, but rather as deadly and insidiously fluid pollution, posing a serious threat to health and safety, not only for us but for future generations.

But which "us" does Jim Day depict? *Who*, specifically, does the Yucca Mountain nuke dump threaten?

A cartoon entitled "Stalker" shows a nervous mother and her school-aged son walking swiftly away from a large, menacing man, who appears to be following them. The man wears a dark trench coat and clutches a baseball bat, although it is clear that he is no baseball player. It is a night scene in a residential neighborhood, implying that nuclear waste can get

Figure 12.4   Stalker.

you where you live. The thug is labeled "Nuclear Power Industry," while the mother's handbag reads, "Nevada" (Day 2002, 55). Here, Day depicts the *my* of "not in my backyard" as innocent Nevada residents threatened in their own neighborhood by a criminal about to commit a crime. Another, similarly themed cartoon shows a mortician and his crew burying radioactive caskets in the living room of an elderly woman. Again, Day figures the threat as male and the defenseless victim as female, and again the immediate threat takes place at home, where one should feel secure.

Whereas these cartoons play upon the domestic theme, another appeals to Nevadans' identification with wild nature.

In this cartoon, a semitrailer truck, hauling a cargo of Nuclear Waste, is shown ripping down a desert highway, belching smoke. The truck's bumper reads, "Congress Trucking," and its trailer sports a smiley face with dead Xs for eyes, displaying the friendly greeting, "Have a nice half life" (Day 2002, 15). From the cab window, the driver yells, "Got 'em!" referring to the bighorn sheep, labeled "NEVADA," that he has just run over and left as road kill. Nevada is represented by the state mammal, the desert bighorn sheep, a charismatic herbivore that is protected in the Desert National Wildlife Refuge immediately east of Yucca Mountain. The *my* in all these cartoons stands for the people of Nevada—imagined as a defenseless

Figure 12.5   Got 'Em!

animal, a frightened mother and child, and an old lady, the weak preyed upon by the strong.

We might expect that since Day represents the *my* of "not in my backyard" as Nevadans, then *backyard* is likely to be the state of Nevada. It is.

One of Day's best known cartoons, entitled "The Dumpster State," features a large dumpster shaped like the state of Nevada, chock-full of dubious contents, including garbage bags labeled "Leaky Landfills" and "Bio-chemical Hazards," a bomb labeled "USAF," old boards labeled "Mining Wastes," a smoking box labeled "Groom Lake—Top Secret," and a bundle of rods labeled "Nuclear Waste" (Day 2002, 53). A human being has apparently also been disposed of, as a pair of legs protrude from the debris, one naked, the other wearing a high-heeled shoe, perhaps suggesting a prostitute. This cartoon and others employ the map-view shape of the state to define the nuclear waste dump *backyard* as the state of Nevada. And this particular cartoon shows nuclear waste to be just one among many activities that trash Nevada, treating it as a dumpster for substances and even people that the rest of the country doesn't want. For some readers, this cartoon will recall the 1962 film *The Misfits*, starring Clark Gable and Marilyn Monroe, with screenplay by Arthur Miller. In the film, Monroe's divorce coach offers this toast: "Well, here's to Nevada, the leave-it state. . . . You want to gamble your money, leave it here. A

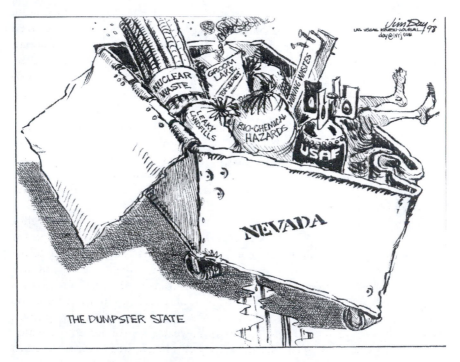

Figure 12.6 The Dumpster State.

wife to get rid of? Get rid of her here. Extra atom bomb you don't need? Just blow it up here and nobody will mind in the slightest. The slogan of Nevada is, 'Anything goes, but don't complain if it went!'" (Miller 2008, 301). Whereas Arthur Miller's lines are an outsider's putdown of Nevada, recycling the hackneyed stereotypes of his national audience, Day's cartoon, run in the local newspaper for the home crowd, summons the power of stigma—"The Dumpster State"—to goad Nevadans to resist exactly such nationally held stereotypes.

Isn't it interesting that the *backyard* of the nuclear waste controversy is consistently imagined as the *entire state of Nevada* when, in fact, Los Angeles is closer to Yucca Mountain than is Reno or Nevada's state capital, Carson City? Why do distant northern Nevadans care more about the Yucca Mountain issue than close Californians do? Because of the way nimby rhetoric has geographically defined *backyard*. Constructing *backyard* politically, along the lines of state government, rather than geographically, according to proximity, is the strategy of choice because opposition to the dump can most effectively be mounted and funded by the state government, in the form of lawsuits, independent scientific reviews, and the state governor's veto power. Furthermore, this strategy keeps Nevadans united against the dump so that Nevada's politicians will be forced to heed an overwhelming mandate by the voters, as indeed they have, repeatedly uniting across party lines to oppose the dump.

The same rhetorical approach of framing the waste dump as a state issue has been taken by an influential nonprofit organization called Citizen Alert, which designed a red-white-and-blue bumper sticker with the slogan "NEVADA IS NOT A WASTELAND," the last word cleverly framed by the trilobed symbol for radioactivity. The slogan not only opposes the proposed Yucca Mountain nuclear waste repository, but it protests the prevailing image of Nevada as a barren wasteland, an image that runs the very real danger of becoming a self-fulfilling prophecy. The fact that this popular bumper sticker quickly appeared on a wide range of vehicles—from beat-up pickup trucks, to sporty SUVs, to buffed Lincoln Continentals, to tricked-out Hondas—demonstrates the rhetorical efficacy of love of place and state-level patriotism to mobilize people across race, class, age, and gender differences.

In this experimental critical reading of nimby literature, I have chosen to analyze editorial cartoons not only because their brevity makes it possible to consider many examples but also because editorial cartoons are an important genre of nimby resistance. Unlike the Yucca Mountain nuclear-waste-dump controversy, which has dragged on for more than a quarter-century, many if not most nimby issues arise swiftly and must be fought immediately. Often there may not be enough time for a nimby book to be written and read. Editorial cartoons reach a broader constituency than many other genres; furthermore, they can be clipped out and taped to refrigerators, pinned to bulletin boards, and posted on office doors. They

employ the powerful weapon of humor and create the iconographic equivalent of catchy slogans, such as "Nevada Is Not a Wasteland" or "Screw
Nevada" or "Mobile Chernobyl." One project for a critical study of nimbyism, therefore, is to collect examples—create a canon—of nimby cartoons.
Such a collection could serve as a training ground for future cartoonists.[5]

Not only are editorial cartoons an important nimby genre in their own
right; they helpfully illustrate the arsenal of rhetorical moves available to
and analyzable in other genres of resistance literature, such as poetry, novels, nonfiction, film, TV, blogs, YouTube videos, and Web sites. They show
the ways that the components of "You do not put that in my backyard"
can be constructed—and to what effect. Thus, close analysis of Nevada's
nuclear nimby cartoons can offer instructive lessons to critics analyzing
other forms and genres of resistance literature and to activists fighting battles in their own backyards.

THE ETHICS AND ENVIRONMENTALITY OF NIMBYISM

But *should* people fight for their own backyards? This question asks us
to reconsider the ethics of nimbyism in general. As we have seen, one tendency in the environmental justice movement is to color nimbys white and
pigeonhole them as economically privileged, regarding nimbyism as a form
of racism that results in social injustice. In this view, nimbyism is a phenomenon—or "syndrome"—that pits people against each other, a zero-
sum game that yields privileged winners and underprivileged losers.

But there is another way to regard nimby-style environmentalism, not
as the power plays of the elite but as the voice of the people against powerful interests. This defense of nimbyism has been articulated by commentators in the UK who object to a government plan announced in 2004 to
ease restrictions protecting greenfields in order to open up these areas to
housing developments to alleviate a national housing shortage. Opponents
to these proposed developments were labeled nimbys, putting their narrow self-interest above the needs of wider society, especially low-income
workers desperate for affordable housing. Employing rhetorical defensive
strategies that we have seen illustrated in Jim Day's editorial cartoons, the
so-called nimbys identified the *you* as big industry—the House Builders
Federation—backed by big government. And they identified themselves—
the *my*—not as members of the affluent but as a wide sector of society. In
other words, these voices of resistance re-spin the battle not as one between
selfish elite and poor wage-earners but as one between the people and the
big business–big government complex.

Moreover, they go one step further and openly reclaim the word *nimby*,
giving it positive valence in much the same way that the GLBT community
has reclaimed the word *queer*, once used pejoratively and *"attrib.,"* now
used self-referentially with pride and a sense of empowerment. In 2006 the

London-based *Ecologist* published an editorial that deconstructs the politics of antinimby propaganda:

> It's not difficult to understand why the government and the big developers who enjoy privileged access to government resent NIMBYism, and why they've sought to make it into something sinister and disagreeable. When the Housebuilders Federation warns that "NIMBYism is rampant and well funded," we know exactly where they're coming from. Nor is it surprising that governments forever seek ways to overcome NIMBYism—invariably by moving the decision making process as far away as possible from the people to be affected by those decisions.
>
> What's harder to understand is why so many otherwise sensible people—campaigners, environmentalists, conservationists and so on—have allowed these self-evidently biased organizations to succeed in turning NIMBYism into a bad word. Why, whenever a local group criticizes a local development, does it feel the need to begin with the disclaimer, "I'm not a NIMBY, but . . ."?
>
> George Orwell understood that control of a debate requires ownership of the language. We shouldn't be embarrassed to call ourselves NIMBYs. On the contrary, if we are not motivated at least partially by a desire to improve our local environment, that is far more shameful. After all—if we're not willing to stand up for our own backyards—who will? (Goldsmith 2006, 5).

Paul Kingsnorth, in an article for *Newstatesman* entitled "Nimbys Are the True Democratic Heroes," similarly observes that "'Nimby' has been the first insult that big developers throw at their opponents . . . [The word] is the propaganda of the powerful" (Kingsnorth 2004, 22). He goes on to champion nimbys as the grassroots base of democracy in a globalizing world:

> In a land, and increasingly a world, where democracy is bought and where the global trumps the local every time, the Nimbys—those prepared to defend what they know and love against the depredations of the distant and the disengaged—are the true heroes. . . .
>
> This is becoming the struggle of the rooted against the rootless; a battle between those who believe that places matter, and those—on the left as well as the right—who see local and national geography as an embarrassing obstacle to a truly global future. This is the struggle of the Mexican Zapatistas and the Welsh road protestors, the Landless Peoples' Movement in Latin America and the family farmers of England, the Narmada Bachao Andolan [dam protestors in India] and the No Airport at Cliffe campaign. Each time, the rallying cry is simple, ancient and deeply democratic: Place matters. This is ours. We decide.
>
> The so-called Nimby, in other words, is practicing the oldest form of democracy—the local variety.

"Not in my backyard," then, is not a cry to be disparaged or dismissed; it is a rallying cry to gladden the heart. (Kingsnorth 2004, 24)

In the U.S., John Cronin and Robert F. Kennedy Jr.'s *The Riverkeepers* likewise seeks to reclaim nimbyism, arguing that "rather than shun the NIMBY label, community groups should wear it as a badge of honor" (Cronin and Kennedy Jr. 1999, 163). Riverkeeper, a nonprofit organization that formed to save the Hudson River, fights its major battles in the courts, using environmental laws to protect diverse community groups—including working-class fishermen and low-income minorities—from pollution. Reaching far beyond its initial home on the banks of the Hudson River, Riverkeeper has become a "model and mentor for the growing Waterkeeper movement that includes more than 180 Keeper programs across the country and around the globe," an inspiring example of nimbys of the world protecting the environment, broadly speaking, by vigilantly protecting local environments on a point-by-point, battle-by-battle basis ("About Us" 2010).[6]

Cronin and Kennedy regard effective nimby resistance as enabled by federal legislation, and they ally nimbyism with the environmental justice movement:

> The new compendium of [post-1970] environmental laws has given civil rights groups weapons with which to fight for their equal rights to a clean and healthy environment. The NIMBY battles moved quickly and easily from working-class communities like Love Canal and Times Beach, Missouri, to African American and Hispanic ghettos that had long been plagued with landfills, highways and paper mills but had never before had the legal standing to divert these facilities away from their neighborhoods. . . . As NIMBY's become conscious of a shared struggle, interest has evolved into a national movement for environmental justice. (Cronin and Kennedy Jr. 1999, 168–169)

Far from indicting nimbys as narrowly selfish, Cronin and Kennedy observe that nimby struggles often *enlarge* their participants' consciousness and sympathies. They introduce another acronym, *NIABY*, to signal this evolution in ethics: "One community's solution should not be another community's problem—NIMBY veterans quickly became 'NIABYs,' 'not in anyone's backyard'" (Cronin and Kennedy Jr. 1999, 169). Additionally, they challenge the assumption that waste must go in *someone's* backyard, the only question being whose; instead, they argue that vigorous nimby opposition creates *positive* pressure for environmentally cleaner technologies: "By 'plugging the toilet,' NIMBY forces industry to move from pollution control to pollution prevention and to consider manufacturing processes that do not produce toxic waste as a by-product" (Cronin and Kennedy Jr. 1999, 169). Ultimately, like their counterparts in the UK, Cronin and Kennedy see nimbyism as a broad-based, multicolored movement for environmental justice that has reenergized environmentalism and that will play a vital role in the future, "citizen empowerment" being "the best hope for preserving the world's natural resources" (Cronin and Kennedy Jr. 1999, 175).

Even in a globalizing world with planetary problems, grassroots resistance to local threats remains an essential component of environmentalism and should be commended, not condemned. So, maybe, rather than criticizing nimby activists, a better approach might be to inspire *more* nimbys, to reclaim nimby for the people, to help nimbys of the world to unite in solidarity, recognize their common cause, and teach each other strategies and rhetoric of effective resistance.[7] The next time someone accuses you of being a nimby, snap back, "Of course I'm a nimby! Why aren't *you*?" Perhaps one day the *OED* will revise its definition of the word:

Nimby, *n.*

orig. *U.S.* Freq. *honorific.* DRAFT REVISION [date to be determined]

1. An attitude ascribed to persons who object to the siting of something they regard as detrimental or hazardous in their neighborhood, while by conviction supporting those who object to similar developments elsewhere. Freq. *self-descrip.*

NOTES

1. "Nimby" is an acronym in the process of becoming a word, whose variants include "NIMBY," "Nimby," and "nimby." I adopt the convention of using all-lowercase letters, "nimby"; however, in quoted passages, I respect the choice of the author.
2. Titus 1989 is a well-documented review of the Yucca Mountain nuclear waste repository issue; I have relied on Titus's essay for basic information.
3. For studies of nimbyism vis-à-vis the proposed Yucca Mountain nuclear waste dump, see Gervers 1987, Kraft and Clary 1991, and Titus 1989.
4. Space does not permit me to analyze here the considerable body of literary texts that treat the Yucca Mountain nuclear waste dump. See Glotfelty 2001 and 2008.
5. Additional future projects might develop critical approaches and discover and catalog nimby literature. I suspect that the vast majority of nimby literature has been published by regional presses and nonprofits, limiting their national visibility. An annotated bibliography of nimby literature would be a valuable contribution to scholarship and a resource for environmental activists.
6. A similar example of how a nimby campaign had beneficial effects beyond its own backyard is the story of Lois Gibbs, who led the Love Canal campaign

to protect her own community. She then founded the Citizens Clearinghouse for Hazardous Waste (subsequently renamed the Center for Health, Environment and Justice) to help other communities fight similar battles. See Shabecoff 2003 for a discussion of Lois Gibbs and defense of nimbyism.

7. A healthy complement to nimbyism would be a widespread, networked IMBY movement—"*in* my backyard"—locally based efforts to envision and enact *desirable* environmental and social futures for particular places. The bioregionalism movement exemplifies this positive approach. See Berg 2009 and McGinnis, ed. 1999. See also Ziser's chapter in this volume.

REFERENCES

"About Us." 2009–2010. *Riverkeeper.* Riverkeeper, Inc. http://www.riverkeeper.org/about-us/ (accessed 3 Aug. 2010).

Behr, Peter. 2010. DOE Delivers its First, Long-Awaited Nuclear Loan Guarantee. *New York Times*, February 17, http://www.nytimes.com/cwire/2010/02/17/17climatewire-doe-delivers-its-first-long-awaited-nuclear-71731.html (accessed 3 Aug. 2010).

Berg, Peter. 2009. *Envisioning Sustainability.* San Francisco: Subculture Books.

Brand, Stewart. 2009. *Whole Earth Discipline: An Ecopragmatist Manifesto.* New York: Viking.

Bullard, Robert D. 2000. *Dumping in Dixie: Race, Class, and Environmental Quality.* 3rd ed. Boulder, Colorado: Westview Press.

Cronin, John, and Robert F. Kennedy Jr. 1999. *The Riverkeepers: Two Activists Fight to Reclaim our Environment as a Basic Human Right.* 1997. New York: Simon & Schuster.

Day, Jim. 2002. *Screw Nevada! A Cartoon Chronicle of the Yucca Mountain Nuke Dump Controversy.* Las Vegas: Stephens Press, LLC.

Dear, Michael. 1992. "Understanding and Overcoming the NIMBY Syndrome." *Journal of the American Planning Association* 58.3, 1–24.

Di Chiro, Giovanna. 1995. "Nature as Community: The Convergence of Environmental and Social Justice." In *Uncommon Ground*, edited by William Cronon, 298–320, 527–531. New York: Norton.

Gervers, John H. 1987. "The NIMBY Syndrome: Is It Inevitable?" *Environment* 29.8, 18–20, 39–43.

Glotfelty, Cheryll. 2001. "Spiritual Testing in the Nuclear West." *Literature and Belief* 21, 221–234.

———. 2008. "In My Backyard: Nevada's Literature of Resistance to Atomic Testing and Nuclear Waste." *Southwestern American Literature* 34, 55–64.

Goldsmith, Zac. 2006. Editorial. *The Ecologist* 36, 5.

Heise, Ursula K. 2008. *Sense of Place and Sense of Planet: The Environmental Imagination of the Global.* New York: Oxford University Press.

Kingsnorth, Paul. 2004. "Nimbys Are the True Democratic Heroes." *Newstatesman*, May 3, 22–24.

Kraft, Michael E., and Bruce B. Clary. 1991. "Citizen Participation and the Nimby Syndrome: Public Response to Radioactive Waste Disposal." *The Western Political Quarterly* 44, 299–328.

McGinnis, Michael Vincent, ed. 1999. *Bioregionalism.* London: Routledge.

Miller, Arthur. 2008. Excerpts from *The Misfits.* In *Literary Nevada: Writings from the Silver State*, edited by Cheryll Glotfelty, 300–302. Reno: University of Nevada Press.

Mitchell, Thomas. 2002. "Dumping on Nevada. Introduction to *Screw Nevada! A Cartoon Chronicle of the Yucca Mountain Nuke Dump Controversy*," by Jim Day, 4–5. Las Vegas: Stephens Press, LLC.

"Obama Administration Announces Loan Guarantees to Construct New Nuclear Power Reactors in Georgia." 2010. U.S. Department of Energy, February 16. http://www.lgprogram.energy.gov/press/021610.pdf (accessed 3 Aug. 2010).

"Secretary Chu Announces Blue Ribbon Commission on America's Nuclear Future." 2010. U.S. Department of Energy, January 29. http://brc.gov/pdfFiles/PressRelease_BRC01292010.pdf (accessed 3 Aug. 2010).

Shabecoff, Philip. 2003. *A Fierce Green Fire: the American Environmental Movement*. 2nd ed. Washington, DC: Island Press.

Smith, Rebecca. 2010. "'Temporary' Home Lasts Decades for Nuclear Waste." *Wall Street Journal*, June 2, A1, http://online.wsj.com/article/SB20001424052748704717004575269111331754570.html#mod=todays_us_front_section (accessed 3 Aug. 2010).

Titus, Dina. 1989. "The NIMBY Syndrome: Dealing with Nuclear Waste." In *Federal-State Conflict in Nevada During the Twentieth Century*, edited by A. Constandina Titus, 162–179. Dubuque, Iowa: Kendall/Hunt Publishing Company.

13 Imagining a Chinese Eco-City

Julie Sze and Yi Zhou

In 2003, you read an article about a Chinese eco-city and say, "This sounds intriguing." Or you might say, "China?" in disbelief, having read for years about the country's disastrous environmental impacts resulting from its manufacturing and economic development policies. The eco-city is supposed to house 500,000 people by 2050, be carbon-neutral and "zero-waste" and based entirely on renewable energy. "Wow," you might think, "I didn't know that was possible."

INTRODUCTION

This chapter is about Dongtan eco-city, announced with fanfare in 2003, its cultural influences, the contributing factors that led to its failure to take root, and its afterlife. Dongtan eco-city was to be located on Chongming Island near Shanghai and was to exemplify a "green" approach to urban design, architecture and infrastructure (including sustainable energy and waste management), and economic and business planning. Arup, a global planning, engineering, and design firm based in London, was going to build Dongtan for the Shanghai Industrial Investment Corporation (SIIC), the investment arm of the Shanghai municipality and one of China's largest real estate developers. The global media adopted Arup's descriptions of Dongtan from the press releases, which claimed that: "Dongtan represents the quest to create a new world." Dongtan was supposed to represent a fundamentally different model for Chinese sustainable urbanism, which explicitly rejected a sequential view of economic development as a precondition for environmental protection. As of June 2010, Dongtan was not built and its future prospects look grim, but its failure nonetheless leaves some fascinating traces for those interested in environmental culture, and for Western environmental critics concerned with transnational discourses of environmental disaster and utopia of which China is the main focus (Chen 2007; Ziser and Sze 2007). Before Dongtan's spectacular flameout, the project was a big political affair.[1] The main *political* question—how a project that was so heavily touted ultimately could be a failure, is outside the scope of this chapter (Moore 2008; Larson 2009; Brenhouse 2010). Here, we consider a related set of *cultural* and *scalar* questions: how did Chongming Island, long considered a rural backwater to Shanghai, become the temporary locus of the world's cutting-edge fantasies about technology and sustainability? What are the *local* impacts of *global* Western fantasies about the presumed solutions to environmental crisis? Whereas much of the focus in U.S. environmental discourse on global environments dwells on the local impacts of development on pollution, the contemporary Chinese political context complicates dominant story lines. Thus, in addition to closely examining the local/global nexus, we also take seriously the complex role of Chinese regional and national development politics that shaped Dongtan, specifically discourses of ecological development in which eco-cities play an important role. Dongtan is not, for example, a story where a local grassroots activist fights successfully against a corporate polluter. This story posits a hero (often a woman) fighting a valiant battle against a corrupt corporate actor or intransigent state regulator. Rather, the (mostly male) actors driving Dongtan are enacting the contested and complicated politics of environmentality and transnational desire.

By *environmentality*, we draw upon political ecologist Arun Agrawal's conceptual framework which he defines as the "union of environment and Foucauldian governmentality." Foucault coined the term *governmentality* to refer to the power of states to govern their populations through a diverse set of techniques and modes of thought by which ideal citizens are produced (Foucault 1991). Agrawal adapts Foucauldian governmentality in relationship to environmental practice, policy, and citizenship to examine the "transformations of power/knowledges, institutions and subjectivities" over time in a village in northern India under British colonialism through to the 1990s (2005, 8). He examines the interplay between "imagination" and social practice (2005, 170). We draw equally from environmentality's *corporate* Disney definition, which is how Agrawal's theoretical analysis becomes operationalized in contemporary transnational environmental politics and culture. If you Google the term *environmentality*, the second page (after Agrawal's Amazon page) that pops up is Walt Disney's Corporate Responsibility home page.[2]

This fusion of Foucauldian and Disneyfied environmentality is particularly fitting in the case of Dongtan. Around the same time that the eco-city was announced, the business press was abuzz that Chongming Island would be chosen as the site of mainland China's first Disneyland site. Although Pudong (a well-developed economic development zone in Shanghai) was ultimately chosen in 2009, Chongming's plausibility as the site for Disneyland and the world's first major eco-city reveals how desired the island was as the locus for the magical and profitable fusion of *fun, environmental concern/respect,* and *business,* specifically tourism and real estate speculation. The multiple logics of corporate environmentality are resonant in Arup's plans *for,* and rhetoric *about,* Dongtan. To environmentality, we add anthropologist Lisa Rofel's framework on "desiring China" to analyze the relationship between neoliberal economy, governmentality, and the formation of new subjectivities (2007). Rofel calls for the importance of

analyzing imagination, representation, and praxis to consider how ordinary people in China engage with neoliberalism (2007). Desire does not
stem from a lack of material objects but is the productive force that creates
neoliberal subjects unleashed by the capitalist machine. Public culture is the
medium that creates the "desire" of neoliberal subjects in China to know
and speak about China's postsocialist reality.

In other words, we suggest that Dongtan captures and enacts the politics
of environmentality and transnational environmental desire. Just as environmentality has dual meanings, transnational environmental desire is a
multilayered discourse and practice. Dongtan is a product of a transnational
collaboration between institutional and individual actors in the United
Kingdom and China, as an example of "best practices" in global sustainability. Another different transnational desire that Dongtan enacts is that
of the eco-city movement, with eco-city planning in locales as diverse as
the U. A. E., Korea, India, and within the U.S.[3] Chongming Island, Dongtan, and eco-cities more broadly are contemporary "magic lands," to use
historian John Findlay's evocative phrase. Findlay, in writing about various
Western U.S. cityscapes, describes magic lands as hyperplanned, "magic
kingdoms" unto themselves that demonstrate how the careful design and
"supervision of new urban forms generated a semblance of order and coherence in a region experiencing enormous change" (1992, 51).

Drawing on photographs, promotional materials, and personal narratives, we argue that transnational corporate culture, global environmentalist subjectivities, and the "imaginative" work of the eco-city idea are
central to shaping Dongtan. Our central text is Arup's promotional book
on Dongtan, which we juxtapose with selected voices of local residents
from Chongming Island and their perceptions of their island's development, ecological and otherwise. To make the case that Dongtan will bring
environmental and social benefits, and be profitable, the book imagines
a narrative drawing upon discourses of technical and scientific expertise,
dystopian fears of Chinese urbanization, and utopian magical thought.

Ultimately, Dongtan represents desires that are neither particular to the
project nor unique to the Chinese context. That is, the desire for Dongtan is
a desire to "have it all," defined as to make money, to have fun, and to help
the environment! The desires that Dongtan represents are those of green or
sustainable capitalist discourse, which suggests that capitalist means are
the best solution to environmental problems. In contrast, we intend to tell
our version of the Dongtan story by highlighting different perspectives and
positionalities in relation to global environmental culture. We were inspired
to highlight different voices and perspectives because our central text uses
this technique to great effect in how it imagines the future of Dongtan. The
first and the last perspective, which you've already encountered, is that of
a Western environmentalist. The second is that of a Western sustainability expert. The third is the reader of the actual Arup promotional book.[4]
The fourth is drawn from selected local voices and views from Chongming

residents. These voices are by no means complete, but they are appropriate given that we are arguing for the central role of stories and storytelling in the tale of Dongtan and its continued afterlife.[5]

CHINESE ECO-CITY ENVIRONMENTALITY: A PARTIAL HISTORY

You are an architect (or engineer) interested in sustainable develop-ment. You lament the decline of big and bold projects in the West, and you are intrigued by the idea of building in China.

This scenario is one that a number of high-profile architects and engi-neers associated with multinational firms have faced in the last twenty years. China's first ecovillage at Huangbaiyu (2001–6) in northeastern China was designed by noted U.S. green architect William McDonough. With a proliferation of first glowing, then damning, publicity, the project failed, according to its resident anthropologist Shannon May, due to the lack of understanding of the local rural Chinese contexts. Some of these contexts were material. For example, the average price of the homes was many times the annual income of the relatively poor rural residents. May argues that many of the global projections of environmental benefits in the village required a fundamental alteration in the practices of the villagers and the economies of the local place. For example, the houses were built with garages for cars even though no one owned a car, and the location of the housing meant that villagers would be cut off from their agricultural fields and sources of income (May 2008). In other words, the site was built with little thought for the actual lives of the villagers and their aspira-tions. Although over forty houses were built, they remain empty and now doomed as a "Potemkin Village."

It would be far too easy to make Huangbaiyu a special case or fail-ure of a particular ambitious eco-architect. Rather, it exemplifies more the perception of some Western experts that China is the preferred nation in which ecological "best practices" can be made heavily dependent upon the nation's political authoritarianism. Journalist Thomas Friedman, in his 2008 bestseller *Hot, Flat and Crowded*, makes this point, in his endorse-ment of the ability of the State Council to ban plastic bags:

If only. . . . If only America could be China for a day—just one day. Just one day! . . . as far as I'm concerned, China's system of govern-ment is inferior to ours in every respect—except one. That is the abil-ity of China's current generation of leaders—if they want—to cut through all their legacy industries, all the pleading special interests, all the bureaucratic obstacles, all the worries of voter backlash, and simply order top-down the sweeping changes in prices, regulations,

> *standards, education, and infrastructure that reflect China's long-term*
> *strategic national interests—changes that would normally take West-*
> *ern democracies years of decades to debate and implement. . . . What*
> *would be so bad? China? Just for one short day?* (2008, 372–373).

Friedman, like McDonough, holds China's political authoritarianism as the *best*—or at least the most efficient—possible pathway to cutting-edge environmentalism, whether defined by a state-level policy to declare, by fiat, better environmental behaviors, or in specific ecodevelopment projects.

Not surprisingly, the experiences of local residents in areas touted for ecodevelopment in China are diverse and uneven. In Huangbaiyu, the subjectivities of the global eco-architect/planner collided sharply with the subjectivities of the local villagers, and the results are clear in the empty houses. Thus, the transnational desire for Huangbaiyu to embody the imagined solution to the problems of global environmental pollution failed, in the face of the lived realities of the local residents (May, forthcoming). There are some substantive differences between Huangbaiyu and Dongtan. For instance, the first was a real inhabited place, while the second was a new city. Huangbaiyu was a rural place touted as an "eco-village," while Dongtan was supposed to be an "eco-city," as befitting its relative proximity to Shanghai. Lastly, Dongtan's environmentality is more aligned with the Disney transnational corporate version of environmentality™—focused on lifestyle, consumption, fun, and profit—than with the Huangbaiyu version. The main difference stems from Chongming's status as part of Shanghai, the richest city in China, and one of the world's rising megaregions (Chen, 2009).

What both projects share is the politics of transnational environmental desire of the builders and planners. Dongtan, like Huangbaiyu, is most saliently understood as a projection of global fantasies of what an ecological life and experience would look like in a rural Chinese context, as Arup's promotional materials illustrate clearly. The builders and planners, despite their words that their project reflects the local values (in the words of the Arup manager, a "Chinese eco-city for Chinese people"), in fact project global fantasies of the local rural ecovillage/eco-city concept. The planners and builders imagine that environmentalism is defined by the advanced technology (of the home to renew itself using local materials in the case of Huangbaiyu), or that the farmers and fisherman near Dongtan will find new markets for their (newly desirable) organic products. While the rhetoric of transnational environmental desire claims to centralize the experiences and worldviews of the locals, the builders and planners are in reality captured by two different perspectives, their own techno-utopian worldview and the mandates of their actual clients.

But this eco-city concept is not just a Western imposition onto a powerless local context. Rather, powerful state actors are also deeply invested in these visions of eco-cities and ecodevelopment, in a broader context where there has been greater awareness and resources aimed at pollution as a result of economic development patterns over the last three decades (Economy, 2004).

DESIRING EXPERIENCES ON "AN IMAGINARY JOURNEY"

Have you tasted homemade cheese? Have you smelt the fragrance of hay in the barn? If not, take a walk from the energy Center to the international eco-farm. The eco-farm is located at the North and next to the modern agricultural district. It consists of a Sino-Italian eco-farm, a Sino-German eco-farm, a Sino-Japanese eco-farm and Dongtan Taiwan folk Village . . . people will be able to visit for the flavor of different places: the Florentine village of the Sino-Italian eco-farm, the picturesque architecture of the Sino-German eco-farm, the Hokkaido buildings of the Sino-Japanese eco-farm, and the aboriginal appeal of the Taiwan folk Village. . . . While appreciating this beautiful vista, as relishing the local fruit, vegetables, locally produced sausages, cheese and beer and hearing oral music, visitors will find themselves back in the good old days of the past, as well as in the 21st century. And all this just in Shanghai . . . (SIIC and Arup, 194–195).

When Dongtan was announced, a 227- page fully bilingual promotional book titled *Shanghai Dongtan: An Eco-City,* written by SIIC and Arup (n.d.), was produced.[6] This book literally illustrates the desire and subjectivities of the planners and investors in the world that they hope to create. Filled with lavish full-page photographs, the book was produced explicitly to promote Dongtan's vision. The opening pages show, on the left page, a map of the region and an unnamed yellow line running from Shanghai over the water to Chongming, through the island close to the eastern edge near the Dongtan site, and then west to the central island, and up to Jiangsu. On the facing page, we are given the brief political history of the project.[7] But before this so-called new world can be created, the planners and client must first pose an important question: What is the problem that Dongtan aims to fix?

The book constructs a narrative that sets up the villain (pollution and urbanization), its victim (the birds), and the saviors (science/technology, architecture, and planning). Dongtan figures as the "natural" (i.e., commonsense) answer to a number of unstated questions: What happens when a city of 500,000 is proposed on ecologically sensitive wetlands where there is no present human population to speak of? What happens when an island like Chongming is connected to Shanghai city and Jiangsu Province? How can catastrophic environmental change be avoided? The book answers its own question for the client and the planner, and for journalists and Western environmentalists. Is it possible to propose a city

of half a million people and promise no ecological harm? The answer—
YES—is evident in the book's insistent focus on the supposed benefits to
the imaginary residents of, and visitors to, Dongtan and to the "environment" itself, specifically the birds that use the wetlands as a major migra-
tory resting ground as they cross over the eastern coast of China. These
benefits—to the imaginary residents and the birds—constitute the central transnational and corporate desire in the project, to imagine a massive development plan that not only does no ecological harm but actually
produces benefits. These hopes undergird the central desires underlying
Dongtan: that a built environment can be at the cutting edge of technology, sustainability, and modernity.

The book opens with short pieces by prominent Western sustainability
thinkers, practitioners and designers, and Arup staff.[8] Collectively, their
pieces discuss the need to design more sustainable cities and posit Dongtan
as the apotheosis of that need, while rejecting the implication that Dongtan
is a utopian project. Rather than the fulfillment of utopianism, Dongtan's
innovations are scientific and technical, and will allow it, in the words of
Gutierrez, to "deliver a more intense development pattern while maintaining or even *decreasing* environmental impacts compared to a business-as-
usual approach" (SIIC and Arup, 27, emphasis added).

The book, soon after, moves from its policy and history approach into
a hybrid photo series/science-fiction tome, changing its genre in distinct
stages. First, it begins with a poem set against an image of natural calm:
"It started as a sand bank / Then it grew into an island / Soon it will hold
the world in awe / And what is it? / It is Dongtan" (28). The first section is
filled with gorgeous full-page photographs of the island's natural beauty.
These include pictures of the riverbanks, goats, oxen, butterflies on a field
of sunflowers, and lastly, a single spoonbill. This section is bookended with
another epigraph which reads: "With a timescale of seven years / we will
/ explore a new possibility of urban development / a new way of life / new
methods of production and more . . . / above all, it is a journey" (48). The
so-called journey then proceeds as a series of specific quests.

First comes "Looking for Shanghai," followed by "Looking for Black-
faced Spoonbill," and then, finally, "Looking for an Eco-City." In short,
this section presents the problems that Dongtan is designed to answer. The
preamble to "Looking for Shanghai" makes this abundantly clear: "Too
much of the world has turned to barren land where mankind has left its
mark," superimposed over the photo image of a desiccated landscape.
"Looking for Shanghai" makes its ideological values clear as it poses the
local equivalent to "mankind's mark" as a series of photos of individual
skyscrapers pasted next to each other. This visible cut and pasting of the
photos of individual skyscrapers rejects the possibility that the hyperur-
banized landscape itself is a panorama. This section also cuts and pastes
highways (88) and street crowds and cars (90) in a manic visual style that
is aimed to produce a sense of fracture and chaos *a la* Blade Runner. The

problem is pollution, and urban alienation, combined with a focus on the scales of China's modernization.[9]

The problems of Shanghai's urban alienation are immediately followed by the presumptive solution in "Looking for Black-faced Spoonbill." This section extols the "natural capital" of the landscape and sketches out the political history of Chongming's development, including the choice made during the 1980s to develop Pudong into Shanghai's economic powerhouse, over Chongming (105). The term *natural capital* is taken from Hawkens and Lovins's influential manifesto (1999). Their concept is that older views of abundant nature as without value under industrial capitalism have not changed to reflect the new context of scarcity of natural resources. Thus individuals, businesses, and governments that can recognize a new paradigm of valuing "natural capital" are positioned to profit in the current political and environmental realities of our age. This analysis dovetails with the local government's attempt to develop Chongming Island as an ecofriendly tourist destination. In other words, Chongming's "natural capital" and its lack of industrial development are a source of new value. A portrait of birds forms the backdrop to the following stated questions: "Do we want Dongtan to be a city with a large number of high-rise buildings? Should we simply follow the usual steps of urban-industrial development? Ought Dongtan's economy be allowed to develop at the cost of its environment? Should we forge ahead in an unsustainable way?" (113). The next page is also populated by birds, but in the cut-and-paste fractured design that visually matches that of the fractured Shanghai landscape (16 squares of bird shots per page). These cut-and-paste visuals, both of Shanghai and the birds, reflect, in part, the subjectivities of Dongtan's planners and builders, positioning the city and the existing natural landscape as problematic partners in their complex project for Dongtan—to both improve upon the existing environment and to make money.

The first two sections of Arup's promotional book ("Looking for Shanghai" and "Looking for Black-faced Spoonbill") *visually* and *rhetorically* set up the problems of intensive urbanization and the potential paradox of sustainable development. The book strains toward answers in its third section: "Looking for an Eco-city." This section contains a number of graphs and computer-generated renderings of Dongtan's development. From the pragmatic and scientific, the book moves into what reads literally like a real estate investment brochure, with images of almost all-white residents exercising with a beautiful waterscape as the aesthetic backdrop. The journey to the imagined eco-city is subtitled "An Imaginary Journey to 2020" (SIIC and Arup, 175). The "we" and "I" taking this "imaginary journey" are visibly racially white, and more often than not, blond. Here, the text reads, "In 2020, we boarded a pleasure boat that brought us from downtown Shanghai to the Nangang Port of Dongtan, which was the starting point where the city began to grow . . . on the wide embankment embracing the port on both sides, I saw guesthouses, hotels, restaurants and stores scattered here and there with people under wide parasols sipping their coffee" (171).

Now the subjectivities of imagined readers take central stage, as do discourses of whiteness. The market for Dongtan eco-city is not the actual transnational financial elites and cosmopolitans who come to Shanghai to work and play. Rather, the image of these transnational elites (imagined as white) is here in the promotional book to signify a particular set of aspirations. In the contemporary Chinese context, whiteness not only represents Western modernity, but more precisely it represents an advanced, developed, and privileged social position and lifestyle in China. The image of whiteness is widely commercialized and dispersed through printed magazines, newspapers, and TV commercials to represent the aspirations of Chinese viewers to a "higher" social status and "better" life (Schein 1994). Schein argues that the significance of whiteness is not in the construction of hierarchies between whiteness/nonwhiteness, Chinese/non-Chineseness, or us/others, but instead it is in how whiteness is mobilized in rhetorics of "improvement" that persist within contesting national and regional discourses. In that regard, this usage of whiteness makes sense given Chongming Island's status as a rural, relatively undeveloped island within close reach to Shanghai that is seen as "needing" improvement and economic development.

In "An Imaginary Journey to 2020," the subjectivities and experiences (nee environmentality) of the imagined Dongtan resident and visitor continue to mingle, and to take center stage. The we/I are "a little tired" but, fortunately, a variety of transportation alternatives are possible: footpaths, boat, horseback, solar-powered vessel, and "of course, hydrogen-powered trolleybuses, cars and motorbikes" (175). The journey continues to the Dongtan science and education zone, where the protagonist may look "back in history seeing a vast sea in the place I had just been through." From this directed change of scene, the protagonist comes to the world-famous natural wetland where "a large flock of seabirds glided past in front of me in the direction of the city, with the clamour of a thousand flapping wings. I accepted this clamour in silence while looking up at the sky at the dark silvery flashes reflected by the wings." Fortunately, he (we assume a male implied reader) is not alone to enjoy this grandeur. A stranger with a telescope shares that "every time I see bird flocks passing by, I can't help holding my breath in awe." After the awe-inspiring moment, the protagonist puts his bike on a bus and works his way back to the port, where he runs into "large numbers of people, some taking the walk on a fisher's dock, some on their way back from the sea, some tasting the newly fished seafood, some angling in private. Among them are . . . an excited crowd of foreign tourists over from Shanghai ready to see this world-famous eco-city with their own eyes" (177). Tourism, appreciation, excitement, and awe come to signify the imagined future of Dongtan, and by extension Chongming Island. In short, the natural landscape complements intensive real estate development to project the future of the island as a mini-Vancouver, or Hong Kong, where the waterscape is a source not of poverty but of improvement and betterment, with the associated inexorable upward spiral in real estate values.

CHONGMING VOICES

Imagine that you are a farmer on Chongming island. You live on the eastern edge of the island. The Shanghai mayor visited in 2008, and you hear that the Chinese prime minister has talked about Chongming. Or, imagine that you are a young office worker in Shanghai who is originally from Chongming. You are proud of your island. What does the development mean?

Now we turn to selected voices of Chongming residents and their perceptions of Dongtan and their island's development more generally. The easiest to track are those of the highly educated, highly technologically adept youth, many of whom have left the island because of the low GDP and lack of employment opportunities (Zhang n.d.). These youth, most of whom have gone to Shanghai to study or work, remain strongly identified with Chongming, which they express through their participation in the Chongming Online Club. The club is an Internet-based forum where Chongming residents can express their thoughts, ideas, happiness, and anxiety about their hometown, reflecting Rofel's argument that one of the central "desires" in China is about the yearning to "know and speak about a post-socialist reality" (2007, 22). Their Chongming identity has been reinforced by Chongming people's "second-class" status in Shanghai, which stems from the long held stigma of Chongming being a poor, alien island. As one indignant "voice" on this forum states: *"I am doing my professional training in Shanghai. They, Shanghainese, all look down upon us Chongming people and call us peasants."* This local identity was further activated in 2004 when Prime Minister Hu Jintao expressed his political vision "to construct [Chongming] into the first class eco-island in the world" (Yu 2010).

As a result, Dongtan eco-city has created a new sense of pride for the dispersed islanders. Many online forum participants expressed yearning for their hometown to gain recognition. As one person wrote: *"Although Chongming is less developed . . . ten years later, we believe that there will be a splendid Chongming in front of us."* Another contributes an opinion: *"The latter project for development is more mature and more suitable to play international games. If Chongming was chosen to develop ten years ago, the result would be like the development of the Shanghai city—a still forest and a concrete city—which did not have the consciousness of building an eco-city. So, I am very proud of being a Chongming person."* Most simply, one writes: *"Chongming, is not only worth living in, it is also a place that has a dream*" (Chongming Online Club 2006/2010). In other words, ecological discourse has also permeated the local discourse of the "dream" for some island residents. The ecological development idea has become the everyday language of some local residents since the project of building Dongtan eco-city has endorsed an imagined ecofuture for them.

At the same time, class and occupational status shape divergent perspectives on the island (Yuan et al. 2003). Some farmers decry the government's limited communication with the local community about the meaning of ecological development. The fifty-four-year-old former peasant Tai'an Ding moved into a new apartment in Chenjia town after his land was confiscated for the development project. He was confused by the concept of the "eco-city." Although his new apartment is under the title of "eco-building," his "new home neither uses renewable energy to provide electricity, nor was it constructed with any special eco-standards" (Moore 2008). Most of the land from the three villages of Chenjia town was confiscated for the development of the Dongtan eco-city. These relocated peasants now have to pay monthly electricity and gas fees as well as go to a market to buy food and vegetables and were granted a township household status and guaranteed a subsidy of 290 yuan (USD42) per month. However, two years after relocations, this subsidy was canceled without explanation and the former peasants unemployed (Song 2008).

Still others complained about the top-down character of the project, which does not put the local community at the center. As one person said on the Chongming Online Club, "Why only the so-called professors, professionals, and the political leaders can speak [for Chongming]? Why have they not listened to our indigenous ideas? Only we have the real speaking rights" (Chongming Online Club 2006/2010). On the other hand, this language of ecology is a very specific index of economic development. Material prosperity is not only the precondition for building the eco-city; it is also the goal. This economic focus of ecodevelopment is clear in debate within the Chongming club: "What is meant by ecology? No development means the best ecology?" Such debates were further pressed when Chongming people had a chance to have an online conversation with Chenlei Peng, the party secretary of Chongming County. Most of them urged him to accelerate the development process and increase incomes. While some did express their desire for protecting the fresh air, unpolluted water, and precious birds, the more significant factors for the meaning of ecological development are in its possible benefits to their economic lives, improvements to their stigmatized image, and possibilities for increased social capital. Therefore, many of them asked Peng about the investment opportunities for Chongming. Dongtan eco-city is, indeed, a utopian fantasy as well as a practical project in the eyes of these particular "ecological fans" from Chongming. The desire for Dongtan cannot be reduced to a cynical ploy of dual corporate and government masters imposing their will on an unwilling populace. The corporate environmentalities of the planner and client generate heated debate and new articulations of environmentalities between different segments of the island populations, who are sharply divided by interest, generation, and age.

CONCLUSION: ECO-CITY ON THE EDGE OF FOREVER

It's 2011, you just finished reading this article, and you are now a little confused/outraged/irritated. Dongtan makes you feel cynical, where you used to feel like optimism was possible.

Eco-city development is flourishing as the scale and scope of environmental damage become clearer to more people and nations throughout the world. The goal of eco-city development to make place-based pathways to environmental change, while laudable, does not come without contradictions or complications. While Western environmentalists may welcome the burgeoning popularity of green capitalist discourse, policy and practice under the auspices of sustainable or ecological development, we suggest that a close examination of Dongtan reveals the urgent need for increasingly theoretical and cultural sophistication in reading ecodevelopments.

In particular, we need to understand eco-cities, within their local, regional, national, and transnational contexts. Eco-cities are not necessarily harmless, or even necessarily beneficial to local environments and populations, and simplistic approval of them from afar is best avoided. Rather, deepening our understanding of the cultural stakes of eco-city development requires unpacking the symbolism behind a very different set of images, fantasies, and subjectivities based in a transnational and corporate environmentality. The fantasy of eco-city development without environmental and social costs through scientific and technological means remains a utopian project likely doomed to failure, particularly in its narrow circumscription of environmental and social values onto particular ecological places. At the same time, ecodevelopments like Dongtan eco-city (even if unbuilt) transform local environments and environmentalities, and they facilitate processes by which ordinary people construct their own desires and subjectivities, in their negotiations with the state, transnational actors, and each other.

In "City on the Edge of Forever," a famous *Star Trek* episode, Bones, in a drugged and paranoid state, enters a time portal and alters the course of human history. Spock and Kirk enter the portal to rescue Bones, and they arrive in Depression-era New York. Kirk falls under the spell of a saintly social worker and pacifist named Edith Keeler, played by Joan Collins. The world as they know it ends when Bones saves Keeler from a traffic accident, because her pacifism delays the U.S. entry into World War II, leading to Nazi victory. Knowing the impact of Bones's action, Kirk, despite his love for Keeler, tackles Bones. In preventing Keeler's survival, Kirk ensures that the world as we know it survives. One violent death prevents countless others.

Dongtan is a little bit like that *Star Trek* episode, and the puzzle of Dongtan is a little bit like Kirk's problem. Should the ends justify the (eco-logical) means? The actual birds, the source of Chongming's ecological dis-tinctiveness, must be sacrificed at the altar of the imaginary birds, for only with the obliteration and death of the actual birds can the imagined future of Chongming begin.

NOTES

1. In 2005, UK Prime Minister Tony Blair and China's President Hu Jintao attended a ceremony in London where Arup and SIIC signed an agreement to expand on their existing partnership to plan and develop Dongtan. Fur-ther, on January 19, 2008, Blair's successor, Gordon Brown, and Shanghai Mayor Han Zheng watched the signing of another landmark memorandum of understanding on Dongtan.
2. Disney's environmentality (trademarked, of course) comes in many forms. First, there is Jiminy Cricket's Environmentality™ Challenge. First launched in 1994, students are "encouraged to develop action projects that target real-world environmental challenges." More than 680,000 children have partici-pated in the Challenge and Challenge winners get a free trip to Disneyland. Environmentality is the fusion of fun with environmental concern, earning the participants a trip to Disneyland (thereby also developing children as loyal Disney consumers). The second category of Disney's environmental-ity derives from Hong Kong's Disneyland, which celebrates "respect for the environment" as "part of how we do business" (Disney Corporation 2010).
3. Masdar is a planned city in Abu Dhabi, in the United Arab Emirates, being built by the Abu Dhabi Future Energy Company and designed by Foster + partners. The majority of seed capital for Abu Dhabi Future Energy Com-pany is provided by the government of Abu Dhabi. Masdar will rely entirely on solar energy and other renewable energy sources, with a sustainable, zero-carbon, zero-waste ecology.
4. As the next section shows, the book is often addressed to a "you," although the presumptive identity of the you is unclear. According to an e-mail cor-respondence with a senior press officer for Arup in May 2010, the book was written to "share learnings," although it was not intended for general sale. It was also produced in line with convention in China to produce a book commemorating big projects.
5. We were also inspired to use this second-person narration from two sources, from Louis Warren (2010) and Timothy Brooks (2005).
6. According to an e-mail correspondence in May 2010, the senior press officer for Arup was unable to confirm how many books were produced, and Arup did not give permission to use images from the book.
7. The yellow line signifies the eventual transportation infrastructure link-ing the three places—Shanghai, Chongming, and Jiangsu. The first part of the project, the Shanghai-Chongming bridge, opened in October 2010. The bridge connects, for the first time, a rural and predominantly poor island, to the megaregion of China's richest city. After the bridge opened, weekend day-trippers from Shanghai reached 100,000 in an island with a total popu-lation of approximately 700,000.
8. Sir Peter Hall, Herbert Girardet and Gary Lawrence, Peter Head, the Direc-tor of Arup, and Alejandro Gutierrez, Dongtan's master planner.

9. The visual problematic of alienation is reminiscent of recent art and photography about China's modernization and its environmental impacts (Ziser and Sze 2007).

REFERENCES

Aggrawal, Arun. 2005. *Environmentality: Technologies of Government and the Making of Subjects*. Durham, NC: Duke University Press.

Brenhouse, Hilary. "Plans Shrivel for Chinese Eco-City." *The New York Times*. June 24, 2010. http://www.nytimes.com/2010/06/25/business/energy-environment/25iht-rbogdong.html?src=busln

Brooks, Timothy. 2005. *Collaboration: Japanese Agents and Local Elites in Wartime China*. Cambridge, MA: Harvard University Press.

Chen, Xiangming, ed. With Zhenhua Zhou. 2009. *Shanghai Rising: State Power and Local Transformations in a Global Megacity*. Minneapolis: University of Minneapolis Press.

Chen, Mel. 2007. "Racialized Toxins and Sovereign Fantasies." *Discourse* 29.2, 367–383.

Chongming Online Club. 2006/2010. I am Pride, I am a Chongming Person. COC. http://tieba.baidu.com/f?z=108779482&ct=335544320&lm=0&sc=0&rn=30&tn=baiduPostBrowser&word=%B3%E7%C3%F7&pn=0

Chongming Online Club. 2010. Is It Reasonable to Build the Bridge in Chenjia Town? COC. http://tieba.baidu.com/f?kz=722428077

Disney Corporation. 2010. *Hong Kong Disneyland*, Sept. 9, 2010. http://park.hongkongdisneyland.com/hkdl/en_US/home/home?name=HomePage

Economy, Elizabeth. 2004. *The River Runs Black: The Environmental Challenge to China's Future*. Ithaca, NY: Cornell University Press.

Gu, Zhuodan. 2009. "Chongming Party Secretary Chenlei Peng Had a Conversation with Internet Users: A Collection of Questions from the Internet Users." *Eastday. Com*, May 18, 2009. http://sh.eastday.com/qtmt/20090518/u1a575741.html

Findlay, John M. 1992. *Magic Lands: Western Cityscapes and American Culture After 1940*. Berkeley: University of California Press.

Friedman, Thomas. 2008. *Hot, Flat, and Crowded: Why We Need a Green Revolution—and How It Can Renew America*. New York: Farrar Straus & Giroux.

Hawken, Paul, Amory Lovins, and L. Hunter Lovins. 1999. *Natural Capitalism: Creating the Next Industrial Revolution*. New York: Little Brown & Company.

Larson, Christina. 2009. "China's Grand Plans for Eco-Cities Now Lie Abandoned." *Environment 360*, April 6, 2009. http://e360.yale.edu/content/feature.msp?id=2138

May, Shannon. 2008. "Ecological citizenship and a plan for sustainable development." *City* 12.2, 237–244.

May, Shannon. Forthcoming. "Ecological Urbanization: Calculating Value in an Age of Global Climate Change." In *Worlding Cities*, edited by Ananya Roy and Aihwa Ong. New York: Blackwell.

Moore, Malcolm. 2008. "China's Dongtan Trial Eco-City Project Was Suspended." *Xingdao Global Newspaper*, Oct. 20, 2008. http://www.stnn.cc/ed_china/200810/t20081020_882305.html

Rofel, Lisa. 2007. *Desiring China: Experiments in Neoliberalism, Sexuality, and Public Culture*. Durham, NC: Duke University Press.

Schein, Louisa. 1994. The Consumption of Color and the Politics of White Skin in Post-Mao China. *Social Text* 41, 141–164.

SIIC and Arup (Zhao Yan and Herbert Girardet). n.d. *Shanghai Dongtan An Eco-City*.

Song, Wenming. 2008. "Mist of Dongtan Eco-City." *China Economist*, Nov. 3, 2008. http://info.cb.com.cn/News/ShowNews.aspx?newsId=20131

Yu, Bingbing. 2010. "An Increased Profit in Land: Chongming Eco-City Is Still Waiting for a Breakthrough." *Shanghai Stock Newspaper*, Jan. 7, 2010. http://www.cnstock.com/paper_new/html/2010–01/07/content_71905939.htm

Yuan, W., P. James K. Hodgson S. M. Hutchinson, and C. Shi. 2003. "Development of Sustainability Indicators by Communities in China: A Case Study of Chongming County, Shanghai." *Journal of Environmental Management* 68, 253–261.

Warren, Louis S. 2010. "Paths Toward Home: Landmarks of the Field in Environmental History." In *A Companion to American Environmental History*, edited by Douglas Cazaux Sackman. Malden, MA: Blackwell Publishing.

Ziser, Mike, with Julie Sze. 2007. "Climate Change, Environmental Aesthetics, and Global Environmental Justice Cultural Studies." *Discourse* 29.2, 3845410.

Zhang, Zhiyuan. n.d. "The Confusion, Reason and Path Breakthrough of Chongming's Economic Development." Shanghai: Shanghai Chongming Government Official Web. http://www.cmx.gov.cn/cmwebnew/node2/node2611/node2693/userobject7ai58483.html

14 "No Debt Outstanding"
The Postcolonial Politics of Local Food

Susie O'Brien

Staying in, living within your means, and getting back to basics. . . . In the spirit of newspaper style sections that make weekly lists of trends that are "hot" or "not," these are three things that have enjoyed a prolonged warm spell, fueled by awareness of global recession and the environmental crisis, not necessarily in that order (von Hahn 2008; Combes 2010). These three prescriptions find perfect confluence in the local-food movement, one of the most visible and growing forms of ecological life politics, manifest in such diverse but related practices as farmers' markets, CSA (Community Supported Agriculture), and variations on the 100-Mile diet.[1] "Life politics" is Anthony Giddens's term for the range of new social movements that differ from earlier forms of collective, emancipatory activism in their focus on aspects of individual practices in everyday life. My use of the term follows Wendy Parkins and Geoffrey Craig's use of it in their book *Slow Living*, to describe the Slow Food movement. Parkins and Craig embrace the term cautiously, tempering its emphasis on "the reflexive project of the self" in the context of global risk culture (Giddens 1991, qtd. in Parkins and Craig 2007, 12) with the ethical imperatives such a culture makes on us, creating "a greater understanding of contingency, chaos and suffering as well as the limits of nature, time and human life, potentially giving rise to values of community, peace and slowness" (Parkins and Craig 2007, 14). Like Parkins and Craig, I approach my subject with a mix of critique and hopeful appreciation for the possibilities it represents. I read the local-food movement, at least in its North American incarnation, as an expression of postcolonial politics. While my argument focuses on the ideological dimension of such politics in a settler-invader society, I also want to recognize the potential a project like local food has to produce positive social change.

While I cite a number of authors (Nabhan [2002]; Pollan [2006]; McKibben [2007]), I focus primarily on Barbara Kingsolver, Steven Hopp, and Camille Kingsolver's bestselling 2007 *Animal, Vegetable, Miracle*, which I read as exemplary of the genre of American local-food writing.[2] My analysis, then, is primarily a textual one, informed by postcolonial and ecocritical theory, as well as a body of interdisciplinary work on alternative food networks that challenges the capacity of what Michael Pollan describes as a "novel hybrid" of "market as movement" (Pollan 2006, 254) to nurture values of either sustainability or social justice. I draw in particular on Rachel Slocum's cogent analysis of the racialization of alternative food practices. Slocum contends that "while the ideals of healthy food, peoples and land are not intrinsically white, the objectives, tendencies, strategies, the emphases and absences and the things overlooked in community food make them so." Whiteness, in Slocum's analysis, defines a particular form of spatial segregation that may function unconsciously, but that also—crucially—is "capable of transforming itself" (Slocum 2007, 523). White spatiality may include a "desire for proximity" (Slocum 2007, 524) whose entanglement with shame does not preclude the possibility of forging real connections across difference; in fact, shame may be a productive force, a point to which I will return below.

Slocum's contention that alternative food practices occupy sites of race and class privilege, that the lines defining these sites are often invisible to participants, and that they can be, and sometimes are, breached, informs my argument that the local-food movement expresses, among other things, white Americans' attempt to come to terms with their place in the ongoing violence of colonialism. A critical part of the backdrop to this argument is that, while localism does not in theory preclude respect for indigenous culture or politics, these elements receive little to no attention in most discussions (Nabhan is a significant exception). I suggest that they are not entirely absent, but refracted into thematic concerns with place, economics, representation, and morality. While tropes of home and domesticity, fortified by a sometimes explicitly Protestant work ethic, echo colonial ideology in surprisingly straightforward ways, local-food discourse also reflects an ambivalent relation to contemporary processes of globalization: critical of global agribusiness, it simultaneously upholds key tenets of neoliberalism in relation to private property and education in particular. It is, like the writing of all uncomfortable beneficiaries of empire, politically ambiguous: progressive—smugly, annoyingly so at times—yet, like all redemption narratives, it acknowledges some sins and omissions while discounting others.

I have suggested that the local-food narrative, which in the case of Kingsolver et al.'s book, along with many others, takes the form of a kind of a pedagogical memoir, may be boiled down, minus a few of the tasty bits, to three general prescriptions with particularly powerful resonance in North American culture today: *stay home, live within your means, and get back to basics.*

* * *

In the first chapter of her book, "Called Home," Kingsolver et al. narrate the start of the family's journey from Tucson to southern Appalachia, a destination chosen for ecological, spiritual, and pragmatic reasons: Kingsolver's ancestors came from nearby, and she grew up in next-door Virginia; her husband, Steven Hopp, a biologist, who contributes scientific sidebars to the book, was born in the area and owns a piece of land that becomes the site of the experiment. As Kingsolver explains: "Now I could spend Memorial Day decorating my ancestors' graves with peonies from my backyard. Tucson had opened my eyes to the world and given me a writing career, legions of friends, and a taste for the sensory extravagance of red hot chiles and five-alarm sunsets. But after twenty-five years in the desert, I'd been called home" (Kingsolver et al. 2007, 3). Though its specifically Christian resonance isn't really extended throughout the book, the biblical allusion gives the concept of "home" a symbolic weight that merits examination. Tucson, where Kingsolver has worked and raised her children, is associated both with extravagant pleasures—a kind of self-indulgent excess— and privation: the desert. It is the place that "opened my eyes to the world" (Kingsolver et al. 2007, 3): worldliness, which connotes both travel and a particular kind of cosmopolitan knowledge, signifies here a sort of fun, but ultimately bad, trip from which one comes down, a bit reluctantly at first, but inevitably and finally gratefully.

The critique of worldliness makes sense in relation to the local-food movement in some obvious ways. First, local-food writing really is on a simple level a kind of antitravel writing, focused most explicitly on the need to reduce the carbon footprint of food—"transporting a single calorie of a perishable fresh fruit from California to New York takes about 87 calories worth of fuel" (Kingsolver et al. 2007, 68)—the same efficiency ratio, as Kingsolver wryly notes, as "driving from Philadelphia to Annapolis, and back, in order to walk three miles on a treadmill in a Maryland gym" (Kingsolver et al. 2007, 68). The "food-miles" argument has taken a hit recently, as some studies suggest that locally produced food is not necessarily the most energy efficient, and that transportation accounts for only a fraction of the environmental cost of food production (see McGregor and Vorley 2007; Bailey 2008; McWilliams 2009). However, global agribusiness is indisputably implicated in the reduction of biodiversity, as industry demand for quick-growing produce that stands up well to travel has resulted in the loss of thousands of heritage crops (Kingsolver et al. 2007, 49). We feel this loss most immediately at the level of taste, but it also has a significant impact on the viability of our future food supply. Gary Nabhan draws a direct connection between biodiversity and "excessive mobility," which he sees as a measure of "homeland insecurity" (Nabhan 2002, qtd. in Delind 2006, 128).

Kingsolver et al.'s book, like others in the genre, places value on human as well as vegetal rootedness in connection with the problem of security. In contrast to the patently *in*secure industrial food system, whose weakness turns up with distressing regularity in cases of BSE or mass salmonella poisoning, local-food economies ensure the health—and not, incidentally, the happiness—of participants, based on the value of neighborliness.

"*Local* is farmers growing trust," as Kingsolver puts it (Kingsolver et al. 2007, 123). Combined with the element of hands-on care that characterizes small-scale farms, the elements of trust and proximity embodied in what Michael Pollan terms "relationship marketing," in which "buyers and sellers look one another in the eye" (Pollan 2006, 24), greatly reduce the risks to people, animals, and environment associated with industrial farming. While Kingsolver, like Pollan, advocates for transparent labeling and rigorous certification processes for organic food, both doubt (with some justification) the capacity and commitment of the FDA to supply the kind of information needed, or to protect the food supply from accidental or deliberate contamination. Without painting any explicitly apocalyptic scenarios, Kingsolver lightly reminds us of the connection between security and self-sufficiency. A survey of agricultural history confirms that "when civilization collapses on itself, as it inevitably does, back we go to the family farm" (Kingsolver et al. 2007, 178). The example of victory gardens, supplied in one of Hopp's sidebars (Kingsolver et al. 2007, 250), makes the point more explicitly. Conceived in response to the German blockage of UK food imports in World War II, the conversion of golf courses, parks, and schoolyards to vegetable gardens was a vivid form of what a friend of Kingsolver calls in another context "edible patriotism" (Kingsolver et al. 2007, 338).

Twenty-first-century "victory gardens" serve diverse aims: in addition to feeding urban populations, they "serve as air filters, help recycle wastes, absorb rainfall, present pleasing green spaces, alleviate loss of land to development . . . reduce fossil fuel consumption, provide jobs, educate kids and revitalize communities" (Kingsolver et al. 2007, 250). This elaboration of functions underlines an important fact: this is an expansive and liberal version of "Homeland Security"—more Obama than Bush (the parallel is accentuated by Michelle Obama's contemporary take on Eleanor Roosevelt's World War II victory garden at the White House [Burros 2009]). And the emphasis on homemaking, with a primary goal of feeding children healthy meals, is self-consciously *post-*, not antifeminist. Kingsolver registers the distinction when recounting a conversation she had about cheesemaking with a woman at a Lebanese market stall. On hearing that Kingsolver has tried it, she says, "'You make cheese *yourself* . . . You are a real housewife.'" "It has taken me decades to get here," Kingsolver notes, "but I took that as a compliment" (Kingsolver et al. 2007, 156). Embracing the role of housewife answers the desire Kingsolver suggests that "a lot of us [have] for a way back home, to the place where care-and-feeding isn't zookeeper's duty but something happier and more creative" (Kingsolver et al. 2007, 127). Stressing the shared and voluntary nature of the division of labor in the Hopp-Kingsolver household, the image here as elsewhere is of "home" not as a place of fixed meanings and identities but a place of possibility and choice.

It is also open to other places and ways of living. Having lived in "some of the world's major cities" confers on Kingsolver what she describes as a kind of "dual citizenship" (Kingsolver et al. 2007, 208), a cosmopolitan perspective that allows her to understand rural suspicions of urbanites and vice versa. It is also staunchly multicultural; like Gary Nabhan, whose experiment in *Coming Home to Eat* (2002) was partly motivated by a trip to visit his relatives in Lebanon, where he came to appreciate the "pleasures and politics" of regional cuisine, Kingsolver draws inspiration from her husband's Italian family, and from the Italian regional food ethic more generally. She recalls of her arrival in Italy, when she saw outside the plane window an elderly farmer with a horse-drawn plow: "For reasons I didn't understand yet, I thought: I've come *home*" (Kingsolver et al. 2007, 243, emphasis added).

The most crucial element of home that emerges in the passages just cited would seem to be this: home is a destination one chooses to come or to return to, rather than a place one has never left and perhaps cannot or will not leave. That is, the meaning of "home" in the local-food narrative is contingent on mobility. This is a constant, subterranean current in Kingsolver's narrative, from her move to Appalachia, to her daughter's departure for college midway through the year, to the family's travels throughout the U.S. and Europe to connect with other devotees of the local. Of the geographically disparate group she meets at a cheesemaking workshop in Vermont, Kingsolver muses that, individual motives notwithstanding,

> we're connecting across geography and time with the artisans of Camembert, the Greek shepherds, the Mongols on the steppes who live by milking their horses—everybody who ever looked at a full-moon pot of white milk and imagined cheese. We're recalling our best memories infused with scents, parental love, and some kind of food magically coming together in the routines of childhood. We're hoping *our* kids will remember us somewhere other than in the driver's seat of the car. (Kingsolver et al. 2007, 140–141)

An interesting thing about this passage is that Kingsolver is deploying one form of mobility—socioeconomic mobility, which extends to the cultural capital of historical knowledge and imagination—in order to condemn another: the fast-food meal eaten in a car. These contradictions highlight a fact that globalization theorists have long noted, which is that the key distinction in the contemporary world is not between global and the local (which always has been, as Doreen Massey puts it, "a conjunction of many histories and many spaces" [Massey 1995, 191]) but between different forms of mobility and stasis. There remain important distinctions between "denizens," who inhabit place precariously, and "citizens," who are free to stay or go (Hammar 1990). Being "on the move" is a condition of modern life, but one whose effects, as Zygmunt Bauman explains, "are radically unequal. Some of us become fully, and truly 'global;' some are fixed in their 'locality'—a predicament neither pleasurable, nor endurable in the world in which the 'globals' set the tone and compose the rules of the life game" (1998, 2). To be "global" is, paradoxically, to be at home in the world in the sense of being not only more secure but more legitimate, both in a general moral sense and a more technical, legal sense, connected to property ownership. These senses come together in the history of colonial homemaking, where the ideology of "good" (civilized) versus "bad" (primitive) mobility was forged. As the entry on "home" in Tony Bennett, Lawrence Grossberg, and Meaghan Morris's 2005 *Keywords* notes: "The nomadism of hunter-gatherer societies,"—their lack of a stable home, in other words—"indicated a lack of civilization, which legitimated colonization as a process of civilizing the savage, and a failure to permanently settle and so effectively own the land . . . justified its expropriation" (Bennett et al. 2005, 163).

The question of legitimacy arises peripherally, and a bit uncomfortably, in Kingsolver's account of Thanksgiving, her favorite holiday because: "As a child of the farmlands I appreciate how it honestly belongs to us" (Kingsolver et al. 2007, 280). The element of ritual thanks is critical to the holiday's meaning: "a day off work just to praise Creation: the turkey, the squash, and the corn, these things that ate and drank sunshine, grass, mud, and rain, and then in the shortening days laid down their lives for our welfare and onward resolve" (Kingsolver et al. 2007, 284). There is, she acknowledges, another version of the story, "the Squanto story,"

> Replayed . . . to death in our primitive grade school pageantry ("Pilgrim friends! Bury one fish beneath each corn plant!"). But that hopeful affiliation ended so badly, I hate to keep bringing it up. Bygones are what they are. In my household credo, Thanksgiving is Creation's birthday party. Praise harvest, a pause and a sigh on the breath of immortality. (Kingsolver et al. 2007, 284)

Kingsolver is no doubt right to cast doubt on the clichéd Thanksgiving story of friendly Europeans and hospitable Indians, but it doesn't explain her rejection of the fuller, more complex story, her subsumption of politics into ecology, of historical violence into the spiritual realm of immortality. Indigenous Americans make another couple of brief (non)-appearances in the text: Kingsolver notes that the Hohokam and Pima once lived harmoniously in the Sonoran desert: "They were the last people to live on that land without creating an environmental overdraft. When the Spanish arrived . . . they set about working up a monumental debt" by, among other things, "withdrawing millions more gallons from the water table each year than a dozen inches of annual rainfall could ever restore" (Kingsolver et al. 2007, 3). Later, Kingsolver laments that "North America's native cuisine met the same unfortunate fate as its native people, save for a few relics like the Thanksgiving turkey" (Kingsolver et al. 2007, 16). If we leave aside the dubiousness of the analogy, it is arguable, and worthy of critical consideration, that the matter of "monumental debt" is addressed in relation to food, instead of—maybe as a proxy for—native people. This concern informs the second mantra of local-food rhetoric: *live within your means.*

This rule informs the accounting practice that factors in all the elements of production, including conventionally disregarded "externalities": the depletion of finite resources used to grow, process, and transport food, the vibrancy of rural communities, and the impact on human health and the environment. In defense of the higher retail cost of local food, which tends to be organic, and to come from small family-run farms, local-food advocates argue that "you can buy honestly priced food or you can buy irresponsibly priced food" (Joel Salatin, qtd. in Pollan 2006, 243). According to the ideal of living within one's means, the most honest and economically efficient way to eat is to grow, gather, hunt, and prepare food oneself; under these admittedly rare circumstances one can be said to have paid "the full karmic price of a meal" (Pollan 2006, 9). In the final chapter of his book, called "The Perfect Meal," Pollan describes a dinner, produced and prepared by him, with assistance from his guests, as coming closest to approaching that goal: the meal "that's been fully paid for, that leaves no debt outstanding" (Pollan 2006, 409). By contrast, the cost of *dis*honest food is "not [or not only?] measured in money," Kingsolver suggests, "but in untallied debts that will be paid by our children in the currency of extinctions, economic unravellings, and global climate change" (Kingsolver et al. 2007, 66). The economic scale used here is simultaneously global and radically local, grounded in an appeal to family values in the form of future generations.

What is not accounted for in any obvious way are debts accruing from the past, or the inequitable distribution of current resources. The issue is defined primarily as a matter of choice: "The main barrier standing between ourselves and a local-food culture is not price," Kingsolver maintains, "but attitude. The most difficult requirements are patience and a pinch of restraint—virtues that are hardly the property of the wealthy" (Kingsolver et al. 2007, 31). A culture of instant gratification is implicated in the swamping of American family farms by global agribusiness: "California vegetables are not the serpent, it's all of us who open up our veins to the flow of gas-fueled foods, becoming yawning addicts, while our neighbourhood farms dry up and blow away. We seem to be built with a faulty gauge for moderation" (Kingsolver et al. 2007, 158). The connotations of the addiction metaphor expose the fault lines in the ideology of personal economic responsibility in a way that recalls media responses to the global financial meltdown, in which individual consumers were alternately portrayed as the victims of corporate corruption and lambasted for not living within their means. There are only two players here: individuals, who are either thrifty or profligate, virtuous or venal, and "the system," which is always by definition corrupt. Elsewhere, Kingsolver explains the farming crisis in terms of an opposition between "people trying to keep work and homes together, versus conglomerates that scoop up a customer's money and move it out of town to a corporate bank account far away. Where I grew up, we used to call that 'carpetbagging.' Now it seems to be called the American way" (Kingsolver et al. 2007, 152) (one might also call it "colonialism" and recall its foundational role in producing "the American way"; Kingsolver doesn't go there). The problem with this binary opposition in which hardworking, thrifty people are pitted against corporate thieves is that it precludes any critical analysis of the capitalist economic system, in which the Protestant ideology of the former provides cover for the activities of the latter.

Kingsolver doesn't take issue with capitalism; in the interests of having her daughter Lily understand her chicken-raising business "genuinely," and not just as "some little kid thing," she explains to her "about capitalization, credit, and investors" and arranges the terms for Lily to pay back the money she has loaned her through the profits of her egg sales. What she objects to isn't the politics of an economy structured around profit and debt but the aesthetics of a "system" that mediates the operation of individual karma, or the possibility of achieving ecological (or spiritual) redemption. Whether or not it is rendered in explicitly Christian terms—and for McKibben (2007) and quite a few of the local-food advocates interviewed in Pollan and Kingsolver's books it is (see Guthman 2007, 263)—the goal of living within one's means is closely bound up with the idea of redemption, the dischargement of debt tantamount to the forgiveness of sin. Excluded in what Pollan identifies as the sometimes "awkward hybrid of the economic and the spiritual" that characterizes local-food rhetoric is any acknowledgment of incommensurable values or the unequal distribution of power (Pollan 2006, 225). The ideological principle of living within one's means diverts to the realm of household economics the properly political questions of: Who has the right to call this place home? On what legal or moral grounds do property claims lie?

Local food rhetoric further precludes consideration of questions like these through an emphasis on *getting down to basics*, a concept that embraces a mixed bag of values, including physical labor, nature, and authenticity, in the name of avoiding aspects of modern culture that are deemed either deceptive, decadent, or both. In parallel to the move back home, Kingsolver's story enacts the localist imperative to get literally down to earth. This involves what she describes as a paradigm shift away from arcane knowledges to a respect for, if not actual participation in, the process of growing food. The point that agricultural knowledge is held in low esteem in contemporary North American culture is reinforced by an analogy of farmers with racial minorities. Growing up in rural Virginia, Kingsolver recalls, "we were all born to our rank, as inescapably as Hindus, the castes being only two: "farm" and "town" (Kingsolver et al. 2007, 206). Although her parents weren't farmers, she was relegated to the category by virtue of simply living in the country. The minority status of farmers is thus a fuzzy one, defined not by socioeconomic status (which would itself be a problematic designation, given the difference between family farms and agribusinesses) but by culture, or the perceived absence of it. In any case, she argues, "the line of apartheid was unimpeachably drawn" (Kingsolver et al. 2007, 206).

Having thus provocatively underlined the magnitude of farmers' exclusion from the mainstream, Kingsolver asserts their unrecognized value through a series of diverse comparisons. "In the grocery store checkout corral," she notes ruefully, "we're more likely to learn which TV stars are secretly fornicating than to inquire as to the whereabouts of the people who grew the cucumbers and melons in our carts" (Kingsolver et al. 2007, 13). Oddly compounding the celebrity obsession problem is the tendency of the urban U.S. middle class to be "more specifically concerned about exploited Asian factory workers [than about American farmers]" (Kingsolver et al. 2007, 208). Kingsolver highlights these skewed American priorities by describing a business meeting with French and Spanish journalists in which the conversation veered sharply from "postcolonial literature to fish markets and the quality of this year's mushrooms or leeks." The Europeans clearly support her belief that, "in the context of a healthy food culture, fish and leeks are as respectable as postcolonial literature. (And arguably more fun)" (Kingsolver et al. 2007, 127).

Thus, by taking their opponents—fornicating TV stars, Asian factory workers, and postcolonial critics—down a peg or two, Kingsolver restores some of the lost status of the farmer. Gary Nabhan goes one better in his book, describing how he planted summer squash seeds

> in the satellite dish perched just outside my garden wall. I had never used it for what most people use satellite dishes for anyway . . . I remembered that old adage for peacemakers: "swords into plowshares," Perhaps I could offer an amendment for today's place makers: satellite dishes into squash planters. We could let the local seeds grow where we had once placed our hope for "keeping in touch with the outside world" (Nabhan 2002, 40–41).

The outside world, with its disturbing menagerie of celebrities, factory workers, and postcolonial critics, isn't just opposed to farming, but, arguably, implicated in its denigration, according to a construction in which the dynamics of postmodern capitalism are rendered as the distortion of the real economy of farming by "fashion and marketing."

Fashion and marketing are implicated in a culture of excess, in which style has come to replace substance, to the detriment of good sense and health, and of taste, which is placed firmly in the realm of biology rather than culture. Pondering consumers' desire to eat exotic, out-of-season, and often flavorless fruits and vegetables, Kingsolver says, "You'd think we cared more about the *idea* of what we're eating than about what we're eating. But then, if you examine the history of women's footwear, you'd think we cared more about the idea of showing off our feet than about, oh, for example, walking" (Kingsolver et al. 2007, 55). Proceeding from the assumption that we can separate *what* we're eating from the *idea* of it, Kingsolver indicts "fashion" (along with its evil agent "marketing") for obscuring the essential truth of food. "So many people were taken in by the pesticide-herbicide propaganda," she quotes an organic farmer noting quizzically; "why would we fall for that?" (Kingsolver et al. 2007, 163). Rather than attempting to answer what is admittedly a complex question, Kingsolver counters industry propaganda with agricultural truth, verifiable by its grounding in local experience. Against the corrupt currency of mass-marketed industrial food, "'locally grown' is a denomination whose meaning is incorruptible" (Kingsolver et al. 2007, 123), a statement that neatly erases the mediating power of language in a way that seems to suggest that local food is somehow simply not just good but *true*. This suggestion is carried by a romanticist strain in Kingsolver's narrative that gives its often scientific rendering of biological fact the currency of immanence—that quality of Romantic writing that critic Alan Liu calls "transcendence sunk in the mundane" (Liu 1990, 93). While Liu is referring to the Romanticist and literary-critical focus on bits of everyday *culture*, Kingsolver transposes this value to nature, in a way that stresses the shared biological characteristics of humans, animals, and vegetables.

In Kingsolver's story, vegetables are protagonists in a cooperative venture in which "we are management; they're labor," employees who "in virtuous green silence work as hard as any chicken or cow" (Kingsolver et al. 2007, 175, 265). They also have feelings: "A too-young [asparagus] plant gets discouraged when you whack off its every attempt to send up new shoots in the spring, abuse that will make the plant sink into vegetable despair and die" (Kingsolver et al. 2007, 28). What is questionable here is not the idea of plants or even food having agency, a proposition that writers such Donna Haraway and Jane Bennett have advanced in compelling ways. However, where they seek to complicate boundaries between nature and technology and extend the multivalent, contradictory, and occult machinations ordinarily associated with culture to the nonhuman world, Kingsolver is doing the opposite: reducing human and nonhuman life to a cheerfully wholesome functionality, evident in this passage about vegetable sex:

> Flowering plants . . . bloom and have sex by somehow rubbing one flower's boy stuff against another's girl parts. Since they can't engage in hot pursuit, they lure a third party, such as bees, into the sexual act. . . . From that union comes the blessed event, babies made, in the form of seeds cradled inside some form of fruit. Finally, sooner or later—because after *that*, what's the point anymore? they die (Kingsolver et al. 2007, 64).

The final zinger can be delivered lightly because the whole scene is implicitly subsumed in the wider drama that queer theorist Lee Edelman calls "reproductive futurism" (Edelman 2004, 4): the zigzagging plotlines of life naturalized (botanized, in this version) in the singular story of boy-meets-girl.

In other places, though, the significatory wildness of sex escapes this heteronormative frame, such as in Kingsolver's description of a bag of store-bought "lipstick-colored organic cranberries" looking "wildly exotic lounging on our counter, dressed in their revealing cellophane bag." She confesses: "All of us, I think, secretly fondled them before Camille cooked them into a gingery sauce" (Kingsolver et al. 2007, 283). Contradicting the claim that "food is not symbolic of anything so much as it is real stuff" (Kingsolver et al. 2007, 339), this image—however humorously conceived—supports Arjun Appadurai's description of food as "both a 'highly condensed social fact' and 'a marvellously plastic kind of collective representation' with 'the capacity to mobilize strong emotions'" (Appadurai 1981, 449). Food's social significance emerges most strongly in those places where Kingsolver insists most strongly on its naturalness—such as her description of the menu for her fiftieth birthday, which included river wines, beer from a nearby microbrewery, local lamb, and strawberry rhubarb crisp. In case the reader missed the significance of that list, she adds: "Here's what we didn't have: the shrimp arranged in a ring like pink poker chips; those rock hard broccoli wedges and lathed carrots surrounding the ubiquitous white dip; the pile of pineapple and melon chunks on a platter. Nobody seemed too disappointed" (Kingsolver et al. 2007, 106). In rejecting what could be called "aspirational food"—staple fare that signals lower-middle-class hospitality with a little bit of fanciness—this passage clearly exemplifies Pierre Bourdieu's argument for the significance of taste in constructing hierarchies of distinction. If any of Kingsolver's guests were disappointed about not getting the shrimp ring, they'd probably hide the fact, not just out of good manners but so as not to betray a lack of taste/class.

The coupling of taste and education, common in alternative food movements, doesn't simply replicate the mode of elitist aestheticism for which "taste," in Bourdieu's formulation, functions as an alibi. Indeed, it arguably counters conventional practices of cultivation (traditionally associated with cerebral rather than corporeal pleasure) with "'appetite and the joys of the body—joys that themselves may be linked to inspiration and imagination'" (Parkins and Craig 2007, 27). The difference is clear. However, emphasizing corporeality over aesthetics does not necessarily decouple taste from class; it merely shifts the stakes, arguably entrenching further the lines of distinction. If the mark of having good taste once was seen as the capacity for enjoyment removed from the realm of physical necessity, now the two realms have been made synonymous, the moral virtue of taste solidified by its association with ecological and personal health. Making taste education more corporeal doesn't make it more democratic, a point that risks being obscured by Kingsolver's seemingly straightforward assertion that the expertise her book seeks to cultivate is useful for "certain kinds of people, namely, the ones who eat" (Kingsolver et al. 2007, 10).

The pedagogical aim of her work, like that of Pollan et al., is based on the premise that better information leads to better choices: "We'd do better if we knew better" (Kingsolver et al. 2007, 8). The key rhetoric of agency here is "choice." Before grade seven, Kingsolver suggests, it is important to expose children to good food on the assumption that "a taste for better stuff is cultivated only through experience" (Kingsolver et al. 2007, 198). On these grounds she is hopeful about the success of farm-to-school programs, in which federal school lunch programs coordinate with local food providers. Research on the success of these programs has been mixed, with one study by Julie Guthman and Patricia Allen suggesting that their aims might be confounded by the same problem that I have suggested is evident in narratives like Kingsolver's, which is an ideological aversion to thinking about structures and institutions. Among the characteristics of these programs in the U.S. is that they are, for example, in their desire to cut out "the middle man," often inimical to existing labor structures within the school food system, relying on the organizational skills of charismatic leaders, and on volunteers, in place of union labor. Structurally, and ideologically, they are in sync with the No Child Left Behind program and the charter school movement in the U.S., which is built around incentives for good schools and penalties for weak ones, and put primary emphasis on the value of parent/customer choice. To the extent that the growing tide of wealthier families to well-funded charter schools in desirable local neighborhoods is weakening the U.S. public school system, the taster's choice model of education is exacerbating the problem that, as Guthman and Allen starkly put it, "Most people in the US lack opportunities to engage in important decisions about food" (Guthman and Allen 2006, 596). Local food, by this reckoning, is not only *not* democratic food; it may in its current form work against it, by contributing, rhetorically and materially, to the disintegration of an education system that, for all its flaws, is still nominally committed to the nurturing of a vibrant public sphere.

The institutional framework of local food, with its hallmark slogans of "independence" and "choice," mirrors an intellectual paradigm defined by the truth of individual knowledge and experience. One way to address the limitations of this paradigm is by countering the ecological idea of localism with the more nuanced understanding of location offered by Haraway's concept of "situated knowledge." Conceived as a critique of the "god-trick" of detached scientific objectivity, "the view from nowhere," situated knowledge also counters the immanent truth of localism with an admission of partiality (Haraway 1988). It is a useful term in its acknowledgment that places are both material and discursive sites, mediated by regulation, rhetoric, and force. Colonialism is a powerful "situating" system, the appropriation of land one of its "most banal but fundamentally important features," as Robert Young has noted (Young 2003, 50). Colonialism initiated (and

globalization continues to drive) circuits of physical and virtual mobility that impact on the construction of place. As Arjun Appadurai points
out, "All locality building has a moment both historical and chronotypic,
when there is a formal recognition that the production of a neighbourhood
requires deliberate, risky, even violent action in respect to the soil, forests,
animals and other human beings" (Appadurai 1986, 183). To really identify with our neighborhoods and localities, to understand how they inhabit
us as much as we inhabit them, it's important to acknowledge the bonds
not just of love and labor but also of violence. Having recognized that the
ground we stand on, our "situation," is defined by operations of power,
myths of self-sufficiency, and pure, impartial knowledge are hard to hold
onto. So where localism seems to promise a recovery of self through communion with the raw material of life, situated knowledge is the recognition
of the impossibility of ever truly giving an account of oneself.

Another way of saying this is that, in Diana Brydon words, "home is
constituted through difference" (Brydon 2007), a concept with particular
saliency in postcolonial societies. We can understand this in the banal sense
that no neighborhood is totally local, that every place is constituted by
ingredients from elsewhere, a process that has been greatly accelerated by
the flows of culture, commerce, and people in the last half century. "I am
the sugar at the bottom of the English cup of tea," the Jamaican-born critic
Stuart Hall jokes (Hall 1997, 48), highlighting the tangle of people, ecology,
and economics that harness home to elsewhere. His comment also serves to
remind us that the meaning of concepts like "home" and "identity" inheres
in the suppressed tension between "self" and "other." Gaining a critical
understanding of this tension requires a shift in conceptual focus from
location to *translation*, understood in the sense not just of the mechanical
substitution of one language for another, but more generally, the process
(never politically innocent) of producing meaning through negotiation with
difference. As Sherry Simon notes, "Translation is a form of regulation. It
allows exchange and incomprehension" and ultimately "depends on the
ability to imagine beyond the borders of one's own experience" (Simon
2006, qtd. in Brydon 2007, 6). The concept of translation critically illuminates Kingsolver's narrative by exposing the seams in its rhetorical claim
to immanence, and disrupting the clean flow of local truth with fragments
of elsewhereness. In the process, it also undercuts the psychic and moral
integrity of the self that is anchored in that truth and reintroduces that
pesky problem of debt.

Something that distinguishes *Animal, Vegetable, Miracle* from much
white postcolonial literature, including Kingsolver's own earlier fiction,
is that it resolutely avoids gestures of liberal guilt. "A thoroughly symptomatic, embarrassed position no one wants to occupy," liberal guilt has
been, at least since the civil rights movement, synonymous with "white
guilt" (Ellison 1996, 345). *Neoliberalism*, Julie Ellison notes, avoids talking about race altogether, based on the claim that to do so would reignite

the social problems associated with racism. This is one response to the helplessness engendered by liberal guilt: "Bygones are what they are," as Kingsolver says (Kingsolver et al. 2007, 284). Ellison, conversely, is interested in the things liberal guilt makes visible, desires, ideas, and concerns that "can be folded into a productive antiracist cultural or political position" (Ellison 1996, 347). Elspeth Probyn makes a similar argument in her consideration of the significance of shame in relation to corporeal politics in general, and eating in particular. A practice in which the boundaries of the self are breached in ways that produce pleasure or disgust, eating has always functioned "as a privileged way by which we know and categorise the other" (Probyn 2000, 70). Writing from Australia, where thinking about food means wrestling with the legacy of Aboriginal displacement, starvation, and forced feeding, as well as contemporary forms of consuming and rejecting otherness, Probyn avers: "Certainly I wouldn't argue that whites eating a curry, or *witjuti* (witchetty) grubs is going to make a jot of difference to the material well-being of 'the other'. However, in thinking about the historical present and the exigency of living well and responsibly within it, alimentary associations may help us better understand the stakes at hand" (Probyn 2000, 103). Conversely, efforts to reduce and simplify those associations may exacerbate the processes of forgetting and exclusion that dog postcolonial cultures.

* * *

Towards the end of her book, in response to critical naysayers, Kingsolver comments that "it's the worst of bad manners—and self protection, I think, in a nervously cynical society—to ridicule the small gesture" (Kingsolver et al. 2007, 346), a charge I take seriously. And after reading in the paper that Monsanto and Dole have embarked on a five-year scientific study to figure out how to make food tastier (Sherr 2009), I shrug and think, why quibble with local food when the alternative is so awful? Well, because the dominant industrial model is *not* the only alternative. While local food has dominated the mainstream media, it represents just one, powerfully symbolic, focus within a raft of food-based movements. The agendas of many of these movements, while not opposed to localism, take up its principles strategically and to varying degrees, insofar as it advances other goals such as democratic participation in food systems, race and gender equity, and sustainable livelihoods for farmers and other food workers. To the extent that it extends its sphere of concern to embrace the interests of this broader constituency, to advocate not just for place but for *rights*-based food systems (Anderson 2008), local food will transcend its current status as a privileged lifestyle choice. It is with this hope in mind that I argue for greater reflexivity in the way local food is debated and promoted. Converting satellite dishes to planters can't protect the sanctuary of the home from the lure of the exotic, the guilty pleasure of the world.

NOTES

1. The term was coined by Vancouver couple Alisa Smith and James MacKinnon, who documented their one-year experiment in local eating in a series of articles that culminated in a book.
2. My analysis is confined primarily to the U.S., where local food resonates quite differently than it does in Europe, for example (see Dupuis, Goodman and Harrison 2006).

REFERENCES

Anderson, Molly D. 2008. "Rights-Based Food and the Goals of Food System Reform." *Agriculture and Human Values* 25.4, 593–608.

Appadurai, Arjun. 1981. "Gastro-Politics in Hindu South India." *American Ethnologist* 8, 494–511.

———. 1996. *Modernity at Large: Cultural Dimensions of Globalization.* Minneapolis: University of Minnesota Press.

Bailey, Ronald. 2008. "The Food Miles Mistake: Saving the Planet by Eating New Zealand Apples." *Reason*, November 4, http://www.reason.com/news/show/129855.html.

Bauman, Zygmunt. 1998. *Globalisation: The Human Consequences.* Cambridge, UK: Polity Press.

Bennett, Jane. 2007. Edible Matter. *New Left Review* 45, 133–145.

Bennett, Tony, Lawrence Grossberg, and Meaghan Morris. 2005. *New Keywords: A Revised Vocabulary of Culture and Society.* Oxford: Blackwell.

Bourdieu, Pierre. 1984. *Distinction: A Social Critique of the Judgement of Taste.* Translated by Richard Nice. Cambridge, MA: Harvard University Press.

Brydon, Diana. 2007. In the Name of Home: Canadian Literature, Global Imaginaries. Transcanada Conference, Guelph, ON, October 11–14, http://myuminfo.umanitoba.ca/Documents/1345/transcan2.pdf.

Burros, Marian. 2009. "Obamas to Plant Vegetable Garden at White House." *New York Times,* March 19, http://www.nytimes.com/2009/03/20/dining/20garden.html.

Combes, Andrea. 2010. "Staying Home to Shelter from Bad Economic Weather." Market Watch, *Wall Street Journal*, March 23. http://www.marketwatch.com/story/staying-home-to-shelter-from-bad-economic-weather-2010-03-23.

Delind, Laura B. 2006. "Of Bodies, Place and Culture." *Journal of Agricultural and Environmental Ethics* 19.2, 121–146.

Dupuis, E. Melanie, David Goodman, and Jill Harrison. 2006. "Just Values or Just Value? Re-Making the Local in Agro-Food Studies." In *Between the Local and the Global: Confronting Complexity in the Contemporary Agri-Food Sector,* edited by Terry Marsden and Jonathan Murdoch. Volume 12 of *Research in Rural Sociology and Development,* 241–268. Amsterdam: Elsevier.

Edelman, Lee. 2004. *No Future: Queer Theory and the Death Drive.* Durham, NC: Duke University Press.

Ellison, Julie. 1996. "A Short History of Liberal Guilt." *Critical Inquiry* 22.2, 344–371.

Giddens, Anthony. 1991. *Modernity and Self-Identity : Self and Society in the Late Modern Age.* Cambridge, UK: Polity Press.

Guthman, Julie. 2004. *Agrarian Dreams : The Paradox of Organic Farming in California.* Berkeley: University of California Press.

———. 2007. "Commentary on Teaching Food: Why I Am Fed Up with Michael Pollan et al." *Agriculture and Human Values* 24, 261–264.

Guthman, Julie, and Patricia Allen. 2006. "From 'Old School' to 'Farm-to-School': Neoliberalism from the Ground Up." *Agriculture and Human Values* 23.4.

Hall, Stuart. 1997. "Old and New Identities, Old and New Ethnicities." In *Culture, Globalization, and the World System: Contemporary Conditions for the Representation of Identity*, edited by Anthony D. King, 31–68. Minneapolis: University of Minnesota Press.

Hammar, Tomas. 1990. *Democracy and the Nation State: Aliens, Denizens, and Citizens in a World of International Migration*. Aldershot: Avebury.

Haraway, Donna. 1988. "Situated Knowledges: The Science Question in Feminism and the Privilege of Partial Perspective." *Feminist Studies* 14.3, 575–599.

———. 2003. *The Companion Species Manifesto: Dogs, People, and Significant Otherness*. Chicago: Prickly Paradigm Press.

Kingsolver, Barbara, Steven L. Hopp, and Camille Kingsolver. 2007. *Animal, Vegetable, Miracle: A Year of Food Life*. New York: HarperCollins.

Liu, Alan. 1990. "Local Transcendence: Cultural Criticism, Postmodernism and the Romance of Detail." *Representations* 32, 75–113.

MacGregor, James, and Bill Vorley. 2007. "Fair Miles": The Concept of "Air Miles" From a Sustainable Development Perspective. Fresh Perspectives: Agrifood Standards and Pro-Poor Growth in Africa. http://www.agr.unipi.it/labrural/Didattica/corso-social-and-environmental-assessment-of-food/fair-miles-kenya-vegetables.pdf.

Massey, Doreen. 1995. "Places and Their Pasts." *History Workshop Journal* 39, 182–192.

McKibben, Bill. 2007. *Deep Economy: The Wealth of Communities and the Durable Future*. New York: Henry Holt.

McWilliams, James E. 2009. *Just Food: Where Locavores Get It Wrong and How We Can Truly Eat Responsibly*. New York: Little, Brown.

Nabhan, Gary Paul. 2002. *Coming Home to Eat: The Pleasures and Politics of Local Food*. New York: Norton.

Parkins, Wendy, and Geoffrey Craig. 2007. *Slow Living*. Sydney: New South Wales Press.

Pollan, Michael. 2006. *The Omnivore's Dilemma: A Natural History of Four Meals*. New York: Penguin.

Probyn, Elspeth. 2000. *Carnal Appetite : Foodsexidentities*. New York: Routledge.

Sherr, Ian. 2009. "Monsanto, Dole to Collaborate on Veggies." *Reuters*, June 24. http://www.reuters.com/article/idUSTRE55N2IL20090624.

Simon, Sherry. 2006. *Translating Montreal: Episodes in the Life of a Divided City*. Montreal: McGill Queen's University Press.

Slocum, Rachel. 2007. "Whiteness, Space and Alternative Food Practice." *Geoforum* 38.3, 520–533.

Smith, Alisa, and J. B. MacKinnon. 2007. *The 100-Mile Diet: A Year of Local Eating*. Toronto: Random House.

Von Hahn, Karen. 2008. "People are Looking for Roots." *The Globe and Mail*, July 26. http://www.theglobeandmail.com/servlet/story/RTGAM.20080725.noticed26/BNStory/lifeStyle/home

Young, Robert. 2003. *Postcolonialism: A Very Short Introduction*. New York: Oxford University Press.

15 Pathways to the Sea

Involvement and the Commons in Works by Ralph Hotere, Cilla McQueen, Hone Tuwhare, and Ian Wedde

Teresa Shewry

In 1975 New Zealand writer Ian Wedde published the poem "Pathway to the Sea" to confront plans by a transnational collection of corporations to place an aluminum smelter on the sand spit and settlement at Aramoana, in Otago, New Zealand. In the poem, the narrator digs a drain to keep "shit" out of the water supply, because when you live in the "universe" there is no "place to chuck / stuff off / of" (1; 12). Wedde suggests that building a drain is a "directed" form of involvement with Aramoana, nonhuman life, the sea, people, and more broadly, the universe (11; 12). Ralph Hotere, one of New Zealand's most important contemporary artists, created the cover art for the first Hawk Press edition of Wedde's poem. In protest, Hotere also dumped black paint over the sign marking the planned smelter site, processed a xeroxed photo of the blackened sign into a painting, and nailed corrugated iron works to power poles on the road to Aramoana. These works were taken down and discarded by police (O'Brien 1997, 101; McQueen 2000a, 43). The social mobilization around Aramoana forced the abandonment of the smelter plans. However, artists' and writers' engagements with Aramoana, including their emphasis on involvement in partly shared environmental, aesthetic, and political spaces, did not stop. Hotere has created many more Aramoana-related works, while Wedde continues to make reference to Hotere's work at Aramoana in his poems, including in "Off / Of (*for Ralph Hotere*)," published in 1984 but initially "given to Ralph Hotere to xerox as a contribution to the travelling exhibition of work by artists opposed to the siting of an aluminium smelter at Aramoana in Otago . . . ," and the 2005 poem "Letter to Peter McLeavey: After Basho" (Wedde 1984, 2005).[1]

In this chapter, I explore how Wedde, along with New Zealand writers Cilla McQueen and Hone Tuwhare, all of whom have collaborated with Hotere, use poetry and art to elaborate what I call *involvements* in shared social and aesthetic spaces related to the sea. I draw the term *involvement* from New Zealand poet Gregory O'Brien's description of Hotere as "an advocate of *involvement*—political, environmental, social and personal"

(1997, 43). For Hotere and his literary collaborators, involvement designates the making of partly directed associations with the sea, or more specifically, with the social forms that shape it, such as oxygen, fish, poets, fishers, water, stories, and images. In recognizing involvement in the sea, these artists move beyond framing the ocean as entirely other to human life, or as a frontier, an idea that has been appearing in New Zealand media recently and that reflects international political and economic interactions and discourses about the sea.[2] As a limiting term, involvement also suggests that they understand the sea as a *commons*, as an environment where they are in the company of others: at times, they try to imagine the sea as entangled among the poems' narrators, fish, birds, waves, and winds, or among specific artists and poets; they mingle this with concern for involvement in a sea that is shared at the scale of "the universe" or the "whole world."

In textual archives at least as early as the Roman Empire, the sea is framed as "common to all life" because the moving waters are unaccountable and resistant to the spatial and temporal scales of property.[3] Contemporary scholars of the commons, such as Vandana Shiva (2002), describe how people's access to environments like the sea is jettisoned or threatened through processes of economic globalization and political governance that privatize or centralize environmental control. Concepts such as community and democracy are important in imagining alternatives in such discussions, but the meanings of such concepts are not inevitable. Arundhati Roy, for example, describes "the ritualistic slaughter of language as I know and understand it" through the use of terms like "'women's empowerment', 'people's participation' and 'deepening democracy'" at an international forum on water, when "the whole purpose of the forum was to press for the privatization of the world's water" (qtd. in Mukherjee 2010, 88).

Through their long-standing interests in collaboration, Hotere, McQueen, Tuwhare, and Wedde maintain complexities in the meanings, potential and actual, of art and environments that are shared with others. Hotere, who has Māori (Te Aupōuri) heritage, is well known for drawing on the work of poets with whom he shares a close, empathetic connection (Mane-Wheoki 1997, 235). Often working in the medium of printmaking, he sometimes gives lithographs the names of poems by particular writers, or incorporates fragments or forms of poems into them. They, in turn, reference his work in poetry. These artists create socialities, places of stretched agency, through which they engage in art and political protest. While these collaborations are in some ways limited, for example, involving specific artists and languages, they are not simply local or national in scale. Gregory O'Brien writes, "Hotere feels a deep affinity with a number of countries (or regions therein) and, in that respect, he seems closer to the notion of the Maori as voyagers rather than as a people rooted to one place. He has produced substantial bodies of work in Spain, Italy, the South of France and Mungo, in the Australian outback" (1997, 76). Hotere has connected art to contexts such as apartheid, Algerian independence struggles, Polaris missiles, the French nuclear program at Mururoa Atoll, the Sangro River War Cemetery, Italy, as well as

New Zealand–based social and environmental struggles. He has written in art in languages that include Arabic, English, French, Italian, Latin, Māori, and Spanish. The poets' works also complicate any single geographic understanding. Tuwhare, who is of Māori (Ngā Puhi) descent, and McQueen, who was born in England, both make connections in poetry between New Zealand localities and varied places internationally. McQueen primarily uses English but draws on other languages, including Māori, while Tuwhare's works involve English, Māori, and limited German. Wedde, in turn, was born in New Zealand but grew up partly in Bangladesh (then East Pakistan) and England. Much of his writing is concerned with different linguistic and cultural traditions, including his work with Palestinian scholar Fawwaz Tuqan on translations of works by Palestinian poet Mahmoud Darwish, and the collection of Māori and English poetry, *Penguin Book of New Zealand Verse* (1985), which he coedited.

Perhaps because they inhabit troubled geographic, cultural, and linguistic spaces, Hotere and collaborating poets concentrate not only on important and sedimented spatial scales but also on how scale is always subject to varied interpretations, how it creates failures in understanding, missing what is "elsewhere," in Wedde's terms (2000, 49). These artists commonly draw on specific spatial arrangements, small and large, that matter in people's lives and for understanding how people, nonhuman life, and environments have survived or have been brutalized. They often repeat place and regional names (Africa, Algérie, Aramoana, Parihaka, Pureora, Mururoa, Sangro) or recurring forms like the sea, windows, and pathways. Yet, they also show that these ways of understanding space are crossed by the tracks of other spatial arrangements. Recognition of limits and differences in understanding is important in the specific collaborations among the artists. It is a way of "leaving space in which the words of others can be heard . . ." (Wedde 1997, 9). Awareness of difference is also important to the broader sense, sometimes articulated in or around the art, that the art works "partake of, rather than simply describe, a darkness that is common to all humanity," in a way that does not elide language, history, and artistic genealogies (O'Brien 1997, 117). These artists extend this concern beyond the human to frame their works as forms of involvement in a sea that is shared with creatures like birds and environmental components like waves. Given this heterogeneous social quality to the sea, scale is an unexhausted, adaptive concern for these artists as they rework ways in which art and environments are shared.

ARAMOANA—PATHWAY TO THE SEA: COLLABORATIONS AMONG HOTERE AND WEDDE

Aramoana is a coastal salt marsh, sand spit, and settlement of about 260 people near the Otago Harbour entrance on the South Island's East Coast. In "Letter to Peter McLeavey," a 2005 poem, Ian Wedde suggests that

Aramoana was saved by an artist who looked at it "so hard / it became beautiful. . ." (61). To understand Wedde's reference, we must reach back to the 1970s, when corporations Fletcher Challenge, CSR Limited, and Alusuisse proposed an aluminum smelter at Aramoana. A social movement to stop the smelter was held together by the place, Aramoana. The specificity of this place's relationship to the smelter—its impending obliteration—is unmistakable. However, an aluminum smelter also points to entanglements that spill well beyond a delineated place. To the south of Aramoana lies the Tiwai Point Aluminium Smelter, owned by Rio Tinto Alcan (New Zealand), which is an operation of the global mining group Rio Tinto, and Sumitomo Chemical Company (Japan). In "Tiwai Sequence," a poem about this smelter, Cilla McQueen notes that it uses the same amount of electricity as Auckland (2000b, 42). Auckland is home to around a third of the people in New Zealand. She also raises concerns that the smelter is creating greenhouse gases and forcing rising sea levels, blowing harmful materials onto the sea and over Bluff, the local town, leaving abandoned stores of dross around the town, and covering the archaeological site of a Māori "toolmaking factory" (2000b, 41–42, 43).

In response to the Aramoana smelter plans, Wedde published "Pathway to the Sea" (1975), a poem where he works through the idea of directed involvement in environments and projects shared with others. The poem is a single, continuous line that runs over twelve pages. Its narrator speaks about working with others to dig a drain in the garden to divert runoff, likely generated by the high rainfall common in New Zealand. This runoff is currently bogging the foundations of a shed, getting into a chicken coop, and could cause overflows in the sewage system. The resulting sludge might also seep into the water supply and so into human bodies. The narrator speculates that this impact on health will draw out council inspectors, who could find the ways local people live "unorthodox or even / illegal. . ." (2). Wedde does not explicitly mention the possibility of drainage eventually reaching the sea, although this is implied by the title, "Pathway to the Sea."

Wedde breaks the story of the drain project to say that he has heard they wanted to put an "ALUMINIUM / SMELTER" at Aramoana and he is concerned that these plans will be renewed:

> [. . .] listen, there's
> birds out there, we're
>   back with those lovers, the buoyancy
>   & updraught of some kind of
> *mutual* understanding of what
>   service is, of the fact that
>   a thing being easy doesn't
> make it available or passive :
>   listen, effort's got to be right
>   directed [. . .] (10–11)

For Wedde, making a drain is a *directed* engagement with Aramoana, the sea, or the universe more broadly because it involves laboriously stopping sludge entering waterways and, presumably, taking a pathway to the sea. Rather than an isolated individual activity, the drain project reflects an understanding and practice that is partly *mutual*, made in and further shaping a commons. The link Wedde draws between birds and mutual dynamics is clarified at an earlier moment in "Pathway to the Sea," when we are told that birds gain buoyancy by flying along in the updraughts of each other's wings (4). "Pathway to the Sea" is an elaboration and analysis of these ideas. Wedde tells of how the process of making the drain is modulated in relation to other people, nonhuman life, and environmental components. As with dirt that washes back into the drain with the rain, this requires compromise (3). These compromises are by no means necessarily easy or productive along the lines that the narrator would like. In fact, he expresses deep resentment that some of the people building the drain abandon the project along the way (6). Wedde simply leaves these conflicts unresolved in "Pathway to the Sea," as refusals of a politics of forced engagement. He further underscores that caring for and enjoying an environment that is shared does not mean obliterating difference into homogeneity when he emphasizes that the state should not interfere in the drainage problem by manifesting in the form of council inspectors and enforcing a singular way of life. The commons is not a term that should be used to imagine wiping out differences among people or social and governmental arrangements.

Ralph Hotere made the cover art for the first edition of "Pathway to the Sea," drawing us towards a further dimension of this poem's engagement with the commons: a history of coordinated projects that stretch among specific writers and artists. The art is a way of *making* a shared project as much as asking for it or waiting for it to arrive. Jonathan Mane-Wheoki identifies two main sources for Hotere's practice of using poetry in lithographs: on one hand, he connects with the Pākehā (New Zealand European) artist Colin McCahon, who wrote lines from poetry into his paintings (1997, 234). On the other hand, the works engage the Māori custom in which "*taonga tuku iho* (treasures handed down from the ancestors) gain significance also from having words 'attached' to them (*he kupu kei runga*). . ." (1997, 235). Mane-Wheoki also notes that since the introduction of reading and writing, this practice has moved to some extent from spoken to written attachments of words.

These collaborative practices involve both coordination and fragmentation among the writers and artist. As Wedde writes, "The collaborations in the art are like a love of conversation. What we love in this art is not so much what it is, as what it has already been" (1997, 11). On one hand, the meanings of these artworks are social, built in a space stretching between companions, rather than unique. On the other hand, a conversation involves the differences of these companions. Without these it would not be required. Wedde's "Pathway to the Sea" and many of Hotere's

Aramoana-oriented works are coordinated around forms, political stances, and aesthetic methods of pathways, ditches, flight paths, and waterways. The lines of "Pathway to the Sea" are narrow and unbroken (without full stops) and so visually flow down the page as a pathway. Critics have also interpreted several kinds of pathways in Hotere's Aramoana works, including in a 1991 installation *Pathway to the Sea—Aramoana*, which Hotere created with artist Bill Culbert and is based on fluorescent light tubes, paua shells, and rocks running thirty meters along the floor (Vangioni 2005, 18). Gregory O'Brien writes that the light running through the installation suggests "the hand-dug ditch which is a central metaphor in Wedde's poem—a human-made line laid on, or dug into, the landscape" (1997, 96). Peter Vangioni, in turn, describes how Hotere and Culbert created thirteen lithographs related to Wedde's "Pathway to the Sea" poem, as well as the *Pathway to the Sea—Aramoana* installation (2005, 18). He suggests that the installation represents the flight paths of Otago Harbour birds, reflecting the words in Māori that Hotere attaches to it and to other works, at least once placing an English translation directly below them: "This is my bird that flies to you a message from where the sun rises. It asks from where have you come? Who are you?" (Vangioni 2005, 18). The words ask the viewer to clarify the pathway they have taken to the sea, to be attentive to their involvement rather than blind or passive, to clarify their singularity but also their relationship to a shared environment. They ask the viewer to understand that they too share in the artwork, that they are an active part in its creation.

As suggested here, while the practices between Hotere and collaborating poets involve coordinations, they do not obliterate differences. The works are marked by the distinctness of the materials that coexist in them, for example, when Hotere writes the poet's names into his works, or when they write Hotere's name into their own works. Hotere's works are intensely formal, places where "language and meaning have been almost extinguished," while the words of the poetry provide somewhat more direct meanings (O'Brien 1997, 13). The different approaches in the paintings "place stresses on each other" and destabilize the certainty of the art (O'Brien 1997, 57). These works challenge "the common-sense assumption that solidarity means homogeneity," as Anna Tsing puts it, suggesting that common projects are creative and wide-ranging because they create not only overlaps but also maintain disagreements, differences, or misunderstandings around purposes, objects, and outcomes of struggle (2005, 245).

How might we move from these specific practices among Hotere and poets to broader ways of engaging the sea as a commons, as an environment shared with nonhuman life and with people around the world? Concern for how to register the nonhuman life of the sea is evident in the dedication of Wedde's "Pathway to the Sea" "to the belief" that Aramoana be left to birds, fish, sand hoppers "& other denizens" who now "possess it" as far as they are "tolerated by men ambitious for / quick solutions & profits."

In his poetry, Tuwhare explores how the sea is shared with sea creatures and marine environmental features, while McQueen engages histories of human presence in the ocean, including in the transborder contexts of colonialism and global capitalism.

CONVERSATIONS AND LOSSES AT SEA

Among the inhabitants of a 1997 poem titled "Kākā Point" by Hone Tuwhare, we find poets. Because the sea is "multi-lingual," these poets share its "collective heart-beat" and find a "mutuality of taste" for fish and chips (78). The sea is a place of enjoyment and sustenance for poets of "all / lands." As a multilingual entity, the sea supports differences and possibly enables people and other forms of life to communicate. Tuwhare's concern with sharing does not mean importing a specific model of communal life around the planet but the chance of conversations among various lifeways. We see a hint of the stakes for Tuwhare later in the poem, when he imagines the return of the seabirds named Tītī or Sooty Shearwater to the waters off Kākā Point. Yearly, these birds undertake a startling migration, flying north from New Zealand and other southern Pacific islands along the western edge of the Pacific to sub-Arctic waters and then returning south along the eastern Pacific. Anxiety that they will not survive washes back across "Kākā Point" in the last line: "Eat well— and mate well—so that your woolly, roly- / poly progeny will thrive in their thousands for us . . ." (79).

Tuwhare in fact lived at Kākā Point, which lies on the coast south of Aramoana and is a place where tensions around the social and environmental status of the sea have been very visible. Just down the road from Kākā Point, the Department of Conservation's (DOC's) efforts to create a marine reserve (Nugget Point / Tokatā) have been contested for years. Nugget Point / Tokatā was first considered for a "no take" reserve, meaning an area where there would be no fishing, by DOC in 1989 and formally proposed as such in 1992; however, the proposal collapsed under pressure from small and commercial fisheries. When I passed through Kākā Point in 2006, the words "no reserve" were painted across the sides of buildings and on signs.

While the marine reserves are primarily a government-run developmental project and articulated in the national context, part of Tuwhare's response in "Kākā Point" involves thinking about the sea as a social entity and site of shared heritage (food, enjoyment, poetry) among people internationally as well as with nonhuman creatures and environmental components like waves.[4] This concern reflects his Māori and Marxist affiliations. Tuwhare, who died in 2008, was one of the only Māori and working-class poets who was being published early in his career (Sharp 1996, 55). He has said in an interview, "We didn't even need Marx and Engels, because Maori people are already natural communists. You know—sharing, and with closer family ties" (Manhire 1988, 273). These family ties bind people, the sea, sky, land, and all life genealogically and so gesture to interactions at vast spatial scales. Marxism provides a different, also spatially expansive, cultural trajectory that Tuwhare brings into dialogue with his concern for life in common. He was a member of the Communist Party ("I made up 50% of the Maori membership!") and has said that Marxism gave him a sense of place and belonging to the working class (Manhire 1988, 271, 270). Tuwhare expresses his clash with property in the form of land as well as contained individuality in "Fifteen Minutes in the Life of Johannes H. Jean Ivanovich," suggesting that his friends have "NO real property to speak of. You'll / find me—in them" (1997, 45). He elaborates that property is tied to staggering hierarchies: "If I owned One Sixth of the World, I should be a high-up rangatira / capitalist (living in the Kremlin). . ." and would fly a flag reading "UP THE INTERNATIONAL WORKING CLASS!" (44). Despite these interests, Tuwhare had an unsettled relationship with the Communist Party, first leaving in protest in 1956 after the Soviet Union's suppression of Imre Nagy's Hungarian government (Sharp 1996, 52). His concern with the possibilities of shared life is threaded through with the question of uneven power and of imposed, homogenous ways of life. These histories do not lead him to abandon but to deepen his concerns for the sea as an entity common to people and other life-forms. In discussing these concerns, I will focus on *Shape-Shifter* (1997), from which "Kākā Point" is drawn and which pulls together Tuwhare's poems and prose works, as well as color paintings by New Zealand artist Shirley Grace. The collection is shaped by the land, water, the wind, trees and birds, significant people in Tuwhare's life, Māori culture and politics, language, colonialism, sex, and love—and, as Robert Sullivan notes, many of the poems are preoccupied with the sea: the collection tastes "salty" (1998, 6).

The narrator of many of Tuwhare's poems in *Shape-Shifter* shares the sea with plants, animals, and environmental components like waves, winds, and the currents. Many of the poems are observations of the interactions of life and environmental components at varying scales, some so small that they are virtually unnoticeable, others filling expanses that are staggeringly vast. In "Big Whale Itch" current, wind, and moon "conspire, to incite the waves / to belt up and war with the land again," shaking the narrator's crib or small, coastal house (16). As all this unfolds, "the great Earth-ball continues on its / course, oblivious to local and minor insurrections" (16). The land finally coaxes the sea to "shut up" by giving it "three billion grains of sand" and the waves retreat (16). Tuwhare ends the poem with the presence of a small life: the narrator examines the sea, hoping to see a ship running into the wind's "shoulder; a lurching sea-animal perhaps— just briefly / imploring the sky to scratch its nose, back, arse. . . ." (16). The sea-animal appears in the middle of the line, and is separated out by two breaks (the semicolon and the dash) so that it does in fact lurch out of the sentence, spilling beyond its smallness and becoming central. Tuwhare is often concerned in this way with relatively differentiated subjects that are nevertheless all caught together, here, warring, conspiring, and negotiating. He is concerned that we sense and acknowledge both the small creatures, given that most of the animals inhabiting the sea are scaled to be missed, at least by humans, and the large agencies that compose the sea, here drawing them to readers' attention by disturbing their hierarchies.

Many of Tuwhare's poems are conversations in which the narrator addresses waves, birds, or Tangaroa (ancestor, sea god). The narrator is often positioned as a person speaking from the crib and is involved but not dominant in the marine life. In "The Sun is a Truant," the narrator interacts with Tangaroa at Kākā Point: "Presently, I shall hold / rhetorical hands with it: kia ora, Ancestor" (83). Meanwhile, black rocks are "slobbering whitely" with the foam of the receding tide that it is abandoning them, but that will return to engulf them emotionally twelve hours later in a "frenzy and furore of embracings—seeded with high / emotional overtones I find . . . excessive" (83). Tuwhare here perhaps takes an oblique swipe at recent dynamics of Pākehā-Māori relations in New Zealand. But this stanza, as in much of Tuwhare's work, primarily works to attribute to the water and the rocks rather than the poet the "high emotional overtones" that are sometimes chased out of poetry by critics concerned about "anthropomorphism." Through the imagery of intimacy, here "seeded," Tuwhare asserts the creativity of these interactions in shaping the sea as well as the poems.

Tuwhare's emphasis on varied creative agents at sea is important because discussions of the commons often emphasize human inheritance, benefit, dilemmas, and agency while positioning everything else in the world as a resource. For example, Tibor R. Machan writes that "when common ownership exists over valuable resources, they will tend to become exhausted" (2001, xvii). The term *resource* has been used to situate nature as an object that is meaningless and passive until transformed by human management into economic profit. Tuwhare provides an alternative approach in recognizing the sea as a shared environment created by and supporting various entities, nonhuman animals, and features like waves and the sun no less than people. As a commons, though, the sea of course also includes people. This is a point that sometimes gets forgotten in the long imaginative histories of the sea as an enigma, threat, and other to human civilization (or in environmentalism's inversion, humans as a threat to be kept out of the sea). For Tuwhare, activities like eating fish and objects like homes on the coasts or boats in the waters should not be left out of the poems: in "Kākā Point," he notes of the power-pole in his view to the sea from the crib, "Second-rate artists / leave it out of their pictures, altogether" (78).

Cilla McQueen's poetry takes Tuwhare's concerns for situating humans in the social spaces of the sea in a way that does not simply condemn them further and into more precarious waters, moving us across time and more

sharply into seas of violence, greed, and loss. She explores people as part
of the sea, from Māori voyaging, to colonial ships, to the fishing and eating of sea creatures, to the sea as taken apart into particles and soldered
back together through the language of physicists, to the transportation of
materials through the waves for institutions such as aluminum smelters.
She often finds "illogical messages / of loss": entire Aboriginal communities destroyed with the arrival of colonists' boats, plague ships traversing
the waves, development projects that cut entire headlands in half (1997b,
108). However, she also moves beyond framing peoples' presences on the
land, coast, and sea over time as inevitably problematic, undertaking the
work of differentiating among ways that people have been involved in
the sea. In exploring this concern here, I will focus primarily on *Markings* (2000b), a collection of McQueen's poetry and drawings. While
McQueen has received less critical attention than Hotere, Tuwhare, and
Wedde, she has published multiple volumes of poetry and was New Zealand's Poet Laureate for 2009–2011. Hotere and McQueen, who married,
collaborated on the aluminum smelter campaign as well as various other
art projects (O'Brien 1997, 103–109).

In *Markings*, McQueen is concerned with arrangements: locations, colors, shapes, flocks, waters, movements, contrasts, relationships, the intimacy of all things. She conceives these shapes as unfolding across vast
durations of time: "In time / things arrange themselves" and are "etched
by light, by love, laughter, / life's abrasion" (61, 62). She often taps the
languages of physics to understand phenomena such as the distinctness and
connection of water, atmosphere, and coast. While this language makes
people impossible to see in the land and seascape, McQueen's poems are
also layered with stories of human presence in the waters across time. We
see this in her short poems of catching and eating sea creatures. "A Wheke"
is addressed to a person who holds an octopus (wheke) that has an "elu-
sive" and "distant power" (36). McQueen describes an intimate, almost
threatening connection to its death: as someone pulls a tentacle from the
octopus, "There's red in the western sky" (36). Two further poems, "Birds"
and "Hearts," describe the catching and eating of mutton birds (the Tītī or
Sooty Shearwater of Tuwhare's "Kākā Point"). "Birds" opens with a communal scene, describing voices and laughter at the table, on a stormy night
for catching young Tītī: "You grab the necks and bite the heads, / killing
swiftly" and then carry the birds home (38). In the poem "Hearts," they
eat the mutton bird hearts that power the animal over the world: "We eat
the power to fly, / succulent stamina of the titi" (39). These poems explore
a community's relationships with the sea and its life, focusing on how they
gather and eat creatures recognized as mysterious, as not fully contained
by humans. These practices support sustenance, enjoyment, and meaning
among people: throughout, "Hearts" is about *we*. In *Markings* McQueen
places these works alongside further poems that provide accounts of large-
scale industrial operations on the sea and coast. Pylons, aluminum smelters,

and large ships dot her poetry, often jarring, associated with an offensive on people, land, birds, plants, and fish. In "The Autoclave," a container ship arrives, "tall as an office block and as foreign to the landscape. . ." (16). The language evokes its homogeneity and vastness. It is clearly opposed to the multiple, varied colors and details of the low-tide environment in the stanza that precedes it (pale yellow, white, pale green, olive, taupe, blue-grey). McQueen then turns to the aluminum smelter at Tiwai Point, emphasizing its power, its militaristic animation: "Pylons walk westward / two by two into the distance. . ." (29).

McQueen's clash with these industrial processes and their impact on people and the environment is not undertaken from a position entirely outside them. To recognize this, we need to understand that the human sociality that I described of "A Wheke," "Birds" and "Hearts" (the "we"), which is supported by the eating of mutton birds and fishing of the wheke, is not homogenous and has partly colonial origins. Many of McQueen's poems refer to how the narrator's colonizing ancestors migrated from the St. Kilda archipelago, Scotland, while her husband's people are Māori. This colonial history cleared space for industrial projects. The smelter at Tiwai Point reflects the spaces of late capitalist globalization. McQueen writes of petroleum coke for carbon anodes arriving at the smelter from California, liquid pitch from Korea, alumina from Australia. But, to understand the use of the place, we must see back to colonialism: "Once this was the site of a Maori toolmaking factory. / Now the aluminium smelter covers the area entirely" (43). McQueen's preoccupation with how important the sea and coast have been to Māori over time gives some sense of just how violently the contemporary arrangement of the coastal and marine space emerged. In "Waituna," for example, as the narrator draws and her dog runs on the beach, the "history of Kati Mamoe and Waitaha," past iwi, "shimmers above the sea." In a while, "you might see a long waka skimming in towards the shore" (47).

McQueen's community in "A Wheke," "Birds," and "Hearts" is partly made possible by colonial and industrial expansion in marine life worlds important to Māori. She further emphasizes this point of intimacy by registering how the materials used in the poems literally rely on industrial processes. In "Tiwai Sequence," a poem about the narrator's visit to the Tiwai Point Aluminium Smelter, McQueen incorporates phrases from the tour guide, such as "Any residue of harmful substances / merely blows out to sea. . ." (41). In part, McQueen imagines *through* materials used to publicly smooth over the aluminum smelter, but she also transforms these materials, makes them speak in unexpected ways. This method can be likened to Hotere's use of demolition materials, including corrugated iron and aluminium, fluorescent lights, paua (abalone) shells, window frames, stainless steel, and lacquer. His uptake of old aluminum and other industrial materials in art is particularly significant, as it suggests a political stance not located outside of capitalism, or more specifically, not fully outside of corporations that mobilize human and nonhuman productivities to build aluminum or fell trees. Rather, Hotere's use of aluminum is an acknowledgment of *involvement* but also an assertion of *difference* in an attempt to redirect shared productive capacities to different ends than the private bank accounts into which much of it swirls in the hands of corporate power structures. In the poem "Baby Iron," McQueen ponders Hotere's reworking of materials like old windows, steel, weathered wood, farm gate timber, and iron. Take it, she writes, and "corrugate it, fuck it up, iron it, ripple it. . ." (1997a, 114). This practice, she suggests, is "something to do with refusing to be afraid" (1997a, 114). These are frightening intimacies but they are also disagreements with and excessive to destructive economic practices.

CONCLUSION

There are fissures between widespread institutional ideals and efforts to even out environmental inequalities, and contemporary marinescapes, places of deep hierarchies through which nonhuman and human life is varyingly valued and abandoned. In this chapter I have looked at how artistic and literary works, made in the shadows of such conditions, interpret the agencies and concerns that might move them beyond practices of domination or isolation in the social spaces of the sea. These artworks, which stretch among Hotere and collaborating poets over more than thirty years, are experiments in imagining environments shared with others, and with artistic forms capable of supporting these environments. Crossing varied scales, they are made through collaborations that are marked by intense engagements among specific artists but that are also understood in relation to wide-ranging contexts and varied kinds of marine life. In these practices, different ways of seeing can be used to reinforce or confront each other, but they can also miss each other completely. Therefore, while the artists work to make shared languages, they also emphasize persistent differences of understanding. Changing attitudes of dejection and hope are evident across this artistic history. For example, in the years between "Pathway to the Sea" (1975) and "Letter to Peter McLeavey: After Basho" (2005), Wedde's tone grows bleaker. The later poem, which remembers Hotere's interventions at Aramoana, also references New Zealand artist Colin McCahon's *Beach Walk* cycle of paintings. This cycle depicts McCahon's walk on Muriwai beach in memory of the New Zealand poet James K. Baxter, whose spirit had traveled along Muriwai as part of the Māori spirit path taken to Cape Reinga (Simpson 1995, 180). Surveying the sand, sky, and waves in "22 *Muriwai*" in "Letter to Peter McLeavey: After Basho," Wedde finds that McCahon may be "weeping again":

> it's because beauty this plain
> doesn't stand a chance, any more
> than his footprints do, the knobbly big toes

pressed more urgently into black sand
on the way back, but written off
all the same
by the same simple waves,
the ones that keep coming (54).

In the water, Wedde reads and simply places side by side precariousness and future desolation, as well as resilience and defiant survival. This quality of reversal appears commonly in these artists' works. It is a reminder of openness, that not all is given, hope held together with possible losses to come.

NOTES

1. In 2008–2009 the United Nations Environment Programme (UNEP), Natural World Museum, and the Museum of New Zealand—Te Papa Tongarewa included thirteen *Aramoana—Pathway to the Sea* lithographs in the international exhibition *Moving Towards a Balanced Earth: Kick the Carbon Habit*. UNEP and Natural World Museum describe the exhibition as involving around twenty-five artists from seventeen countries and "designed to generate awareness of global climate change and issues regarding the environment while inspiring a positive change in people's attitudes and actions toward the environment." Te Papa Tongarewa's publicity material situates the *Aramoana—Pathway to the Sea* lithographs as a collaboration of Bill Culbert and Ralph Hotere, based on Wedde's poem "Pathway to the Sea" and works by New Zealand poets Tangirau Hotere and John Caselberg.
2. For example, in "Submarine Frontiers," an article in *New Zealand Geographic*, Ian Wright describes the government's efforts to shift the country's seabed boundaries further out beyond the existing Exclusive Economic Zone through the United Nations Convention on the Law of the Sea (Wright 2006).
3. Referring to book I of the *Digest* of Justinian, which attributes this statement to *Institutes* of Marcianus, an author of the second century AD, Daniel Heller-Roazen finds that "The oldest recorded legal document on the status of the waters in the West tells us that the sea is a being of this kind, irreducibly common, by natural law, to all living things" (2009, 61).
4. Although it is awkward to frame these creatures simply as nonhuman, I want to recognize them as relatively autonomous from human actions. I say awkward because, on one hand, human activities are altering the composition and temperature of sea water and its exchanges with the atmosphere, shaping fish populations, changing submarine topologies, and so on, while on the other, in a different time scale, life on Earth, including human, is tied to oceanic productivities such as the creation of oxygen. I use the terms *nonhuman* and *human* with reservation here to set up useful but not absolute distinctions.

REFERENCES

Heller-Roazen, Daniel. 2009. *The Enemy of All: Piracy and the Law of Nations.* New York: Zone Books.

Machan, Tibor R. 2001. *The Commons: Its Tragedies and Other Follies.* Stanford, CA: Hoover Institution Press.

Mane-Wheoki, Jonathan. 1997. "Hotere—Out the Black Window." *Landfall* 194, 233–240.

Manhire, Bill. 1988. "Ready to Move: Interview with Hone Tuwhare." *Landfall* 42, 262–281.

McQueen, Cilla. 1997a. "Baby Iron." In *Hotere: Out the Black Window. Ralph Hotere's Work with New Zealand Poets*, by Gregory O'Brien, 114. Auckland and Wellington: Godwit and City Gallery Wellington.

———. 1997b. "Sangro River Cemetery." In *Hotere: Out the Black Window. Ralph Hotere's Work with New Zealand Poets*, by Gregory O'Brien, 108. Auckland and Wellington: Godwit and City Gallery Wellington.

———. 2000a. "Dark Matter: Ralph Hotere and Language." In *Ralph Hotere: Black Light: Major Works Including Collaborations with Bill Culbert*, edited by Cilla McQueen, Priscilla Pitts, Mary Trewby, John Walsh, and Ian Wedde, 39–47. Wellington and Dunedin: Te Papa Press and Dunedin Public Art Gallery.

———. 2000b. *Markings*. Dunedin: University of Otago Press.

Mukherjee, Upamanyu Pablo. 2010. *Postcolonial Environments: Nature, Culture and the Contemporary Indian Novel in English*. New York: Palgrave Macmillan.

O'Brien, Gregory. 1997. *Hotere: Out the Black Window. Ralph Hotere's Work with New Zealand Poets*. Auckland and Wellington: Godwit and City Gallery Wellington.

Sharp, Iain. 1996. "When a Poem Kicks: Tuwhare's River Talk." *Landfall* 191, 50–61.

Shiva, Vandana. 2002. *Water Wars: Privatization, Pollution, and Profit*. Cambridge, MA: South End Press.

Simpson, Peter. 1995. Candles in a Dark Room: James K. Baxter and Colin McCahon. *Journal of New Zealand Literature: JNZL* 13: 157–188.

Sullivan, Robert. 1998. "Engaging all the Senses, *Shape-Shifter*, Hone Tuwhare." *New Zealand Books* 8, 6.

Te Papa Tongarewa—The Museum of New Zealand. n.d. Bill Culbert and Ralph Hotere. http://collections.tepapa.govt.nz/exhibitions/CarbonHabit/resource.aspx?irn=618 (accessed August 27, 2010).

Tsing, Anna Lowenhaupt. 2005. *Friction: An Ethnography of Global Connection*. Princeton, NJ: Princeton University Press

Tuwhare, Hone. 1997. *Shape-Shifter*. Wellington: Steele Roberts.

United Nations Environment Programme and Natural World Museum. n.d. "Moving Toward a Balanced Earth; Kick the Carbon Habit," http://www.unep.org/art_env/Documents/natural_world_museum.pdf (accessed August 27, 2010).

Vangioni, Peter. 2005. "The Lively Surface." In *Hotere: Empty of Shadows and Making a Shadow: Lithographs by Ralph Hotere*, edited by Peter Vangioni and Jillian Cassidy, 13–19. Christchurch: Christchurch Art Gallery.

Wedde, Ian. 1975. *Pathway to the Sea*. Christchurch: Hawk Press.

———. 1984. *Georgicon*. Wellington: Victoria University Press.

———. 1997. "Where Is the Art that Does This?" In *Hotere: Out the Black Window. Ralph Hotere's Work with New Zealand Poets*, by Gregory O'Brien, 8–11. Auckland and Wellington: Godwit and City Gallery Wellington.

———. 2000. "Trouble Spots: Where is Ralph Hotere?" In *Ralph Hotere: Black Light. Major Works Including Collaborations with Bill Culbert*, edited by Cilla McQueen, Priscilla Pitts, Mary Trewby, John Walsh, and Ian Wedde, 49–59. Wellington and Dunedin: Te Papa Press and Dunedin Public Art Gallery.

———. 2005. "Letter to Peter McLeavey: After Basho" in *Three Regrets and a Hymn to Beauty*, 40–67. Auckland: Auckland University Press.

Wright, Ian. 2006. "Submarine Frontier." *New Zealand Geographic* 78. http://www.nzgeographic.co.nz/articles.php?ID=157 (accessed August 27, 2010).

Afterword

AN INTERVIEW WITH ELAINE SCARRY

The questions for this interview were written by Ken Hiltner, Stephanie LeMenager, and Teresa Shewry. The interview was conducted by Ken Hiltner in Cambridge, MA, December 2009.

Ken Hiltner: Nuclear weapons represent perhaps the greatest single threat to the welfare of our species and planet. Even the detonation of a single nuclear weapon could result in extraordinary environmental devastation for an entire region of the earth. Nonetheless, environmentalists rarely engage with this threat today. Why do you think that this might be the case?

Elaine Scarry: In a way, that's a really hard question because it's got a lot of different parts to it. I think the major reason environmentalists and few other people engage with nuclear weapons is because they're invisible and that the threat is simply off everyone's attention, and so the few people who do try to call attention to it are themselves just left alone and they're not covered in the news, and you can't build up any critical mass. For example, there's one group that you may know about called Nuke-Watch in Luck, Wisconsin, which is a small group of people, who for years and years and years were protesting the aerial that was used to communicate with our deeply submerged submarines. And eventually, that aerial was taken out, just a couple of years ago. The group has continued to do a newsletter, and as long as that aerial was there, ironically, the problem of the existence of our nuclear weapons was known to at least the people in that area of Wisconsin; but you had the physical evidence right there. But that's rare: There's no aerial in Cambridge, Massachusetts, you don't see the missile silos, and therefore it simply can't enter people's consciousness. When it does, it just is not reported. For example, in the late 80s, there was a group in Concord, California, that had tried to stop the nuclear weapons trains—trains carrying any materials connected to nuclear weapons. One person in charge of it eventually sat on the railroad tracks, and he actually lost both his legs doing this. He was part of a small group of people who were just relentless in saying this is real, this is our responsibility to stop this. And yet outside of Northern California you'd be hard-pressed to find anyone aware of that. His name was Brian Wilson.

There are [vocal] environmentalists; there's a group at Oakridge, Tennessee, that meets every summer. But again, it gets very badly dispersed, or very easily dispersed. On the other hand, I think that when something starts getting done about nuclear weapons, then because people do love the environment, and because people either are dedicated environmentalists, or at least like to think they are (that is, those who don't really do it with life passion; many people think of themselves as being lovers of the environment) that energy, that elaborately developed love of the physical environment, can be pulled into play.

In fact, at one point I was part of a group of people who were doing a law case against nuclear weapons . . . I should back up and say that I had started trying to formulate a case, using the Constitutional provisions that require declaration of war by the Congress, as a way of having a case. Now, a little bit further down the road, a couple months later, I joined up with some people who already had a case developed, and we worked together on a case that was held in the 9th circuit in California, and we had two Congressional plaintiffs saying their right or obligation to oversee the entry into war was being abridged by our presidential first use policy. And the judge ruled that the case was not yet ripe for decision, by which he did not mean that we weren't close enough to nuclear war; he meant that in his view we needed more Congressional plaintiffs. I think he was wrong about that, but nonetheless that's what he thought, and he said this is an issue on which the Supreme Court may one day have to make a ruling. I believe it is an issue on which the Supreme Court will have to make a ruling. But the point I wanted to get to about the environment was, when I was back in Philadelphia working on my East Coast version of the same case, the law firm that had offered to help me pro bono had decided that the only laws that would help us establish standing in a court were environmental laws, and in particular, cases that had already been done on trying to get to the population standing to appear in court. In that way, environment surfaces in interesting ways.

To address the other part of your question, I think you could either mean environmentalists in general, or you could mean environmentalists within the university. If you mean within the university, then I think that is something that has puzzled me not with environmentalists, but with almost every other school of literary criticism. Just rotate your mind through things that have been of concern to people in the last 20 or 30 years, and I don't mean necessarily of concern to me, actually most of them are fields in which I have not participated, but think of people talking about colonialism. What could be a more major example of colonialism than what the United States did with the Marshall Islands, testing on Bikini? Instead, we look at more subtle instances of colonialism where we've had a bad attitude, or where we've exploited people economically. Those may not be so subtle, but compared to using somebody's island to test our weapons, it's pretty subtle. And yet . . . very seldom do you see people who are concerned about post-colonialism talking about that. Or, if you take another school of criticism, feminism, again, what would be a better example of a world that is almost exclusively male invented, and in which there's no room or place for a female voice? For example, although we have gender openness in many parts of the military, nuclear submarines have no women allowed on them. I don't know about the silos, the land-based and air-based silos, but I am guessing that there's not a high portion of females, nor do females have much of a place in developing the bomb, even if they, like Lisa Ratner for example, were very important in understanding radioactivity. So, it is a kind of mystery. However, I feel confident that an audience can be gotten ready for something, or participants can be gotten ready for something, before they know quite what their object is. [The work to] develop in people a kind of concern for the world is itself a good, even if it doesn't explicitly have the object yet of eliminating nuclear weapons.

KH: It is now clear that global climate change is inevitable. However, it is not certain that, outside of testing, even a single nuclear weapon will ever again be detonated. Do you think that the relative risks involved here play a role in the fact that the threat of nuclear weapons to the planet is often ignored by environmentalists?

ES: I do think that. And, here again, the invisibility of the weapons is a big, big part of the problem. The way you phrase the question, it is not certain that a single nuclear weapon will ever be used again. It is not certain, although most people when they have to guess the probability of one being used, if you change the question from their own lifetime, to their children's lifetime, to their grandchildren's lifetime, they begin to say certain use, or either accidental detonation or certain use. But again, here is a place where the fact that the population is completely excluded from any knowledge about nuclear weapons makes us unable to assess what the risk is. So we know that, as I said during [my keynote address at the 2009 "Beyond Environmentalism"] conference, Eisenhower, at least twice, in the 1954 Taiwan Straits Crisis, and again in the 1959 Berlin Crisis, contemplated using an atomic weapon. And it isn't just as though somebody mentioned that in a list of possible responses. They were discussing it very concretely. Again, we know that Kennedy three times considered nuclear weapons. McNamara, in the film *Fog of War*, says that at least three times we came within a hair's breadth of using them and only luck, not intelligence or diplomacy, kept us from catastrophe in the case of Cuba, the one instance any of us know about. LBJ contemplated using them to preempt China getting them; Nixon said he contemplated using them three times other than Vietnam, and we also have the record of his contemplating dropping them on North Vietnam, so that's four times. However, in each of those cases, with the exception of the Cuban missile crisis, there's a huge time lag between the president considering using [nuclear weapons] and when we find out about it. So, it's thirty years later that we find out about it, or twenty-eight years later, and the kind of security we feel from ordinarily being in ignorance is just reenacted by the security we feel from this near-miss happening thirty years ago. I think it is a false sense that the risk is small that puts it off the radar of environmentalists. But I think that's very, very misinformed. I also think that Bertrand Russell was right when he said the higher the injury is, the lower the risk has to be before you're obligated to address it; since the injury is so huge here, the obligation would be high even if the risk were small, and I don't see how it could be small, given the numbers.

KH: The civilian use of nuclear power is seriously being considered today, alongside solar, wind, and a range of other options, as a form of alternative energy because it produces fewer carbon emissions than the burning of fossil fuels. What do you think of nuclear power as a "green" alternative?

ES: I don't know the answer to that. I think probably you know a lot more about that [than I do]. The idea that [nuclear power is] clean is something that I, in an uneducated way, tend to accept. Now activists, such as those in Luck, Wisconsin, think that we're not being given an honest story about whether it's clean or not. They follow [news about] where nuclear waste goes, and what it's doing to the rabbits, and what it's doing to the flora and fauna. And, so, one question is: How can we even be sure that we're getting accurate information? When you think of the debacle of getting corn as fuel for cars, and then it had this terrible effect on rice prices and so forth, you just would want an awful lot of people to sign off on the idea that it's clean before you accept it. And then, of course, there are the problems like Chernobyl and Three Mile Island. I happened to be in Europe, in Germany, during the year that Chernobyl exploded. I wasn't there right when it happened, but I was there in the months following. I know that in the markets they would have to have signs up saying [products were] nuclear free. The accounts I've seen of Chernobyl are horrifying. Of that place itself, once in a while you'll hear something like the oddity of the fact that lichens apparently can survive by absorbing a huge amount of radioactivity; lichens absorbed, without peril to themselves, a huge amount of radioactivity at Chernobyl. On the other hand, unfortunately, the reindeer, which don't survive well, were injured by [radioactivity from Chernobyl]. But lichens are also very adept at taking up heavy metals that we would all accept as terrible pollutants.

The bottom line is that in my own work I am exclusively focusing on nuclear weapons because they have no other purpose but to injure massively. As to the question of the nuclear reactors, I just remain puzzled. I am also from a coal mining family. My grandfather was an anthracite coal miner. I am aware of all the costs of some of the alternative kinds of fuel, too, and I see how little of the actual story of these other fuels is being given accurately. *The Boston Review* recently had an article on coal that just gave you about 100 times as much information about what the truth is with the coal industry than most media accounts. I am in the position of needing to learn a lot more about that issue.

KH: A repeated criticism of Al Gore's *An Inconvenient Truth* (both the book and the film) was that it did much to reveal the problems associated with global climate change, but offered little in the way of solutions. Confronted with the threat of nuclear weapons, what can we as individuals do to combat it?

ES: I think that when we say that all Al Gore did was bring attention to [global climate change] without providing solutions—bringing attention to it is half the solution, or maybe three-fourths the solution. Or, put the other way, there is no solution if you haven't started by making people aware of it. So, to me, his having been able to do that is just a miracle. So, everything else is premised on that. Now the same would be true on nuclear weapons. It may well be that President Obama can make people aware that this is something that has to be done. He is up against a reigning orthodoxy that not only tolerates nuclear weapons and pretends they don't exist, but even has an account of them as bringing about peace. For example in today's *Financial Times*, there's an article by Martin Wolf, who is a very smart economist, that just in passing credits nuclear weapons with there not having been any wars. And that just is the way the world has come to see them. So, someone like Obama or anyone else who might have the power to get people to see that we've got a big, big problem, that's half the battle at least. Now, once that's done, I do think that the Constitutional provisions can be used to absolutely make the military go into a receivership in the courts, for example. I'm not speaking against the military, but it's just that they happen to be the group that has access to the nuclear weapons. But if you had a court ruling that our whole nuclear weapons arrangement was incompatible [both] with the Constitutional requirements for a Congressional declaration of war, and with the Second Amendment requirement that whatever injuring power the country had, had to be equally distributed across all the people of the country, then the courts could also order the military arsenal, the ships and planes, to go into a state of receivership in the courts until things could be redesigned and straightened out in a way that made it, again, constitutionally possible.

There are so many things that argue on the side of getting rid of nuclear weapons, like the fact that the rest of the world wants us to get rid of them, and the fact that environmentalists and people that care about the environment want us to get rid of them, and the fact that there are these technical, legal provisions, you might not even have to act on it. You might just have to say, "We've got a problem here," and therefore a president or anybody trying to get his or her own population to get rid of these things, would be able to explain that it isn't just a matter of whether we personally like it or not, there's the matter of the law that's got to be followed. And that, in combination with other things, might help move us towards the position that many other countries are in, countries that have signed non-proliferation treaties and agreed not to have them. It really isn't unthinkable to undo them; it's very thinkable to undo them. In a way, it seems to me as though it can't be done. But that's something like the Berlin Wall coming down: in two hours, suddenly it's open. And the world is changing. This seems like something that cannot be repaired, and yet it could be that at a certain point enough things are ready and converge, and three days later, the nuclear weapons are gone. Or, rather, slowly disassembled.

KH: Nuclear weapons are rarely mentioned in environmental literary studies, which is paying much greater attention to, for example, climate change. In fact, concern for nuclear weapons seems to have gone relatively quiet throughout the humanities in recent years. Can you speak to the ecological and social impact of nuclear weapons in our world, in potential but also in terms of what has already been damaged and destroyed?

ES: Of course, part of what has been damaged and destroyed are places like the island of Bikini, or the similar area in the Sahara where the French tested their weapons (I don't know about the radiation levels or the destruction of life there as well as I know what happened at Bikini). However, I think that a lot of what has happened may not be known. We know of real damage. We know of people who track the waste from weapons and could fill in a lot here about the damage that's already been done. Here and there there are lots of local pockets of people who know the damage. But even without that environmental damage, [there is] damage to us as a country. I feel that our whole citizenry, because of being read out of the whole responsibility for the defense of the country, has suffered a diminution in civic stature; by that I don't mean that we all ought to be ready to go to war, but whether we go to war ought to be up to us. And we're the ones who ought to be discussing it, rather than turning on the TV and learning from the president whether we're going to go to war. This is our responsibility, and in the history of the United States, the responsibility for carrying out these decisions always went hand in hand with civic stature. So the right to vote in the Fifteenth Amendment is extended to blacks, primarily on the argument that 180,000 blacks had fought in the Civil War and could not therefore be denied the right to vote, even though they then of course had tremendous problems getting that realized. The Nineteenth Amendment, giving women the right to vote—not as strongly as in the case of the Fifteenth Amendment, but very, very elaborately, women's authority to be able to vote was argued on the basis that they had the capacity for self-defense, that they had participated in munitions factories, that they could contribute to the defense of other people. This is in pageant plays, suffrage plays, and suffrage ceremonies, and there were songs like "Onward Christian

Soldiers," [which] was used as a pageant song. And then the Twenty-Sixth Amendment, lowering the voting age from 21 to 18 in this country, was done on the basis that the Vietnam generation, both those who fought in Vietnam and those who protested the war in Vietnam, had earned for that generation and all later generations the right to vote at a younger age. And so, if you just look at that civic stature, and then just [wonder] what happens now, when as a country we can't even talk about things like Iraq. As I was arguing at the "Beyond Environmentalism" conference, once you have an executive office that's making decisions about atomic war and has the power of life and death over millions of people in its hands, he's going to be very impatient with getting any authorization for conventional war, and all that led to the disappearance of the draft. So what are the losses? The losses are real in terms of spent weapons, the environment that has been hurt, the lack of courage in the U.S. population and lack of civic stature, and also the lack of capacity for self-defense by many other people on earth. There are exceptions, like the Swiss with their shelter system. [The Swiss] have absolutely decided that they are going to be able to find a way to carry out acts of self-defense regardless, but that is very rare. I think they now have a shelter system that protects 114% of their population, whereas in Germany it's 3% and in certain Scandinavian countries, it's I think between 20 and 40% of the population covered if there's a nuclear war.

KH: There are so many things about nuclear weapons that seem difficult to grasp, including just what these weapons are capable of doing; that they really are here with us, ready to unleash all their deadly potentials at every moment; the speed at which they operate. Can you talk about the imaginative difficulties of nuclear weapons, and whether you see the arts or literary studies as relevant in helping us engage them in any way?

ES: Well, I think that the imaginative difficulty comes from what we already talked about: invisibility. Also, there's a tremendous confusion in people's minds between the unreality something has by being genuinely unreal, and the unreality it has from not yet having happened, by its being in the future. Those two are very confused. The other thing that I think weighs in here, and it comes up in one of your later questions, is the fact that a nuclear weapon doesn't have any incremental sequence. Global warming does have an incremental sequence, even if it's accelerated. But with nuclear weapons it's kind of nothing or all. There's no space in between to say, "Gee, I think something is happening here that we need to reverse." It's just not there, and then one day it is there. I don't know about the role of art because I can imagine that there could be a novel that was the equivalent to nuclear weapons that *Uncle Tom's Cabin* was to slavery. That's very unusual within the arts to be able to do something like that, but there certainly could be such a work where suddenly everybody would just get it. So, that could happen. In the meantime I think that it's hard for people, talking now not about art, but literary criticism, and maybe art itself too, that they tend to be a bit ret-rospective rather than prospective. So, if something terrible happened and yet the world survived and there still were universities, certainly it would be something that people in the Humanities would be talking about. But unfortunately it's retrospective and this is terrible because you can't do any-thing about injuries that have already happened. The only injuries you can prevent are the ones that haven't yet happened, but that kind of prospective thinking is hard for us.

Maybe all the work on global warming will help not only with global warming, but with being able to think prospectively here too. Bertrand Russell, in one of his books written for lay people as well as for philoso-phers (*Has Man a Future?*), talks about the incredible stupidity of having invented nuclear weapons. Then he begins to imagine, "If I were before the God Osiris and pleading for the right of humanity to be able to go on living, even though it had done something so inexcusable as to invent these things, what would I say?" And one of the things he says is that the creation of the arts shows in mystic miniature what human beings can do, and that Osiris ought to take that as a sign of the potential for people, who despite this sort of cruelty of having made these weapons, are capable of something better. So, that might be one way of thinking of the arts.

KH: There is much talk right now in environmental literary studies about globalization and of the decreasing power of the nation state. But with nuclear weapons this seems complicated because the power to make and detonate these weapons is concentrated in only some national places and in the hands of particular people. What forms of governance do you see in relation to nuclear weapons?

ES: Well, this is a very important question and I think a very complicated question. I'll answer it first focusing on the nation-state and then I'll try to focus it imagining a global governor, rather than nation-state governance. So, for me the nation-state is an important unit, and I see it as danger-ous that people are very impatient with the nation-state now. However, for good reason they're impatient with the nation-state. The nation-state has done a million things wrong; it bullies, it uses its sway to get things. But to me, the idea of something that is transnational is actually atavistic because there's no way to do it and enlist the consent of millions of people. Instead what you're talking about is a small number of people who are able to have transnational conversations with other very gifted people, or very wealthy people, or very mobile people. And so, you don't have any way of making sure that the views you're urging are not just your own views, but the views of millions of people. The nation-state is a way of, for better or for worse, making sure that you've got a huge amount of your population signed on to whatever it is you're doing. Often I've been involved in conversations, sometimes with people of other countries, about international rights, and there will be 20 people in the room and everybody will be talking about how limited the nation-state is. And the nation-state is limited, but we're 20 people in a room and we may think of ourselves as representing all of France and the United States and Germany and China, but we're just one person from China, one person from the United States, and one person from France. It is just tremendous arrogance to think that we've got anything like the belief system of everybody behind us. And who will enforce any agreements that we come up with, even if we come up with enlightened agreements that really are done on behalf of everybody? I mean everything that was ever meant by patriarchy is in that model, where I am going to decide what is good for the rest of the people. I think in general, the whole issue of globalization has to be careful that it's not getting seduced into just scoffing at anything that's national, like mere constitutions, the only things you can use as a brake on certain wrong-doings, or mere laws. I say keep the nation-state and use the social contract that it has to make sure that you can never have the kind of weapons you have. I am sure those social contracts can also be enlisted in solving global warming.

But if you could persuade me otherwise and say, no, we really need a global government, and obviously I believe a lot in the United Nations as a second brake on injuring. [The UN has] to be a back-up brake to the injuring prohibitions that occur in national law. The way this has normally worked is presidents have often said that it's easier to get an authorization from the UN than to get it from your own Congress, so go to the UN. Well, that's wrong: You should have to go to your own country *and* the UN because the UN basic treaty says nothing in this treaty can ever be taken to abridge or short-circuit the home constitution. However, let's say that you could eliminate national governments, and you could have a global government. Also, let's say that somebody came up with a reason for having nuclear weapons. For example, it's conceivable to me that it really could be that only nuclear weapons could be shot against an incoming meteor that was the size of the planet that was going to kill us. Maybe nuclear weapons really could deflect that. But if you were then going to have those weapons, I think you would have to have a global government that was really chosen by lottery—some people or one person this year, or this decade. The people in charge of this [global government are] going to involve one person from the region we now call China, one person from the region we now call x, y, and [they would be] chosen by lottery because to say we'll have it, but we'll be in charge, is to just use [nuclear weapons] as this tremendous permanent threat against the world's people.

KH: What kind of pathway ahead do you imagine is possible and desirable in the face of nuclear weapons? Where today do you see people working to seek alternatives to life in the shadow of these weapons?

ES: You know, the problem with nuclear weapons is that there is no right of exit. There's no place on earth where you're free of the threat of [nuclear weapons]. That's a deep part of what's wrong with it. I mean, social contract always allowed for right of exit: If you don't like the country, you can leave the country. There is no way to leave the situation of being subject to a nuclear threat. Now lots of countries have tried to make themselves nuclear free zones. So, if we looked at a map of the parts of the land and ocean that are now covered by nuclear free weapons treaties, it starts to cover a large part of the earth. For example, there's the recent treaty for the Southern Americas and Mexico, the Treaty of Tlatelolco, and then for Africa it's Pelindaba. Then there's the Treaty of Bangkok for South Asia and the Treaty of Rarotonga for the South Pacific. Of course the United States wants these other countries to sign these nuclear free zones because it means they won't have nuclear weapons, and supposedly our part is to say, "We won't use weapons against these countries." Further, we won't threaten to use them unless they assist a country that uses them, develop research, etc. Now a big problem is: Are our nuclear ships allowed to transit through their waters? I think the answer is yes. And so, these other countries are declaring nuclear free, but there's no assurance. I mean it may decrease the possibility that we use [nuclear weapons] against them, but so long as we have the nuclear weapons there is no such thing as absolute assurance. When New Zealand did its real nuclear free protocols, the United States punished it by saying it would no longer share surveillance information with it, it would no longer act in the same security relations with it, because New Zealand, unlike these other places, really said, "And by the way, don't ever bring your ships into our waters." The attempt to stand outside this thing is very, very difficult. To some extent, Switzerland has found a way of standing outside it by requiring every house to have a fall-out shelter. Now Switzerland even gave to the population a right to vote on whether people who abstain from building the legally required fall-out shelter in their house for whatever reason have to pay money to contribute to the public shelters that will protect people who don't have their own. A huge turn-out occurred and 80% of the population said they have to contribute a high tax to contribute to a public shelter. That is a kind of vertical evacuation. Rather than being able to stand outside the borders of the area that can be subjected to nuclear fall-out or a nuclear weapon, they have gone down into the ground, and they have done this not only by providing shelters for their population, but by providing elaborate shelters for cultural property. They mapped every object that has to be saved, the pathway it has to go on, [figured out each] staircase it has to be carried up. They've got the whole thing mapped out. They themselves say that we're not as close to nuclear war as we were in the past, but they continue to keep the whole system in operation.

KH: Do you happen to have any thought on the historical relationship between nuclear testing programs and the development of the science of ecology?

ES: It's an interesting question, and I don't know the answer to that. Whether the science of ecology started developing in relation to it. I mean what do you think of the science of ecology? Do you think of it as [starting with] Rachel Carson?

KH: That's what I was getting at. While the word "ecology" was coined in 1866 by Ernst Haeckel, I am thinking of the modern ecological awareness that Rachel Carson popularizes in the mid-1960s, which was already emerging in the 1950s. Coincidentally this was also . . .

ES: . . . the atomic age. And I know that when she wrote jacket notes for Debussy's "Le Mer," she's talking about how the ocean takes us out of time because it connects us with all of time. She ends the sequence by just referring to our own time as the atomic age. Even though her major work is on chemical pollutants, it certainly is very much coinciding with a period in which we not only had atomic weapons, but where the population in general was very aware of this. And she's also very aware in her writing of the abridgement of consent that comes when chemicals like that are being used without people understanding what has gone into them. [This] would certainly also be true of atomic weapons. She quotes this 19th century naturalist, Richard Jefferies is it? . . . who talks about the . . . I can't remember the exact phrase . . . the "astonishing beauty of earth." She has a whole essay about his insight that we're only truly alive, or we're most truly alive, when we're seeing the beauty of something. But the real answer to question nine is I don't know the answer.

KH: In Part II of *On Beauty and Being Just,* you raise questions of stewardship relevant to both traditional and current goals of many environmentalists. Would it be fair to say that in this book you raise fundamental problems of environmental aesthetics?

ES: I think so. Because one thing that I talk about there is that an attribute that yokes together beauty and justice is the important attribute of symmetry. I [also] talk about other ways in which the two are yoked, such as the kind of decentering, the kind of unselfing that Simone Weil and Iris Murdoch talked about, that is necessary to working for justice; you [must] stop seeing yourself at the center of the world. Other things yoke together beauty and justice, but one that I believe in very strongly that people sometimes think I'm just saying metaphorically, is the issue of symmetry. Symmetry is absolutely fundamental to justice. In that book I talk about Rawls's definition of fairness as requiring a symmetry in all our relations to one another. But you could take many other models other than Rawls. For example, Plato [suggested that] crimes ought to be commenced with punishment, something we still haven't figured out how to do correctly, but we recognize that there ought to be a symmetry. Or we talk about how work and compensation ought to be symmetrical. Hume talked about the regulation of expectations and their fulfillment as symmetrical. So symmetry is very important, and even though in the modern world we like to talk about how asymmetry is very interesting, and haunting, and being off balance, really it's a tiny amount of asymmetry in the midst of overwhelming symmetry. Part of the reason why environmental aesthetics and environmental justice can escape people is because we, especially in the United States, don't think of symmetry as an interesting attribute. We don't think of symmetry as an interesting attribute because, as so many people have pointed out, we own so much of the wealth, and the asymmetry in the weapons even exceeds the asymmetry in wealth. And so we say, "Well symmetry, that's really not so interesting, let's talk about asymmetry." But [imagine] if you were to really recover the sense of how important symmetry is to beauty, and how important it is to justice. Aristotle said more beautiful even than the evening star, or the morning star, is the symmetry of justice. If you could recover that, it would lead to environmental justice.

Now I understand there are tremendous complications, and I think it comes up in one of your other questions, which is the fact of China pointing out that we've had our Industrial Revolution and we've allowed the western countries to squander the resources, and now suddenly we want to talk about the environment, while they're just starting to get their population with a strong scaffolding under them economically. But there could be compromises; that is, it could be that the west would have to give up or share a lot of its wealth or technology or power so that China wouldn't have to take the earth through the same things that we did in the west in order to bring about the same level of economic well-being.

KH: To what degree do you recognize the environmental movement as, indeed, *moved* by the sort of "vibrant self-interest and self-survival" attributable to those who would wish to protect beautiful things, such as plants and blossoms? How might aesthetic fairness, in your terms, directly contribute to problems of justice that must be worked out at the level of national and international governance, such as the capping of carbon emissions, the decommissioning of nuclear submarines, etc.?

ES: Well, certainly I think, if I understand the question correctly, the environmental movement is just directly motivated by an awareness of the beauty of the world. I can hardly even think what the alternative explanation would be but that self-evident importance of the thing continuing to exist and thrive, whether the thing is a tree or a plant or a stream. I think that absolutely [the environmental movement is] motivated by the aliveness, or the kind of reciprocal feeling of aliveness that happens when you come into the presence of something beautiful. That it either is alive, it raises your own standard for what will count as perceptual acuity, which is the felt fact of aliveness, and conversely it protects, it increases your feeling of wanting to be a steward and protect it and carry it forward in time. Even if it's inanimate, like a painting, you're conferring on it the rights of aliveness or the rights of not being injured that we would normally accord only to something alive. I think that is very directly used in the environmental movement as a direct appeal to people's felt experience. It's much less true of the nuclear area, but I think it would be a very successful thing to enlist in the nuclear area. My own work is on the legal constraints that we can bring to bear on calling back all these weapons and getting rid of them. But I think that the people who have been most successful in getting people to care about nuclear weapons have made an argument from the beauty of the earth, like Jonathan Shell's *Fate of the Earth* and Rachel Carson, even though [her work is] not as elaborately in the atomic area. But I can easily imagine it, if you could get people from zero to step, let's say, forty, in concern about nuclear weapons, you could easily have brilliant commercials of the kind you sometimes see in environmental literature where you just show the blue sky, and then someone says, "Help rid the world of nuclear weapons." [We must] make that link to get people used to the reflex that whenever they see something beautiful [it's a] reminder to try and stop these things, just as it's a reminder to try and undo global warming. The problem with beauty right now is just that the only people who use it for advertising are people who want you to buy something. So that there's this association if you see something beautiful, you should buy it. And that's not the advertisers' fault, it's because everybody else has vacated the field. So in universities they could say when you see something beautiful it's the call to educate yourself, or when you see something beautiful it's a call to reduce injuries in the world; people would very easily get that link. "When you see something beautiful, buy it," is just the result of the simple way that beauty has entered the commercial world.

KH: Do we inevitably confront apocalypse when we meet problems that have a weak aesthetic dimension—such as global climate change or Ohio-class nuclear submarines? Threats whose availability to the senses is delayed? More specifically, does environmental "apocalypse" arise out of environmental problems that evade the human senses, their "intense somatic pleasure[s]," the urgent call to fairness that such pleasures may bring?

ES: So, I think if I understand the question that the answer is certainly yes. In a way we've kind of been addressing it. Either the time frame is too long, as with global warming, or too short, as with the on-off button of the nuclear weapon, for people to comprehend the enormity of the problem. I guess it's a little bit like the idea of aesthetic distance in the theater. It was often said (there are lots of exceptions to this) that in the theater you have to be at the right aesthetic distance in order to experience the play. If you're too close, you see the safety pins on the costumes and it ruins the effect, and if you're too far away everything is miniaturized and so you can't accept it. And I think that this question may well be right, that apocalypse is what happens for all those things that are happening at a distance—it incapacitates us because they're outside our own sensory horizon, either by being much too long or much too short.

KH: Can ugliness—not the absence or denial of beauty but actual insult to it, for example a landscape of mine tailings—generate ethical fairness? Have environmental movements in the US and Western Europe been too quick to posit a cause-effect relationship between insults to beauty and remediative ethical action?

ES: I don't think [the response] could be too quick. I think people should, when they see insults to the environment, call for immediate remediative ethical action. I see beauty and injury as the opposites of one another. Here, the question says ugliness, but for me the opposite of beauty is always injury, and that seems to be the way the question is formulated too. I think either one of those can cause the incitement to remedial action because they're both the same. Either out of the beauty of the world you perceive what it would mean to injure it, or you see the injury directly, and you want to restore it. I think that the problem is once the injury is done, like the clean-up of the Valdez spill, the chance to restore it is so hard. Of course the Valdez spill is nothing compared to [the detonation of] nuclear weapons: there would be no way to undo it or clean it up.

KH: How might "aesthetic fairness" and the self-survival linked to the decentering of self through beauty be reconciled to theoretical science, which often speaks with foremost authority upon environmental issues but does so in a language that fails to direct the imagination of the ordinary reader toward creating analogues to life, virtual vitality or beauty?

ES: That one I might need to think about more. On the one hand, there have been [organizations] like the Bulletin of the Atomic Scientists [that] have been trying to engage the imagination of the ordinary reader, maybe without success. And I think that, as Al Gore pointed out in his movie, it's not that the literature wasn't working away saying that we've got a big problem, it was that it was being misreported or it was going through this preposterous grid of "there must be two sides to the question" and "let's hear the pro and con, and weigh them in the balance." In the case of nuclear weapons, often the only time people will listen is if you've got somebody who invented the bomb then regretting it. I'm glad the people who partici- pated in the invention of it do regret it, and I'm glad that their words carry, but the people who have as much right to speak about that are any human beings on the earth, any creature on earth, any plant on earth. It shouldn't be up to the few people who have been authorized to injure to then point out that it's not such a good idea. In recent years, [we've heard from] "The Four Horsemen," Kissinger and three other Secretaries of State who now say we have to get rid of nuclear weapons; I'm so thankful that they are saying it. On the other hand, these people who sat there and tolerated this while they were in office don't by that gain some special knowledge to say this, when every single person on earth has the right to be saying this.

Contributors

Lawrence Buell is the Powell M. Cabot Professor of American Literature at Harvard University. He is the author of *Literary Transcendentalism* (1973), *New England Literary Culture* (1986), *The Environmental Imagination: Thoreau, Nature Writing, and the Formation of American Culture* (1995), *Writing for an Endangered World: Literature, Culture, and Environment in the United States and Beyond* (2001), *Emerson* (2003), and *The Future of Environmental Criticism* (2005). He is coeditor, with Wai Chee Dimock, of *Shades of the Planet: American Literature as World Literature* (2007). *Writing for an Endangered World* won the Popular Culture and American Culture Associations' Cawelti Prize for the best book of 2001 in the field of American Cultural Studies; *Emerson* won the 2003 Warren-Brooks Award for outstanding literary criticism. Professor Buell won the 2007 Jay Hubbell Award, Modern Language Association, American Literature Group, for lifetime contributions to American literary studies.

Elaine Scarry is the Walter M. Cabot Professor of Aesthetics and General Theory of Value at Harvard University. Professor Scarry's interests include nineteenth-century British novel, twentieth-century drama, theory of representation, language of physical pain, structure of verbal and material making in art, science, and the law. She is the author of *On Beauty and Being Just* (1999), *Dreaming by the Book* (1999), *Resisting Representation* (1994), *Literature and the Body* (1988), and *The Body in Pain: The Making and Unmaking of the World* (1985). Among her many awards, *Dreaming by the Book* won the Truman Capote Award for Literary Criticism.

Byron Caminero-Santangelo is Associate Professor at the University of Kansas. He is coeditor, with Garth Myers, of *Environment at the Margins: Literary and Environmental Studies in Africa* (Forthcoming, University of Ohio Press) and author of *African Fiction and Joseph Conrad: Reading Postcolonial Intertextuality* (SUNY Press, 2005). Some of his recent articles include "In Place: Tourism, Cosmopolitan Bioregionalism, and Zakes Mda's *The Heart of Redness*," *Postcolonial Ecologies: Literatures of the Environment* (Oxford UP, forthcoming);

"Different Shades of Green: Ecocriticism and African Literature," *African Literature: An Anthology of Criticism and Theory* (Blackwell, 2007); "Of Freedom and Oil: Nation, Globalization, and Civil Liberties in the Writing of Ken Saro-Wiwa," *Research in English and American Literature* (2006).

Allison Carruth is Assistant Professor of English and participating faculty member in Environmental Studies at the University of Oregon. Her research interests include contemporary fiction and media, environmental criticism, food studies, and globalization theory. She has published essays in *Modern Fiction Studies, Modern Drama, Modernism/Modernity,* and in a forthcoming collection entitled *Postcolonial Ecologies.* Her current book manuscript, *Monsanto's Garden: Food, Power and the Global Imaginary,* argues that the food system profoundly shapes aesthetic responses to globalization in United States and Anglophone culture from World War I to the present. Additional works in progress include an environmental critique of social networking media, an essay on Seamus Heaney's digital poetics, and a second book project that traces artistic and literary interventions in the science of genetic engineering.

Jill H. Casid is Associate Professor of Visual Culture Studies in the Department of Art History at the University of Wisconsin–Madison. As a historian, a theorist of visual culture, and a practicing artist in photo-based media, her work explores the productive tensions between theory, the problems of the archive and the writing of history, issues of gender, race and sexuality, and the performative and processual aspects of visual objects and imaging. Her research in visual studies and in vision and aesthetics includes her book *Sowing Empire: Landscape and Colonization* (2005) and her forthcoming book *Shadows of Enlightenment—* both with the University of Minnesota Press. She has just begun a new book project, "The Volatile Image: Other Histories of Photography," that reconsiders photography as a complex and unstable medium. Professor Casid directs the new Visual Culture Center at the University of Wisconsin–Madison.

Cheryll Glotfelty is Professor of Literature and Environment and Chair of the Literature & Environment graduate program at the University of Nevada, Reno. She and Harold Fromm coedited *The Ecocriticism Reader: Landmarks in Literary Ecology* (1995), an acclaimed and widely taught text that introduced the field of environmental criticism to its first generation of practitioners. Glotfelty is a cofounder and past president of the Association for the Study of Literature and Environment (ASLE), which recently awarded her an honorary lifetime membership for her pioneering work. She has published widely on ecocriticism, environmental literature,

Western American literature, literature by women, and bioregionalism. In 2006, Glotfelty was named Nevada Professor of the Year by the CASE-Carnegie Foundation. Glotfelty's love of the Great Basin propelled her into a twelve-year research project, culminating in publication of *Literary Nevada: Writings from the Silver State* (2008).

Ken Hiltner is Associate Professor of English at the University of California, Santa Barbara, where he directs the Early Modern Center. His first book, *Milton and Ecology* (Cambridge University Press, 2003), explored the ideological underpinnings of our current environmental crisis by way of Milton's radical reevaluation of dualistic theology, metaphysical philosophy, and early modern subjectivism. He has recently edited a collection of essays, *Renaissance Ecology: Imagining Eden in Milton's England* (Duquesne University Press 2008), in which the contributors consider, through both literature and the visual arts, the question of how human beings in the Renaissance imagined an ideal relationship with the earth. His next book project, entitled *What Else Is Pastoral? Renaissance Literature and the Environment.* (forthcoming from Cornell University Press in 2011), expands the arguments of *Milton and Ecology* into a broader ecocritical consideration of Renaissance literature from Petrarch through the seventeenth century. He also has over a dozen essays published or in the works.

Jennifer C. James is Associate Professor of English and Director of the Africana Studies Program at the George Washington University in Washington, DC. She is the author of *A Freedom Bought with Blood: African-American Literature of War, the Civil War–World War II*, published by the University of North Carolina Press in 2007. She is also the author of several articles and book chapters including " 'Civil' War Wounds: William Wells Brown, Violence and the Origins of African American War Fiction" in *The African American Review* and the forthcoming "Blessed are the Warmakers: Martin Luther King, Vietnam and the Black Prophetic Tradition," in *Writing War Across the Disciplines,* to be published in 2011 by the University of Toronto Press. She recently coedited a special topic issue of *MELUS*, entitled *Race, Ethnicity, Disability and Literature*. Her interests include exploring the legacy of slavery on black social-justice philosophy in the twentieth and twenty-first centuries.

Stephanie LeMenager is Associate Professor at the University of California, Santa Barbara, where she teaches English and Environmental Studies and served as Director of the American Cultures and Global Contexts Center from 2007 to 2010. LeMenager's first book, *Manifest and Other Destinies* (U. Nebraska, 2004), won the 2005 Thomas J. Lyon Award for Best Book in Western Literary Studies and was reissued in paperback in

2008. LeMenager has published several journal articles and book chapters, in *American Literary History, American Literature, ELH, Qui Parle*, the *Cambridge History of the American Novel*, and the *Oxford Handbook of Nineteenth-Century American Literature*. She is completing a book manuscript treating the convergence of climate change, peak oil, and food scarcity as a challenge to environmental imagination, titled *This Is Not a Tree*.

Timothy Morton is Professor of Literature and the Environment at the University of California, Davis. He is the author of *The Ecological Thought* (Harvard, 2010), *Ecology without Nature* (Harvard, 2007), seven other books and over sixty essays on ecology, philosophy, culture, literature, and food.

Susie O'Brien is Associate Professor of English and Cultural Studies and Associate Director of the Institute on Globalization and the Human Condition at McMaster University, Hamilton, Ontario. Her teaching and research interests are in postcolonial literature and culture, globalization, and green cultural studies. Her published work includes essays in *Cultural Critique, Interventions: International Journal of Postcolonial Studies, Modern Fiction Studies, Mosaic*, and *South Atlantic Quarterly*, and a textbook, *Popular Culture: A User's Guide* (2nd ed. 2009), coauthored with Imre Szeman. Her current projects focus on the postcolonial politics of local food, and the concept of resilience in ecology and culture.

Paul Outka is Associate Professor of English at University of Kansas, where he specializes in nineteenth-century U.S. literature and culture, literature and science studies, and ecocriticism. He has published articles in *Contemporary Literature, The Mickle Street Review, Interdisciplinary Studies in Literature and the Environment, The Journal of American Studies,* and elsewhere. In 2004–05, Outka was awarded a full-year American Council of Learned Societies/Andrew W. Mellon Junior Faculty Fellowship for his book project examining the intersection between the construction of racial identity and natural experience in nineteenth- and early twentieth-century America. *Race and Nature: From Transcendentalism to the Harlem Renaissance* was published in 2008 by Palgrave Macmillan. In 2009 the book won the Association for the Study of Literature and the Environment's (ASLE) biennial prize for the best book of ecocriticism published in 2007–2008.

Alfred K. Siewers is Associate Professor of English at Bucknell University and author of several articles and book chapters in addition to the books *Strange Beauty: Ecocritical Approaches to Early Medieval Landscape* (Palgrave Macmillan, 2009) and *Tolkien's Modern Middle Ages*, coedited with Jane Chance (Palgrave Macmillan, 2009). Professor Siewers teaches and researches environmental approaches to literature, premodern/medieval and Celtic literature, fantasy literature, and traditions of nature in English poetics and epic from Chaucer to Coleridge and Cooper. He is Nature and Human Communities Initiative faculty coordinator at the Bucknell Environmental Center, and senior fellow at the Environmental Residential College.

Teresa Shewry is Assistant Professor of English at the University of California, Santa Barbara. She has a PhD in Literature from Duke University (2008) and an MA in English and BA in Japanese from Victoria University, New Zealand (2002). Her research interests include environmental studies, Pacific and Asia Pacific cultures, postcolonial theory, and critical theory. She is completing a book manuscript, *Possible Ecologies: Literature, Nature, and Hope in the Pacific*, which is about the literary making of hope around damaged ecologies, lost lifeworlds, and marginalized peoples of the Pacific Rim. Shewry is also working on the politics and poetics of ecology and geological time scales and lifeworlds in media, fiction and film; the engagements of literature and film with criminalized fishing economies in the Pacific; and the environmentalist experience of certain marine places and creatures as abandoned in globalization.

Julie Sze is Associate Professor of American Studies at the University of California, Davis, and the founding director of the Environmental Justice Project for the John Muir Institute for the Environment. Her book *Noxious New York: The Racial Politics of Urban Health and Environmental Justice* won the 2008 John Hope Franklin Publication Prize, awarded annually to the best published book in American Studies. Sze's research investigates environmental justice and environmental inequality; culture and environment; race, gender, and power; and community health and activism. She has published on a wide range of topics such as energy and air pollution activism; toxicity; the cultural politics of the Hummer; and on environmental justice novels and cultural production. She has been interviewed widely in print and on the radio, including in *Newsweek*, *Asian Report*, and *Grist Magazine.*

Edward M. Test is Assistant Professor at Boise State University. His recent publications include "Seeds of Sacrifice: Amaranth, the Gardens of Tenochtitlan and Spenser's Faerie Queene," in *A Companion to the Global Renaissance, 1550–1660* and "The Tempest and the Newfoundland Cod Fishery," in *Global Traffic: Discourses and Practices of Trade in English Literature and Culture from 1550 to 1700*. He has also published a volume of poetry, *Fata Morgana,* and translated three volumes of poetry: *Torn Awake* (by Forrest Gander), *The Zoo Father* (by Pascale Petit), and *Appalachia* (by Charles Wright). Professor Test's current project considers the role that literary representations of New World flora and fauna (by Spenser, Shakespeare, Jonson, and others) played in what he aptly describes as the "marketing of an environment."

Beth Fowkes Tobin is Professor of English at Arizona State University and author of three books: *Colonizing Nature: The Tropics in British Arts and Letters, 1760–1820* (U of Pennsylvania P, 2005), winner of the Eighth Annual Susanne M. Glasscock Book Prize for best book of interdisciplinary humanities scholarship; *Picturing Imperial Power: Colonial Subjects in Eighteenth-Century British Painting* (Duke UP, 1999), winner of the Best Book on British Art before 1800, presented by the Historians of British Art; and *Superintending the Poor: Charitable Ladies and Paternal Landlords in British Fiction, 1770–1860* (Yale UP, 1993). She is the editor of the Oxford Classics' Eliza Haywood novel, *Miss Betsy Thoughtless* (1997), and *History, Gender and Literature*, a collection of essays (U of Georgia Press, 1994). She is working on a book on natural history collecting in the eighteenth century, a project for which she recently received a scholar's award from the National Science Foundation.

Priscilla Solis Ybarra is Assistant Professor in the Department of English at the University of North Texas, where she teaches courses on Latina/o literature and environmental literary studies. She has published several articles on the environmental aspects of Chicana/o writing, discussing writers such as Jovita González, Gloria Anzaldúa, Cherríe Moraga, Jimmy Santiago Baca, and Arturo Longoria. She enjoys traveling and offering lectures on her research, with recent trips including Washington state, New Mexico, and Vancouver Island, as well as to Scotland and Japan. Her current book-in-progress, *Medioambientes/Environments: A Literary History of Chicana/o Environmental Writing from 1848 to the Present*, is the first study to engage a long-range environmental literary history of Chicana/o writing. She has taught courses for the Departments of English at Texas Tech University, Rice University, the University of California, Los Angeles, and for American Studies at Yale University.

Yi Zhou is a graduate student in Anthropology at the University of California, Davis. She studied at the University of Sydney and received her master's degree in Asian Studies. Currently, she is pursuing a research project on Women's Studies and popular culture in China.

Michael G. Ziser is Associate Professor of English at the University of California, Davis. Ziser's research addresses questions about the image and agency of nonhuman nature in North American writing and visual arts, engaging along the way with ecocriticism, agrarianism, ecophenomenology, food studies, science studies, media studies, religious studies, and bioregionalist thought and practice. His book *Continent Ajar: Environmental Practice and Early American Writing* (forthcoming, Cambridge UP) proposes a new theoretical and methodological approach to producing more-than-human literary histories. As inaugural director of the UC Davis Environmental Humanities Research supercluster, Ziser has worked to bring faculty and graduate students from different disciplines together to discuss environment-related work of common interest. Ziser serves as the reviews editor for Eighteenth-Century Studies and as area editor for the forthcoming *Boom: A Journal of California Studies*.

Index